Palgrave Literary Dictionaries

CW00376702

General Editors: **Brian G. Caraher and Estelle Sh**
Founding Editor: **Malcolm Andrew**

This series provides readers with concise and reliable guides to individual authors or groups of authors. Entries are arranged alphabetically and include topics and issues on literary works, fictional characters, place, historical, political and social contexts, intellectual influences, genre and critical traditions. Entries are cross-referenced as appropriate. Each Dictionary will include a practical introduction, bibliography of recommended further reading and a chronology of key events.

Titles include:

Malcolm Andrew
THE PALGRAVE LITERARY DICTIONARY OF CHAUCER

Valerie Purton and Norman Page
THE PALGRAVE LITERARY DICTIONARY OF TENNYSON

Forthcoming:

Martin Garrett
THE PALGRAVE LITERARY DICTIONARY OF BYRON

Palgrave Literary Dictionaries
Series Standing Order ISBN 978–0–333–98779–7 (Hardback) 978–0–230–20035–7 (Paperback)
(*outside North America only*)

You can receive future titles in this series as they are published by placing a standing order. Please contact your bookseller or, in case of difficulty, write to us at the address below with your name and address, the title of the series and the ISBN quoted above.

Customer Services Department, Macmillan Distribution Ltd, Houndmills, Basingstoke, Hampshire RG21 6XS, England

---

Also by Malcolm Andrew

THE POEMS OF THE PEARL MANUSCRIPT (edited with Ronald Waldron)

THE *GAWAIN*-POET: An Annotated Bibliography 1839–1977

TWO EARLY RENAISSANCE BIRD POEMS (editor)

VARIORUM CHAUCER: *The General Prologue* (edited with Charles Moorman & Daniel J. Ransom)

GEOFFREY CHAUCER: *The Canterbury Tales* (revised version of edition by A.C. Cawley)

Palgrave Literary Dictionaries
The Palgrave Literary Dictionary of Chaucer

Malcolm Andrew

First published in hardback 2006
First published in paperback 2009 by
PALGRAVE MACMILLAN

Palgrave Macmillan in the UK is an imprint of Macmillan Publishers Limited, registered in England, company number 785998, of Houndmills, Basingstoke, Hampshire RG21 6XS.

Palgrave Macmillan in the US is a division of St. Martin's Press LLC, 175 Fifth Avenue, New York, NY. 10010

Palgrave Macmillan is the global academic imprint of the above companies and has companies and representatives throughout the world.

Palgrave® and Macmillan® are registered trademarks in the United States, the United Kingdom, Europe and other countries.

ISBN-13: 978–0–333–99808–3 hardback
ISBN-13: 978–0–230–23148–1 paperback

This book is printed on paper suitable for recycling and made from fully managed and sustained forest sources. Logging, pulping and manufacturing processes are expected to conform to the environmental regulations of the country of origin.

A catalogue record for this book is available from the British Library.

Library of Congress Cataloging-in-Publication Data

Andrew, Malcolm.
    The Palgrave literary dictionary of Chaucer / Malcolm Andrew.
       p. cm.—(Palgrave literary dictionaries)
    Includes bibliographical references and index.
    ISBN 978–0–333–99808–3 (cloth) 978–0–230–23148–1 (pbk)
       1. Chaucer, Geoffrey, d. 1400 – Encyclopedias. 2. Poets, English – Middle
English, 1100–1500 – Biography – Encyclopedias. I. Title. II. Series.

PR1903.A53 2006
821'.1—dc22   2005045603

10 9 8 7 6 5 4 3 2 1
18 17 16 15 14 13 12 11 10 09

Printed and bound in Great Britain by
CPI Antony Rowe, Chippenham and Eastbourne

Contents

Series Editors' Foreword

The purpose of the *Palgrave Literary Dictionaries* is to provide the reader with immediate access to reliable information on some of the major authors of literature written in the English language. These books are intended for a readership including students, graduate students, teachers, scholars, and advanced general readers. Each volume will be dedicated either to an individual author or to a group of authors. It will offer a concise reference guide, consisting mainly of entries presented under headwords arranged in alphabetical order. The entries will vary in length from about 10 to about 3000 words, depending on the significance of the particular topic. The topics will include the literary works, individuals, fictional characters, genres, traditions, events, places, institutions, editors, and scholars most relevant to a full and sophisticated understanding and appreciation of the author (or authors) in question. The more substantial entries will include suggestions for further reading, full particulars of which will be supplied in a selective bibliography. Access to information will be facilitated by extensive cross-referencing.

We trust that volumes in this series will be judged by their effectiveness in providing quick, clear, and convenient access to reliable and scholarly information.

BRIAN G. CARAHER & ESTELLE SHEEHAN
SERIES EDITORS'
QUEEN'S UNIVERSITY BELFAST

Preface

This book is intended to provide the reader with swift and convenient access to scholarly information about the works, life, and times of Geoffrey Chaucer, presented in succinct and cogent form. It consists mainly of about 720 entries, arranged under headwords in alphabetical order. These headwords have been carefully chosen. They cover topics and issues which include the following: each of Chaucer's works; major fictional characters in these works; writers who influenced Chaucer or were influenced by him; people and places of significance in Chaucer's life and works; relevant genres and literary traditions; the most significant manuscripts and editions; the most distinguished scholars and editors (up to *c.* 1950); and historical, social, and political contexts.

The selection of the topics and issues covered in the entries has, inevitably, been limited by the relatively compact scale of this book; it is also at least somewhat subjective. It has, however, been carefully and consistently related to the texts of Chaucer's works and to the events of his life and times. An outline of the latter is provided in the brief chronology (pp. xiv–xvi).

Access to the information contained in the entries is facilitated by cross-references of two distinct kinds. Nearly 300 headwords serve only as cross-references to one or more relevant entries. Within each entry, asterisks are used to indicate the existence of another potentially relevant entry on a related topic. (The latter method is not used to indicate the existence of entries on Chaucer or any of his works, since it will hardly be necessary to draw these to the reader's attention.)

Each entry begins with a brief definition. While this comprises the whole entry in a minority of cases, in most it introduces an account which varies in length from a few dozen to three thousand words. The length of any particular entry is intended to be appropriate to the relative significance and complexity of its topic. Plentiful allusions to Chaucer's works are provided. These make use of abbreviated titles, as listed in the table of abbreviations (pp. x–xiii). In order to avoid any potential confusion, all abbreviated titles appear in italics (whatever the length of the work in question). Line references are provided whenever allusions are made to specific passages, lines, or words. While these refer specifically to the text printed in *The Riverside Chaucer*, they should allow the reader to locate the relevant passage in any good edition. Translations of the titles of works in Latin are provided, but only in the main entry in which they are cited (normally that on the author of the work in question).

The longer entries and those on the more significant topics end with suggestions for further reading. These refer to the brief selective bibliography, with which this book concludes.

Acknowledgements

The genesis of the *Palgrave Literary Dictionary of Geoffrey Chaucer* has been somewhat strange and notably protracted. About fifteen years ago, a publisher contacted me to ask whether I thought there was a need for a handbook on Chaucer. After reviewing the relevant publications then available, I responded by observing that the term 'handbook' was used to describe books of several different kinds, and that (in my view) the most useful addition to these would be a Chaucer dictionary. When the publisher proceeded to ask me whether I wished to submit a proposal for such a volume, my answer was negative – essentially because I was then both involved in other projects and carrying a heavy burden of management duties in my university. During the following years, I found, nonetheless, that the idea of such a volume slowly took shape in my mind. I discussed it with several scholars in the field, and gradually compiled a list of potential headwords. When I happened to meet Eleanor Birne – then a commissioning editor with Palgrave – in the autumn of 2000, and mentioned the idea to her, she responded with enthusiasm. The outcome, five years later, is not only the present volume but also a fledgling series.

In the early stages of this project, Queen's University provided me with a part-time research assistant, Lisa English, to help me keep my research alive during a year of particularly heavy management duties. As well as assisting with another project, she did some valuable work on my list of headwords and created some computer files which served me very well. During the early stages of the project, I also benefited from the support and advice of various scholars, especially Al David, Tony Edwards, and the late David Burnley. Several other colleagues have kindly provided specific information: thanks are due to James Binns, Bruce Campbell, Brian Caraher, Kevin De Ornellas, Rosalind Field, Judith Green, Stephen Kelly, Linne Mooney, Desmond O'Rawe, Derek Pearsall, Estelle Sheehan, Karen Smyth, and John Thompson. I have enjoyed working with three Palgrave editors – first Eleanor Birne, then Emily Rosser, and finally Paula Kennedy.

Throughout this project – and, indeed, throughout my career – I have been exceptionally fortunate in the support I have received from my wife and family. I am particularly grateful to my wife, Lena, not only for taking care of me so well, but also for granting me the space to get on with my work.

MALCOLM ANDREW
QUEEN'S UNIVERSITY BELFAST

Abbreviations

1. Works by Chaucer

ABC	*An ABC*
Adam	*Chaucers Wordes Unto Adam, His Owne Scriveyn* (also known as *Adam Scriveyn*)
Anel	*Anelida and Arcite*
Ariadne	*The Legend of Ariadne* (*LGW*)
Astr	*A Treatise on the Astrolabe*
Bal Compl	*A Balade of Complaint*
BD	*The Book of the Duchess*
Bo	*Boece*
Buk	*Lenvoy de Chaucer a Bukton*
CkP	*The Cook's Prologue*
CkT	*The Cook's Tale*
Cleopatra	*The Legend of Cleopatra* (*LGW*)
ClP	*The Clerk's Prologue*
ClT	*The Clerk's Tale*
Compl d'Am	*Complaynt d'Amours*
CT	*The Canterbury Tales*
CYP	*The Canon's Yeoman's Prologue*
CYT	*The Canon's Yeoman's Tale*
Dido	*The Legend of Dido* (*LGW*)
Equat	*The Equatorie of the Planetis*
For	*Fortune*
Form Age	*The Former Age*
FranP	*The Franklin's Prologue*
FranT	*The Franklin's Tale*
FrP	*The Friar's Prologue*
FrT	*The Friar's Tale*
Gent	*Gentilesse*
GP	*The General Prologue*
HF	*The House of Fame*
Hypermnestra	*The Legend of Hypermnestra* (*LGW*)
Hypsipyle	*The Legend of Hypsipyle* (*LGW*)
Hypsipyle and Medea	*The Legend of Hypsipyle and Medea* (*LGW*)

KnT	*The Knight's Tale*
Lady	*A Complaint to His Lady*
LGW	*The Legend of Good Women*
LGWP	*The Prologue to the Legend of Good Women*
Lucrece	*The Legend of Lucrece (LGW)*
MancP	*The Manciple's Prologue*
MancT	*The Manciple's Tale*
Mars	*The Complaint of Mars*
Medea	*The Legend of Medea (LGW)*
Mel	*The Tale of Melibee*
MelP	*The Prologue to the Tale of Melibee*
MercB	*Merciles Beaute*
MerE	*The Epilogue to the Merchant's Tale*
MerP	*The Merchant's Prologue*
MerT	*The Merchant's Tale*
MilP	*The Miller's Prologue*
MilT	*The Miller's Tale*
MkP	*The Monk's Prologue*
MkT	*The Monk's Tale*
MLE	*The Epilogue to the Man of Law's Tale*
MLIntro	*The Introduction to the Man of Law's Tale*
MLP	*The Man of Law's Prologue*
MLT	*The Man of Law's Tale*
NPE	*The Epilogue to the Nun's Priest's Tale*
NPP	*The Nun's Priest's Prologue*
NPT	*The Nun's Priest's Tale*
PardIntro	*The Introduction to the Pardoner's Tale*
PardP	*The Pardoner's Prologue*
PardT	*The Pardoner's Tale*
ParsP	*The Parson's Prologue*
ParsT	*The Parson's Tale*
PF	*The Parlement of Foules*
Philomela	*The Legend of Philomela (LGW)*
Phyllis	*The Legend of Phyllis (LGW)*
PhyT	*The Physician's Tale*
Pity	*The Complaint unto Pity*
Prov	*Proverbs*
PrP	*The Prioress's Prologue*
PrT	*The Prioress's Tale*
Purse	*The Complaint of Chaucer to His Purse*

Ret	*Chaucer's Retraction*
Rom	*The Romaunt of the Rose*
Ros	*To Rosemounde*
RvP	*The Reeve's Prologue*
RvT	*The Reeve's Tale*
Scog	*Lenvoy de Chaucer a Scogan*
ShT	*The Shipman's Tale*
SNP	*The Second Nun's Prologue*
SNT	*The Second Nun's Tale*
SqIntro	*The Introduction to the Squire's Tale*
SqT	*The Squire's Tale*
Sted	*Lak of Stedfastnesse*
SumP	*The Summoner's Prologue*
SumT	*The Summoner's Tale*
Th	*The Tale of Sir Thopas*
Thisbe	*The Legend of Thisbe (LGW)*
ThP	*The Prologue to Sir Thopas*
Tr	*Troilus and Criseyde*
Truth	*Truth*
Ven	*The Complaint of Venus*
WBP	*The Wife of Bath's Prologue*
WBT	*The Wife of Bath's Tale*
Wom Nobl	*Womanly Noblesse*
Wom Unc	*Against Women Unconstant*

2. Books of the Bible

Acts	Acts of the Apostles
Cor.	Epistle of St Paul to the Corinthians
Dan.	Daniel
Eccles.	Ecclesiastes
Exod.	Exodus
Gen.	Genesis
Jer.	Jeremiah
Macc.	Maccabees (Apocrypha)
Matt.	Gospel according to St Matthew
Sam.	Samuel
Song of Sol.	Song of Solomon

3. Miscellaneous

c.	circa
d.	died
fl.	flourished
m.	metrum (in *Bo*)
MED	*Middle English Dictionary*
MS	Manuscript
OED	*Oxford English Dictionary*
p.	prosa (in *Bo*)
RR	*La Roman de la Rose* (references are to the edition of Langlois: see Bibliography)
STC	*A Short Title Catalogue of Books Printed in England, Scotland, & Ireland . . . 1475–1640*, ed. A.W. Pollard and G.R. Redgrave. Second edn, rev. W.A. Jackson, F.S. Ferguson, and Katharine F. Pantzer, 3 vols (London: Bibliographical Society, 1976–91).

Chronology

c. 1312	Birth of Chaucer's father, John Chaucer.
1313	Birth of Boccaccio.
1321	Death of Dante.
1327	Accession of Edward III.
1328	Edward III marries Philippa of Hainault.
1337–1453	The Hundred Years' War between England and France.
1338	Completion of Boccaccio's *Il Filostrato* (main source for *Tr*).
early 1340s	Birth of Chaucer, probably in London.
1341	Completion of Boccaccio's *Teseide* (main source for *KnT*).
1348–49	England ravaged by the Black Death.
1357	Chaucer in service as a page in the household of Elizabeth, Countess of Ulster, wife of Prince Lionel.
1359–60	Chaucer experiences military service in the retinue of Lionel in France; ransomed after being captured at the siege of Reims.
1360–69	Peace between England and France, following the Treaty of Brétigny.
c. 1365–66	Chaucer marries Philippa Roet, eldest daughter of Sir Paon de Roet and sister of Katherine (later Katherine Swynford, eventually the third wife of John of Gaunt).
1366	Death of Chaucer's father, John Chaucer.
1367	Birth of Richard of Bordeaux, later Richard II.
by 1367	Chaucer in service as an esquire in the household of Edward III.
c. 1367	Birth of Chaucer's elder son, Thomas.
late 1360s	Chaucer translates all or part of *Le Roman de la Rose*, as *Rom*.
1367	Death of Blanche, Duchess of Lancaster (September), subsequently commemorated by Chaucer in *BD*.
1369	Death of Queen Philippa (August).
1369, 1370	Chaucer experiences military service with John of Gaunt in northern France.
1370s	Chaucer writes *ABC*, *Anel*, *HF*, and the stories which later became *SNT* and *MkT*.
1372	Philippa Chaucer in service in the household of Constance, second wife of John of Gaunt.

1372–73	Chaucer travels to Genoa and Florence on dipomatic business; this visit to Italy probably brings him into contact with works by Dante, Petrarch, and Boccaccio.
1374	Chaucer appointed controller of customs for hides, skins, and wools in the port of London; granted lease for a dwelling above Aldgate; granted a daily pitcher of wine by Edward III and an annuity by John of Gaunt. Death of Petrarch.
1375	Death of Boccaccio.
1376	Death of Edward, the Black Prince (June).
1377	Death of Edward III (June); accession of Richard II.
1378	Chaucer travels to Lombardy on diplomatic business. Richard II confirms Chaucer's annuities.
1380	Chaucer released from threat of legal action regarding a potential accusation of rape by Cecily Champain. Birth of his younger son, Lewis.
early 1380s	Chaucer writes *PF* and *Palamon and Arcite* (which became *KnT*).
1381	Death of Chaucer's mother. Marriage of Richard II and Anne of Bohemia (May); the Peasants' Revolt (June).
mid-1380s	Chaucer translates the *De consolatione philosophiae* of Boethius (as *Bo*) and writes *Tr* and *LGW*.
1385	Chaucer becomes a Justice of the Peace for Kent and is appointed to the county's commission of the peace.
1386	Chaucer retires from his position as controller of customs and relinquishes his lease on the dwelling above Aldgate. Serves as member of parliament for Kent. Gives testimony in the legal action between Sir Richard Scrope and Sir Robert Grosvenor.
1386–89	Period during which the powers of Richard II are curbed, and Chaucer appears to be out of favour.
1387	Death of Chaucer's wife, Philippa.
c. 1387–1400	Chaucer writing *CT*.
1389	Chaucer appointed clerk of the king's works.
1391	Chaucer resigns clerkship of the king's works; appointed deputy forester of North Petherton (Somerset); writes *Astr*.
1392	Composition of *Equat* (possibly by Chaucer).
1394	Death of Queen Anne. Chaucer granted a royal annuity; revises *LGWP*.
1395	Thomas Chaucer marries Maud Burghersh.

1396   Richard II marries the French princess Isabella (aged 6). John of Gaunt marries Katherine Swynford.

1397   Chaucer granted a tun (272 gallons) of wine yearly by Richard II.

1399   Deposition of Richard II; accession of Henry IV, who confirms Chaucer's annuities. Chaucer leases a house in the precinct of Westminster Abbey.

1400   Chaucer dies; buried in Westminster Abbey. His remains are subsequently moved to 'Poet's Corner'.

A

abbot *see Prioress's Prologue and Tale, The*

ABC, An

Devotional poem of 184 lines, addressed to the Virgin *Mary. *ABC* survives, complete or in fragmentary form, in 16 manuscript copies, and is attributed to Chaucer in four of these. The title was supplied by *Skeat. The poem is written in an eight-line stanza, rhyming ababbcbc, which Chaucer uses elsewhere in *MkT* (and in *Form Age* and *Buk*). Each of its 23 stanzas begins with a different letter of the alphabet, progressing from A to Z (but omitting the modern letters J, U, and W). *ABC* constitutes a prayer of petition to the Virgin, based on a poem in *Deguilleville's *Le Pèlerinage de la Vie Humaine*. The speaker's appeal for the Virgin to intercede on his behalf makes notable use both of legal terminology and of a great wealth of images and symbols representing the relationship between the petitioner and the Virgin. There is no evidence to support the statement made by *Speght in his second edition (1602), to the effect that *ABC* may have been written at the request of the Duchess *Blanche, who died in 1368. Indeed, Chaucer's use of the deca-syllabic line in this poem suggests a somewhat later date of composition, perhaps in the late 1370s. *ABC* invites comparison with the invocations to the Virgin in *PrP* (VII.467ff./ B^2.1657ff.) and *SNP* (VIII.29ff.).

Further reading: V.J. Scattergood in Minnis (1995).

Abigail *see* **Bible; David**

Absolon

Parish clerk and admirer of *Alison in *MilT*. Absolon is portrayed as affected and effeminate, with his elaborately styled hair, fancy clothes, and squea-mishness. Though he suffers humiliation at the hands of *Nicholas, his rival for the affections of Alison, he eventually takes revenge in a notably decisive manner. His name would have been rare in medieval England and suggests an association with the biblical Absalom, son of David, known for his luxu-riant hair (2 Sam.14–15), to whom passing allusions (also as 'Absolon') occur in *LGWP* (F.249, 539/G.203) and *ParsT* (X.639).

1

Accidie *see* Sloth

Achates

Trusted companion and armour-bearer of *Aeneas. In *Dido* (*LGW* 963ff.) Chaucer describes how Achates accompanies Aeneas to *Carthage, where they meet *Venus disguised as a huntress. Achates is also mentioned, in the context of the same story, in *HF* (219ff.).

Achilles

Foremost Greek hero of the Trojan war. Achilles is named several times in *Tr*, most notably when he kills *Hector and *Troilus (5.1548–61, 1800–06). Passing allusions, mainly concerning his martial prowess, occur in various other works, including *SqT* (V.239), *NPT* (VII.3148/B².4338), *MLT* (II.198), and *BD* (329). The death of Achilles, resulting from his unfortunate love for *Polyxena, is briefly described in *BD* (1064–71). His mistreatment of his previous love, *Briseyde, is mentioned in *HF* (398) and *MLIntro* (II.70–71).

Adam

The first man (according to the *Bible). Adam is mentioned, mainly in connection with the Creation and the Fall, in various works. A brief account of the Fall constitutes the second of the Monk's 'tragedies' (*MkT* VII.2007–14/B².3197–204). Its implications, especially with regard to the origins of sin, are considered in *ParsT* (X.322–36, 682), where Adam and *Eve are accused of *Gluttony (X.819), as they are in *PardT* (VI.505–11). The suggestion that the Fall was brought about when Adam paid heed to the bad advice of a woman is made (evasively) in *NPT* (VII.3256–66/B².4446–56). Allusions to the creation of Eve as a companion for Adam occur in several texts, including *ParsT* (X.925–9), *Mel* (VII.1103–4/B².2293–4), and *MerT* (IV.1325–32).

Adam Scriveyn see Chaucers Wordes unto Adam, His Owne Scriveyn; Adenet le Roi *see* **Squire's Introduction and Tale, The**; Adrastus *see* **Seven Against Thebes**; Adriane, Adryane *see* **Ariadne**

Aegeus

King of *Athens and father of *Theseus. In *KnT* (I.2836–52) Aegeus utters a bleakly fatalistic speech following the death of *Arcite. His position as the father of Theseus and his death are mentioned in *Ariadne* (*LGW* 1944, 2178).

Aegidius, St *see* Giles, St

Aegyptus

King of Egypt and brother of Danaus, king of Argos. *Ovid's *Heroides* tells the story of the rivalry between these two brothers. The 50 sons of Aegyptus marry the 50 daughters of Danaus, who instructs his daughters to kill their husbands on their wedding night. All obey except *Hypermnestra. She spares her husband *Lynceus, who later kills Danaus. Chaucer tells part of this story in *Hypermnestra* (*LGW* 2562ff.), but reverses the identities of the two brothers, making Aegyptus the father of Hypermnestra and Danaus the father of Lynceus.

Ælla *see* Alla

Aeneas

Son of *Venus and *Anchises. Passing references to Aeneas occur in *Tr* (2.1474), *BD* (733), and *MLIntro* (II.64). The first of these alludes to the legend linking him with *Antenor in the betrayal of *Troy to the Greeks. The others allude to the story of his affair with *Dido, which Chaucer relates in *LGW* (924ff.) and *HF* (239ff.). In both accounts, Chaucer shows a sophisticated awareness of the differences between the story as told by *Virgil and as told by *Ovid – the former tending to sympathise with Aeneas, the latter with Dido. *HF* also describes the flight of Aeneas from Troy (166ff.) and his journey to Hades in search of his father *Anchises (439ff.). Later in *HF* (1485) there is an allusion to his representation by Virgil as 'Pius [noble] Eneas'.

Aeneid *see* Virgil

Aeolus

Mythical god of the winds. During the Middle Ages he was represented as a trumpeter, and it is in this form that he appears in *HF* (1567ff.) – with two clarions, proclaiming either good or bad reputation.

Aesculapius

Ancient Greek god of medicine. While the inclusion of this name in the list of authorities known to the *Physician (*GP* I.429) has often been taken ironically – to suggest ignorance or pretension – it is worth noting that several medical treatises were attributed to Aesculapius during the Middle Ages.

Aesop

(6th century BC)
Semi-mythical author of fables. The name of Aesop was attached to several collections of fables during the Middle Ages. Chaucer's single allusion to 'Isope' in *Mel* (VII.1184/B².2374) – a quotation to the effect that one should not trust a past enemy – was derived from his source, *Renaud de Louens. The influence of the Aesop tradition is reflected in *NPT*, which is based on a *beast fable, and in *MancT* and *MerT*, of which (partial) Aesopic analogues exist. Passing allusions to Aesopic fables occur in several other works, including *KnT* (I.1177–80), *RvT* (I.4054–5), *WBP* (III.692), and *Tr* (1.257–8): see explanatory notes in Benson (1987).

African *see* Scipio the Elder

Against Women Unconstant

*Ballade of 21 lines, uncertainly attributed to Chaucer. Though *Wom Unc* is not ascribed to Chaucer in any of the manuscripts in which it survives, it has normally been included in collected editions (often, however, in sections reserved for works of dubious authenticity). *Wom Unc* consists of three *rhyme royal stanzas. Its title was modified by *Skeat from one given by *Stowe; it has also appeared under the title *Newefangelnesse*. While the latter is a word which Chaucer may have coined (see *OED*, *MED*), the anti-feminist sentiments of *Wom Unc* are hardly typical of his work. The refrain echoes that of a ballade by *Machaut.
   Further reading: Pace and David (1982); V.J. Scattergood in Minnis (1995).

Agamemnon

Leader of the Greeks in the Trojan war. A passing allusion to him as such occurs in *Tr* (3.382). There are brief accounts of two stories associated with

Agamemnon – the return of *Helen and the sacrifice of his daughter (Iphigenia) – in *Bo* (4, m.7.1ff.), where he is also named Atrides (i.e. son of Atreus).

Agaton

Supposed author of a story concerning *Alceste. The allusion to Agaton in connection with the transformation of Alceste (*LGWP* F.526/G.514) has been taken to signify either the *Symposium* of *Plato or a Greek tragedian mentioned by *Dante (*Purgatorio* 22.107).

Alan

One of the young scholars in *RvT*. Alan and his companion, *John, are scholars of *Soler Hall, *Cambridge. Their origins in the north of England are reflected in the use of various dialect words and forms (see *RvT* I.4022ff. and note in Benson, 1987: 850). They are first cheated by *Simkin, the dishonest miller of *Trumpington, and then take comic revenge on him. Though they are represented as a pair, Alan emerges as the more resourceful and impetuous of the two.

Alan of Lille

(*c.* 1116–1202)
French author, also known as Alanus de Insulis. Chaucer was familiar with the two philosophical allegories written by Alan, *De planctu naturae* ('On the complaint of Nature') and *Anticlaudianus* ('Against Claudianus'). The former provides the basis for the figure of *Nature in *PF*, as Chaucer duly acknowledges (*PF* 316). The latter, echoed in the account of the heavens in *HF* (964ff.), is also acknowledged (*HF* 986).

Albertanus of Brescia

(*c.* 1193–*c.* 1270)
Writer on moral and legal matters. Chaucer was indebted to three works by Albertanus, all written in Latin prose during the mid-thirteenth century. *Mel* is based on a French translation, by *Renaud de Louens, of his *Liber consolationis et consilii* ('The book of consolation and counsel'). The discussion

of marriage in the early part of *MerT* (IV.1311ff.) reflects the influence of his *De amore et dilectione Dei* ('On the love and dearness of God'). The comments on silence, towards the end of *MancT* (IX.325ff.) draw on his *De arte dicendi et tacendi* ('On the art of speaking and being silent').

Albion *see* Brut

Alceste

Queen of *Thessaly; exemplary virtuous woman in *LGW*. In *LGWP* (F.241ff./G.173ff.), Alceste defends the poet-narrator against the accusation of the god of *Love – essentially, that *Tr* and *Rom* are unsympathetic to love and to women – and instructs him to make amends by writing tales of virtuous women (which come to constitute *LGW*). The story of Alceste's goodness and of how she was turned into the daisy which becomes her symbol is later summarized (F.510ff./G.498ff.). The notion that she represents *Anne of Bohemia was proposed by *Tyrwhitt, but no longer attracts much support. Passing references to Alceste as a woman of exemplary virtue also occur in *MLIntro* (II.75), *FranT* (V.1442), and *Tr* (5.1527, 1778).

Alcione

Daughter of *Aeolus and wife of *Ceyx. The story of how Ceyx drowns at sea and of Alcione's need to face this loss forms a significant episode in *BD* (62ff.). It is based on *Ovid's *Metamorphoses* (11.410ff.).

Alecto *see* Furies

Alexander

(356–323 BC)
Alexander the Great, king of Macedonia. An account of Alexander's life and death is included in *MkT* (VII.2631ff./B^2.3821ff.). This account conforms to the tale's theme of the fall of princes, and describes how Alexander was poisoned by his own followers. An allusion to a well-known anecdote on the nature of power, supposedly told to Alexander, occurs in *MancT* (IX.226–34). He is mentioned briefly in several other works, including *BD* (1059–60) and *HF* (913–15).

Alexandria

Egyptian city. The capture of Alexandria in 1365 is mentioned twice: in the brief 'tragedy' of *Pierre de Lusignan (*MkT* VII.2392/B².3582) and among the campaigns on which the *Knight has served (*GP* I.51). Passing allusions to Alexandria occur in *BD* (1026) and *CYT* (VIII.975).

Algarsif *see* Cambyuskan

Algeciras

Seaport in *Granada. The siege of Algeciras ('Algezir'), a Moorish stronghold which fell to Christian forces in 1344, is included among the campaigns on which the *Knight has served (*GP* I.56–7).

Algus

(fl. 9th century)
Arabian mathematician. Algus ('Argus') is mentioned in *BD* (435–42) as the inventor of Arabic numerals.

Alhazen

(c. 965–1038)
Arab author of a work on optics. A passing allusion to Alhazen ('Alocen') occurs in *SqT* (V.232).

Alice *see* Alison; Wife of Bath

Alisaundre *see* Alexandria

Alison

Female protagonist of *MilT*. The portrayal of Alison is derived from the stereotype of the young woman married to an old man – in this case, *John the carpenter. The celebrated set-piece description of Alison (I.3233ff.) stresses her attractiveness, liveliness, and sexuality. In the course of the tale, she becomes the object of competition between three men – her husband, her lover *Nicholas, and her admirer *Absolon.

The *Wife of Bath is also called Alison and Alice (the latter presumably an abbreviated form), though these names occur only once each (*WBP* III.804, 320). Her close friend is, likewise, called both Alison and Alice (*WBP* III.530, 548).

Alkaron *see* Koran

Alla

King of Northumbria and husband of *Custance in *MLT*. Alla may be identified with the historical Ælla (d. 588), king of Deira (the southern part of Northumbria). He is portrayed as a just ruler and a faithful husband.

alliterative verse

Traditional English verse, associated mainly with the north and the midlands. The movement sometimes termed the 'Alliterative Revival' occurred during the second half of the fourteenth century. It consisted mainly of narrative poetry written in a long alliterating line which had evolved from the four-stress alliterative metre of Old English verse. The best alliterative poems, especially *Piers Plowman* and *Sir Gawain and the Green Knight*, are among the finest written in English during the Middle Ages. Even the poems of more modest quality – which tend to be insular and prolix – have particular strengths, especially in powerful descriptions of violent events. While dialect evidence indicates that most of this poetry was written in the north and the north-west midlands, several alliterative poems have connections with London – where, incidentally, *Richard II had an entourage from Cheshire during the last years of his reign. Most significantly, William *Langland, the author of *Piers Plowman*, came from the south-west midlands and seems to have lived in London for some time.

Chaucer uses alliteration (though not the alliterative long line) in passages from *Cleopatra* (*LGW* 635ff.) and *KnT* (I.2601ff.) – both, notably, descriptions of conflict. The refusal of the Parson, as a 'Southren man', to 'geeste "rum, ram, ruf, by lettre" ' (*ParsP* X.42–4) clearly constitutes an allusion to alliterative poetry (cf. 'geeste' in *MelP* VII.933/B^2.2133). Any assumption that it reflects contempt on Chaucer's part should, however, be qualified by the following line, in which the Parson states that he regards 'rym' (i.e. rhyming poetry) as 'but litel bettre'.

Almachius *see* Cecilia, St; *Second Nun's Prologue and Tale, The*

Almagest *see* Ptolomy; Alocen *see* Alhazen; Amazons *see* Scythia

Ambrose, St

(339–97)
Bishop of Milan; one of the four doctors of the early church (along with SS *Augustine, *Jerome, and *Gregory). Ambrose is quoted on martyrdom in *SNT* (VIII.270–83) and on penitence in *ParsT* (X.83–4).

Amorous Complaint *see* *Complaynt d'Amours*

Amphiaraus

One of the *Seven Against Thebes. Allusions to the death of Amphiaraus ('Amphiorax') occur in *Tr* (2.105, 5.1500) and *Anel* (57). In *WBP* (III.741) he is said to have been included in *Jankin's *'book of wicked wives', as an example of a man betrayed by his wife.

Anchises

Father of *Aeneas. Anchises is mentioned several times in *HF* and in *Dido*. Both poems describe how he was carried from the flames of *Troy on his son's shoulders (*HF* 168–73; *LGW* 943–4). *HF* (439–50) also provides a brief account of Aeneas' journey to Hades in search of his father.

Andreas Capellanus

(fl. late 12th century)
French author. Andreas Capellanus wrote a Latin treatise on 'courtly love', usually known as the *De amore* ('On love'). While it is unlikely that Chaucer

knew this work directly, it may have influenced him indirectly, perhaps through *Jean de Meun's part of *RR.

Andromache *see* Hector

Anelida

Queen of Armenia; abandoned lover of *Arcite in *Anel*. Anelida is portrayed as a young, beautiful, and faithful woman, deceived by a false and cynical lover.

Anelida and Arcite

Poem of 357 lines, combining narrative and *complaint. *Anel* survives in 12 manuscripts, and is attributed to Chaucer in three of these (two of which were written by *Shirley). The title is editorial. *Anel* comprises an invocation (21 lines), the story (189 lines), and the complaint of *Anelida (147 lines). In several manuscripts, the story is headed with an epigraph from the *Thebaid* of *Statius concerning the return of *Theseus to *Athens with *Hippolyta and *Emily (a shorter version of which appears as an epigraph in some manuscripts of *KnT*). Though the story begins with a brief account of these events (cf. *KnT* I.875ff.), it focuses on the love of Anelida for the unworthy *Arcite, who leaves her for another lady. The complaint of Anelida takes the form of a letter to Arcite, in which she expresses her sorrow and sense of betrayal. Thus both the story and the complaint have strong similarities with *LGW*.

The invocation and the story are written in *rhyme royal stanzas, which Chaucer may well have been using for the first time. The complaint, on the other hand, consists of nine-line and 16-line stanzas (12 of the former and two of the latter). In terms of structure and metre, it is the most complex and intricate passage in Chaucer's works, with a proem and strophe precisely matched by the following antistrophe and conclusion, the use of only two rhymes in most of the stanzas, and a mixture of octosyllabic and decasyllabic lines in the two 16-line stanzas. *Anel* is unfinished, and ends with a (rhyme royal) stanza promising a continuation of the story in which Anelida visits the temple of Mars. This suggests that Chaucer considered basing the unwritten conclusion on a passage from *Boccaccio's *Teseida*, later used for the description of the temple of Mars in *KnT* (I.1967ff.). While the invocation is, indeed, based on the *Teseida* (and probably constitutes Chaucer's first borrowing from this poem, which was to prove so influential in his work), its allusions to further sources (Statius and *Corinna) are misleading: no other significant source for *Anel* has been found. It has generally been supposed that this is a fairly early work, written around 1380, possibly between *HF* and *PF*.

Further reading: V.J. Scattergood in Minnis (1995).

Anne

Sister of *Dido. Anne (called Anna in Virgil and Ovid) is mentioned as her sister's counsellor and confidante in *Dido* (*LGW* 1168ff., 1343ff.) and in *HF* (364ff.).

Anne of Bohemia

(1366–94)

First wife of *Richard II. Anne, the daughter of the Holy Roman Emperor Charles IV, was born in Prague on 11 May 1366. She married Richard in Westminster Abbey on 20 January 1382. It is thought that she sympathized with the radical religious views of her compatriot Jan Hus and of John *Wyclif – sympathies which Chaucer himself is often assumed to have shared. Anne died of the plague, childless, on 7 June 1394 at the royal palace of *Sheen, which Richard had demolished the following year as a mark of respect. Her monument and effigy, designed by Henry *Yevele, can still be seen in Westminster Abbey.

Several references to Anne have been identified in Chaucer's work. The most explicit of these occurs in *LGWP* (F.496–7), where *Alceste stipulates that the finished book should be presented to 'the quene' – presumably Anne. This statement may have given rise to the claim of *Lydgate in his *Fall of Princes* (1.330–36) that Chaucer wrote *LGW* at Anne's request. In the revised version of *LGWP* (G), the reference to the queen has been removed, presumably following Anne's death. It has been suggested that the last part of *PF* may refer to the negotiations concerning the betrothal of Richard and Anne. The allusion to the letter A in *Tr* (1.171) probably constitutes a compliment to her. An allusion to the wrecking of Anne's ship shortly after her arrival in England on 18 December 1381 has been detected in *KnT* (I.884).

Anne, St

Mother of the Virgin *Mary. It is specifically in this role that St Anne is addressed in *MLT* (II.641) and *SNP* (VIII.70). Her name also occurs in an oath in *FrT* (III.1613).

Anselm, St

(1033–1109)
Theological writer and Archbishop of Canterbury. St Anselm is quoted on
the pains of hell in *ParsT* (I.168–72).

Antenor

Trojan who betrays *Troy to the Greeks. A brief allusion to Antenor as a
traitor occurs in *BD* (1119–20). The sequence of events which brings
about the exchange of Antenor, then a prisoner of the Greeks, for *Criseyde
is described at length in the fourth and fifth books of *Tr*.

Anthony *see* Antony; *Anticlaudianus see* Alan of Lille

anti-feminist writing

Tradition of writing which satirized women and warned men against
marriage. Chaucer's work shows an extensive knowledge of anti-feminist
writing and a lively engagement with the issues it raises. The origins of this
tradition are complex. Classical literature provided satire on the foibles of
women and debate on whether a wise man should marry (as well as praise of
good women and loyal wives). Christian writing – almost entirely by celibate
male clerics – struggled to reconcile some of the attitudes to sexuality in the
Old Testament with subsequent dogma, and expressed suspicion of women
and female sexuality in general, while praising virgin saints and martyrs. It
contrasted the flawed and pernicious femininity of *Eve with the perfect and
redemptive femininity of the Virgin *Mary. Throughout the later Middle
Ages, vernacular literature, religious and secular, reflects a continuing interest in these matters, setting the idealized female figures of the Virgin and the
romance heroine against their flawed counterparts.

Chaucer's engagement with anti-feminist writing is apparent throughout
his work, and especially in *CT*. The most sustained and conspicuous
encounter with it occurs in *WBP*, where the Wife of Bath takes issue with
the clerical view of women and female sexuality, both in general and as
represented in the texts contained in *Jankin's *'book of wicked wives'.
Elsewhere in *CT*, issues of love and marriage and of the conduct relating to
them, recur – though mainly in less polemical terms. Thus, for example, the
traditional debate on marriage is used in *MerT* (IV.1252ff., 2237ff.), while *ClT*
provides an account of a wife who confounds the anti-feminist stereotype.

Such themes and concerns are not limited to the *'marriage debate', conducted in the tales of the 'marriage group': they emerge in the first fragment of *CT* and continue throughout. They are also reflected in Chaucer's earlier work. *BD*, *HF*, and *PF* all deal, in one way or another, with love and the assessment of related female (and male) conduct. These matters are, of course, central to *Tr*. Chaucer's (supposed) criticism of women in *Tr* and *Rom* provides the ostensible reason for his being asked to write *LGW*, which mainly comprises the stories of women wronged by faithless male lovers – and may thus be seen as a counterblast to traditional anti-feminist prejudices.

Readers from the fifteenth century onwards have generally felt that Chaucer's work reflects a predominantly sympathetic view of women. While the development of feminist criticism since the 1960s has generated a wide range of opinions on this matter, Chaucer's critical engagement with the anti-feminist tradition has never been in doubt.

Further reading: Blamires (1992).

Antigone

One of the nieces of *Criseyde in *Tr*. Criseyde's three nieces, Antigone, Tharbe, and Flexippe, are introduced during the second book of *Tr* (2.816). While Antigone sings a love song relevant to the current situation of Criseyde (2.827ff.), the other two play no significant part in the story.

Antiochus

(d. 163 BC)
Antiochus Epiphanes VI, king of Syria. The story of his pride, affliction, and horrible death, based on the apocryphal Book of Maccabees (2 Macc. 9), is told as one of the *Monk's 'tragedies' (*MkT* VII.2575ff./B².3765ff.). An allusion to the story of *Apollonius of Tyre, in which Antiochus is guilty of raping his own daughter, occurs in *MLIntro* (II.81–9).

Antony

(c. 83–30 BC)
Mark Antony, Roman statesman and husband of *Cleopatra. In *Cleopatra* (*LGW* 580 ff.), Chaucer describes how Antony (also 'Antonius') abandons his wife – the sister of Octavian (subsequently the emperor *Augustus) – to marry Cleopatra, and how he is defeated by Octavian in the naval battle of

Actium, after which he commits suicide. A passing allusion to the death of Antony occurs in *KnT* (I.2032).

Apius

Evil judge in *PhyT*. The lust and cynicism of Apius lead to the death of the innocent maiden *Virginia. Apius eventually commits suicide.

Apollo *see* Phoebus

Apollonius of Tyre

Hero of romance. The statement in *MLIntro* (II.81–9), to the effect that Chaucer has not told tales of incest such as that of Apollonius (in which *Antiochus rapes his daughter) has sometimes been taken as a barb directed at *Gower, who had included this story in his *Confessio Amantis* (8.271ff.).

Appius *see* Apius

April

The month of April. The best-known allusion to April in Chaucer's work, at the beginning of *CT* (*GP* I.1), associates it with spring, showers, renewal (both physical and spiritual), and a particular moment in astronomical time. More specific astronomical allusions – to 12th and 18th April respectively – occur in *Mars* (139) and *MLIntro* (II.5–6). Elsewhere, in addition to the use of April to indicate a literal but less exact date (as in *Tr* 3.360), it is mainly associated with spring (as in *Tr* 1.156) or rain (as in *Anel* 309).

Aquitaine *see* Chaucer, Geoffrey; Edward, Prince of Wales; France

Arcite

Theban prince in *KnT* and *Anel*. Arcite is based on Arcita in the *Teseida* of *Boccaccio. In *Anel*, he is 'false Arcite', an unworthy man who wins the heart of *Anelida with feigned love and then betrays her. He appears as a different and more developed character in *KnT*. Here he is portrayed, with *Palamon, as one of a pair of cousins and sworn 'brothers', who are captured in war and become rivals in love. While Chaucer represents the two of them as essentially similar in background and outlook (notably reducing the contrasts between the characters in Boccaccio), Palamon is, perhaps, the more reflective and Arcite the more pragmatic – a distinction suggested by their respective adherence to *Venus and to *Mars. In order to remain close to *Emily, the object of his (and Palamon's) love during a period of banishment, Arcite adopts the name and identity of Philostrate. This name, signifying 'one vanquished in love', is (curiously) altered from that in the *Teseida* (Penteo), and modelled on the title of Boccaccio's *Il Filostrato*, the main source of *Tr*.

Argonautica see **Valerius Flaccus**

Argus

All-seeing man of ancient Greek myth. Passing allusions to Argus occur in *KnT* (I.1390), *WBP* (III.358), *MerT* (IV.2111), and *Tr* (4.1459). (This is also the name of the man who built *Jason's ship, the *Argo*, mentioned in *LGW* 1453.) *See also*: **Algus**.

Argyve

Mother of *Criseyde. Argyve is mentioned only once (*Tr* 4.762). Criseyde's mother remains unnamed in the main sources of *Tr*, and Chaucer appears to have derived this name from Argia in the *Thebaid* of *Statius. There she is the wife of Polynices (one of the *Seven Against Thebes), herself mentioned briefly in *Tr* (5.1509).

Ariadne

Daughter of *Minos and abandoned lover of *Theseus. The story of how Ariadne ('Adriane') and her sister *Phaedra help Theseus to defeat the *Minotaur and escape from *Crete, and how Theseus subsequently abandons Ariadne and leaves with Phaedra is told in *LGW* (1886ff.) as an example of male treachery. A summary of the story occurs in *HF* (405ff.) and a passing allusion to it in *MLIntro* (II.67). In *Phyllis* (*LGW* 2394ff.), Chaucer compares the treatment of Ariadne by Theseus to that of *Phyllis by his son *Demophoön.

Aries

First sign of the Zodiac, the Ram. References to Aries (also 'Ariete') and the Ram appear in formal allusions to the season or date in *GP* (I.8), *SqT* (V.51, 386), and *Tr* (4.1592, 5.1190). Aries also features in the calculations of the clerk of Orléans in *FranT* (V.1282). Numerous allusions to Aries, mainly of a technical kind, occur in *Astr*.

Arion

Mythical harper and poet. Two allusions to Arion (also 'Orion') occur in *HF* (1005, 1205), the first of which mentions his transformation into the constellation Lyra.

Aristotle

(384–322 BC)
Ancient Greek philosopher and scientist. Some of Aristotle's vast body of work on philosophical and scientific subjects was accessible to western Europe in the late Middle Ages, mainly through Latin versions of Arabic translations. In *GP* (I.295) the *Clerk is described as someone who prefers books on 'Aristotle and his philosophie' to worldly goods. Lady *Philosophy refers to Aristotle's *Physics* in *Bo* (5.p.1.62–4). Aristotle is cited on optical matters in *SqT* (V.233) and *Bo* (3.p.8.40), and on eternity in *Bo* (5.p.6.30). The allusion to 'Etik' in *LGWP* (F.166) has been taken to signify either Aristotle's *Ethics* or Horace (see note in Benson, 1987: 1062). Aristotle is mentioned briefly in *HF* (759) as an authority on sound.

Armorica

Ancient name for a coastal region of *Brittany and Normandy. The setting for *FranT* is termed both Armorica (V.729, 1061) and Brittany (V.729, 810, etc.). An allusion to Armorica as the home of Oliver de Mauny, one of those who betrayed *Pedro I of Castile, occurs in *MkT* (VII.2388/B^2.3578).

Arnaldus de Villanova

(*c*. 1235–*c*. 1314)
Authority on medicine and alchemy. Chaucer cites Arnaldus on the subject of alchemy in *CYT* (VIII.1428–9) – specifically mentioning his *Rosarie* (i.e. *Rosarium*), though the material in question appears to have been derived,

rather, from his *De lapide philosophorum* ('Concerning the philosophers' stone').

Arrius *see* Latumyus; Arsechiel *see* Arzachel

Artemisia

Example of a good wife, mentioned in *FranT*. Artemisia ('Arthemesie'), who was renowned for her chastity and built a fine tomb for her husband, is included among the exemplary women specified by *Dorigen (V.1451–2).

Arthur

Legendary British king and founder of the Round Table. The Arthurian setting so prevalent in medieval romance is used by Chaucer only in *WBT* (III.857), where Arthur himself is mentioned merely in passing (882 etc.), as he is in *Rom* (1199). Chaucer shows no interest in the deeds of the knights of the Round Table, likewise a major topic of medieval romance. He does, however, allude briefly to the Arthurian knights *Gawain and *Lancelot.

Artois *see* Flanders

Arveragus

Husband of *Dorigen in *FranT*. Arveragus is represented as a man concerned both to fulfil his chivalric duties as a knight and to maintain integrity in his conduct as a husband. His offer to Dorigen of an egalitarian marriage, in which he would relinquish his right to conventional male dominance, is conspicuous, and open to a wide range of interpretations – not least regarding how effective the agreement proves when the tale reaches its crisis. The name Arveragus has been compared to that of Arviragus in the *Historia regum Britanniae* of *Geoffrey of Monmouth, the Celtic associations of which would accord with a *Breton lai.

Arzachel

(*c.* 1029–*c.* 1087)
Astronomer from Toledo. Arzachel was associated with the Toledan tables, which indicated the positions of the planets – termed 'Arsechieles tables' in *Astr* (2.45.2) and 'tables Tolletanes' (i.e. Toledan) in *FranT* (V.1273).

Ascanius

Also known as Julius; son of *Aeneas and *Creusa. In *Dido* (*LGW* 1128ff.), Ascanius is mentioned as a member of his father's company. Allusions to the story of how Aeneas saved him from the sack of *Troy occur both here (941) and in *HF* (178) – where Chaucer appears (mistakenly) to regard Julius ('Iulo') as another son of Aeneas.

Astrolabe *see* Treatise on the Astrolabe, A

Atalia

City in present-day Turkey. Chaucer includes Atalia ('Satalye') among the campaigns on which the Knight has fought (*GP* I.58) – an allusion to the capture of this city by *Pierre de Lusignan in 1361.

Athalus *see* Attalus; Athene *see* Pallas Athene

Athens

Principle city of ancient Attica, setting for *KnT*. Chaucer emphasizes that the action of *KnT* takes place mainly in Athens, which is ruled by *Theseus. It is also significant in *LGW*: in *Ariadne* (1886ff.), the people of Athens are in thrall to *Minos; in *Philomela* (2228ff.), it is the original home of *Philomela and *Procne; and in *Phyllis* (2394ff.), *Demophoön, son of Theseus, plays a substantial role. Passing allusions to Athens occur in several other works. The most notable of these concern the colonnade associated with the teaching of philosophy (*Bo* 5.m.4.2), and the burning of the temple of Isis (*HF* 1844–5 – where Athens is mentioned in error for Ephesus).

Atropos *see* Fates

Attalus

(d. 133 BC)
Attalus III, king of Pergamos. In *BD* (663), Attalus ('Athalus') is credited with the invention of chess – an idea derived by Chaucer from *RR* (6691–2).

Attila

(406–53)
King of the Huns. An allusion to the death of Attila, from a nosebleed caused by drunkenness, occurs in *PardT* (VI.579–81).

Auchinleck MS

Manuscript containing a miscellany of romances and didactic works in English. The Auchinleck MS (National Library of Scotland MS 19.2.1) is generally dated *c*. 1330–40, and has been taken to represent the literary tastes of the growing bourgeoisie of late medieval London. The eponymous heroes of three of the romances contained in this manuscript are mentioned in *Th* (VII.897–902/B².2087–92): *Horn, *Guy of Warwick, and *Bevis of Hampton.

Augustine, St

(354–430)
Bishop of Hippo; one of the four doctors of the early church (along with SS *Ambrose, *Jerome, and *Gregory). The enormous authority of St Augustine (also 'Austyn') as a writer on theology and the moral life is reflected in the fact that, though none of his works constitutes an actual source for *ParsT*, he is cited there more than twenty times, on a range of topics including sin, penitence, and the love of God (e.g. X.97, 368, 383, 958–9). Similar allusions occur in *Mel* (VII.1617–18, 1643–5/B².2807–8, 2833–5). He is cited on divine foreknowledge in *NPT* (VII.3241/B².4431) and (as 'the Doctour') on *Envy in *PhyT* (VI.117). More controversially, Chaucer states in *LGW* (1689–91) that Augustine felt compassion for *Lucrece (see note in Benson, 1987: 1070). The monastic rule associated with his name is mentioned in *GP* (I.187); allusions to it occur in *Rom* (6583 etc.). In *ShT* and its subsequent link (VII. 259, 441/B².1449, 1631) 'Seint Austyn' is invoked in a blessing and an oath.

Augustus Caesar

(63 BC–14 AD)
First Roman emperor. In *Astr* (1.10), Chaucer states that 'Cesar Augustus' named the month of August after himself. 'Augustus' was, in fact, a title conferred on Octavian, and it is by the latter name that Chaucer identifies him elsewhere – as an emperor out hunting in *BD* (368), and (more significantly) as the conqueror of *Antony and *Cleopatra in *LGW* (624ff.).

Aurelian

(215–75)
Roman emperor. The story of *Zenobia in *MkT* describes how she is defeated by Aurelian, who parades her in triumph through the streets of *Rome (VII.2351ff./B².3541ff.).

Aurelius

Young squire, admirer of *Dorigen in *FranT*. Aurelius appears at first to conform to the stereotype of the love-struck squire, pining hopelessly for an unattainable lady (cf. *Damian in *MerT*). His subsequent conduct is, however, more distinctive – particularly his ultimate generosity, based on sympathy not just for Dorigen but also for her husband, *Arveragus. Appropriately for a character in a *Breton lai, Aurelius has a Roman name with British associations.

Aurora see **Peter of Riga; Austin** *see* **Augustine, St**

Avarice

One of the *Seven Deadly Sins. A section of *ParsT* (X.739ff.) provides a detailed definition of Avarice and specifies remedies against it. Counsel against Avarice is also provided by *Prudence in *Mel* (VII.1597ff./B².2787ff.) and by Lady *Philosophy in *Bo* (especially 2.p.5). The *Pardoner offers a cynical account of his approach to preaching on this subject (*PardP* VI.389ff.). The depiction of a figure representing Avarice is described in *Rom* (207ff.).

Averroës

(1126–98)
Spanish philosopher and scientist. The inclusion of Averroës among the authorities whose work was known to the *Physician (*GP* I.433) reflects his authorship of a medical encyclopedia, translated into Latin as the *Colliget*.

Avicenna

(980–1037)
Persian scientist. Avicenna's authorship of the vast medical encyclopedia translated into Latin as the *Canon* explains his inclusion in the list of authorities

known to the *Physician (*GP* I.432). The allusion to him in *PardT* (VI.889–94) may reflect his particular eminence as an expert on poisons.

Ayash

Town in present-day Turkey. In *GP* (I.58) the Knight is said to have fought at Ayash ('Lyeys') – an allusion to the capture of this town by *Pierre de Lusignan in 1367.

B

Babylon

City on the Euphrates. Babylon was the capital of a province of the Assyrian empire. Allusions to it as the principal seat of *Nebuchadnezzar and as a city captured by *Cyrus the Great occur in *MkT* (VII.2149/B².3339) and *SumT* (III.2082) respectively. It serves as the setting for *Thisbe* (*LGW* 706ff.) and is mentioned in *BD* (1061) as a city of fabulous wealth.

Bacchus

Roman god of wine. Passing allusions to Bacchus occur in several of Chaucer's works. While in some of these (e.g. *PF* 275) the reference is to the god himself, in others (e.g. *PhyT* VI.58) it is to Bacchus as a symbol of wine.

Bailly, Harry *see* Host

Balade of Complaint, A

Poem of 21 lines, probably written in imitation of Chaucer during the early fifteenth century. *Bal Comp* survives in a single manuscript (MS Additional 16165), copied by *Shirley, in which it is not attributed to Chaucer. At one time *Skeat argued, on grounds of style and quality, that it was by Chaucer, but later changed his mind. Most editors have included it among poems of doubtful attribution. *Bal Comp* comprises three stanzas of *rhyme royal – and, strictly speaking, lacks the requisite rhyme-scheme and refrain of the true *ballade. In it, the poet expresses his devotion to an unnamed lady.
Further reading: V.J. Scattergood in Minnis (1995).

Balade of Pity, A see Complaint to his Lady, A

Balat

Town in present-day Turkey. The Knight is said to have fought with 'the lord' of Balat ('Palatye') against 'another hethen in Turkye' (*GP* I.64–6). It has generally been supposed that this alludes to the campaigns of *Pierre de Lusignan in the region during the 1360s.

Baldeswelle *see* Bawdeswell

ballade

Form used in lyric poetry. The ballade is one of the characteristic forms of French courtly lyric. It normally consists of three stanzas, each comprising eight octosyllabic lines, rhyming ababbcbc. The same rhymes are used throughout, and the final line of each stanza is identical, and thus serves as a refrain. Ballades often end with an *envoy, addressing some such figure as a lady or a prince. While many of Chaucer's lyrics are based on the ballade, these are all written in the decasyllabic line. Chaucer uses the form freely, modifying it in various ways. Several of his ballades, such as *Truth* and *Sted*, are written in the *rhyme royal stanza; some (like *Sted*) with envoys, others (like *Truth*) without. Some, such as *Buk*, lack the repeated rhymes. While *Scog* is a double ballade (i.e., a lyric consisting of two connected ballades), *For* and *Ven* are triple ballades. Among Chaucer's lyrics, the closest to a pure ballade is, perhaps, *Ros* (despite the fact that it lacks an envoy). A ballade in rhyme royal stanzas is incorporated into *LGWP* (F 249ff./G 203ff.). The envoy at the end of *CIT* (IV.1177ff.) constitutes a double ballade in six-line stanzas.

Basil, St

(*c*. 330–79)
St Basil the Great, bishop of Caesarea. He was the principal monastic legislator of the Eastern Church – a role similar to that of St *Benedict in the Western Church. A quotation from his works is included in *ParsT* (X.221).

Bath *see* Wife of Bath

Bawdeswell

Village in north Norfolk. Bawdeswell ('Baldeswelle') is mentioned in *GP* (I.620) as the home of the *Reeve.

Bayard

Horse's name. Bayard is the name of a horse associated with Charlemagne, and suggests, more generally, the colour bay. It occurs three times in Chaucer's works – in *Tr* (1.218), *RvT* (I.4115), and *CYT* (VIII.1413). The last of these alludes to the proverbial blindness of Bayard: see Whiting (1968: B.71).

beast epic

Extended, episodic form of *beast fable. The beast epic comprises a series of stories, developed from beast fables, involving the adventures of Reynard the Fox and Isengrim the Wolf. It appears that the story of the cock and the fox in *NPT* reflects the influence of this genre, in which a mock epic manner was often used.

beast fable

Brief tale in which human characteristics are portrayed by animals. The beast fable is associated particularly with the name of *Aesop. It typically consists of a narrative followed by a moral comment – the latter expressed in terms of practical common sense rather than of pure morality. The story of *NPT* is ultimately derived from a beast fable, though closer to the form in which it occurs in *beast epic. Some slight influence from beast fable may also be detected in the treatment of the *crow in *MancT* and of the birds in *PF*.

Becket, St Thomas à *see* Thomas à Becket, St

Bel Acueil

Personification, representing the lady's welcome to the lover in *RR*. The rendition of this name in Fragment B of *Rom*, 'Bialacoil', differs conspicuously from that in Fragment C, 'Fair-Welcomyng'. Bel Acueil is described as a handsome and gracious young man (see especially *Rom* 2979ff.).

Belmarye *see* Benmarin

Belshazzar

King of Babylon. The story of Belshazzar's Feast and of his downfall, based on the Book of Daniel (chap. 5), is related in *MkT* (VII.2183ff./B².3373ff.).

Benedict, St

(*c*. 480–*c*. 550)
St Benedict of Nursia, author of the Benedictine Rule (for the regulation of monastic life). He is mentioned (as 'Seint Beneit') in this connection, together with St *Maurus, in *GP* (I.173). His name is invoked in a charm against evil spirits in *MilT* (I.3483).

Beneit *see* Benedict, St

Benmarin

A north African country, corresponding approximately to present-day Morocco. Chaucer includes Benmarin ('Belmarye') among the places where the Knight has campaigned (*GP* I.57), though the date of the implied conflict is uncertain. A passing allusion in *KnT* (I.2630) associates Benmarin with lions.

Benoît de Sainte-Maure

(fl. mid-12th century)
Author of *Le Roman de Troie* (*c*. 1160), one of the sources of *Tr*. Benoît transformed his own relatively brief sources, the chronicles of *Dares and of *Dictys, into a rich and complex narrative of the Trojan wars, extending to over 30,000 lines in octosyllabic couplets. The *Roman* was translated into Latin prose by *Guido delle Colonne in the late thirteenth century. Since Chaucer knew both texts, it is not always possible to ascertain which he is using at any particular (relevant) point in *Tr*. The distinctive contribution of Benoît to the development of the story of Troilus does, however, remain clear. It is in Benoît's poem that the passionate love of Troilus for Briseida (the original of *Criseyde) and his sense of loss when she deserts him – elements which become crucial in subsequent versions of the story, including *Tr* – appear for the first time.

Berchorius, Petrus *see* Bersuire, Pierre; Bernabò
see Visconti, Bernabò

Bernard of Gordon

(*c*. 1258–*c*. 1330)
Medical authority (also known as Bernard Gordon) associated with Montpellier. The inclusion of Bernard among the authorities known to the

*Physician (GP I.434) reflects his authorship of the medical compendium *Lilium Medicinae*.

Bernard, St

(1090–1153)
Abbot of Clairvaux and authority on theological and moral matters. St Bernard is cited in the invocation to the Virgin in *SNP* (VIII.30) and is quoted several times in *ParsT* (e.g. X.130, 274), mainly on the subject of contrition. The proverbial allusion (see Whiting B.255) to 'Bernard the monk' in *LGWP* (F/G.16) probably signifies St Bernard.

Bersuire, Pierre

(1290–1362)
French scholar and encyclopedist. Bersuire (also known as Petrus Berchorius) was the author of a vast encyclopedia, the *Reductorium morale* ('The restoration of morals'). The fifteenth book of this work was a commentary on Ovid's *Metamorphoses*, known as the *Ovidius moralizatus* ('Ovid moralized'). Its first chapter, entitled *De formis figurisque deorum* ('On the forms and figures of the gods'), provides information on the pagan gods. Chaucer used this material especially in *KnT*.

Bertrand du Guesclin

(*c.* 1320–80)
French nobleman and military leader. In *MkT* (VII.2383–5/B².3573–5) Chaucer alludes to the role of Bertrand in the murder of *Pedro I of Castile.

Berwick

Berwick upon Tweed, Northumbria. The phrase 'fro Berwyk into Ware' (*GP* I.692) occurs in a passage on the skills of the *Pardoner. It should probably not be taken literally (as an indication of the area in which the Pardoner operates), since *Ware is just 20 miles north of London, while Berwick is in the far north of England.

Beryn, The Tale of

Fifteenth-century addition to *CT*. *The Tale of Beryn* comprises a prologue (732 lines), sometimes termed the 'Canterbury Interlude', and a tale (over

3000 lines), told by the *Merchant as the first offering on the return journey. It survives in a single (highly idiosyncratic) manuscript, dating from the mid-fifteenth century, but may have been written considerably earlier – perhaps as early as *c.* 1410. The anonymous author shows detailed knowledge not just of *CT* but also of the shrine of St *Thomas in Canterbury cathedral, and may well have been a local cleric. The prologue describes the arrival of the pilgrims in Canterbury, their visit to the shrine, and their stay overnight at a local inn. This provides the setting for a story in the style of a *fabliau, which relates how the *Pardoner (clearly regarded by the author as heterosexual) makes advances to a barmaid and is duped by her. The tale, based on a French original, is set in ancient Rome, and offers an account of the progress of Beryn, from an ill-spent youth, through various misfortunes (notably at the hands of unscrupulous merchants), to prosperity and happiness.

Further reading: Bowers (1992).

Bevis of Hampton

Hero of romance. An allusion to Bevis occurs in *Th* (VII.899/B².2089), in a stanza containing the names of several other heroes, all of whom are said to have been surpassed by Sir *Thopas. Like *Guy of Warwick, Bevis was the hero of a romance translated into English from Anglo-Norman, and preserved in the *Auchinleck MS.

Bialacoil *see* Bel Acueil

Bible

Sacred book of Christianity, much cited in Chaucer's work. Though Chaucer was not primarily a religious poet, his work clearly reflects the ubiquitous influence of the Bible in late medieval Christendom. It contains over five hundred allusions to more than fifty books of the Old Testament, the New Testament, and the Apocrypha. Eight of these are cited more than twenty times each: Genesis, the Psalms, Proverbs, the Song of Solomon, Ecclesiasticus, the Gospels according to St Matthew and to St John, and St Paul's First Epistle to the Corinthians. The Bible provided Chaucer not only with authoritative views and sayings on a great diversity of topics, but also with a vast range of stories and exemplary figures.

For a writer living in western Europe during the late Middle Ages, the Bible signified the Vulgate. This was the version of the Bible in Latin, based partly

on earlier translations, compiled by St *Jerome at the request of Pope
Damasus during the final decades of the fourth century, and completed at
the beginning of the fifth. Chaucer would also have been aware of a
tradition of biblical interpretation and exegesis, conducted by a series of
writers including St Jerome, St *Augustine, and St *Gregory, which had been
partially codified in the twelfth-century *Glossa Ordinaria*.

The Bible serves as a source of authority in various works, though nowhere
more emphatically than in *ParsT*. Here it is used repeatedly to illustrate, confirm, or reinforce the moral judgements and exhortations which constitute
the essential matter of the tale. Formulae such as 'for Job seith' (X.134),
'remembreth yow of the proverbe of Salomon' (155), 'as Seint Poul seith'
(162), and 'alle thise thynges been preved by hooly writ' (313) occur
throughout. The Bible is, however, also cited as an authority in more dubious contexts. The *Pardoner stresses that he uses 'hooly writ' as his 'witnesse'
(*PardT* VI.483), and states three times over (578, 586, 742) that the views
expressed in his sermons can be validated by checking in the Bible. The
*Wife of Bath describes how her fifth husband, *Jankin, searches out a text in
Ecclesiasticus to endorse his anti-feminist prejudices (*WBP* III.650–53).
Earlier in her prologue, she has herself offered conspicuously partial
interpretations of various biblical texts in order to justify her own opinions
(e.g. 26–34). She refers to the process by which individuals 'glosen, up and
doun' (26) – suggesting that texts can be interpreted in different ways, and
thus used to support a diversity of views. Indeed, the verb 'glosen' is used
elsewhere by Chaucer to mean not just 'interpret', but also 'deceive' (as in
MkT VII.2140/B[2].3330). The cognate words 'glose' and 'glosynge' can, likewise, signify not only 'interpretation' but also 'deception' (as in *SqT* V.166).
A passage in *SumT* (III.1788–96) may suggest that it can be difficult to distinguish genuine interpretations from false ones. In *GP*, two less specific
allusions to the authority of the Bible appear at least somewhat ambiguous.
While the statement to the effect that the study of the *Physician 'was but
litel on the Bible' (I.438) does not express disapproval but could imply it, the
assertion that 'Crist spak hymself ful broode in hooly writ' (739) ostensibly
represents plain speaking as a potential justification for obscenity.

The Bible provided Chaucer with a great range of exemplary stories
and figures, and of resonant passages and concepts. This is, perhaps,
most apparent in *MkT*, where seven of the seventeen 'tragedies' draw on biblical and related material: those of Lucifer (see *Satan), *Adam, *Samson,
*Nebuchadnezzar, *Belshazzar, *Holofernes, and *Antiochus. While the brief
narratives of *MkT* tend to concentrate on the best-known characteristics or
experiences of their subjects, other significant aspects of these exemplary

lives may be emphasized elsewhere. Thus, for instance, Samson is cited in *PardT* (VI.554–5) solely as an example of someone who never drank wine – a point which warrants only the briefest mention in *MkT* (VII.2055/B².3245). The particular approach to an exemplary story adopted in a given context may also influence the treatment of its secondary characters. While *Delilah is cited as a treacherous wife in *MkT* and elsewhere (*BD* 738, *Wom Unc* 16), *Judith, who is treated somewhat unsympathetically in *MkT* (as the killer of Holofernes) appears elsewhere as an admirable and heroic woman (e.g. *MLT* II.939–42, *Mel* VII.1099/B².2289). Allusions such as these to Delilah and Judith clearly both depend upon and reflect the familiarity of the story in question. Numerous similar examples occur in Chaucer's work – among them, allusions to *Daniel as an interpreter of dreams (e.g. *NPT* VII.3127–9/B².4317–19; *ParsT* X.126), to Abigail as a wife who provided good advice (*MerT* IV.1369–71; *Mel* VII.1100/B².2290), and to *Judas as the betrayer of *Christ (e.g. *CYT* VIII.1000–09; *ParsT* X.616). In some cases, allusion to a biblical figure or concept may serve to enrich the representation of a character – as with *Absolon (in *MilT*), whose name echoes that of an ill-fated figure in the Old Testament, known for his beautiful hair. *MilT* contains allusions to several Christian concepts (including the Annunciation) and echoes of various biblical passages (notably Song of Sol. 4:9–12, 5:1), which may seem somewhat startling, given the tale's subject-matter and pervasive amorality. The sustained echoing of passages from the Song of Solomon (especially 2:10–12, 4:7–12) in a speech by the cynical and worldly *January in *MerT* (IV.2138–48) is, perhaps, still more disturbing and challenging, particularly when his speech, though full of scriptural resonances, is dismissively referred to as 'swiche olde lewed wordes' (2149).

Further reading: Besserman (1988).

bibliography *see* **Studies in the Age of Chaucer**;
biography *see* **Chaucer, Geoffrey**

Black Death

Plague which severely affected England in 1348–49. This plague, later termed the Black Death, was carried from Asia to Europe by trading vessels. During the course of 1348–49, it killed perhaps a third of the population of England. The bacillus of the plague – which existed in two forms, bubonic and pneumonic – was carried by black rats and transmitted to humans by fleas. Though the Black Death signifies the outbreak of 1348–49, the plague recurred periodically (as in 1368, when one of its victims was the Duchess *Blanche).

Chaucer makes only passing references to the Black Death in his work. He mentions how the thief *Death, sought by the three 'rioters' in *PardT*, operates through the plague (VI.675–9). When, in *GP* (I.605) he states that the farm workers fear the *Reeve like 'the deeth', this may be a specific allusion to the Black Death. Other authors provide much fuller accounts: two which would have been known to Chaucer are those of *Machaut in *Le Jugement dou Roy de Navarre* (on the plague in Reims) and of *Boccaccio in the *Decameron* (which describes how a group of young aristocrats flee the plague in Florence and tell a series of tales).

Black Prince *see* Edward, Prince of Wales

Blake, William

(1757–1827)
Poet and artist; painter of a picture of Chaucer's Canterbury pilgrims. Though the idea of representing the pilgrims in a painting originated with Blake, his own painting of this subject did not appear until 1809, a year after that of Thomas *Stothard. To accompany his picture Blake wrote a 'Descriptive Catalogue', in which he provided a commentary on his representation of the pilgrims, together with some negative comments on the ways in which Stothard deviated from Chaucer's descriptions. In addition to the light it sheds on Blake's painting, this account offers some exceptionally perceptive interpretation of *GP* as a text. Blake produced an engraving of his painting in 1810. A reproduction of this picture is provided by Spurgeon (1925: 2, facing p. 44).

Blanche

(1341–68)
Duchess of Lancaster and first wife of *John of Gaunt, commemorated by Chaucer in *BD*. Blanche was the younger daughter of Henry Grosmont, Duke of Lancaster – in his day the most prominent man in England after the king. Since Henry had no sons, Blanche was co-heir with her sister, Maud, to her father's estates and titles. The fact that Maud was childless also proved significant in due course. Blanche married Gaunt, fourth son of *Edward III, in 1359. During the next few years, Henry and Maud died (in 1361 and 1362 respectively); thus Gaunt and Blanche became Duke and Duchess of

Lancaster. When Blanche died, on 12 September 1368, she had borne five children, of whom three survived: Philippa (later Queen of Portugal), Elizabeth, and Henry (later *Henry IV). Blanche was buried in *St Paul's cathedral, where her husband had a fine tomb built for her by Henry *Yevele.

The main connection between Blanche and Chaucer is (of course) *BD*. Chaucer's own reference to this poem in *LGWP* (F.418/G.406) clearly identifies the lady whose death is mourned there. *BD* also contains several allusions to Gaunt and to Blanche, including a pun on her name (948). The portrayal of Blanche in *BD* stresses her beauty, grace, and kindness – a view which, while doubtless somewhat idealized, must have had sufficient basis in fact to seem appropriate to those who had known her. There is, however, no evidence to support the attractive assertion of *Speght (1602), that Chaucer wrote *ABC* for Blanche's use.

Blean; Bobbe-up-and-Doun *see* Harbledown

Boccaccio, Giovanni

(1313–75)

Italian writer. Boccaccio was a prolific author, who wrote both poetry and prose. While it remains possible that Chaucer met Boccaccio during his first visit to *Italy in 1372–73, this seems unlikely, given the great disparity of age and status between the two men at that time. There can, however, be no doubt as to the impact of Boccaccio's work – especially his two early poems, the *Teseida* and the *Filostrato* – on Chaucer. Scholars have agreed that these sophisticated secular poems, which Chaucer probably encountered during his second visit to Italy in 1378, had a profound influence on his development as a writer. *Il Teseida delle Nozze d'Emilia* (*c*. 1340–41) is an epic romance, consisting (like *Virgil's *Aeneid*) of 9896 lines arranged in twelve books. Chaucer based *KnT* on this work – though he makes highly selective use of his source, and produces a far briefer, more coherent poem. He also drew on the *Teseida* for passages in several other works, including the opening of *Anel*, the temple of Venus in *PF* (211ff.), and the apotheosis of Troilus in *Tr* (5.1807ff.). *Il Filostrato* (*c*. 1338) is based on an episode added by *Benoît de Sainte-Maure to the 'history' of the Trojan wars. From this material, Boccaccio developed the story of the ill-fated love of Troiolo and Criseida, creating in the process the character of the go-between, Pandaro. Chaucer's *Tr* is, of course, based on the *Filostrato* – though it represents a notably longer and more reflective version of the story.

Several other works by Boccaccio influenced Chaucer in various ways. The *Decameron*, written in the early 1350s, comprises a collection of one hundred prose tales, told over a period of ten days by ten different tellers. While it seems almost certain that Chaucer was indebted to this work for some aspects of the frame story in *CT*, none of Boccaccio's tales seems to have provided a direct source for any of Chaucer's. Scholars have concluded that Chaucer probably read all or part of the *Decameron* during his visit to Italy in 1378, but did not possess a copy of this work. A tale from the *Filocolo*, an early prose romance, appears to have been the main source of *FranT*. Chaucer may also have been indebted to Boccaccio's later work in Latin prose, *De casibus virorum illustrium* ('On the fates of illustrious men') for the idea of *MkT*, in which the 'tragedy' of *Zenobia is based on a story told in Boccaccio's broadly similar *De claris mulieribus* ('On famous women').

Chaucer's works do not contain any allusions to Boccaccio. This seems strange, particularly since he refers, with notable explicitness, to the other Italian poets to whom he was indebted, *Dante and *Petrarch. The issue is further complicated by the fact that Chaucer twice acknowledges the mysterious author *Lollius as his source in *Tr* (1.394; 5.1653). It seems improbable that he could have been unaware of the name of a writer whose works he clearly knew well. Most scholars have therefore concluded that Chaucer chose not to reveal his indebtedness to Boccaccio – for reasons which remain uncertain.

Boece

Chaucer's translation of the *De consolatione philosophiae* of *Boethius. The text of *Bo* is preserved in nine manuscripts. Chaucer's authorship has never been in doubt: he mentions *Bo* among his works in both *LGWP* (F.425/G.413) and *Ret* (X.1088). In *Adam* (2) he expresses concern that *Bo* should be copied accurately – which may suggest an intention that it should be disseminated. The title reflects the normal spelling of 'Boethius' in Middle English.

The *De consolatione philosophiae* comprises five books. Each of these contains several sections, written alternately in prose and verse – the former termed 'prosa', the latter 'metra' (singular 'metrum'). Though Chaucer retains this structure in *Bo*, he translates the entire work in prose. Scholars have regarded the *De consolatione philosophiae* in various ways: as a Platonic dialogue, a consolation, or an example of prison literature. In it, Boethius describes a conversation between himself, as a wretched prisoner, and a figure of great authority, Lady *Philosophy. By means of this encounter,

Boethius represents himself as gradually becoming reconciled to his loss of power and fortune, and to the cruelty and injustice with which he has been treated. In the process, the *De consolatione philosophiae* confronts some of the essential dualities of human experience (good and ill fortune, happiness and sorrow, fame and ignominy, freedom and bondage) and engages with some fundamental issues, above all those of free will and predestination. Lady Philosophy refutes the assertion of Boethius to the effect that divine foreknowledge precludes human free will by maintaining that, while God knows everything, this knowledge exists in an eternal present, and does not prevent individual humans from making significant choices during their timebound existence (5.2–6). She urges Boethius to turn from the transitory pleasures and temptations of life, represented by the fickle goddess *Fortune, to the tranquil certainties of the divine order (especially books 2 and 3). It is striking that this case, here and throughout the work, should be made entirely without recourse to arguments based on the Christian concept of salvation.

The ideas and issues explored in the *De consolatione philosophiae* have particular resonance elsewhere in Chaucer's work, especially in *Tr*, *KnT*, and a group of 'Boethian' lyrics (*Form Age*, *For*, *Truth*, *Gent*, and *Sted*). The lengthy and agonized reflections of Troilus on the subject of free will (*Tr* 4.958ff.) are closely based on the arguments of Boethius mentioned above. Likewise, the 'first mover' speech by Theseus towards the end of *KnT* (I.2987ff.) is derived from expositions of universal order by Lady Philosophy (*Bo* 2.m.8, 3.p.10, 4.p.6). Both works are full of Beothian echoes and allusions. The theme of patient endurance, which recurs throughout *CT*, reflects the more general influence of Boethian concerns.

Though Chaucer translates Boethius both closely and carefully, he bases his version not only on the Latin text of the *De consolatione philosophiae*, but also on the French translation of *Jean de Meun. It is conspicuous that Jean translates the 'metra' of Boethius into prose, and it seems probable that Chaucer followed his lead in this particular. Chaucer also draws on several commentaries, notably that of Nicholas *Trevet. He includes various glosses, derived from commentaries, in the text of *Bo*; modern editions generally print the relevant lines in italics. Some scholars have conjectured that Chaucer may have worked from a composite manuscript which contained the text of the *De consolatione philosophiae* in Latin, Jean de Meun's French translation, and extracts from various commentaries.

It has generally been supposed that Chaucer was working on *Bo* in the early 1380s, either immediately before or during the period in which he wrote *Tr*. The allusion in *LGWP* (see above) indicates that *Bo* was completed before *c.* 1386. It is echoed by *Usk in his *Testament of Love*, which suggests that it was in circulation before 1388.

Boethius

(*c.* 480–524)

Anicius Manlius Severinus Boethius, philosopher and statesman. Boethius served as consul of Rome under the Ostrogothic king Theodoric the Great, but fell from favour, and was imprisoned and executed in *Pavia. He was canonized as St Severinus. While in prison, he wrote the *De consolatione philosophiae* ('On the consolation of philosophy'), which was translated by Chaucer as *Bo*. This work had been one of those translated into Old English by King Alfred in the late ninth century, and proved immensely popular and influential throughout the Middle Ages. Boethius was also significant as the author of commentaries on *Aristotle and *Plato and of works on a range of theological issues and other subjects including arithmetic and music. Outside of *Bo* itself, Boethius is cited by Chaucer on various topics: on predestination and on music in *NPT* (VII.3242, 3294/B[2].4432, 4484), on true nobility in *WBT* (III.1168), and on the swiftness of thought in *HF* (972).

Bologna

Italian city. Bologna is mentioned in passing as a location in *CIT* (IV.686, 763, etc.).

Boloigne *see* Bologna; Boulogne

Book of the Duchess, The

Elegiac *dream vision on the death of *Blanche, Duchess of Lancaster. Chaucer refers twice to *BD* elsewhere in his work, terming it 'the book of the Duchesse' in *Ret* (*CT* X.1086) and 'the Deeth of Blaunche the Duchesse' in *LGWP* (F.418/G.406). This identification is confirmed by coded allusions to Blanche and to her bereaved husband, *John of Gaunt, within the poem itself (*BD* 948, 1318–19).

While *BD* clearly serves to commemorate Blanche, the precise date of its composition remains uncertain. One of the manuscripts in which it survives (Bodleian Library MS Fairfax 16) contains a statement, apparently in the hand of John *Stow, to the effect that *BD* was written at the request of John of Gaunt. There is, unfortunately, no means of corroborating this claim;

even if there were, it would not (as it stands) indicate whether the poem was composed in the immediate aftermath of Blanche's death or (as some commentators have suggested) on the occasion of a subsequent annual commemoration. It might, however, seem unlikely that a poem which stresses the intense grief of the widower would have been written after Gaunt's second marriage, in September 1371. All of this suggests that *BD* may be included among the earliest of Chaucer's surviving works.

While the essential theme of *BD* is apparent, its structure is quite intricate. The opening introduces a narrator suffering from chronic lovesickness, and thus unable to sleep – which leads him to read, and relate, *Ovid's story of *Ceyx and *Alcyone (lines 62–230). When he finally falls asleep (after some comic byplay with *Morpheus, the god of sleep), he enters a Maytime dream world, in a chamber with beautiful stained glass – from which he emerges into a wood where the emperor *Octavian is hunting the hart, and follows a lost puppy to a secluded spot (231–442). This serves as the setting for the crucial encounter between the narrator and the *Man in Black, which occupies the remainder of the poem, except for a brief conclusion (1311–34). Several aspects of this encounter seem clear enough: that the lengthy preamble has served to distance it from the mundane world, that wordplay between 'hart' and 'heart' links hunting with the pursuit of love, and that the Man in Black represents the bereaved John of Gaunt. The manner of the narrator's questions and the level of understanding they imply do, however, present a significant challenge to interpretation. The key issue arises from the fact that, though the narrator initially overhears the Man in Black lamenting the death of his lady (475ff.), he proceeds to behave as though he were unaware of this until just before the end of the poem, when the Man in Black finally utters the blunt statement, 'she ys ded' (1309). Responses to this apparent contradiction have been notably varied. It has been taken to indicate qualities in the narrator ranging from extreme obtuseness to subtle psychological insight, and to reflect either his understanding of the initial lament as generic or his sophisticated handling of the substantial gap in social status between himself and the Man in Black. What remains clear, however, is that, by asking a series of questions and showing due deference, the narrator facilitates a description by the Man in Black of the process by which he wooed and won the love of Blanche, and a moving celebration of her qualities and her life. Once the stark fact of her death has been articulated, the narrator briefly mentions the (symbolically appropriate) ending of the hunt, and the poem draws rapidly to a close.

The matter and style of *BD* reflects Chaucer's profound indebtedness to the French genre of the 'dit amoureux'. It is written in the *octosyllabic couplet characteristic of this form (with the exception of the two brief embedded lyrics in lines 475–86 and 1175–80). Chaucer's most substantial borrowings are from *Machaut's *Le Jugement dou Roy de Behainge* (for material used in the description of Blanche), and from *Froissart's *Le Paradys d'Amour* (for the account of the lovesick narrator). He was, of course, also indebted to Ovid's *Metamorphoses* for the story of Ceyx and Alcyone – though his treatment of this story reflects both his own modifications (especially the omission of the final metamorphosis), and the influence of several other versions, including those in the *Ovide moralisé*, Machaut's *Le Dit de la Fonteinne Amoreuse*, and Froissart's *Le Paradys d'Amours*. It has generally been supposed that the statement in *MLIntro* (II.57) to the effect that Chaucer wrote on 'Ceys and Alcione' in his youth may allude to an earlier version of this episode. Despite the extent of Chaucer's indebtedness to the source material, *BD* remains distinctive – especially for its bold combination of poignancy with humour.

BD survives in three manuscripts. The text in the edition of *Thynne (1532) is also significant, and provides a passage missing from the manuscripts (31–96) – an omission which presumably reflects the loss of a leaf from a manuscript early in the process of transmission.

Further reading: Minnis (1995); Windeatt (1982).

Book of the Lion, The

Lost work by Chaucer. In *Ret* (X.1087), Chaucer includes among his works 'the book of the Leoun'. It has been conjectured that this was a translation or adaptation of *Machaut's *Le Dit dou Lyon*, a possible echo of which occurs in *BD* (387–99). *Lydgate mentions *The Book of the Lion* as a work by Chaucer in *The Fall of Princes* (1.319).

'book of wicked wives'

*Anti-feminist compilation owned by *Jankin in *WBP*. Jankin is said to enjoy reading from a collection of anti-feminist and anti-matrimonial works, bound in a single volume and termed his 'book of wikked wyves' (III.669ff.). This includes works by Walter *Map, *Theophrastus, St *Jerome, *Tertullian, *Trotula, *Héloïse, and *Ovid. While this particular compilation is fictional, it was relatively common in the Middle Ages to gather materials on any given subject into a single volume.

Further reading: Hanna and Lawler (1997).

Bordeaux

City on the river Garonne in south-western France. The allusions to Bordeaux in *GP* (I.397) and *PardT* (VI.571) associate it with the production of wine.

Boughton

Small town on the *Canterbury Way, a few miles from Canterbury. Chaucer describes how the pilgrims are joined at 'Boghtoun under Blee' (i.e. in the lee of the Blean forest) by a *canon and his yeoman (*CYP* VIII.556). While the former soon departs, the latter becomes a member of the group and, as the *Canon's Yeoman, proceeds to tell a tale.

Boulogne

Seaport in north-eastern France. The pilgrimage sites said to have been visited by the *Wife of Bath include Boulogne (*GP* I.465) – associated with an image of the Virgin which, according to legend, had arrived in a rudderless boat.

Bowe *see* Stratford atte Bowe

Bradshaw, Henry

(1831–86)
Chaucerian scholar. Bradshaw was a Fellow of King's College, Cambridge, and had responsibility for rare books in the University Library. For many years, he worked on an edition of Chaucer; after his death, this was completed and brought to publication by *Skeat. Bradshaw also provided advice, particularly on the manuscripts of *CT*, to *Furnivall – thus making a significant contribution to the publications of the *Chaucer Society. He is chiefly remembered for the 'Bradshaw Shift': the proposal that Fragment VII of *CT* should be shifted to follow Fragment II. Thus, in the terminology of the Chaucer Society, it follows Group B^1, and becomes Group B^2. This idea is based on the fact that references to places along the *Canterbury Way occur in an appropriate sequence, with the exception of those to *Sittingbourne (*WBP* III.847) and *Rochester (*MkP* VII.1926/B^2.3116) – which can be corrected by the proposed 'shift'. While this hypothesis was adopted by Furnivall and Skeat, and has attracted some subsequent support, many

scholars have felt that Chaucer's references to places along the road are less consistent and literal than Bradshaw supposed. A particular legacy of the 'Bradshaw Shift' is the use in several editions (as in this book) of two sets of line numberings for Fragment VII/Group B², reflecting the two positions in which this section of the text may be placed.

Bradwardine, Thomas

(*c.* 1290–1349)
Oxford theologian. Bradwardine became chancellor of *St Paul's cathedral in 1337 and Archbishop of *Canterbury shortly before his death. He is cited in *NPT* (VII.3242/B².4432) on the subject of predestination – on which he had written an authoritative and staunchly conservative treatise.

Bredon, Simon *see Equatorie of the Planetis, The*

Breton lai

Brief *romance, typically involving love and magic. In *FranP* (V.709–15), the *Franklin defines the tale he is about to tell as a Breton lai. Chaucer was probably familiar with English versions of the Breton lais composed by Marie de France during the twelfth century. These are relatively brief and simple romances, which tend to be particularly concerned with high ideals, to involve supernatural occurences, and to show more interest in feelings than in events. While *FranT* broadly conforms to these expectations, it appears not to have been based on actual Breton sources.

Briseyde

Wronged lover of *Achilles. Passing allusions to the cruelty of Achilles to Briseyde (Briseis in *Homer's *Iliad* and Ovid's *Heroides*) occur in *MLIntro* (II.70–71) and in *HF* (398).

Brittany

Principality in north-west France, setting for *FranT*. The ancient name *Armorica is also used in *FranT* with reference to this region. A passing allusion to the *Shipman's knowledge of the coast of Brittany occurs in *GP* (I.409).

Bromholm

Bromholm Priory, Norfolk. The oath on the holy cross of Bromholm, uttered by *Simkin's wife during the fracas at the end of *RvT* (I.4286), alludes to the relic of the true cross, preserved during the later Middle Ages at Bromholm Priory.

Bruges

City in medieval *Flanders (now in Belgium). Bruges was a flourishing port during the late Middle Ages. (Magoun [1961: 41] states that it remained accessible from the North Sea until 'the final silting up of the Zwijn in 1490'.) It is the destination to which the *merchant in *ShT* (VII.55, 300, etc./B².1245, 1490, etc.) travels on business. In *Th* (VII.733/B².1923) the brown stockings worn by Sir *Thopas come from Bruges – not unreasonably, since he is said to have been born in Flanders (718–20/1908–10).

Brut

Legendary founder of Britain. An allusion to Brut as the founder of 'Albyon' (i.e. Britain) occurs in *Purse* (22).

Brutus (1)

(fl. 510 BC)
Lucius Junius Brutus; traditionally, founder of the Roman republic. In *LGW* (1862), Brutus swears revenge on *Tarquinius for his crime against *Lucrece. A passing allusion to Brutus (possibly signifying Marcus Junius Brutus: see below) occurs in *Bo* (2.m.7.19).

Brutus (2)

(c. 85–42 BC)
Marcus Junius Brutus, responsible for the assassination of *Julius Caesar. In the 'tragedy' of Julius Caesar (*MkT* VII.2671ff./B².3861ff.), the role of Brutus is treated unsympathetically. The allusion to him as 'Brutus Cassius' (2697/3887) reflects the erroneous belief that Brutus and Cassius (Cassius Longinus) were the same person (a misconception which occurs in the work of several medieval writers). In *FranT* (V.1448–50), *Dorigen notes that Portia, wife of Brutus, commits suicide rather than continuing to live after his death.

Bukton *see Lenvoy de Chaucer a Bukton*

Burghersh, Maud

(d. 1437)
Wife of *Thomas Chaucer. Maud was the daughter and co-heiress of Sir John Burghersh of Ewelme (Oxfordshire).

Burne-Jones, Sir Edward *see* **Morris, William; Burnellus the Ass** *see* **Nigel of Longchamps**

C

Caesar *see* **Augustus Caesar; Julius Caesar**

Caesarius of Heisterbach *see* ***Summoner's Prologue
and Tale, The***

Calchas

Trojan soothsayer; father of *Criseyde in *Tr*. Calchas is mentioned several
times early in the first book of *Tr* (1.64ff.), as a traitor who has foretold the
fall of *Troy and fled to the Greeks, abandoning his daughter. He reappears
in the fourth book (4.57ff.), when a truce provides him with the opportunity
to request that his daughter should be included in an exchange of prisoners.
The exchange of Criseyde for *Antenor (who ironically proceeds to betray
the Trojans) is, of course, the crucial event which brings about the parting of
*Troilus and Criseyde.

Calliope *see* Muses

Cambalo

Younger son of king *Cambyuskan in *SqT*. Cambalo is mentioned in passing
early in the tale (V.31) and again – apparently in connection with the story of
his incestuous relationship with his sister, *Canacee – near its end (V.667-9).

Cambises

(d. 522 BC)
King of Persia. The evil conduct of Cambises is briefly described by friar
*John in *SumT* (III.2043ff.), to exemplify the dangers of wrath – in this case,
exacerbated by drunkenness.

Cambridge

University town. *RvT* is set in *Trumpington, near Cambridge ('Cantebrigge',
'Cantebregge'); its two young male protagonists, *Alan and *John, are

scholars at *Soler Hall (*RvT* I.3921, 3990). Otherwise, Chaucer does not refer to Cambridge as a university (and pays rather more attention to *Oxford). There is no basis for the assertion, made by some early biographers, that Chaucer studied at Cambridge.

Cambyuskan

Genghis Khan, king of the Tartars; father of *Canacee in *SqT*. Other members of his family – his wife, Elpheta, and his sons, Algarsif and *Cambalo – are mentioned briefly (V.29–31, 663–9). Cambyuskan is represented as a noble and benign king in the twentieth year of his reign, and described presiding at exotic festivities.

Campaneus *see* Capaneus

Canacee

Female protagonist of *SqT*. Canacee (also 'Canace') is the beautiful daughter of king *Cambyuskan. *SqT* relates how she receives the gift of a magical ring which enables her to communicate with birds, and goes on to describe at length her sympathetic treatment of a (female) falcon wronged in love. Since she is presented as a model of decency and moderation, her association with the story of her incestuous relationship with her brother *Cambalo seems somewhat problematic. Allusions to this story occur in *LGWP* (F.265/G.219) and in *MLIntro* (II.77–80). While the former could suggest that Chaucer had considered including it as one of his legends, the latter states that he would not tell such a wicked story – perhaps pointedly, since *Gower had done so in the *Confessio Amantis* (3.143ff.).

Canon

Master of the *Canon's Yeoman; fleetingly one of the Canterbury pilgrims. *CYP* opens with a description (VIII.554ff.) of how the pilgrims are overtaken at *Boughton by a canon and his yeoman (that is, personal servant). While the Canon's Yeoman remains a member of the group and soon becomes the teller of a tale, the Canon quickly flees, apparently fearing that his failure as an alchemist will be exposed. This duly happens in *CYT*.

canon

Fraudulent alchemist in *CYT*. The second part of the tale (VIII.972ff.) describes how the canon uses faked experiments to dupe a foolish priest, to whom he sells a worthless alchemical recipe for £40. While the similarities between him and the *Canon are conspicuous, the *Canon's Yeoman insists that they are distinct individuals (1088–91).

canon (of Chaucer's works) *see* Chaucer, Geoffrey

Canon's Yeoman

Pilgrim and teller in *CT*. There is no portrait of the Canon's Yeoman in *GP*, since he does not join the pilgrimage until the beginning of his own prologue (VIII.1ff.). There he quickly exposes the failure of his master, the *Canon, as an alchemist – precipitating his hurried departure from the company. The Canon's Yeoman presents himself as someone who has been both impoverished and disfigured by his master's obsession with experiments which prove dangerous and unsuccessful. His tale provides a detailed account of these failures before proceeding to describe the fraudulent activities of an alchemist who is also a *canon.

Canon's Yeoman's Prologue and Tale, The

Quasi-confessional prologue and moral tale from Fragment VIII of *CT*. *CYP* begins with a brief allusion to the preceding *SNT*, before going on to describe how the pilgrims are overtaken at *Boughton by a *Canon and his personal servant, the *Canon's Yeoman. This establishes the situation for a lengthy prologue (longer than any in *CT* except *WBP*). *CYP* is a lively and contentious text, which shares some characteristics with the 'confessional' prologues of the *Wife of Bath and the *Pardoner – though in this case the speaker's revelations mainly concern the activities of his master rather than himself. While the opening description of the two newcomers' horses, soaked in sweat after their pursuit of the pilgrims, seems largely for comic effect, the allusion to how the Canon's forehead 'dropped as a stillatorie' (VIII.580) anticipates the accounts of alchemy later in *CYP* and in *CYT*. The Canon's request to join the company initiates a conversation between the *Host and the Canon's Yeoman, in which the latter first boasts about his master's learning and skill, claiming that he could pave the road to

Canterbury with silver and gold. When, however, the Host responds by expressing puzzlement regarding the Canon's poor clothes, the Canon's Yeoman reveals that his master's obsessive experiments with alchemy have, in fact, reduced them to a poverty-stricken life among the criminal fraternity, as well as causing the discoloration of his own face (657ff.). Overhearing some of this conversation, the Canon attempts to silence his servant, but finds that (with the Host's support) he proves defiant. The Canon then flees, fearing that he will be shamed by revelations regarding his life as an alchemist. This fear proves well founded: such revelations constitute the first part of *CYT* and underlie the tale as a whole.

The relationship between *CYP* and *CYT* is not entirely straightforward. While the first part of the tale consists of the Canon's Yeoman's account of his life with the Canon, and their fruitless alchemical experiments, the second part (972ff.) describes the activities of another *canon, a dishonest alchemist. Thus the first part of the tale acts as a kind of prologue to the second. Commentators have speculated that the latter may initially have been written as a separate work, and subsequently modified for inclusion in *CT* with the composition of *CYP* and the first part of *CYT*. This hypothesis derives some credibility from the presence of a passage, early in the second part of the tale (992–1011), which appears to represent an address by Chaucer (rather than a fictional narrator) to an audience of canons. It does, however, lack supporting evidence from the manuscripts: they consistently present *CYT* as a single work, and most of them do not even divide it into two parts. The absence of *CYP* and *CYT* from the *Hengwrt MS has led to the somewhat extreme conjecture that they are entirely spurious. This has attracted little support.

The essential theme of *CYP* and *CYT* is the failure of alchemy to fulfil its purpose of transmuting base metals into silver and gold. The emphasis of the account in *CYP* and the first part of *CYT* does, however, differ significantly from that in the second part of *CYT*. Whereas the former concentrate on the Canon's unsuccessful experiments, mentioning only briefly that his activities can cause financial losses to others (673–82), the latter constitutes an exposure of deliberately fraudulent conduct, through which the crafty canon fleeces a naive priest. While *CYP* and the first part of *CYT* summarize the theory of alchemy and offer a highly particularized account of the materials and equipment involved in the practice of it, the second part of *CYT* provides a description, with clear and specific details, of the procedures followed by the canon in his faked experiments. Both the former and the latter focus on the activities of a canon who practises alchemy, though the Canon's Yeoman states plainly that they are not one and the same person (1088–91).

Alchemy is represented throughout as a 'cursed craft' (830) which harms everyone associated with it. Various allusions to fiends, hell, and *Judas (e.g. 705, 861, 884–5, 1000–9, 1159) serve not only to support this impression but also to provide an emphatic contrast with *SNT*. This is reinforced by several specific parallels: thus, for instance, the early allusion to the Canon, sweating profusely after his vigorous ride (577–81) contrasts with the assertion (made only a little earlier) that St *Cecilia did not shed one drop of sweat in her boiling bath (519–22) – a fiendish piece of equipment echoed in the alchemical apparatus of *CYT*.

This tale does not conform to the conventions of any particular genre, but offers what purports to be a kind of reportage, exposing the evils of alchemy. Commentators have suggested that it may refer to the activities of a contemporary alchemist, William Shuchirch, a canon of St George's Chapel at Windsor, who was accused of dishonest conduct. The allusions to life in the squalid suburbs, frequented by criminals (657–62), have some parallels to that described in *CkT*, but are hardly typical of *fabliau. The moral condemnation of alchemy reflects official attitudes: clergy were repeatedly banned from practising it, as in the prohibition issued by Pope John XXII (*c.* 1322). (The fact that the alchemists in *CYP* and *CYT* are clerics may, therefore, constitute a deliberate irony.) Chaucer's account of alchemy reflects a good deal of knowledge – which could have been gleaned from alchemical textbooks such as those he cites and paraphrases (1428ff.), though much of it would have been available in encyclopedias. No source for this tale has been identified. The only analogue written earlier than *CYT* is a story by Ramón Lull (*c.* 1232–1315), which was almost certainly unknown to Chaucer.

It has generally been assumed that *CYP* and *CYT* were written late in Chaucer's career – though some commentators maintain that the second part of the tale was originally a discrete work, later adapted for *CT* (see above). The manuscripts contain few significant variants, other than the omission of a couplet (1238–9) in the *Ellesmere MS.

Further reading: Cooper (1996); John W. Spargo in Bryan and Dempster (1941).

Canterbury

County town of *Kent; archiepiscopal see; destination of the pilgrimage in *CT*. The shrine of St *Thomas à Becket was located in Canterbury cathedral. Allusions to it as the destination of the pilgrimage in *CT* occur in *GP* (I.16, 22, 769, etc.) and in *CYP* (VIII.624).

Canterbury Tales, The

Unfinished collection of tales, written during the final phase of Chaucer's career. *CT* consists of a sequence of stories, told within the framework of a (fictional) pilgrimage. The story collection, as a narrative form, would have been familiar to Chaucer from such examples as *Ovid's *Metamorphoses*, the *Seven Sages* (an anonymous work from the late twelfth century), *Boccaccio's *Decameron* (*c.* 1350), and *Gower's *Confessio Amantis* (the first version of which was completed in 1390). He had already composed one such collection, *LGW*, and may well have written another, subsequently revised as *MkT*. The common feature of all these works is, simply, that they comprise a sequence of stories. *CT* does, however, share some more particular characteristics with the *Decameron*, in which the stories are told by ten different tellers, who also engage in discussion with each other. While the extent of Chaucer's familiarity with the *Decameron* remains uncertain, it seems likely that he would have gained some knowledge of it during his visits to *Italy. Scholars believed until quite recently that one of the defining features of *CT*, the use of the pilgrimage frame, might have been derived from the *Novelle* of another Italian author, Giovanni Sercambi; it has, however, now been established that this was not written until *c.* 1400 (the year of Chaucer's death). In *CT*, the pilgrimage supplies the fictional occasion for the assembly of a notably mixed group of individuals, who become the tellers of the tales. Both the substantial number and the social mix of these tellers contribute to the distinctive character of *CT*. It is striking that the pilgrims are introduced and described in *GP* (I.43ff.) as a group of individuals before Chaucer reveals that they will become the tellers of a series of tales. The idea of a tale-telling contest, established towards the end of *GP* (761ff.), provides additional motivation both for telling the tales and for discussing them. These discussions take place in various prologues and epilogues, which also serve to connect one tale with another, and are often referred to as 'links'.

The variety of the tellers is matched by the variety of their tales. While collections of stories are commonly restricted to a single type of story – such as the 'tragedies' of *MkT* or the stories of unfortunate women in *LGW* – *CT* comprises a remarkable diversity of genres. These include *romance, *fabliau, *exemplum, *saint's life, and *beast fable, as well as various kinds of moral tales and tracts. Some of the genres, especially romance, appear in several distinct guises; some of the tales, notably *MerT* and *NPT*, mingle features from several genres. This generic range calls for considerable stylistic variety. Most of *CT* is composed in the *decasyllabic couplet pioneered by Chaucer, which proves an admirably flexible medium, adapting to a great diversity of subjects and moods. Chaucer also uses several stanzaic forms – notably the *rhyme royal stanza in some of his more serious tales, but also an eight-line stanza in *MkT* and a variety of tail-rhyme stanzas in the burlesque *Th*. The two tales most akin to moral treatises, *Mel* and *ParsT*, are written in prose.

The traditional collection of stories tends not only to be restricted to a single story type but also to promote a clear and consistent moral message. Again, *CT* offers a contrast. From the outset, Chaucer qualifies the authority associated with the voice of the author by attributing the tales to a large group of narrators. In the course of the ensuing tales, a variety of themes emerge, each initially presented by an individual – and clearly fallible – narrator, in the context of a particular tale. It is a distinctive feature of *CT* that a theme presented in one tale will recur for reconsideration in another, and that ideas and issues are explored, challenged, revised, and reiterated throughout. This applies not just to the familiar case of marriage (which some critics have taken to constitute a *marriage debate) but also to a great range of major and minor themes and topics, including destiny and free will, the position and role of women, love and courtship, patience, professional integrity, the elusiveness of language, truth and promises, the suffering of the innocent, *'gentilesse', and the nature of fiction. Discussions, arguments, and quarrels, based on these and other matters, take place not just within the tales but also in the links, which record both the responses of the pilgrims as a fictional audience and their various encounters and exchanges with each other as individuals. For these reasons, it is in the nature of *CT* to be pluralistic and indeterminate – at least until the final sequence of *ParsP*, *ParsT*, and *Ret*.

Chaucer left *CT* in an unfinished state. The outline of the tale-telling contest initially proposed by the *Host in *GP* (I.790–5) stipulates that each pilgrim will tell two tales on the way to Canterbury and two on the way back, which would have produced a vast sequence of some 120 tales (admittedly, not many more than the 100 of the *Decameron*). Later, when the Host invites the Franklin to tell a tale (V.696–9), he refers to the less substantial and specific requirement of telling 'a tale or two'. By the time Chaucer wrote *ParsP* (X.24–5), this has apparently been further reduced to a single tale on the way to Canterbury. The programme was not completed, even in this truncated form. *GP* provides portraits of 26 pilgrims, seven of whom (the Yeoman, the Plowman, and the five Guildsmen) have no tales. Three additional pilgrims – the Nun's Priest and the Second Nun, who are mentioned but not described in *GP* (163–4), and the Canon's Yeoman, who joins the company en route (VIII.554ff.) – go on to tell tales, while the pilgrim

Chaucer tells two (*Th* and *Mel*, the latter an alternative offering after the former has been interrupted by the Host).

Texts of these 24 tales and the various prologues and linking passages that introduce and connect them are preserved in some 83 manuscripts, of which 55 contain much or all of the work. While some tales are connected by links, others are not; thus, *CT* survives in a series of narrative blocks, often termed 'fragments'. The correct order of these is by no means certain. Whereas *CT* clearly begins with Fragment I (comprising *GP*, *KnT*, *MilT*, *RvT*, *CkT*, and the relevant links) and clearly ends with Fragment X (comprising *ParsP*, *ParsT*, and *Ret*), the correct sequence of the intervening fragments remains unclear. Indeed, it seems likely that Chaucer made no final decision on the order of the tales. The order familiar to most readers – that adopted in the *Riverside Chaucer – is derived from the early and authoritative *Ellesmere MS, and supported by several others. The numbering of fragments with Roman numerals from I to X reflects this sequence. The other well–known order, associated with the *Chaucer Society, uses the term 'groups' rather than 'fragments', and designates these with capital letters from A to I. It attempts to match the order of the tales and related links to the allusions made in the text to places along the *Canterbury Way, in a sequence which is logical in these terms but lacks manuscript support. The two orders are indicated in the table below.

Fragment	*Group*	*Tales, Prologues, Epilogues, etc.*
I	A	General Prologue, Knight, Miller, Reeve, Cook
II	B¹	Man of Law
III	D	Wife of Bath, Friar, Summoner
IV	E	Clerk, Merchant
V	F	Squire, Franklin
VI	C	Physician, Pardoner
VII	B²	Shipman, Prioress, *Sir Thopas*, *Melibee*, Monk, Nun's Priest
VIII	G	Second Nun, Canon's Yeoman
IX	H	Manciple
X	I	Parson, Retraction

Throughout this book, references are to Fragments I–X, with subsidiary references, where appropriate, to Groups A–I.

These uncertainties reflect not only the incomplete state of *CT*, but also the fact that the text was in need of revision and correction. A few examples will suffice to indicate the kinds of issues involved. The Man of Law expresses the intention of speaking in prose (*MLIntro* II.96), but then tells a tale in verse; while the female teller of *SNT* sounds like a man (*SNP* VIII.62), the male teller of *ShT* sounds like a woman (VII.1–19, 433–4/B².1191–1209, 1623–4). These three cases may well constitute loose ends left when Chaucer altered his initial plans: probably, to attribute *Mel* to the Man of Law, *SNT* to one of the male clerics, and *ShT* to the Wife of Bath. It seems reasonable to deduce from the existence of *NPT* and *SNT* that Chaucer might have inserted portraits of these two pilgrims into *GP* (presumably at the point where they are briefly mentioned, 163–4). Finally, the implication of the passage in *MancP* (IX.11–14), where the Host expresses the wish that the Cook should tell a tale, may well be that *CkP* and the fragmentary *CkT* (I.4325ff.) would have been cancelled.

Revisions such as these indicate, among other things, that *CT* occupied Chaucer for a considerable period of time. Commentators have generally assumed that he began work on the project after completing (or abandoning) *LGW*, around 1386–87, and continued with it until near the end of his life in 1400. The pilgrimage itself has traditionally been supposed to have taken place in 1387; since it is clearly fictional, this does, however, seem more or less irrelevant. The major sources and analogues provide little help with dating: in addition to Ovid's *Metamorphoses*, Boccaccio's *Decameron*, and Gower's *Confessio Amantis* (all mentioned above), the most significant influences on *CT* as a whole are those of the *Bible and *RR* – with which Chaucer was, of course, familiar throughout his career. More specific dates for some individual tales can be tentatively proposed on the basis of specific sources: see entries for individual tales. The allusions in *LGWP* (F.417–30/G.405–18) would seem to indicate that *KnT* and *SNT* were originally written as individual works, and later incorporated into *CT*. It has been suggested, without such compelling evidence, that the same may be true of some other tales, notably *MkT* and part of *CYT*.

The unfinished state of *CT* provides various opportunities for both scribes and later poets to supply additional material. The former compose a range of spurious links, which are gathered by Bowers (1992). These include one in which the Cook finishes off his incomplete tale in a single couplet, and then goes on to tell the *Tale of Gamelyn* (see **Cook's Prologue and Tale, The**). The most ambitious addition to *CT* is the *Tale of *Beryn*. This comprises a comic prologue, describing the activities of some of the pilgrims in Canterbury, and a tale, told on the return journey by the Merchant. In the *Siege of Thebes*, *Lydgate represents himself as the narrator of a prologue and tale, again told on the return journey. Two entirely different poems appear as the **Plowman's Tale*: while one is a miracle of the Virgin written by *Hoccleve, the other consists of a prologue and a Lollard dialogue on ecclesiastical corruption. Endings for the interrupted *SqT* are provided by

*Spenser in the fourth book of the *Faerie Queene* and by the early seventeenth-century poet John Lane.

Illustrations depicting the Canterbury pilgrims appear in three manuscripts: the Ellesmere MS, Cambridge University Library MS Gg.4.27, and the fragmentary Rosenbach Library (Philadelphia) MS 1084/2. Only those in the Ellesmere MS represent anything approaching a complete set – the Cambridge and Rosenbach manuscripts containing just six and three illustrations respectively. The Ellesmere miniatures are significant not only because they are early and of considerable quality, but also because their details reflect an attentive reading of the text, especially the portraits in *GP*. Woodcuts depicting the pilgrims, possibly derived from manuscript illustrations, appear in several early printed editions. Several later editions contain illustrations, of which the most interesting is, perhaps, that of the *Tabard in *Urry's edition of 1721. A well-known illustration of the pilgrims leaving Canterbury on their return journey occurs in a manuscript of Lydgate's *Siege of Thebes*. This partly anticipates the familiar picture of the pilgrims setting out from Southwark by William *Blake, and the broadly similar work of his contemporary Thomas *Stothard. Among later editions of Chaucer, by far the finest illustrations are contained in the magnificent Kelmscott Chaucer, produced by William *Morris.

A tradition of relatively free translations or modernizations of individual tales is inaugurated by *Dryden at the very end of his life (1700). This is continued during the eighteenth century by *Pope and various other writers. At the beginning of the nineteenth century, *Wordsworth initiates a tradition of relatively close translation, which has continued until the present day. The best known and most successful translation of *CT* into modern English is that of *Coghill (1951), who was also involved in several stage adaptations. Translations into numerous other languages have appeared since the mid-nineteenth century. The most significant treatment of *CT* in film is that of *Pasolini (1972). For further information, see Ellis (2000) and Malcolm Andrew in Ellis (2005).

Further reading: Cooper (1996).

Canterbury Way

Pilgrimage route from London to *Canterbury. An allusion to the 'Caunterbury Weye' occurs in *MancP* (IX.3). Elsewhere it may be suggested in the phrase 'by the weye', which is used repeatedly toward the end of *GP* (I.771, 774, etc.) and also appears in *FrP* (III.1274). The following places on the Canterbury Way are mentioned in *CT*: the *Watering of St Thomas (*GP* I.826), *Deptford (*RvP* I.3906), *Greenwich (*RvP* I.3907), *Sittingbourne (*WBP* III.847), *Rochester (*MkP* VII.1926/B².3116), *Boughton (*CYP* VIII.556), and *Harbledown (*MancP* IX.2). The fact that Sittingbourne and Rochester seem to be in the wrong order led *Bradshaw to propose a modification to the order of the fragments of *CT* (the 'Bradshaw Shift'). The total length of the Canterbury Way is just under 60 miles. For a description of the route, see Magoun (1961: 48–53).

Capaneus

One of the *Seven Against Thebes. Allusions to the death of Capaneus (also 'Cappaneus', 'Campaneus') occur in *Anel* (59) and *Tr* (5.1504–05). In *KnT* (I.912ff.) his widow is the 'eldeste lady' who appeals for the help of *Theseus against *Creon.

Carpenter

One of the *Guildsmen in *GP*. It is also significant that *John, the cuckolded husband in *MilT*, should be a carpenter, since this leads the *Reeve, who was trained as a carpenter (see *GP* I.613–14), to take the depiction of John as a personal slight.

Carthage

Phoenician city near present-day Tunis. The story of *Dido, told in *LGW* (924ff.) and in *HF* (219ff.), is set in Carthage. Several passing allusions to Carthage occur elsewhere: in connection with Dido (*BD* 732); as an exotic place (*PF* 44, *BD* 1062); and with reference to its destruction by the Romans in 146 BC (*FranT* V.1399–1400; *NPT* VII.3365/B².4555). The allusion to 'Cartage' in connection with the Shipman in *GP* (I.404) has generally been taken to signify Cartagena in south-east Spain.

Cassandra

Female prophet; daughter of *Priam. In *Tr* (5.1450ff.) Cassandra interprets *Troilus' dream, explaining that the boar signifies *Diomede. A passing allusion to her prophecy of the fall of *Troy occurs in *BD* (1246–9).

Cassiodorus

(*c*. 480–*c*. 580)
Flavius Magnus Aurelius, monastic writer. Chaucer quotes the *Variarum* ('Miscellanies') of Cassiodorus several times in *Mel* (VII.1196, 1348, 1438, etc./B².2386, 2538, 2628, etc.), on a range of topics including deception, revenge, and poverty. These quotations are derived from the main source of *Mel*, the *Livre de Melibée et de Dame Prudence* of *Renaud de Louens.

Cassius Brutus *see* Brutus

Cato (1)

(fl. 3rd century?)
Dionysius Cato, supposed author. Cato's *Disticha* (or *Distichs*) was a collection of maxims in Latin verse, written by an unknown author and widely used for the teaching of grammar. Chaucer cites Cato ('Cato[u]n') several times in *CT* (mostly in *Mel*), on subjects including flattery (*Mel* VII.1181/B².2371), wealth (*Mel* 1602–4/2792–4), marriage (*MilT* I.3227–8), and dreams (*NPT* VII.2940–1, 2971–81/B².4130–1, 4161–71).

Cato (2)

(2nd century BC)
Marcus Porcius Cato, Roman orator. Passing allusions to Cato occur in *Bo* (2.m.7.19; 4.p.6.233).

Catullus

(*c*. 84–54 BC)
Gaius Valerius Catullus, Roman poet. A passing (and secondhand) allusion to Catullus – whose work was almost certainly unknown to Chaucer – occurs in *Bo* (3.p.4.11).

Caxton, William

(*c*. 1422–91)
First printer of works by Chaucer. Caxton, who was the first printer of books both in England and in the English language, set up his press in the

precincts of Westminster Abbey in 1476. Prior to that he had lived for many years on the continent, mainly in Bruges, and had worked as a mercer, an administrator of foreign trade, and a diplomat before turning to the relatively new trade of printing. He published several books in Bruges – including his own translation of *Le recueil des histoires de Troye*, the first printed book in English – before returing to England. There his press was a great success, producing over 100 volumes. These included seven volumes of Chaucer's work: two of *CT*, one each of *Bo* and *Tr*, and three slim volumes of minor poems.

Though he was not an editor in the modern sense, Caxton took considerable care with his texts, and wrote various prologues and epilogues to the works he published, including Chaucer's. In one of these he explains that his second edition of *CT* was produced in response to criticism to the effect that the first edition had been based on an unreliable manuscript. Since this criticism was justified, it is unfortunate that Caxton did not base his second edition on a fresh transcription of the more reliable manuscript to which he then had access, but simply used this to correct his first edition. Nonetheless, Caxton made a substantial contribution to the process of disseminating the works of Chaucer.

Further reading: Beverly Boyd in Ruggiers (1984).

Cecilia, St

(fl. 3rd century)
Virgin martyr of the early Roman church; heroine of *SNT*. Chaucer portrays Cecilia as a woman of exceptional courage and singlemindedness, whose faith enables her to insist on a celibate marriage with her husband Valerian; to convert him, his brother Tiburce, and the Roman official Maximus; to defy secular authority in the person of the prefect Almachius; and to endure torture and martyrdom.

Ceffi, Filippo

(fl. early–mid-14th century)
Translator of *Ovid's *Heroides* into Italian. It has been suggested that *LGW* reflects the influence of Ceffi's translation, mainly in *Hypermnestra* and *Ariadne*. Parallels between Chaucer and Ceffi could, alternatively, indicate that they both used manuscripts of the *Heroides* with similar glosses.

Cenobia *see* Zenobia; *Ceys and Alcione see* Book of the Duchess, The

Ceyx

Husband of *Alcione in *BD*. The story of Ceyx and Alcione, based on *Ovid's *Metamorphoses* (11.410ff.), constitutes a substantial episode in *BD* (62ff.).

'Ch' Poems

French love lyrics speculatively attributed to Chaucer. The notation 'Ch' appears beside 15 poems preserved in a manuscript containing several hundred French poems from the mid-fourteenth century (University of Pennsylvania MS French 15). It has been suggested that these might have been written by Chaucer in his youth. All fifteen are, however, conventional love lyrics, without any particular sign of the characteristics and concerns which emerge in Chaucer's English poetry. Texts (with parallel translations) and discussion of these poems are provided by Wimsatt (1982).

Champain, Cecily

(fl. late 14th century)
Woman who threatened Chaucer with an accusation of rape. A document from the court of Chancery in May 1380 (see Crow and Olson, 1966: 343–7), recording that Cecily Champain released Chaucer from all actions *de raptu meo* ('concerning my rape'), was discovered by *Furnivall in 1873. For the next 75 years or so, commentators tended to argue that the term *raptus* could signify abduction, and that the document probably pertained to a case in which a young person was abducted for financial reasons – as had happened to the poet's father, John *Chaucer. Evidence regarding the use of the word *raptus* in legal documents, presented in two articles published in the late 1940s, rendered this interpretation virtually untenable. It could not, however, provide a clear indication of what had actually happened in this case. The most likely explanation would seem to be that Chaucer had an affair with Cecily Champain, and that she threatened to accuse him of rape in order to secure a settlement from him. Three documents dating from June and July 1380 (also printed in Crow and Olson) appear to record arrangements whereby Chaucer makes such a settlement by proxy. It has been

suggested that the poet's younger son, Lewis *Chaucer, who was born around 1381, could have been the offspring of this (supposed) union. For further particulars, see Pearsall (1992: 135–8).

Charlemagne *see* Oliver; Bayard

Chaucer, Agnes (1)

(d. *c.* 1381)
Chaucer's mother. Agnes was the daughter of John de Copton, and married John *Chaucer probably in the late 1330s. She had previously been married to John Heron. Though there is no definite evidence of her having any children other than Chaucer himself, a document from the seventeenth century (cited in Crow and Olson, 1966: 288–9) states that Simon Manning of Cudham married Katherine, a sister of Geoffrey Chaucer. (It has also been suggested that Elizabeth *Chaucer could have been Chaucer's daughter or sister.) Shortly after the death of John Chaucer in 1366, Agnes married Bartholomew Chappel.

Chaucer, Agnes (2)

(fl. late 14th–early 15th centuries)
Possible daughter of Chaucer. She is mentioned as a lady in waiting at the coronation of *Henry IV.

Chaucer, Alice

(d. 1475)
Chaucer's grand-daughter. Alice was the daughter of Thomas *Chaucer and Maud *Burghersh. After two childless marriages and twice becoming a widow, she married William de la Pole, Earl (later Duke) of Suffolk in 1430. Her husband, who supported the Lancastrian cause in the dynastic conflicts then current, was killed in 1450. Alice subsequently made the conspicuously pragmatic manoeuvre of arranging a Yorkist alliance for their eldest son, John (b. 1442), with his marriage to Elizabeth, second daughter of Richard, Duke of York. His descendants pursued a claim to the throne for several generations. Alice was buried in a fine tomb which still survives in the parish church of Ewelme (Oxfordshire).

Chaucer, Elizabeth

(fl. late 14th century)

Possible daughter (or sister) of Chaucer. This conjecture is based on the survival of three documents concerning a nun, variously named Elizabeth Chausier, Chaucy, and Chausir (see Crow and Olson, 1966: 545–6). Despite the variation in the spelling of the surname, these documents probably refer to the same person. They record the following events: her nomination as a nun at the Priory of St Helen, London (1377); a warrant of *John of Gaunt for expenses and gifts when she became a nun at Barking Abbey (1381); and her vow of obedience to the new Abbess of Barking (1397). It is the second of these that suggests a possible connection between 'Elizabeth Chaucy' and Chaucer (whose name is also spelt thus in some records). The speculation that the generosity of John of Gaunt indicates his paternity would seem unwarranted (in this case as in that of Thomas *Chaucer).

Chaucer, Geoffrey

(early 1340s–1400)

English poet. This account is arranged in two main sections, dealing respectively with Chaucer's life and with his works (canon and chronology), followed by a brief section on portraits of him.

Life. The early biographies of Chaucer contain many errors and misconceptions, and establish numerous myths which survived until well into the nineteenth century. These include the following notions: that Chaucer was of noble birth; that he studied at Oxford or Cambridge; that he had a house near the royal residence at Woodstock; and that he lived in exile for some years during the reign of *Richard II. Most of these (and other) erroneous ideas can be traced back to the earliest biographies, written in Latin by John Leland (*c.* 1545) and John Bale (1548, 1557–9). The first biography of Chaucer in English is that prefaced to the edition of *Speght (1598). Though this draws on the documentary research of John *Stow, it retains numerous errors. A glance at the fanciful biography of Chaucer by William Godwin (1803) will demonstrate that these survived – and, in some cases, were elaborated – during the seventeenth and eighteenth centuries. The first biography to reflect a truly scholarly approach to documentary evidence is that by Sir Nicholas Harris Nicolas, attached to the Aldine edition of 1844. During the middle and later decades of the nineteenth century, scholars such as *Furnivall and *Skeat developed this approach. Their labours culminated in the publication by the *Chaucer Society of the *Life-Records of Chaucer* (1900). A radically revised and extended version of this work was prepared by a team of scholars during the early years of the twentieth century, and published belatedly as *Chaucer Life-Records* (ed. Crow and Olson) in 1966.

All subsequent biographies have been based on these life-records – a substantial body of documentary evidence regarding Chaucer's life and work in royal and public service. The information this provides is extensive but patchy: thus, for instance, while it can indicate the dates of Chaucer's journeys abroad on diplomatic business and specify the exact amounts of the annuities he received, it makes no mention of his work as a writer and does not reveal the date or place of his birth. It does, however, indicate that his father was John *Chaucer, a successful wine merchant, whose family came from Ipswich but had been living in *London since the late thirteenth century. John and his wife, Agnes *Chaucer, owned property in Thames Street, just north of the river in Vintry ward, one of the most prosperous parts of London. Chaucer was probably born and raised there.

The most specific evidence regarding Chaucer's date of birth comes from his own testimony, given in connection with the legal action between Sir Richard *Scrope and Sir Robert Grosvenor in 1386 (see Crow and Olson: 370–4). Here Chaucer describes himself as over forty – which suggests that 1345 would be the latest possible date for his birth. The earliest records tend to corroborate this. Chaucer is first mentioned as a boy, probably a page, in the household of *Elizabeth de Burgh, countess of Ulster, during the years 1356–59 (see Crow and Olson: 13–22). In 1359, Elizabeth's household was merged with that of her husband, *Lionel of Antwerp. Chaucer experienced military service under Lionel's command on an expedition to *France in 1359–60, during the course of which he was captured near Reims but soon released (see Crow and Olson: 23–8). He later took part in several further military expeditions to France.

While there is no definite evidence regarding Chaucer's education, scholars have taken the learning so evident in his work to suggest that he attended a good school, such as that attached to *St Paul's cathedral. As a junior member of a royal household, he would have been trained in the essential requirements of courtly life, would have travelled a good deal, and may have received instruction from a tutor. After his return from France in 1360, Chaucer disappears from the records for several years. During this period he may have remained a member of Lionel's household; if, however, there is any basis for the tradition that he studied law at the Inner Temple – which goes back to the edition of Speght (1598) – then this study would probably have been undertaken during the early 1360s. Such training would, incidentally, have proved highly relevant to the administrative work for which Chaucer was later responsible, especially as controller of customs and clerk of the king's works. He reappears in the records in 1366, apparently travelling to Spain with three companions (see Crow and Olson: 64–6). While it has often been pointed out that this journey could have been a pilgrimage to *Santiago de Compostella, some scholars detect a more secular purpose, associating it with *Edward, the Black Prince, and the movement of his troops into Castille – which has led to speculation that Chaucer could have spent some time in the service of Edward in Aquitaine during the early 1360s.

A document of September 1366 (see Crow and Olson: 67) indicates that by then Chaucer was married to Philippa *Chaucer, who was herself to provide service in several royal households. By 1367 he had become an esquire in the household of the king, *Edward III – in which capacity he would have been one of several dozen young men expected to act as messengers and undertake a variety of duties. In 1368 Chaucer spent more than three months abroad. While his destination and business are unknown, some scholars have speculated that he may have travelled to *Pavia, in connection with the second marriage of Lionel (whose first wife, Elizabeth, had died in 1363), to Violante Visconti.

Chaucer definitely visited Italy in 1372–73. He was sent on a diplomatic mission, accompanying two Italian merchants to Genoa in order to conduct negotiations on trade between Genoa and England (see Crow and Olson: 32–40). The fact that Chaucer was sent on such a mission may well suggest a prior knowledge of Italian. In this connection, it has been pointed out both that his father traded with Italian merchants and that there were several Italians living in London's Vintry ward. The records indicate that he also visited Florence (without giving any specific reason for this visit). Scholars have, however, generally supposed that Chaucer first encountered the works of *Dante on this visit to Italy, and it is notable that he identifies Dante with Florence in *WBT* (III.1125–6). In 1378, Chaucer made a second journey to Italy, on a diplomatic mission to negotiate on military matters with Bernabò *Visconti, the lord of Milan (see Crow and Olson: 53–61). It has been suggested that he may have had the opportunity to use the fine libraries of the Visconti on this occasion. Chaucer's two visits to Italy were exceptionally important for his development as a writer: they brought him into contact with works not only by Dante, but also by *Petrarch, and (above all) by *Boccaccio, which were to have a profound influence on his own work.

Meanwhile, his career in royal and public service had developed in a significant manner, with his appointment in 1374 to the position of controller of customs (see Crow and Olson: 148–270). This was a position of genuine significance. Chaucer was responsible for the taxes levied in the port of London on the export of wool and leather, which represented a substantial source of income to the crown. He held this post for twelve years, during which time he lived, free of rent, in a nearby apartment over Aldgate, one of the main gates in the city walls. (There is, incidentally, no means of knowing whether Chaucer was at home when a group of rebels entered London through Aldgate during the *Peasants' Revolt of 1381.) In 1382 he was appointed to an additional position, that of controller of petty customs, which included import and export duty on wine. During his journeys abroad, Chaucer was permitted to appoint deputies to take care of these posts.

In 1380 Chaucer was involved in a case which has caused some embarrassment among scholars. Records indicate that a young woman, Cecily *Champain, had threatened to accuse him of rape, and that she received a substantial settlement through intermediaries (see Crow and Olson: 343–7). While the circumstances of the case are not entirely clear, it seems at least possible that Chaucer had an affair with Cecily and that she became pregnant. This has led to speculation that she could have been the mother of Chaucer's son, Lewis *Chaucer, who was probably born in 1381. Curiously enough, the parentage of Chaucer's elder son, Thomas *Chaucer, has also attracted conjecture: in this case, the speculation – based on far less substantial grounds – that he might have been fathered by *John of Gaunt. It is not known whether Chaucer had any other children, though two women, named Elizabeth *Chaucer and Agnes *Chaucer, have been identified as possible daughters (see Crow and Olson: 541–6).

The late 1380s appear to have brought a low ebb in Chaucer's fortunes, both personal and professional. His wife appears in the records for the last time in June 1387, and probably died later that year. He seems to have been out of favour in the period 1386–89 – during which *Richard II was involved in a power struggle with a group known as the Appellants, and lost much of his personal authority. Chaucer's tenure of the post of controller of customs and his tenancy of the Aldgate apartment came to an end. It seems probable that he moved out of London, to live just to the south of the city, in the northern part of Kent – possibly in *Greenwich, since he makes a jesting allusion to the dubious inhabitants of this small town in *RvP* (I.3907). Several other developments indicate a growing connection with Kent. Chaucer was a Justice of the Peace for the county between 1385 and 1389, became a member of its commission of the peace in 1385, and was elected as one of its two Knights of the Shire (i.e., members of parliament) in 1386.

Richard II regained power in May 1389. Within two months, Chaucer had been appointed clerk of the king's works (see Crow and Olson: 402–76).

This was perhaps the most demanding and certainly the best paid post of his career, though one which he held for only two years. It involved the supervision of building and maintenance at ten royal residences, including the Palace of Westminster and the Tower of London. In addition to such regular duties, Chaucer supervised specific projects such as the construction of lists for the Smithfield tournament of 1390. During the same year, he was robbed by highwaymen while travelling between royal manors with money for employees' wages (see Crow and Olson: 477–89). The end of his tenure of the position of clerk was followed immediately by another royal appointment, as deputy forester of North Petherton, Somerset (see Crow and Olson: 494–9). This involved the administration of an area which included moorland, cultivated fields, and villages as well as forest. It is, however, not known whether the tradition that Chaucer lived at Park House in North Petherton has any basis in fact.

The last years of Chaucer's life were, again, affected by royal politics. In 1397, Richard moved against the Appellants, and set in motion a chain of events which culminated in his own deposition by the future *Henry IV in 1399. It seems that Chaucer did not suffer unduly from the change of regime: though there was a brief delay in the payment of his annuities (probably reflecting nothing more sinister than administrative problems), these were continued, and even increased, by the new king. It may be noted that, during the course of his career, Chaucer received annuities from three kings – Edward III, Richard II, and Henry IV – as well as from John of Gaunt (see Crow and Olson: 123–43, 271–4, 303–39, 514–34). In December 1399, Chaucer took a lease on a dwelling within the precincts of Westminster Abbey (see Crow and Olson: 535–40). He died the following year. The precise date of his death is not known: it is recorded as 25 October 1400 on his tomb, but since this was not constructed until the mid-sixteenth century, its evidence may not be reliable (see Crow and Olson: 547–9). Chaucer was buried in the Abbey. Though this reflected his status as a servant of the crown rather than as a poet, the area known as 'Poets' Corner' subsequently developed around his tomb.

Works (canon and chronology).   Scholarly editions of Chaucer's complete works from that of *Skeat (1894) onwards provide a generally reliable indication of the range of his extant writings in poetry and prose. There has never been any doubt regarding the authorship of most of these works. Earlier editions did, however, often include various works not by Chaucer – not only spurious additions to *CT*, such as The *Plowman's Tale and The Tale of *Beryn, but also such works as The Assembly of Ladies (by an unknown poet), *The Testament of Love* (by *Usk), *The Book of Cupid* (by *Clanvowe), and *The Testament of Cresseid* (by *Henryson). This could cause significant misunderstandings – as, for instance, when *Wordsworth translates *The Book of Cupid* (also known as *The Cuckoo and the Nightingale*) in the belief that it was by Chaucer. Such misconceptions were resolved through the efforts of nineteenth-century scholars, especially those associated with the Chaucer Society. It is significant that Skeat's great edition of 1894 was supplemented in 1897 by a volume containing texts of most of the works which had previously been incorrectly attributed to Chaucer.

The most valuable evidence regarding authorship comes from statements and allusions by Chaucer himself and by several well-informed contemporaries and near-contemporaries, including *Lydgate and *Shirley. Chaucer provides partial lists of his own works in *LGWP* (F.417–30/G.405–20) and *Ret* (X.1085–8), and offers some more discursive comments in *MLIntro* (II.45–89). In the F-text of *LGWP*, which is generally dated around 1385–86 and believed to be the earlier of the two versions, *Alceste attributes numerous works to Chaucer: *HF*, *BD*, *PF*, and *Bo*; various lyrics ('balades, roundels, virelayes'); and two other works ('the love of Palamon and Arcite' and 'the lyf ... of Seynt Cecile'), generally taken to be early versions of *KnT* and *SNT* respectively. She also names a work which has not survived, *'Origenes upon the Maudeleyne' – presumably a translation of the *De Maria Magdalena*, a homily attributed to Origen. The equivalent passage in the G-text of *LGWP* (414–15), which is believed to be a revised version dating from *c.* 1394, adds another lost work, 'Of the Wreched Engendrynge of Mankynde' by 'Pope Innocent' – doubtless a translation of the *De miseria conditionis humane* of *Innocent III. Alceste goes on (*LGWP* F.431–41/G.421–31) to indicate that Chaucer wrote *Tr* and translated *RR. The latter attribution clearly has a substantial bearing on the authenticity of the three surviving fragments of *Rom*. In *Ret*, Chaucer acknowledges authorship of *Tr*, *HF*, *LGW*, *BD*, *PF*, *CT*, *Bo*, and various lyrics and other unspecified works. He also mentions an additional lost work, 'the book of the Leoun' – probably a version of *Machaut's poem, *Le Dit dou Lyon*. In *MLIntro*, the Man of Law states that Chaucer wrote about 'Ceys and Alcione' in his youth, and goes on to discuss *LGW*, mentioning various women whose stories are told in that work. The former presumably constitutes an allusion to the account of this Ovidian story in *BD* (62ff.). The latter is problematic, since it includes both legends that exist and legends that do not – and thus suggests that several legends which once formed part of *LGW* have been lost (though it may also be possible that they were never written).

While the Chaucer canon has, in the main, been stable for more than a century, several issues regarding the authenticity of individual works remain unresolved. Current editions of the complete works include various pieces and passages, the authorship of which is in doubt. In his first edition (1933), *Robinson placed five lyrics – *Wom Unc*, *Compl d'Am*, *MercB*, *Bal Comp*, and *Prov* – in a separate section, headed 'poems of doubtful authorship'. In *The Riverside Chaucer* (Benson 1987), an edition based on Robinson's work, *Prov* has been omitted from this section, the heading of which has become 'poems not ascribed to Chaucer in the manuscripts'. A majority of present-day scholars would, nonetheless, tend to regard *MercB* as genuine. The authorship of the three surviving fragments of *Rom* is still a matter of debate. The most widely accepted view would be that Chaucer was probably respon-sible for Fragment A, possibly for Fragment C, and definitely not for Fragment B. It also seems likely that most or all of the 'supplementary propo-sitions' at the end of *Astr* were not written by Chaucer. Opinion regarding another treatise on astronomy, *Equat*, remains divided. The ascription to Chaucer, proposed in Price (1955) has been supported by some scholars and rejected by others; the only edition of the complete works to include *Equat* is that of Fisher (1977).

The chronology of Chaucer's works is difficult to establish in anything more specific than broad outline. Just one work, *Astr*, contains clear evidence of the date at which it was written (1391). Only one of Chaucer's major poems is unequivocally occasional – *BD*, which responds to the death of the duchess *Blanche in September 1368; even so, the precise date of composi-tion remains conjectural. For the most part, the attempt to establish a chronology has been based on other kinds of evidence – Chaucer's allusions to his own works, the influence on him of the works of other writers, his allusions to individuals and events, and his stylistic and technical develop-ment – all of which tend to be somewhat inexact.

On the basis of such evidence – gathered, considered, and applied over many years – scholars have, nonetheless, reached a broad consensus regard-ing the outline chronology of Chaucer's work. This may be summarized as follows. In his youth, Chaucer probably wrote love poems in the style of French poets such as *Machaut, some of which may have been in French (and, presumably, not unlike the *'Ch' poems). The composition of *BD* in *c.* 1368–70 may well have been preceded by a full or partial translation of *RR, some of which survives in *Rom*. During the next period of his life (*c.* 1370–80), Chaucer's works would have included *ABC*, *Anel*, some lyrics (such as *Pity* and *Lady*), the life of St Cecilia (which became *SNT*), most of the 'tragedies' which later comprised *MkT*, and *HF* (*c.* 1378–80). In the fol-lowing years (*c.* 1380–86) he produced *PF* (*c.* 1380–82), the story of Palamon and Arcite (later revised as *KnT*), *Bo*, *Tr*, *LGW*, and various short poems, including *Mars, Venus,* and the 'Boethian' lyrics – *For, Form Age, Truth, Gent,* and (possibly) *Sted.* During the remainder of his life (*c.* 1387–1400), he concentrated on *CT,* while also revising *LGWP* (*c.* 1394) and writing *Astr* and several lyrics (including *Scog, Buk,* and *Purse*). The various tales and links have been tentatively assigned to successive stages in the development of *CT* – which may be loosely termed early (late 1380s), middle (earlier 1390s), and late (later 1390s). Examples of the elements probably composed in each of these stages include the following: *GP, MilT,* and *RvT* in the first; *WBP, MerT,* and *FranT* in the second; and *NPT, ParsT,* and *Ret* in the third. The text of *CT* does, however, reflect an exceptionally complex process of composition and revision, which renders all such judgements elusive and provisional.

Specific information on dating and (where relevant) issues of attribution and authenticity is provided in the entries on individual works.

Portraits.   Since lifelike portraiture had not become the norm even at the end of the Middle Ages, the fact that several apparently accurate portraits of Chaucer have survived from the period just before and soon after his death seems extraordinary. One such portrait is that contained in an early copy of *Hoccleve's Regement of Princes,* which dates from *c.* 1412 (British Library MS Harley 4866). It depicts Chaucer, with a forked beard and a thoughtful expression, holding a rosary and wearing a pen-case around his neck. Remarkably, Hoccleve provides a comment on this portrait (in lines 4992–8), stating that it represents a good likeness. Chaucer's appearance here is strikingly similar to that in the equestrian portrait placed alongside the opening of *Mel* in the *Ellesmere MS, which may have been produced before Chaucer's death. It has been suggested that these two portraits may be based on a common exemplar – which would, no doubt, have been executed during Chaucer's lifetime. His appearance is similar both in the celebrated frontispiece of the *Corpus Christi MS and in various portraits in other manuscripts. Depictions of Chaucer – in which his appearance is, again, broadly similar – appear in printed editions from that of Speght (1598) onwards. An account of this topic is provided by Pearsall (1992: 285–305), who supplies reproductions of the most significant portraits and a list of those produced before the beginning of the eighteenth century.

Further reading: Spurgeon (1925); Benson (1987); Pearsall (1992).

Chaucer, John

(*c.* 1312–66)
Chaucer's father. John is named by Chaucer as his father in a deed of 1381 (see Crow and Olson, 1966: 1–2). He was a prosperous wine merchant and a

freeman of the city of London. Between 1347 and 1349 he held the office of deputy in the port of Southampton to the king's chief butler. In 1324 he had been abducted by his aunt, Agnes de Westhall, who attempted to marry him to her daughter, Joan, in order to secure an inheritance. The abduction was foiled, and John later married Agnes de Copton.

Chaucer, Lewis

(b. *c*. 1381)
Probably Chaucer's younger son. Chaucer states that *Astr* was written for 'Lowys my sone', who was then aged ten (*Astr* Prol. 1, 24). Since *Astr* was probably written in 1391, this would suggest that Lewis was born around 1381. The close coincidence of this date with that of Chaucer's alleged rape of Cecily *Champain (1380) has led to speculation that Lewis was the off-spring of their (supposed) union. Claims that he might have been Chaucer's godson rather than his son seem to have been motivated mainly by embar-rassment about this episode: it is more likely that Lewis's rather unusual name identifies him as the godson of Chaucer's friend Sir Lewis *Clifford. The allusions to *Oxford in *Astr* (Prologue 10, 106) have been taken to sug-gest that Lewis may have been at school there. A document dated 1403, in which Thomas *Chaucer and 'Ludowicus Chaucer' are named together as members of a garrison at Carmarthen castle (see Crow and Olson, 1966: 544–5) would seem to confirm that Lewis was indeed Chaucer's son.

Chaucer, Mary

(fl. early 14th century)
Chaucer's paternal grandmother. She was the widow of John Heron (or Heyron) when she married *Robert Chaucer, who died *c*. 1314. Their son *John Chaucer, Chaucer's father, who was born *c*. 1312 was, therefore, probably brought up by Mary and her third husband, Richard Chaucer (apparently a cousin of Robert).

Chaucer, Philippa

(d. *c*. 1387)
Chaucer's wife. It is probable, though not entirely certain, that Philippa Chaucer was a daughter of Sir Paon de *Roet. If so, she was a sister of Katherine *Swynford, the long-term mistress (and, belatedly, third wife) of *John of Gaunt. Scholars have generally supposed that she can be identified

with the 'Philippa Pan', mentioned between 1356 and 1358 in the accounts of the household of *Elizabeth de Burgh, of which Chaucer was also a member. She subsequently served in two further royal households – those of Queen *Philippa and *Constance of Castile – and received annuities from Edward III and Richard II, and both annuities and gifts from *John of Gaunt. A document from September 1366 indicates that she and Chaucer had become a married couple. The latest record of Philippa Chaucer dates from June 1387; it has therefore been assumed that she died not long after this. For relevant documents and comment, see Crow and Olson (1966: especially 13–17, 67–93, 94–100, 126–7, 131–2, 271–4).

Chaucer Review, The

Quarterly journal. *The Chaucer Review* has been publishing scholarly articles on Chaucer and his work since 1966.

Chaucer, Robert

(*c.* 1288–*c.* 1314)
Chaucer's paternal grandfather. Robert Chaucer was a mercer who moved to London from his family home in Ipswich (Suffolk). He was originally known as Robert Malyn or Robert de Dynyngton, and probably adopted the name Chaucer (or le Chaucer) when he became the beneficiary of his master, the London mercer John le Chaucer, who was killed in 1302.

Chaucer Society

Victorian society for the promotion of Chaucerian scholarship. The Chaucer Society was founded by *Furnivall in December 1867. Its most significant contribution to the development of Chaucerian scholarship was the publication, between 1868 and 1902, of numerous transcripts from manuscripts containing works by Chaucer. The best known of these is *A Six-Text Print of Chaucer's Canterbury Tales* (1868–77), which appeared in fascicle form and provided a parallel text from six manuscripts, including the *Ellesmere MS and the *Hengwrt MS. The fragments of the text are presented in the sequence devised by *Bradshaw (incorporating the 'Bradshaw Shift') – a sequence subsequently identified with the Chaucer Society. The Society's publications – especially the 'Six-Text' print of *CT* and similar volumes containing texts of other works by Chaucer – greatly facilitated the work of later editors, especially *Skeat.

Chaucer, Thomas

(*c.* 1367–1434)
Chaucer's elder son. Thomas Chaucer was acknowledged as Chaucer's son during his lifetime, and described himself as such in a legal document of 1396 (see Crow and Olson, 1966: 541). The fact that he leased the tenement in Westminster where Chaucer had lived at the end of his life may even indicate that he took an interest in his father's works. While this is only conjectural, Thomas's public life is a matter of record. He enjoyed the patronage of *John of Gaunt from early in his life, and went on to build a successful career which included service as a member of parliament. His marriage in 1395 to Maud *Burghersh, brought him considerable wealth. It was facilitated by a gift of £100 from Gaunt, which has led to speculation that Thomas was his illegitimate son (by Philippa *Chaucer). This speculation gains piquancy from the fact that Katherine *Swynford, who was almost certainly Philippa's sister, was the long-time mistress and, ultimately, third wife of Gaunt. It is generally felt to be unlikely but not impossible, and may perhaps be related to *Speght's unsubstantiated assertion that Thomas was not really Chaucer's son. These conjectures could be linked with the coat of arms on Thomas's tomb in the parish church of Ewelme (Oxfordshire), which quarters the arms of Roet (for his mother) with those of Burghersh (for his wife) rather than with those of Chaucer. This may, however, indicate that Chaucer never acquired arms or that Thomas preferred to identify with his more socially prestigious connections.

Chaucerians *see* English Chaucerians; Scottish Chaucerians

Chaucers Wordes unto Adam, His Owne Scriveyn

Poem of seven lines. *Adam* consists of a single *rhyme royal stanza and survives in only one manuscript, written by *Shirley (MS Trinity College Cambridge R.3.20). It provides an example both of Chaucer's wit and of his concern regarding the accurate transmission of his work (compare *Tr* 5.1793–9). Recent research has identified the scribe mentioned in this poem as Adam *Pynkhurst.

Chauntecleer

Cock in *NPT*. Chauntecleer is based on Chantecler in the *beast epic, *Le Roman de Renart*. In *NPT* he becomes a splendid comic figure – magnificent, vain, and uxorious. While his debate with his favourite 'wife', *Pertelote, reflects his intellectual pretensions, his encounter with the fox, 'daun' *Russell, demonstrates a susceptibility to flattery which almost proves fatal.

chaunte-pleure

Proverbial song. An allusion to this song, which encapsulates the idea of things beginning in joy and ending in sorrow, occurs in *Anel* (320).

Chester, Thomas *see* Lybeaus Desconus; *Thopas, The Prologue and Tale of Sir*

Chichevache

Legendary lean cow. Chichevache, which was said to feed on patient wives and therefore have little to eat, is mentioned in the *envoy at the end of *ClT* (IV.1188).

children

Several unnamed characters in *CT*, notably: the seven-year-old boy murdered in *PrT*; the son and daughter of *Grisilde in *ClT*; the children of *Ugolino in *MkT*; the baby boy who occupies the cradle in *RvT*. *See also*: **Maurice**.

Christ

The son of God and saviour of humankind, according to Christian doctrine. Chaucer's work contains many allusions to Christ, whose name appears as 'Crist', 'Jhesu Crist', and 'Jhesu(s)', and in various formulae such as 'oure Lord Jhesu Crist' and 'Crist our king'. The words or deeds of Christ are cited or quoted in numerous allusions to the *Bible (e.g., *LGW* 1879–82; *WBP* III.9–13; and *ParsT* X.115). A wide range of more general references to Christ's role in relation to morality and devotion appear in various works (including *MLT* II.538–9; *PrT* VII.513–15/B².1703–5; and *SNT* VIII.120–6). Specific allusions to Christ's suffering also occur (as in *PardT* VI.498–501; *MelP* VII.943–5/B².2133–5; and *ParsT* X.256–9). Prayers or addresses to Christ are common (as in *HF* 492–4; *Tr* 5.1863–9; and *MLT* II.283–4). The works of

Chaucer also contain a great range of blessings, invocations, exhortations, and exclamations involving the name of Christ (e.g. *HF* 271; *MilT* I.3483–5; *WBP* III.365; *PardT* VI.658; and *CYT* VIII.1122).

Christopher, St

(3rd century ?)
Early Christian martyr. The story of St Christopher carrying the child Jesus across a river on his shoulders was well known in the Middle Ages. The 'Cristopher' medallion worn by the Yeoman (*GP* I.115) may have a particular aptness, since he is described as a forester (I.117) and St Christopher was the patron saint of foresters.

chronology (of Chaucer's works)
see **Chaucer, Geoffrey**

Cicero

(106–43 BC)
Marcus Tullius Cicero, Roman writer on rhetoric and moral matters. Chaucer's knowledge of Cicero is mainly indirect: most of the allusions to 'Tullius' (the name by which Cicero was usually known during the Middle Ages) come from his sources. These include numerous citations (many of which are actually misattributions) on a range of moral issues in *Mel* (e.g. VII.1165, 1335ff./B².2355, 2525ff.). Three allusions are independent of any known source: those to Cicero as an authority on rhetoric in *FranP* (V.722); to his views on friendship in *Scog* (47); and to the *Somnium Scipionis* ('The dream of Scipio'), the last part of his *De re publica* ('On the republic'), as preserved by *Macrobius, in *PF* (31).

Cipio(u)n *see* **Scipio the Younger**

Circe

Enchantress in Greek legend. The story in which Circe ('Circes', 'Cerces') changes the followers of *Ulysses into animals is summarized and interpreted in *Bo* (4.m.3.1ff.). Passing allusions to her as an enchantress occur in *HF* (1272) and *KnT* (I.1944).

Clanvowe, Sir John

(1341–91)
Writer, soldier, and diplomat. Sir John Clanvowe was a knight of the king's chamber under *Richard II, and served both in military campaigns against the French and on various diplomatic missions. He is one of a group of *Lollard Knights with whom Chaucer was associated. Two of his works survive: a poem and a prose treatise. *The Book of Cupid* (also known as *The Cuckoo and the Nightingale*), a dream vision of 290 lines comprising a debate between the two birds, opens with a quotation from *KnT* (I.1785–6) and strongly reflects the more general influence of Chaucer's work, especially *PF*. *The Two Ways* is a brief treatise which advocates following a way of life based on the values of the New Testament, and shows marked *Lollard sympathies.

Clarence, Duchess of *see* Elizabeth de Burgh;
Clarence, Duke of *see* Lionel of Antwerp

Claudian

(370–c. 404)
Latin poet. Allusions to Claudian occur in *MerT* (IV.2232–3), *HF* (449, 1507–12), and *LGWP* (G.280). These all reflect his authorship of the unfinished poem *De raptu Proserpina* ('On the rape of Proserpine'), some of which is set in the underworld.

Claudius *see* Physician's Tale; Virginius

Cleo *see* Muses

Cleopatra

(69–30 BC)
Queen of *Egypt; wife of Mark *Antony. The story of Cleopatra was not well known in the Middle Ages, and its inclusion as the first legend in *LGW* (580 ff.) is, therefore, by no means predictable. The legend describes how Cleopatra and Antony marry, despite his existing marriage to Octavia, sister of Octavian (who later becomes the emperor *Augustus), and thus set in train a course of events which leads to defeat by Octavian at the sea battle of Actium. Following the suicide of Antony, Cleopatra arranges her own

celebrated suicide in a pit of snakes. Brief allusions to Cleopatra occur in *PF* (291) and *LGWP* (F.259, 566/G.213, 542).

Clerk

Pilgrim and teller in *CT*. The portrait of the Clerk in *GP* (I.285ff.) represents him as a devoted scholar from *Oxford, and is placed between those of the *Merchant and the *Sergeant of Law. Commentators have regularly taken this to imply a contrast between their worldliness and acquisitive attitudes and his unworldliness and indifference to money. There seems to be no hint in *GP* of the later exchange between the Clerk and the *Wife of Bath, which develops during the course of *WBP*, *WBT*, and *ClT*. While it is often supposed that the two other Oxford scholars in *CT*, *Nicholas (*MilT*) and *Jankin (*WBP*) represent contrasts to the Clerk, some critics detect the suggestion that he interprets the Wife's account of the latter to include implied criticism of himself. The position of such men is considered by various commentators. They point out that 'clerks' might either go on to become priests, or remain in minor orders – in which case they could undertake various kinds of administrative work and were allowed to marry. Though the portrait has generally been taken as a wholly or largely positive statement, various reservations have been expressed regarding its implications: that the Clerk seems intellectual rather than pious; that his usefulness to society is not clear; that his unworldliness seems slightly absurd; and that his poverty is at odds with his apparent extravagence in the purchase of books. Nonetheless, a great majority of commentators have responded positively to the portrait, seeing genuine praise for the Clerk especially in the final lines, which describe his reticence, virtuous discourse, and dedication to learning and teaching.

Further reading: Andrew (1993); Mann (1973).

clerks *see* scholars

Clerk's Prologue and Tale, The

Prologue and exemplary tale from Fragment IV of *CT*. Fragment IV opens with the *Host's request that the *Clerk should tell a tale – and, moreover, that this should be 'som murie thyng of aventures' which avoids the 'heigh style' (IV.15–20). Though the Clerk agrees, and assures the Host of his obedience, the tale he proceeds to tell could scarcely be termed 'murie' and, if not

unduly elevated in style, is notable for its formality and restraint. Alone
among the tellers, the Clerk begins by specifying his source, stating that he
learnt his tale in *Padua from the 'lauriat poete' *Petrarch (26ff.). He goes on
to summarize the proem of Petrarch's story, *De obedientia ac fide uxoria
mythologia* ('A fable of obedience and wifely faithfulness'), which establishes
the setting of the tale in *Saluzzo. It is, indeed, true that Chaucer based *ClT*
on this work, written by Petrarch in 1373, incorporated into his *Epistolae
seniles* ('Letters of an old man'), and revised the following year. Petrarch's
version of the story constitutes a fairly free translation (from Italian into
Latin) of the last tale in *Boccaccio's *Decameron*. Chaucer also used an anonymous French translation of Petrarch's tale, *Le Livre Griseldis*. The story is
believed to have origins in folktale.

At the beginning of *ClT*, Chaucer switches from the *decasyllabic couplets
of the prologue to *rhyme royal stanzas. *ClT* has seemed broadly appropriate
to its teller: it is a serious and thoughtful tale, which relates a harrowing
series of events in a restrained but compassionate manner. (More specific
connections emerge only at the end of the tale: see below.) In generic terms,
ClT may be regarded as an *exemplum – though one incorporating some
features associated with the *saint's life, together with the happy ending typical of *romance. The story does, of course, deal with some extreme conduct:
*Walter's testing of *Grisilde and her acceptance of her lot seem excessive by
virtually any standards. While this poses a challenge to readers, it seems that
Chaucer was not disposed to minimize such problems. A comparison
between his version and that of Petrarch reveals Chaucer making some
significant modifications which do nothing to reduce tensions: increasing
the pathos of Grisilde's suffering (e.g. 547ff., 645ff., 813ff.), making the censure of Walter more explicit (e.g. 456–62, 617–23, 785ff.), and giving greater
emphasis to religious symbolism (e.g. 206–7, 440–1, 871–2). The mingling of
diverse generic features also contributes to the difficulties of formulating a
coherent interpretation. While views vary considerably, most critics accept
that the tale should be read as an exemplum rather than an allegory (which
would tend to result in an identification between Walter and God). They
have regularly pointed out its orderly structure, which emphasizes repetition
and reversal, and its dominant themes: obsessive doubt and relentless testing
on the one hand; superhuman obedience, patience, and endurance on
the other.

The end of *ClT* (1163ff.) brings a conspicuous change in tone and style.
The Clerk acknowledges that women such as Grisilde are rare, expresses good
wishes to the *Wife of Bath and her ilk, and introduces the *envoy. This passage (1177ff.) comprises six stanzas of six lines each, with only three rhymes;

it thus constitutes a double *ballade. It is notably sardonic in tone, arguing that women like Grisilde exist only in fiction, and encouraging real women to defy their husbands. Some commentators have felt that the voice of the Clerk has been replaced here by that of Chaucer – as the heading 'Lenvoy de Chaucer' seems to imply. Be that as it may, the last two stanzas of *ClT* and the envoy serve to establish a connection between *ClT* and the *Wife of Bath. In the process, the tale becomes a riposte to the views expressed in *WBP* – especially the assertion that no clerk will speak well of any women other than saints (III.688–91) – and (at least potentially) part of the *'marriage debate'. This serves to set the views and conduct of the Wife in opposition to the views of the Clerk and the conduct of Grisilde. It may also suggest that the Clerk detects an implied identification between himself and the Wife's fifth husband, *Jankin (also an Oxford clerk). Nonetheless, there are striking areas of agreement between these two contrasting tellers. While *WBP* mounts an open assault on male sovereignty, *ClT* may be seen to undermine it in a more subtle manner. Not dissimilarly, while *WBT* asserts a crucial principle concerning *'gentilesse' – that true nobility is reflected in conduct rather than indicated by birth – *ClT* may be taken to demonstrate that this is so.

In the absence of any particular evidence, commentators have generally supposed that the composition of *ClT* dates from the period in which Chaucer was probably working on the tales of Fragment III, the early to mid-1390s. *ClT* is, however, copied as a separate poem more frequently than any other tale, which has raised the possibility that it was written as an independent work and subsequently incorporated into the Canterbury scheme. The fact that its relationship with the pilgrimage framework is apparent only in *ClP* and at the end of the tale might be adduced in support of this view. On the other hand, *ClT* almost always follows Fragment III in manuscripts of *CT*. The ending of the tale shows signs of revision. It has been suggested that the comments of the Host (sometimes termed the 'Host stanza' and generally included as lines 1212a–g) would originally have been placed at the end of the tale (following 1162). Such revision could have involved several other elements: the reworking of these comments in a later passage (*MkP* VII.1891–4/B².3081–4), the change in the tale assigned to the Wife of Bath (from *ShT* to *WBT*), and the composition of *MerP*. It is, at least, clear that the comments of the Host here would have disrupted the link, in which the first line of *MerP* echoes and responds to the last line of the envoy of *ClT*.

The anonymous French translator (see above) seems to have been responsible for dividing the story into sections: while the first five of the divisions in *ClT* are derived from this version, the sixth appears to be scribal. With the exception of the signs of revision already mentioned, the text of *ClT* contains relatively few variants of any particular significance.

Further reading: Cooper (1996); Thomas J. Farrell and Amy W. Goodwin in Correale and Hamel (2002).

Clifford, Sir Lewis

(*c.* 1330–1404)
Soldier and courtier; one of the *Lollard Knights. Clifford had a long record of service in the households of *Edward, Prince of Wales and *Joan of Kent before becoming a knight of the king's chamber under *Richard II. He was a friend of *Deschamps, who entrusted Clifford with the task of delivering to Chaucer a copy of a poem in his praise. The fact that Chaucer's younger son was named Lewis *Chaucer suggests that Clifford may have been his godfather.

Clio *see* Muses

Cloune, William de

(d. 1377)
Abbot of the Augustinian Abbey of Leicester. Cloune has been proposed as a model for the *Monk, as described in *GP* (I.165ff.), especially since he was renowned for hunting the hare (cf. I.191–2). This hypothesis has attracted little support.

Coghill, Nevill

(1899–1980)
Scholar and translator. Coghill is best known for his translation of *CT*, which was originally written for radio broadcasts and was first published in 1951. He also produced a translation of *Tr* (1971), and collaborated in adaptations of *CT* for television and as a musical.

Cologne

German city. The pilgrimage destinations to which the *Wife of Bath is said to have travelled include Cologne (*GP* I.466), location of the reliquary of the Three Kings.

Collatine

Husband of *Lucrece. Collatine receives relatively little attention in Chaucer's account of the rape of Lucrece (*LGW* 1680ff.), though the story can be taken to imply that his initial boasting of his wife's virtue is unwise.

Colle

Magician. Colle is mentioned in *HF* (1277–81), in a passage on magic and illusion. He has been tentatively associated with *Orléans. For additional information see note in Benson (1987: 987).

Colonne, Guido delle *see* Guido delle Colonne

complaint

Genre of lyric poetry. Chaucer wrote numerous complaints: *Anel*, *Mars*, *Venus*, *Pity*, and *Lady*, as well as the dubiously attributed *Bal Comp* and *Compl d'Am*. For him, the complaint appears to have been less a matter of form than of style and theme: it reflects and comments on the sorrow, melancholy, or discontent expressed by the poet or narrator. The complaint occurs widely in the works of Chaucer's French contemporaries, especially *Granson. The evidence presented in the *MED* suggests that Chaucer initiated the relevant sense of the French word 'complaint' in English.

Complaint of Chaucer to His Purse, The

*Ballade and *envoy of 26 lines. *Purse* survives in 11 manuscripts, only five of which include the envoy. It consists of three *rhyme royal stanzas followed by an envoy of five lines (rhyming aabba). The title is a translation of a French title which appears in several manuscripts. Chaucer displays notable skill in the main body of *Purse*, using the same three rhymes throughout, sustaining word play between various senses of 'heavy' and 'light', and providing a witty parody of the conventional love complaint by addressing his purse as his lady. The envoy, which transforms an engaging reflection on money and worth into a begging poem, is addressed to *Henry IV. It has been taken to indicate a date in the first few weeks of his reign (during the autumn of 1399) and to reflect the financial difficulties which Chaucer may have experienced before his annuities, cancelled at the deposition of *Richard II, were restored by the new king (for particulars, see

Benson 1987: 1088). The title provided by *Shirley (in British Library MS Harley 7333) does, however, describe *Purse* as a poem addressed to King Richard. While this has led some commentators to conclude that the envoy was added to a poem written somewhat earlier (a view which can be supported by its absence from several manuscripts), others have argued for the integrity of the poem as it stands.

Further reading: Pace and David (1982); V.J. Scattergood in Minnis (1995).

Complaint to His Lady, A

Love lyric of 127 lines. *Lady* survives in two manuscripts, and is attributed to Chaucer by *Shirley. The title was supplied by *Skeat; the alternative title, *A Balade of Pity* is used in some editions. *Lady* appears as a continuation of *Pity* in both manuscripts, but has regularly been printed as a separate poem. It is, however, clearly unfinished, and may comprise several fragments. The four parts of the poem are unified only by their general subject and style – unrequited love, lamented in a conventional manner – and are notably varied in form. Part I (lines 1–14) consists of two *rhyme royal stanzas; parts II and III (lines 15–39) comprise, respectively, a single stanza and two stanzas in 'terza rima'; and part IV (lines 40–127) is written in a ten-line stanza similar to the nine-line stanza used in *Anel* (apart from a single eight-line stanza, lines 50–7, which may result from scribal error). It has generally been supposed that *Lady* is a fairly early work, in which Chaucer experiments with various metrical forms.

Further reading: V.J. Scattergood in Minnis (1995).

Complaint of Mars, The

Poem of 298 lines, combining narrative and *complaint. *Mars* survives in eight manuscripts, and is attributed to Chaucer by both *Shirley and *Lydgate. The title was provided by *Skeat. *Mars* comprises three rather loosely connected parts: a proem in praise of love, sung by a bird on St *Valentine's day (lines 1–28); the story of the ill-fated love affair between *Mars and *Venus (lines 29–154); and the complaint of Mars, expressing regret at the loss of love (lines 155–298). While the proem and the story are written in *rhyme royal stanzas, the complaint is written in an intricate nine-line stanza (rhyming aabaabbcc) – with an introductory stanza followed by 15 stanzas arranged in five groups of three. It has been suggested that the proem was written to link the story and the complaint, and that these had previously existed as unrelated pieces. The story is based on a well-known episode from *Ovid's *Metamorphoses* (4.167ff.), in which Vulcan discovers Venus (his wife) making love with Mars. Chaucer assigns the role of Vulcan to *Phoebus (the sun), and presents the story simultaneously in human and astronomical terms, with Mars and Venus moving into conjunction, Phoebus approaching, and Venus fleeing as Phoebus overtakes Mars. Some commentators have identified the implied astronomical positions with those actually prevailing in the spring of 1385. Others, following a suggestion in a collophon written by Shirley (in Trinity College Cambridge MS R.3.20) have taken *Mars* (and *Venus*) to reflect an illicit relationship between John Holland (who became Earl of Huntingdon in 1388 and subsequently Duke of Exeter in 1397) and either Isabel of York or Elizabeth of Lancaster (both daughters of *John of Gaunt). Recent commentators have tended to envisage any such allusions in the context of court entertainments (rather than as pointers to an actual affair). *See also*: **Complaint of Venus, The**.

Further reading: V.J. Scattergood in Minnis (1995).

Complaint unto Pity, The

*Complaint of 119 lines. *Pity* survives in nine manuscripts and is ascribed to Chaucer by *Shirley. The title comes from a manuscript (Bodleian Library Oxford MS Bodley 638). This poem comprises 17 *rhyme royal stanzas, the first nine of which provide a narrative while the last eight present the complaint itself – a structure which may be compared to that used in *Anel* and *Mars*. Though *Pity* is a conventional complaint about unrequited love, it is unusual in Chaucer's work both for its pervasive mood of gloom and frustration and for its extensive and insistent use of allegory (especially in abstractions such as Pity and Cruelty). The complaint itself takes the form of a legal document ('bill'), presented by the narrator as though in a court of law. This use of legal language and metaphor has been compared to that in *ABC*. While there is no specific evidence for dating, the conventional nature of *Pity* has led to a general assumption that it represents fairly early work.

Further reading: V.J. Scattergood in Minnis (1995).

Complaint of Venus, The

Love lyric of 82 lines. *Venus* survives in eight manuscripts, two of which attribute it to Chaucer. The title appears in two manuscripts. *Venus* comprises a triple *ballade with an *envoy, each ballade consisting of three eight-line stanzas, and the envoy of a single ten-line stanza. While the poem is based on a sequence of ballades by *Granson, Chaucer has changed the speaker from a man to a woman. The three ballades in *Venus* reflect, from a specifically female viewpoint, on the worthiness of the beloved, on tribulations caused by jealousy, and on renewed and reiterated commitment. Though nothing in the text identifies the speaker as Venus or provides a link with *Mars*, both connections have the authority of several manuscripts, including that written by *Shirley. *Venus* has, therefore, been associated with the (supposed) affair to which allusions have been detected in *Mars*. The envoy offers a complimentary acknowledgement to Granson while lamenting the lack of rhymes in English – somewhat disingenuously, since *Venus* displays Chaucer's consummate skill in managing a severely restricted rhyme scheme. The reference in the envoy to Chaucer's advanced age (lines 76–8) has led to the suggestion that it may be a later addition to the poem, the main body of which is generally assumed to have been written in the mid-1380s. *See also*: **Complaint of Mars, The**.

Further reading: V.J. Scattergood in Minnis (1995).

Complaynt d'Amours

*Complaint of 91 lines, uncertainly ascribed to Chaucer. *Compl d'Am* is preserved in three manuscripts. Its title appears in one of these; it is also known as *An Amorous Complaint*, on the basis of the subtitle in another. The poem was first attributed to Chaucer by *Skeat in 1901 (after the publication of his great edition). Though the manuscripts in which it survives all contain poems definitely by Chaucer (including *Mars*, *Truth*, *Fortune*, and *Pity*), the attribution has not been generally accepted. Most commentators take *Compl d'Am* to be the work of an imitator of Chaucer; complete editions tend to include it among poems of doubtful authenticity. It consists of 13 *rhyme royal stanzas, and presents a conventional complaint about unrequited love. The final stanza suggests that it was written as a poem for St *Valentine's day, and includes (85–6) an echo of *PF* (309–10).

Further reading: V.J. Scattergood in Minnis (1995).

constable *see* Hermengild; Constance *see* Custance

Constance of Castile

(1356–94)
Second wife of *John of Gaunt. Constance (Costanza) was the elder surviving daughter of *Pedro I, king of Castile and Leon. She became the second wife

of Gaunt in September 1371. This was, however, an essentially dynastic mar-
riage, and in due course Constance withdrew to live in a small court in
Leicestershire, while her husband lived with his mistress, Katherine
*Swynford. Constance had two children: John, who died in childhood, and
Catherine (1372–1418), also known as Catalina, who became queen of
Castile and Leon. Records indicate that the poet's wife, Philippa *Chaucer,
was a member of Constance's household (see Crow and Olson, 1966: 68,
85–7, 271–2).

Constantinus Africanus

(d. 1087)
Medical authority. Constantinus was born in Carthage, worked at the medical school of Salerno, and ended his life as a monk at Monte
Cassino. Though he was essentially a translator of medical texts from Arabic
to Latin, he was sometimes credited with the authorship of the works he
translated. This may be the case in *MerT* (IV.1810–11), where he is
mentioned as the author of *De Coitu* ('On coitus'), and termed a 'cursed
monk' – presumably on account of the pragmatic view of sex taken in this
work. His name also appears in the list of authors known to the Physician
(*GP* I.431).

Cook

Pilgrim and teller in *CT*. The portrait of the Cook is the shortest in *GP*
(I.379–87), and mainly comprises an account of culinary expertise, as
reflected in the preparation of a wide range of foodstuffs. If the allusion to
the running sore on the Cook's leg has the effect of qualifying this praise,
that process is developed in *CkP* (I.4344ff.) and *MancP* (IX.3ff.). In the
former, the *Host accuses the Cook of unscrupulous and unhygienic prac-
tices in his shop – accusations which are not denied. In the latter, the Cook
appears as a drunkard, which would tend to qualify the apparent approval in
the portrait (382) for his knowledge of London ale. His name, 'Hogge'
(i.e. Roger) of *Ware (which he provides in *CkP* I.4336) may also contribute
to this process, since one Roger Knight, a cook from Ware, was accused of
disreputable conduct in contemporary records. The opening of the portrait
has often been taken to indicate that the *Guildsmen have hired the Cook to
prepare their food on the pilgrimage.

Further reading: Andrew (1993); Mann (1973).

Cook's Prologue and Tale, The

Comic prologue and incomplete tale from the first fragment of *CT*. Like *MilP* and *RvP*, *CkP* opens with a response to the preceding tale. The *Cook interprets *RvT* as a tale about the dangers of having lodgers in one's home (an interpretation which could be extended to *MilT*). He offers to tell a tale of his own: 'a litel jape that fil in oure citee' (I.4343). While accepting this offer, the *Host engages in some banter about the poor standards of hygiene observed by the Cook – who cheerfully admits the truth of these assertions, but warns that his tale may feature an innkeeper. In the process, he names himself as Roger of *Ware and the Host as Harry Bailly (I.4336, 4358), thus augmenting information already provided in *GP*. The exchange between the Cook and the Host implies professional rivalry (an impression confirmed and developed in *MancP*), and suggests how – as in the case of the *Miller and the *Reeve – such tensions could spill over into the tales.

On the basis of *CkP*, it might seem reasonable to anticipate that *CkT* will be a *fabliau about an innkeeper, set in *London. Such expectations are realized only in part. The tale is set in London, and opens in fabliau style, broadly similar to that of *MilT* and *RvT*. It immediately introduces its protagonist, the apprentice *Perkin, a young man with a conspicuously dissolute lifestyle. After some 30 lines, a considerable change of tone occurs, as the tale describes – in a notably aphoristic and somewhat moralizing manner – how Perkin's master dismisses him, and he goes to live with a companion whose wife works as a prostitute.

Since *CkT* breaks off at this point, it is possible only to speculate as to how it might have developed. A few commentators have maintained that the tale is, in fact, complete as it stands; others have suggested that more may have been written, but lost at an early stage of transmission. While both the *Ellesmere and the *Hengwrt manuscripts leave space for a continuation, the latter includes a marginal gloss, to the effect that Chaucer wrote no more of the tale. Some manuscripts add a couplet, in which the Cook abandons *CkT* and proceeds to narrate the *Tale of Gamelyn* (text in Skeat, 1894: 4.645–67). This is a romance of 902 lines, definitely not by Chaucer, the story of which (as derived from Thomas Lodge's *Euphues*) was used by *Shakespeare in *As You Like It*. Commentators from *Skeat onwards have conjectured that the *Tale of Gamelyn* was found among Chaucer's papers, and that he may have been planning to use it as source material – possibly for a tale to be told by the *Yeoman. Two fifteenth-century manuscripts provide conclusions to *CkT* – both moralistic in tone; one very brief, the other more substantial (texts in Bowers, 1992: 33–9). The Host's subsequent assertion that the Cook must tell a tale (*MancP* IX.3ff.) has sometimes been taken to indicate an intention on Chaucer's part to cancel *CkP* and *CkT*. It has generally been assumed that the composition of these texts occurred at much the same time as that of *RvT*.

Further reading: Cooper (1996); John Scattergood in Correale and Hamel (2002).

Copton, Agnes de *see* Chaucer, Agnes (1)

Corinna

(3rd century BC)
Female Theban poet. Though 'Corynne', mentioned as a source for *Anel* (21) should probably be identified with Corinna, the significance of this acknowledgement remains unclear.

Corpus Christi MS

Manuscript of *Tr*, well known for its splendid frontispiece. Corpus Christi College, Cambridge, MS 61 is among the most authoritative manuscripts of *Tr*, and has normally been used as the base text for critical editions. It contains a beautiful and celebrated frontispiece, the foreground of which apparently depicts Chaucer reading, from a lectern in the form of a pulpit, to a courtly audience in a formalized outdoor setting. The background shows a group of figures emerging from a city, and may represent the sequence in *Tr* which describes how *Criseyde is transferred to the Greek camp. This fine manuscript, which dates from the early fifteenth century, also contains numerous spaces for illustrations which were not carried out.

Costanza of Castile *see* Constance of Castile

Creon

King of Thebes. Early in *KnT* (I.931ff.), Chaucer describes how Theseus defeats and kills Creon, following the latter's refusal to allow the Theban widows to bury the bodies of their husbands (six of the *Seven Against Thebes). Creon is also mentioned briefly in *Anel* (64) and in *Hypsipyle and Medea* (*LGW* 1661).

Crete

Mediterranean island, setting for *Ariadne* (*LGW* 1886ff.). Crete is identified in various works as the kingdom of *Minos (*LGW* 1866, 1894) and *Pasiphae (*WBP* III.733), and as the place where *Theseus slew the *Minotaur (*KnT* I.980).

Creusa

Wife of *Aeneas, mother of *Ascanius, and daughter of *Priam. In *HF* (174ff.) and *Dido* (*LGW* 940ff.) Chaucer describes how Creusa is lost while fleeing from the sack of Troy. The former account also mentions that her spirit advises Aeneas to pursue his destiny in Italy.

Criseyde

Female protagonist of *Tr*; lover of *Troilus, to whom she eventually proves unfaithful. Criseyde is represented as a beautiful and aristocratic young Trojan widow, placed in a vulnerable position by the fact that her father, *Calchas, has foreseen the fall of *Troy and defected to the Greeks. Though Chaucer could not alter the essential facts of the established story – that Criseyde became Troilus' lover, was sent to the Greek camp, and there transferred her affections to *Diomede – he represents her with notable sympathy. He does so, in part, by stressing the pressures put on her by four men: Calchas, who requests that she should be returned to him; Troilus, who asks for her love; her uncle, *Pandarus, who presses her to accept Troilus; and Diomede, who insists that Troy will fall and that she should accept him as her lover. Criseyde is based on Criseida in *Boccaccio's *Il Filostrato*, but is a more complex and thoughtful character. At her best, in book 3, she appears as a tender and devoted lover. The final book describes the sad process by which she succumbs to the bleakness of her situation, becomes duplicitous, and forsakes Troilus.

Crisippus

Unidentified author. Crisippus is mentioned among the anti-feminist writers included in *Jankin's *'book of wicked wives' (*WBP* III.677). It appears that the name was derived from St *Jerome's *Epistola adversus Jovinianum* (1.48), but the author is otherwise unknown.

Croesus

(d. *c.* 546 BC)
King of Lydia. The account of his fall in *MkT* (VII.2727ff./B².3917ff.), based mainly on **RR* (6489ff.), places emphasis not on his fabulous wealth but on the foretelling of his death by hanging – in a dream interpreted by his daughter Phania ('Phanye'). Croesus is also mentioned briefly in *KnT* (I.1946), *NPT* (VII.3138/B².4328), *Bo* (2.p.2.60), and *HF* (105).

crow

Foolhardy informer in *MancT*. The pet crow of *Phoebus is a white bird, who can sing beautifully and has been taught to speak by his master. He informs Phoebus – truthfully but unwisely – that his wife has been unfaithful, thus precipitating her death and his own punishment (through which he loses his beautiful voice, his white feathers, and his home).

Cupid *see* Love, god of

Curry, Walter Clyde

(1887–1967)
Chaucerian scholar. Curry is mainly known for his pioneering book, *Chaucer and the Mediaeval Sciences* (1926), in which he used material from classical and medieval scientific writing to illuminate various allusions in Chaucer to topics such as medicine, dream lore, and physiognomy.

Custance

Heroine of *MLT*. Custance is represented as a virtuous woman, whose trials and tribulations result entirely from the actions of others. Chaucer's portrayal of her reflects the conventions of the *saint's life in its emphasis on the strength of her faith, the patience with which she accepts suffering, and her dedication to converting heathens. Her complaint against women's thraldom to men (II.286–7) strikes a conspicuously radical note. This could be related to Chaucer's decision to change her name from Constance (as in his main source, *Trevet's chronicle) to Custance – which suggests a concern that she should not function simply as the personification of a virtue.

Cynthia *see* **Diana**

Cyrus

(6th century BC)
Cyrus the Great, king of Persia. Allusions to the capture of *Croesus by Cyrus occur in *MkT* (VII.2727–34/B².3917–24) and *Bo* (2.p.2.58–63). The behaviour of 'irous Cirus' is cited by the friar *John in *SumT* (III.2079–88) to exemplify the dangers of wrath.

D

Dalida *see* **Delilah**

Damascien

Medical authority of uncertain identity. Since several writers on medicine were known by this name in the Middle Ages, the identity of the Damascien mentioned in *GP* (I.433), among those whose work was known to the *Physician, remains uncertain. It has, however, generally been supposed that this signifies either Mesuë the Elder or Serapion the Elder. Mesuë the Elder (d. 857) was a Christian working in Baghdad, renowned mainly for a treatise on ophthalmology. Serapion the Elder, likewise a Christian, worked in Damascus during the second half of the ninth century, and produced two medical compilations. *See also*: **Serapion**.

Damasus, St

(*c.* 304–84)
Pope Damasus I. 'Seint Damasie' is cited in *ParsT* (X.788).

Damian

Young squire, admirer of *May in *MerT*. The portrayal of Damian draws on the stereotype of the young squire in love with the unattainable lady (compare *Aurelius in *FranT*). In this case, however, the lady – May, wife of Damian's lord, *January – proves notably attainable.

Danaus *see* **Aegyptus**

Danger

Personification in *Rom*, representing a lady's reticence. Danger is one of the guardians of the Rose (*Rom* 3018ff.), along with *Shame and *Wicked Tongue. The portrayal of Danger reflects the romance stereotype of the crude and ugly peasant (see, especially, *Rom* 3130ff.). Passing allusions to Danger as a personification occur in *PF* (136), *Tr* (2.399, 1376), *LGWP* (F.160), and *MercB* (16, 26).

Daniel

Old Testament prophet. Daniel appears as a prophet, scholar, and interpreter of dreams in the stories of *Nebuchadnezzar and *Belshazzar, which are told as two of the Monk's 'tragedies' (*MkT* VII.2143ff./B².3333ff.). Brief allusions to him as an interpreter of dreams occur in *NPT* (VII.3127–9/B².4317–19) and *ParsT* (X.126) – the latter with specific reference to the dream of Nebuchadnezzar.

Dante

(1265–1321)

Dante Alighieri, Italian poet. References to Dante occur in five of Chaucer's works: *HF* (450), *LGWP* (F.360/G.336), *WBT* (III.1125–7), *FrT* (III.1520), and *MkT* (VII.2460–2/B².3650–2). While these mainly concern Dante's great sacred poem, *La Divina Commedia* (*The Divine Comedy*), one of them (that in *WBT*) also alludes to his earlier work, the *Convivio*. The three parts of the *Divine Comedy*, the *Inferno*, the *Purgatorio*, and the *Paradiso*, describe Dante's journey through hell and purgatory, with *Virgil as his guide, and then through paradise. In two of Chaucer's references (those in *HF* and *FrT*), Dante and Virgil are cited together as authorities on hell. Two more – those in *LGWP* and *MkT* – acknowledge indebtedness to passages from the *Inferno*: respectively, some comments on envy at court and the story of *Ugolino (*Inferno* 13.64–5; 33.1ff.). The references in *MkT* and *WBT* are notably similar and respectful – terming Dante 'the grete poete of Ytaille' and 'the wise poete of Florence'. The reference in *WBT* also constitutes a more general acknowledgement of Dante's views on true *'gentilesse', as expressed in the *Convivio* (5.15.19–38) and in the *Purgatorio* (7.121–3).

Among Chaucer's works, the influence of the *Divine Comedy* is most apparent in *HF*. Since there is no sign of such influence in *BD* (*c.* 1369–70) and *HF* cannot have been written before 1374, it has generally been supposed that Chaucer first encountered the *Divine Comedy* during his visit to *Italy in 1372–73. Commentators have also argued that *HF* suggests Chaucer's response to the magnitude of Dante's celebrity and, more specifically, to his assertion that writing in the vernacular could rival the eloquence of that in *Latin (made in several works, and later endorsed by *Petrarch). Various passages reflect the influence of the *Divine Comedy*, none more so than the proem to book 3 (*HF* 1091–1109), which constitutes an imitation of a passage in the *Paradiso* (1.13–27). This evident respect for Dante does not, however, inhibit Chaucer from offering, in the account of his notably verbose guide, the *eagle, a parody of a passage from the *Purgatorio* (9.19–30).

While various echoes of Dante occur elsewhere in Chaucer's work, these mainly function as individual borrowings (rather than serving as components of a thematic entity); the following examples are among the most significant. The story of Ugolino in *MkT* (VII.2407ff./B².3597ff.), mentioned above, constitutes a radically modified version of that in Dante's *Inferno*. A prayer to the Virgin in the *Paradiso* (33.1ff.) underlies passages in both *SNP* (VIII.36ff.) and *PrP* (VII.474–80/B².1664–70). The inscriptions over the gate of the garden of love in *PF* (127–40) are partly derived from that over the portal of hell in the *Inferno* (3.1–3). In *Tr*, the prohemium of book 2 (1–6) and that of book 3 (45) both echo a passage from the *Purgatorio* (1.1–3, 7–9), while Troilus' words in praise of love and the final address to the Trinity (3.1261–7; 5.1863–5) draw on prayers from the *Paradiso* (33.14–18; 14.28–30). In *Lady*, Chaucer attempts a few lines (15–22) in 'terza rima', the form used by Dante throughout the *Divine Comedy*.

Dares

(5th century?)
Dares Phrygius, author of an account of the Trojan war. The *De excidio Troiae historia* ('History of the fall of Troy') is presented by Dares as an eyewitness account from the Trojan viewpoint, and was was regularly linked in the Middle Ages with that of *Dictys on the Greek side. It survives only in a sixth-century Latin translation. The account of Dares is a succinct and pragmatic military chronicle, though it does offer some character portrayal. It mentions such matters as the martial exploits of *Troilus and the treachery of *Calchas, and includes a brief description of Briseida (the original of *Criseyde). Allusions to Dares as an authority on the Trojan war occur in *Tr* (1.146, 5.1771) and in *HF* (1467). He is cited on the death of *Achilles in *BD* (1070). Chaucer would probably have known Dares only indirectly: through the twelfth-century verse translation of *Joseph of Exeter, and the works of *Benoît de Sainte-Maure and *Guido delle Colonne.

Dart, John *see* Urry, John

Dartmouth

Seaport in south Devon. Dartmouth ('Dertemouthe') is mentioned in *GP* (I.389) as the probable home of the *Shipman. On the basis of this allusion and that to the *Maudelayne* (*GP* I.410), an identification of the Shipman with Peter *Risshenden has been proposed.

David

Old Testament king of Judaea; supposed author of the Psalms. Numerous citations of David as author of the Psalms appear in *CT*, especially *ParsT* (e.g. X.125, 193) and *Mel* (e.g. VII.1198, 1303–4/B².2388, 2493–4). David's defeat of Goliath (I Sam. 17) is mentioned as an example of divinely-inspired strength agains the odds in *MLT* (II.932–8). Allusions to the story of Abigail's delivery of Nabal from David (I Sam. 25) occur in *Mel* (VII.1100/B².2290) and *MerT* (IV.1369–71).

De coitu see **Constantinus Africanus;** *De consolatione philosophiae* see **Boethius;** *De contemptu mundi* see **Innocent III;** *De miseria conditionis humane* see **Innocent III;** *De planctu naturae* see **Alan of Lille**

Death

Personified abstraction in *PardT*. The three 'rioters' are told that Death has caused many to die of plague, and set out to find and kill him (VI.670ff.). Following directions from the *old man, they discover a hoard of gold, which leads to their own deaths, at each other's hands. The allusion to 'the deeth' in *GP* (I.605) is sometimes taken to signify the plague.

decasyllabic couplet

Form used by Chaucer in much of his mature work. While some of Chaucer's early poetry was written in *octosyllabic couplets, he appears to have abandoned this form after the composition of *HF*. His first poem in decasyllabic couplets may have been *Palamon and Arcite*, almost certainly an early version of *KnT*. They are used throughout *LGW* and for much of *CT*. The earliest surviving decasyllabic lines by Chaucer may well be those in which the eight-line stanzas of *ABC* are composed. The *rhyme royal stanza, which first appears in Chaucer's work in *PF* and parts of *Anel*, also consists of decasyllabic lines: indeed, the last four lines of a rhyme royal stanza comprise two decasyllabic couplets. Most significant of all, Chaucer developed the decasyllabic couplet as the basic form of his mature narrative poetry. Though decasyllabic lines were quite common in French and not unknown in English verse, Chaucer appears to have been the first poet to write decasyllabic couplets in English. The influence of this innovation on subsequent English poetry was profound.

Decretum

Compilation of canon law and related material. The *Decretum* was assembled by the Italian monk Gratian in the mid-twelfth century. Chaucer cites it as 'the Book of Decrees' in *Mel* (VII.1404/B². 2594) and, less specifically, in *ParsT* (X.931, 941). Each of these allusions is derived from the relevant source.

Dedalus

Mythic Greek craftsman. Dedalus constructed the Labyrinth, in which the *Minotaur was kept. He is mentioned briefly four times in Chaucer's works – as the designer of the labyrinth in *HF* (1920–1) and *Bo* (3.p.12.156), as a skilful craftsman in *BD* (570), and as the father of *Icarus in *HF* (919).

Deguilleville, Guillaume de

(fl. *c.* 1330–60)
French poet. Deguilleville was a Cistercian monk who wrote a long allegorical poem in three parts, based on the idea of pilgrimage. Chaucer translated a prayer from the first part of this poem, *Le Pèlerinage de la Vie Humaine*, as *ABC*.

Deianira

Wife of Hercules. The 'tragedy' of Hercules (*MkT* VII.2095ff./B².3285ff.) relates how Deianira inadvertently causes her husband's death by giving him a poisoned shirt, but does not blame her for this. The attribution of blame is, however, clearly implied by her inclusion among the examples in *Jankin's *'book of wicked wives' (*WBP* III.724–6). Allusions to Deianira as a sorrowing woman – with reference to the episode in which she comes to believe that Hercules loves someone else (see *Ovid, *Metamorphoses* 9.134ff.) – occur in *MLIntro* (II.66) and *HF* (402).

Deiphobus

Son of *Priam and *Hecuba; brother of *Troilus. Deiphobus is portrayed positively in *Tr* – as the favourite brother of Troilus and a well-meaning supporter of *Criseyde (albeit one manipulated by *Pandarus). He is mentioned in *HF* (444) among those seen in Hades by *Aeneas.

Delilah

Wife of *Samson. The betrayal of Samson by Delilah ('Dalida') is described in *MkT* (VII.2063ff./B².3253ff.). She is included (though not named) in *Jankin's *'book of wicked wives' (*WBP* III.721–3) , and mentioned briefly in *BD* (738) and *Wom Unc* (16).

Delphi

Site of the temple and oracle of *Apollo. In *FranT* (V.1077) *Aurelius promises to make a pilgrimage to the temple if his prayers are answered. An allusion to the visit of *Calchas to the oracle (which prophesies the fall of *Troy) occurs in *Tr* (4.1411).

Demophoön

King of *Athens, son of *Theseus, and false lover of *Phyllis. In *LGW* (2394ff.), Chaucer tells how Demophoön ('Demopho[u]n'), driven ashore in *Thrace on his way home from the Trojan wars, is greeted with hospitality by *Phyllis, who then falls in love with him. The legend goes on to describe how he leaves for home and breaks his promise to return and marry her – as a consequence of which she commits suicide. Demophoön is represented as an unfaithful lover, like his father (who betrayed *Ariadne in a similar way). A summary of the story occurs in *HF* (388–96), and passing allusions in *BD* (728–31), *MLIntro* (II.65), and *LGWP* (F.264/G.218).

Denis, St

(d. *c.* 250)
Bishop of Paris and patron saint of France. In *ShT* (VII.151/B².1341), the monk, *John, swears by 'Seint Denys of Fraunce' – with some appropriateness, since the tale is set in the town of *Saint-Denis.

Deptford

Small town on the *Canterbury Way, just over four miles from *London bridge. An allusion to Deptford, together with *Greenwich, occurs in *RvP* (I.3906).

Deschamps, Eustache

(*c.* 1345–*c.* 1406)
French poet. Deschamps was mainly a writer of lyric poetry on political and moral subjects, though he also wrote a long satirical poem on marriage (*Le Miroir de Mariage*). While echoes of his work have been detected in Chaucer – especially in the lyrics, *LGWP*, and the discussion of marriage in *CT* – the influence is general rather than particular. The most notable connection between the two poets is the *ballade written by Deschamps in praise of Chaucer (text in Spurgeon, 1925: 3, Appendix B.16–17). In the opening lines, Deschamps addresses Chaucer as Socrates in philosophy, Seneca in morals, Aulus Gellus in practical matters, and Ovid in poetry, going on to term him 'grant translateur' – probably in recognition of *Rom*.

devil

Character in *FrT*. The devil appears as a hunter in pursuit of human prey, but nonetheless behaves more scrupulously than the corrupt *summoner – whose failure to understand and heed the devil's advice paradoxically leads him to hell.

Deyscorides *see* Dioscorides

Diana

Roman goddess of chastity, hunting, and the moon. In *KnT* (I.2051ff.), Chaucer provides a fine description of the temple of Diana, which is decorated with symbols of hunting and chastity, and with depictions of appropriate stories. *Emily expresses devotion to Diana (I.2272ff.), requesting (in vain) that she should be permitted to remain a virgin. Elsewhere, passing allusions to Diana include that in *PF* (281), where values contrary to her own are represented in the temple of *Venus. 'Cynthia', another name for Diana, is applied to the moon in *Tr* (4.1608, 5.1018).

Dictys

(1st century AD?)

Dictys Cretensis, author of an account of the Trojan war. The *Ephemeris de historia belli Troiani* ('Journal of the history of the Trojan war') of Dictys was regarded in the Middle Ages as an eyewitness account from the Greek viewpoint and a counterpart to that of *Dares from the Trojan perspective. The surviving text is a Latin translation dating from the fourth century. Dictys concentrates on military matters and takes a rational approach. He mentions *Troilus (without any great emphasis) but not *Criseyde (or any equivalent figure). An allusion to Dictys – together with *Homer and Dares – as an authority on the Trojan war, occurs in *Tr* (1.146); another, to 'Tytus' (*HF* 1467), in the context of writers on Troy, probably signifies Dictys. He would have been known to Chaucer only as a name, through the works of *Benoît de Saint-Maure and *Guido delle Colonne.

Dido

Queen of *Carthage and abandoned lover of *Aeneas. The story of Dido's love affair with Aeneas and of her suicide after his departure is told in *LGW* (924ff.) and in *HF* (239ff.). Both accounts end with an expression of loss by Dido (in the form of a letter in *LGW*); both show considerable sympathy for her, while recognizing that her story can be seen as that of a wronged woman (as in *Ovid) or as that of a man whose sense of public duty saves him from self-indulgence (as in *Virgil). Passing allusions to Dido occur in *BD* (731–4), *MLIntro* (II.64), and *PF* (289).

Diomede

Son of *Tydeus; Greek warrior who replaces *Troilus as the lover of *Criseyde in *Tr*. Diomede is not mentioned until the fifth and final book of *Tr*, except for the prediction at the beginning of the fourth book (4.8–14), to the effect that his fortunes are about to rise as those of Troilus decline. Though he constitutes (in some senses) the hero's rival, the portrayal of Diomede is not predominantly negative. Chaucer describes him as courageous (e.g. 5.799–803) and emphasizes his noble lineage (e.g. 5.930–8), but represents him as somewhat cynical and manipulative in his wooing of Criseyde (5.771ff., 841ff.).

Dioscorides

(fl. 1st century AD)

Pedanios Dioscorides, pharmacologist. Dioscorides worked as a military physician in *Rome. His inclusion among the medical authorities known to the *Physician (*GP* I.430) reflects the great success of his herbal, which remained the standard text on medical materials for many centuries.

Doctour of Phisik *see* Physician

Donegild

Evil mother-in-law of *Custance in *MLT*. Donegild resents the marriage of Custance to her son, *Alla. Her letters to the absent Alla, falsely informing him that his new-born son is a fiendish monster, lead to the banishment of Custance and her baby. When, on his return, Alla discovers the truth, he has Donegild put to death.

Dorigen

Wife of *Arveragus in *FranT*. Dorigen is represented as a noble lady and a devoted wife. Chaucer emphasizes that her rash promise to *Aurelius, which brings the tale to its crisis, is paradoxically motivated by concern for her husband. Interpretations of both this and various other aspects of Dorigen's conduct within her egalitarian marriage to Arveragus have ranged from sympathetic to hostile – not least those of the long sequence of virtuous women whose examples she contemplates during the crisis (V.1355ff.). The form of her name suggests Celtic origins, appropriate to a *Breton lai.

Douglas, Gavin *see* Scottish Chaucerians

Dread

Personification of fear in *Rom*. Dread serves as a watchman in the castle of *Jealousy (*Rom* 3958ff.).

dream vision

Poem written in the form of a dream. This was a significant and varied genre, in which some of the most influential poems of the Middle Ages were composed – among them, *RR. In addition to *Rom* (his partial translation of *RR*), Chaucer wrote four poems which may be categorized as dream visions: *BD, HF, PF,* and *LGWP.* Such poems typically describe how the dreamer falls asleep (at or near the beginning) and awakes (at the end); they often concern some aspect or aspects of love, feature strange and symbolic settings, and include an encounter with a figure of authority. The conventions of the genre facilitate a sense of identification between poet and dreamer, and provide a significant freedom from the demands of plausibility. The dream lore inherent in these poems reflects the influence of the commentary of *Macrobius on the *Somnium Scipionis* (mentioned by Chaucer on several occasions). The broader issue of the veracity of dreams forms the subject of the central debate between *Chauntecleer and *Pertelote in *NPT.* This involves traditions not only of classical learning but also of biblical interpretation – as the citation (in *NPT* VII.3127–35/B^2.4317–25) of such examples as the prophetic visions of Daniel (Dan. 7–12) and Joseph's interpretations of Pharoah's dreams (Gen. 41) suggest.

Dryden, John

(1631–1700)
Poet and playwright; translator of several works by Chaucer. Dryden produced four translations from Chaucer: *Palamon and Arcite,* based on *KnT; The Wife of Bath Her Tale; The Cock and the Fox,* based on *NPT;* and *The Character of a Good Parson,* an expanded version of the portrait of the *Parson in *GP.* They were published in his *Fables Ancient and Modern,* which appeared in 1700, shortly before his death. These are notably free translations, in which Chaucer's works are recreated in Dryden's own poetic idiom. They were well received, and started a trend of free translations from *CT* which lasted throughout the eighteenth century. In the preface to the *Fables* (text in Spurgeon, 1925: 1.272), Dryden asserts that Milton was the 'Poetical Son' of *Spenser, who bore an equivalent relationship to Chaucer.

Dryden also wrote *Troilus and Cressida: Or, Truth Found Too Late,* a revised version of *Shakespeare's *Troilus and Cressida* (which was partly based on *Tr).*

Du Guesclin, Bertrand *see* **Bertrand du Guesclin; Dunbar, William** *see* **Scottish Chaucerians**

Dunmow

Town in Essex. An allusion to the local custom of Dunmow – where a flitch of bacon could be claimed by any couple who had been married for a year and a day without quarrelling – occurs in *WBP* (III.217–18).

Dyer *see* **Guildsmen**

E

eagles

Guide figure in *HF*; one female and three male eagles in *PF*. *HF* (529ff.) describes how the eagle seizes the poet-narrator, transports him to the heavens, and offers him instruction on the nature of the universe. In *PF* (372ff.), a 'formel' eagle is wooed by three 'tercel' eagles.

Early English Text Society *see* Furnivall, Frederick J.; Skeat, Revd Walter W.

editions *see* printed editions

Edward III

(1312–77)

King of England, 1327–77. Edward, son of Edward II and Isabella of France, was born on 13 November 1312. He succeeded to the throne at the age of 14 in 1327, following the deposition of his father. A year later, he married *Philippa of Hainault, who bore him 12 children. After her death in 1369, Edward became increasingly feeble-minded and withdrawn from public life, and fell progressively under the influence of his manipulative mistress, Alice Perrers, and a small group of sycophantic courtiers. Nonetheless, his reign has generally been regarded as relatively successful and harmonious – especially by comparison with those of Edward II and *Richard II, which immediately preceded and followed it.

At some point in the 1360s, Chaucer moved from the household of *Lionel of Antwerp to that of Edward III, where he progressed to the rank of esquire. During the years 1371–73 he was a member of Edward's private household (*secreta familia*), and would have had some personal contact with the king (though perhaps not much, since there were several dozen such esquires). Chaucer regularly travelled abroad on royal business and received annuities from the king. After his appointment in 1374 to his post in the customs, he would have spent little time at court, but remained a member of the king's household.

Edward, Prince of Wales

(1330–76)
Edward of Woodstock, eldest son of *Edward III and *Philippa of Hainault; father of *Richard II. Edward was born on 15 June 1330, and became successively Earl of Chester (1333), Duke of Cornwall (1337), Prince of Wales (1343), and Prince of Aquitaine (1362). His marriage in 1361 was not the conventional dynastic arrangement, but a somewhat controversial love-match with the Countess *Joan of Kent. She bore Edward two sons, Edward (d. 1370) and Richard. Edward, Prince of Wales, was famed for the great victories he achieved during the *Hundred Years' War, which are celebrated in his biography, written (in verse) by an anonymous writer known as the Chandos Herald around 1385. His military reputation has been encapsulated in the well-known name, 'the Black Prince', coined for him during the sixteenth century. It has been suggested that during the mid-1360s, when Chaucer's movements are difficult to trace, he may have spent some time in the service of Edward in Aquitaine. Edward's splendid tomb and effigy, by Henry *Yevele, can be seen in Canterbury cathedral.

Edward, St

(1003–66)
King Edward the Confessor (reigned 1042–66). The *Monk suggests in passing that he might relate the life of St Edward as his tale (*MkP* VII.1970/B².3160), but then turns to other subjects. Edward the Confessor was a popular saint in the later Middle Ages, and was held in particular reverence by *Richard II.

Egeus *see* Aegeus; Egiste *see* Aegyptus

Egypt

The Egypt of the ancient and biblical world. In *LGW* (580ff.), Egypt is identified as the country of which Cleopatra is queen. The allusions to the Old Testament story of Joseph as an interpreter of dreams (Gen. 41) in *BD* (281) and *NPT* (VII.3133/B².4323), and to the ascetic life of John the Baptist in *Rom* (7000) mention Egypt as a location. *BD* (1207) also includes a passing reference to the plagues of Egypt (Exod. 7–12).

Eglentyne *see* Prioress

Elephant, Sir

Giant in *Th*. Sir Elephant ('Olifaunt') makes a brief appearance in *Th* (VII.807ff./B².1997ff.). His name, which is doubtless intended to satirize similarly absurd names in popular romance, reappears with *Spenser's giant Ollyphant in the *Faerie Queene* (3.7.48; 3.11.3–4).

Eleyne *see* Helen; Eleyne, St *see* Helen, St; Eligius, St *see* Loy, St

Elizabeth de Burgh

(1332–63)
Countess of Ulster and first wife of *Lionel of Antwerp. Elizabeth was the daughter and heiress of William de Burgh, Earl of Ulster. As a consequence of her marriage to Lionel, the third son of *Edward III, she became, in due course, Duchess of Clarence. Surviving records indicate that Chaucer was a member of her household, probably a page, in 1357 (see Crow and Olson, 1966: 13–18). It is generally supposed that this is a post he occupied from roughly 1356 until 1359.

Ellesmere MS

Manuscript of *CT*. The Ellesmere MS (Ellesmere 26 C 9 in the Henry E. Huntington Library, San Marino, California) is one of the earliest manuscripts of *CT*, probably dating from *c.* 1400–05. Scholars believe that it was compiled shortly after the *Hengwrt MS and was written by the same scribe – recently identified as Adam *Pynkhurst. While these are generally regarded as the two most authoritative manuscripts of *CT*, their special qualities differ. Hengwrt is valuable, above all, for the authenticity of its text, but shows signs of hasty compilation. Ellesmere, on the other hand, is a sumptuous manuscript, which was clearly produced with great care. The text shows signs of editorial intervention, but offers what has proved the most acceptable tale order (see entry on the **Canterbury Tales**). Ellesmere has been used as the base text by most editors from *Skeat onwards.

This manuscript is also exceptional for its miniatures, which depict the pilgrims (including Chaucer) and are placed in the margin at the beginning of each tale. (Thus those pilgrims who do not tell tales are not depicted.) The miniatures reflect attentive reading of the text, especially *GP*, and represent numerous details from the portraits, such as the Cook's 'mormal', the Summoner's inflamed skin, the Wife of Bath's hat and spurs, the Reeve's dappled grey horse, and even the Monk's greyhounds (I.386, 624–7, 470–3, 616, 190).

Further reading: Stemmler (1979).

Eloi, St *see* Loy, St; Eloise *see* Héloïse; Elpheta *see* Cambyuskan

Eltham

Royal manor, approximately eight miles south-east of London bridge. Eltham is mentioned, together with *Sheen, in *LGWP* (F.497).

Emetreus

King of India. Emetreus appears in *KnT* (I.2155ff.) as an exotic figure with one hundred followers, supporting *Arcite at the tournament.

Emily

Sister of *Hippolyta, wooed by *Palamon and *Arcite in *KnT*. Though based on Emilia in the *Teseida* of *Boccaccio, Emily is a more stereotypical figure: the idealized young lady, for the love of whom two young knights contend. The description of her early in the poem (I.1033ff.), just before Palamon and Arcite fall in love with her, with its emphasis on conventional beauty and purity, serves to establish this impression. Thus there may be an element of surprise when Emily – who has apparently accepted the decision regarding her marriage, made without consultation by *Theseus (I.1845ff.) – prays to *Diana that she should always remain a virgin. Once her appeal has been rejected, however, there is no further hint of opposition to the decisions of Theseus, which ultimately lead to marriage with Palamon. A passing allusion to Emily, similar to one early in *KnT* (I.871), occurs in *Anel* (38).

Emperor of Rome

Father of *Custance in *MLT*. He may be identified with the Byzantine emperor Tiberius Constantinus (d. 582). Though his role in the tale is relatively slight, he appears as a well-meaning father and a just ruler.

English *see* **French**

English Chaucerians

English poets influenced by Chaucer. This term echoes the more widely-used term *'Scottish Chaucerians', and is unsatisfactory for much the same reason: that it tends to exaggerate the dependence of these poets on Chaucer and to underestimate the diversity of their work. Chaucer was, in fact, already being echoed by contemporary writers, such as Thomas *Usk and Sir John *Clanvowe. The term 'English Chaucerians' is, however, generally applied to the poets of the next generation, notably John *Lydgate and Thomas *Hoccleve, and to several later fifteenth-century poets, including the authors of various works erroneously attributed to Chaucer (such as *The *Plowman's Tale* and *The Assembly of Ladies*). The term has occasionally been extended to early sixteenth-century poets who admired Chaucer and were influenced by his work, among them Stephen Hawes (d. *c.* 1523) and John Skelton (*c.* 1460–1529).

envoy

Formal address at the end of a poem. Most of Chaucer's lyrics written in the *ballade form end with envoys. In *Sted* and *Purse*, these address the reigning monarch – Richard II and Henry IV respectively. Two lyrics, *Buk* and *Scog*, are written in the guise of extended envoys. The most interesting envoy in Chaucer's work is, however, 'Lenvoy de Chaucer', which appears at the end of *ClT* (IV.1177ff.), addressing women and offering a radical interpretation of the preceding tale.

Envoy to Bukton see *Lenvoy de Chaucer a Bukton*; *Envoy to Scogan* see *Lenvoy de Chaucer a Scogan*

Envy

One of the *Seven Deadly Sins. A section of *ParsT* (X.484ff.) deals with Envy and the remedies for it. The initial definition offered there, attributed to St *Augustine, also occurs in *PhyT* (VI.113–17). The painting of a figure representing Envy is described in *Rom* (248ff.).

Ephesus *see* **Athens**

Epicurus

(341–270 BC)

Greek philosopher. The Epicurean view of pleasure is summarized and rejected by Lady *Philosophy in *Bo* (3.p.2.77–82). A passage in *MerT* (IV.2021–30), on the pursuit of pleasure by *January, has sometimes been taken to identify this with Epicurean values – and thus to imply censure of such values. Interpretations of the significance of the allusion to the *Franklin as 'Epicurus owene sone' (*GP* I.336) have been notably varied, ranging from positive (good-natured generosity) to negative (foolish worldliness).

Epistola adversus Jovinianum see **Jerome, St**; *Epistola Valerii ad Rufinum* see **Map, Walter**

Equatorie of the Planetis, The

Astronomical treatise, uncertainly attributed to Chaucer. *Equat*, which survives in a unique manuscript, Peterhouse (Cambridge) MS 75.I (now in the Cambridge University Library), was discovered in 1951 by Derek J. Price. In the introduction to his edition, published in 1955, Price argues that *Equat* could well be a work by Chaucer, written as a companion piece to *Astr*. It comprises an account of the construction and use of the *equatorium planetarum*, an instrument for calculating the positions of the planets (and thus a larger and more complex instrument than the astrolabe). The source of *Equat* may be a lost Latin treatise by Simon Bredon of Merton College, Oxford, who died in 1372. The attribution to Chaucer depends mainly on a marginal inscription, 'radix Chaucer', which appears beside calculations based on a date ('radix') in December 1392. Price compares this to a possible signature by Chaucer on a customs house document from 1378, and suggests that *Equat* could be a holograph. The fact that the date used in *Equat* (1392) is so close to that used in *Astr* (1391) has been taken to support the case, and has led to speculation that *Equat* could have replaced parts 3 to 5 of *Astr* (which were apparently planned but not written). *Equat* may also contain an allusion to *Astr* (C.29–30 in Price's edition). While scholarly opinion on this attribution remains divided, it is notable that Fisher (1977) is the only editor so far to have included *Equat* in an edition of the complete works of Chaucer.

Further reading: Price (1955).

Erinyes *see* **Furies; Esculapius** *see* **Aesculapius**

Euripides

(*c.* 485–406 BC)
Greek tragedian. Euripides is mentioned in *Bo* (3.p.7.25), where Lady
*Philosophy cites a line from his play *Andromache* (420). Chaucer would not
have known the work of Euripides.

Eurydice *see* **Orpheus**

Eve

The first woman (according to the *Bible). Eve is mentioned, alone or as the
wife of *Adam, in several works. Most of these allusions concern the
Creation or the Fall, and some – including that to the creation of woman in
Mel (VII.1103–6/B^2.2293–6) and the brief account of the Fall in *MkT*
(VII.2007–14/B^2.3197–204) – do not refer to Eve by name. The fullest
account of the implications of the fall occurs in *ParsT* (X.322–36, 682); here
(X.819), as in *PardT* (VI.505–11), she and Adam are accused of *Gluttony. In
NPT (VII.3256–66/B^2.4446–56) and *MLT* (II.365–71), Eve is blamed for caus-
ing the Fall – a view to which the *Wife of Bath objects strongly (*WBP*
III.713–20). Eve's more positive role as the companion of Adam is described
in *MerT* (IV.1325–32) and *Mel* (see above). The allusion to the teller of *SNT* as
an 'unworthy sone of Eve' (*SNP* VIII.62) has attracted attention, since it may
suggest that the tale was initially written for a male teller.

exemplum

Illustrative story, used especially in sermons. The exemplum (plural
'exempla') was intended to provide an apt illustration of a moral point. Such
stories were regularly gathered into collections for the use of preachers. In
CT, *PardT* is introduced specifically as an exemplum (*PardP* VI.329ff.), used
by the *Pardoner to illustrate the moral *radix malorum est cupiditas* ('greed is
the root of [all] evils'). Several other tales, though not related to the context
of a sermon, clearly have an exemplary function and quality – among them
FrT, *ClT*, and *MancT*.

F

fable *see* **Aesop; beast fable**

fabliau

Short comic tale, typically involving sex and trickery. The fabliau (plural 'fabliaux') came to prominence on the continent of Europe during the thirteenth century. While most surviving examples are French, fabliaux were also written in several other languages, including Italian, German, and Latin. They are, essentially, brief comic poems which relate stories of mundane contemporary life, featuring stereotyped characters from the lower and middle orders of society, involved in material and sexual competition, exchange, and deception. Their prevailing attitude is fundamentally amoral: while they sometimes offer aphoristic comments, these are concerned with being careful rather than with being good. Thus they tend to provide an opposing view to that of *romance – with its exotic settings, aristocratic protagonists, and elevated ideals. Nonetheless, they appear to have been written largely for the amusement of learned and aristocratic audiences. Chaucer's application of the genre – which is virtually unknown in English outside of his work – seems notably astute and original. He uses the plots, situations, and characters typical of fabliau in several of the *CT*, mainly in tales attributed to tellers of relatively modest social standing and relatively unscrupulous attitudes, such as the *Miller and the *Reeve. In *MilP* (I.3169) he refers to the forthcoming *MilT* as a 'cherles tale', going on to state that the Reeve and some others will tell similar tales. In fact, three tales – *MilT, RvT,* and *ShT* – may be termed fabliaux (though they are supreme examples of the genre). Several others reflect the influence of fabliau to a greater or lesser extent, and in a variety of ways – notably *SumT, MerT,* and the fragmentary *CkT*.

Fair-Welcomyng *see* **Bel Acueil**

Fairy

Fairyland. The term Fairy ('Fayerye' etc.) is used to signify the classical underworld, the land of fairies, and perhaps the Arthurian otherworld, Avalon. In *MerT* (IV.2038ff.), *Pluto and *Proserpina are described as king and queen of Fairy. In *Th* (VII.790ff./B².1980ff.), the hero visits the land of the fairies in pursuit of his love, the 'elf-queene' ('elf' and 'fairy' apparently being synonymous). The allusion to the possible return of *Gawain from 'Fairye' in *SqT* (V.95–6) may suggest Avalon. It may, however, merely reflect the more general association of the world of Arthurian romance with fairies, evident at the beginning of *WBT* (III.857ff.).

Fals-Semblant

Personification of hypocrisy in *Rom*. Fals-Semblant is based on Faus Semblant in *RR* – a shape-changer, able to assume the form of lay or ecclesiastical men or women, but particularly associated with the guise of a friar, whose cynicism is revealed in his 'confession' (*RR* 10,887ff.; *Rom* 5817ff.). This reflects (among other things) the views of writers opposed to the friars, such as *Guillaume de St Amour. It has been acknowledged that the portrait of the *Friar in *GP* (I.208ff.) and the account of the *Pardoner's conduct in *PardP* are indebted to the confession of Faus Semblant in *RR*.

Fame

Allegorical figure in *HF*. Fame is represented as a goddess, the sister of *Fortune. Chaucer describes how she dispenses either fame or infamy to those who petition her, without any regard for their true deserts (*HF* 1520ff.).

Fates

The Parcae, controllers of human life in classical myth. They were envisaged as three sisters, Clotho, Lachesis, and Atropos – responsible respectively for spinning, measuring, and cutting the thread of life. The Fates are mentioned in *Tr* (3.733–5, 5.3) and *LGW* (2580), in the latter case as 'Wirdes' (from Old English *wyrd* [fate]). Individual allusions to Atropos and Lachesis also occur in *Tr* (4.1208, 1546–7; 5.7).

Femenye *see* Scythia; fiend *see* devil

Finisterre

Cape Finisterre, north-west Spain. In *GP* (I.408), the *Shipman is said to be familiar with the coast from *Gotland (in the north) to Finisterre (in the south).

Flanders

Countship under French rule, corresponding roughly to the western half of present-day Belgium. Chaucer probably had a personal connection with Flanders, since his wife was almost certainly the daughter of the Flemish knight, Sir Paon de *Roet. Flemish towns mentioned in Chaucer's work or otherwise relevant include Ghent (birthplace of *John of Gaunt), Poperinghe (birthplace of Sir *Thopas according to *Th* VII.720/B².1910), *Bruges, and *Ypres. The identification of Flanders as the setting for *PardT* (VI.463) has been taken by some scholars to reflect the reputation of the Flemings for drunkenness. In *GP* (I.85–6), the *Squire is said to have campaigned in Flanders, Artois, and Picardy (the latter two being regions of France to the south of Flanders) – probably an allusion to the abortive expedition of 1383, led by the militant bishop of Norwich, Henry le Despenser, against supporters of the pope in Avignon (during the *Great Schism). The *Merchant in *GP* (I.272) wears a Flemish hat, which may suggest trading activities (also indicated in allusions to Bruges and Ypres). The deadly attacks on prosperous Flemish traders in London during the *Peasants' Revolt are mentioned briefly and somewhat flippantly in *NPT* (VII. 3393–6/B².4583–6). A Flemish proverb is used by the *Cook in *CkP* (I.4357; see Whiting [1968] P.257).

Flexippe *see* Antigone; Fletcher, John *see* Shakespeare, William

Former Age, The

Moral lyric of 63 lines. *Form Age* survives in two manuscripts, one of which (Cambridge University Library Ii.3.21) interpolates it into the text of *Bo* (following 2.m.5). Its title was supplied by Skeat. *Form Age* consists of eight stanzas of eight lines each (as used in *MkT*); a line missing from the seventh stanza (in both manuscripts) explains why the total length should be 63 rather than 64 lines. In this uncharacteristically bleak poem, Chaucer contrasts the corruption of his own times with a former golden age of primeval simplicity. *Form Age* is often included – along with *For, Truth, Gent,* and *Sted* – in a group of 'Boethian' lyrics, all of which deal with issues addressed in the *De consolatione philosophiae* of *Boethius. It draws specifically on *Bo* 2.m.5 (see above), and also reflects the influence of *RR (8325ff.) and of *Ovid's *Metamorphoses* (1.89ff.). While *Form Age* has often been dated in the 1380s because of its connection with *Bo*, some scholars have interpreted it as a comment on the final years of *Richard II's reign (*c.* 1397–99).

Further reading: Pace and David (1982); V.J. Scattergood in Minnis (1995).

Fortune

Fickle goddess in *Bo* and other works. The figure of Fortune was developed from Fortuna, the Roman goddess of good fortune. In the second book of the *De consolatione philosophiae* of *Boethius, she comes to represent worldliness and the instability of all worldly good fortune, in contrast to the stable and unworldly values of *Philosophy. Elsewhere in Chaucer's work, she is identified with the arbitrariness and transience of power, success, and happiness. The protagonists of the 'tragedies' which comprise *MkT* are envisaged as victims of Fortune; those of several other works, notably *Tr* and *KnT*, are seen at times in much the same way. In *For*, she is accused of fickleness and responds to this accusation. Passing allusions to the arbitrariness, instability, and cruelty of Fortune occur throughout Chaucer's work. These are sometimes associated with the idea of Fortune's wheel, the turning of which reduces the protagonist from good to ill fortune (e.g. *KnT* I.925; *MkT* VII.2397–8/B^2.3587–8), or the gifts of Fortune, which prove transient and illusory (e.g. *MerT* IV.1314–15; *Bo* 2.p.5.5).

Fortune

Philosophical lyric of 79 lines. *For* survives in 10 manuscripts, in one of which (Cambridge University Library Ii.3.21) it is interpolated into the text of *Bo* along with *Form Age*. The title is editorial. In some manuscripts, *For* has a subtitle, 'Balades de Visage sanz Peinture' ('ballades on a face without painting'), on which see Benson (1987: 1084). It comprises a triple *ballade and an *envoy, each ballade consisting of three eight-line stanzas, and the envoy of a single seven-line stanza. *For* is based on the idea of a lawsuit, with a plaintiff stating his case against *Fortune, who duly responds. It has strong links with the *De consolatione philosophiae* of *Boethius – stronger than those in any of the other 'Boethian' lyrics (*Form Age*, *Truth*, *Gent*, and *Sted*). While the association with *Bo* has encouraged a dating in the 1380s, the envoy has often been taken as a later addition. It has been interpreted as an appeal for funds, directed to the three dukes (Lancaster, York, and Gloucester) who in 1390 controlled gifts given on behalf of *Richard II. This would strengthen the view of *For* as a begging poem (cf. *Purse* and *Scog*).

Further reading: Pace and David (1982); V.J. Scattergood in Minnis (1995).

fox *see* **Russell**

France

Country corresponding roughly to present-day France and the western half of Belgium. By comparison with England, France was a wealthy country with a large population. It was, however, not politically cohesive: the pricipalities (*Flanders, *Brittany, and Burgundy) had considerable autonomy, and Aquitaine (which comprised a large area around Bordeaux) was under English rule. The *Hundred Years' War between England and France began a few years before Chaucer's birth and lasted, intermittently, until more than half a century after his death. Thus, for much of his life, the country of his birth was at war with the country whose literature, culture, and language provided many of the earliest and most significant influences on his work. Two of his tales are set in France: *ShT* near Paris and *FranT* in Britanny. *See also*: **French**.

Franklin

Pilgrim and teller in *CT*. The portrait of the Franklin in *GP* (I.331ff.) follows that of the *Sergeant of Law. The first line appears to indicate an association between the two pilgrims – generally assumed to have been professional, on the basis of the public offices the Franklin is said to have held (355–9). The fact the offices mentioned here include those of Justice of the Peace and Knight of the Shire, both of which had been held by Chaucer, has sometimes been taken to suggest that the portrait reflects Chaucer's own career in public service. These allusions have also provided the basis of several attempts to identify a model for the portrait, none of which has proved particularly convincing. They have, moreover, been considered – along with the terms 'franklin' and 'vavasour' (360), and the account of the Franklin's life-style – as evidence of his implied social status. Though commentators would agree that he is portrayed as a member of the country gentry, assessment of his precise status remains divergent – ranging from relatively high (not far below that of the *Knight) to relatively low (in which case he can be deemed a parvenu). Such assessments have a significant influence on interpretation of the Franklin's concern for *'gentilesse', which emerges after his (apparent) interruption of *SqT* and is developed in *FranT*. The portrait's account of his life-style appears to be a celebration of hospitality, good cheer, and the frank enjoyment of food and drink. While many commentators read it in this way, others have detected a range of negative connotations, especially gluttony, social climbing, and lack of spirituality. They tend to stress the allusion to *Epicurus (335–8) and sometimes refer to satire on gluttony and on the conduct of administrators. Despite such reservations, the portrait is often regarded as one of the most attractive in *GP*.

Further reading: Andrew (1993); Mann (1973).

Franklin's Prologue and Tale, The

Prologue and *Breton lai from Fragment V of *CT*. *FranT* is clearly linked to the preceding *SqT*. It has generally been supposed that the *Franklin interrupts the *Squire, before going on to praise his *'gentilesse' and contrast this with the unseemly conduct of his own son. In the process, the Franklin establishes one of the central themes of his tale. (Thus the appearance in some manuscripts – including the *Hengwrt MS – of *MerE* and *SqIntro* as a prologue to *FranT* is plainly inappropriate.) The Franklin uses *FranP* to indicate that his tale will be a Breton lai (see below) and to apologize for his shortcomings as a teller – in an apology for ignorance of rhetoric which, ironically, displays striking rhetorical sophistication.

FranT opens with an account of how *Arveragus woos *Dorigen, and of how, in their eventual marriage, he relinquishes traditional male 'maistrie'. This is followed by a substantial passage of comment (V.761ff.), not strictly necessary to the story itself, which argues strongly in favour of freedom, patience, and mutuality in marriage. Thus, although the Franklin does not overtly engage with the *Wife of Bath, the *Clerk, or the *Merchant, his argument clearly takes up issues raised earlier by them. In the initial formulation of the concept of the *'marriage debate', *FranT* was regarded as the final contribution, and supposed to represent Chaucer's own opinions. While few commentators would now accept this theory in full, it remains clear that *FranT* articulates a distinctive and idealized view of marriage. This is severely tested by the main events of the story – the separation of Arveragus and Dorigen, caused by his determination to fulfil his chivalric duties (806ff.); Dorigen's rash promise to the unwelcome suitor, *Aurelius (989ff.); the help provided to him by the scholar from *Orléans, and his consequent success in meeting her stipulation that the rocks should be removed (1239ff.); the responses of Dorigen and of Arveragus to the resulting dilemma (1341ff.); and even the final resolution (1493ff.). Interpretations of the tale have been conspicuously varied. What might be termed the traditional reading would see the Franklin as a wise teller, and the main protagonists as essentially decent individuals, who struggle to respond in a civilized manner to the challenges they encounter. More negative readings tend to regard the

Franklin as a social climber, presenting an impractical (and, arguably, improper) view of marriage, which clearly fails his confused and self-indulgent protagonists. Thus, for instance, Dorigen's 'complaint' (1355ff.) can be taken to reflect the anguish of a genuine dilemma or to reveal vacillation and self-delusion. Similarly, the determination of Arveragus that she should keep her word can be taken to demonstrate uncompromisingly high principles or a complete lack of judgement. The tale ends with a traditional debating point, the teller asking his audience which of the three men whose actions resolved the dilemma – Arveragus, Aurelius, and the clerk of Orléans – was the most 'fre' (that is, generous of spirit). The posing of this question, and possibly even its formulation (which notably omits Dorigen) may serve not just to encourage debate but also to suggest that the issues involved are complex, elusive, and resitant to absolute judgements.

While *FranT* clearly contributes to the discussion of marriage, both within the 'marriage group' and in *CT* as a whole, it also suggests various links with several other tales. The most prominent of these is, perhaps, that with the preceding *SqT*. While the well constructed and relatively brief *FranT* offers a contrast to the loosely woven and potentially very long *SqT*, both are concerned with 'gentilesse' and with ideals of conduct. The motif of the 'love triangle', which had previously featured in *KnT*, *MilT*, and *MerT*, reappears in *FranT*. The parallel with *MerT* may seem particularly close, despite the marked contrast in tone between the two tales, since in each case the 'triangle' consists of a knight, his wife, and a squire. Dorigen's questioning of providence, prompted by her feelings about the rocks on the coast of *Brittany and her concern for the safety of her husband (865ff.), may also serve as a reminder of the extensive consideration of divine providence in *KnT*.

The Franklin introduces his tale as a Breton lai (*FranP* V.709–15). Its relative brevity, concern with love, interest in the supernatural, and emphasis on feelings rather than action have generally been regarded as typical of this sub-genre of romance. Chaucer seems to have taken some care in creating the impression of a pagan setting in ancient Brittany, referring to places such as *Armorica (729) and *Kayrrud (808), and providing appropriate names for his protagonists. The Breton setting does not appear in the analogues, which comprise folktales concerning rash promises and, especially, two versions by *Boccaccio of the same story – one in the *Decameron* (10.5), the other in the *Filocolo* (4.31–4). Though the latter has often been regarded as the main source of *FranT*, it lacks some of the tale's most significant features, including the removal of the rocks, the motivation of Dorigen, and the knight-lady-squire triangle. Various passages in the tale are indebted to texts on which Chaucer often drew: the discussion of marriage (761ff.) to

*RR (9391ff.), Dorigen's questioning of providence (865ff.) to *Boethius (*De consolatione philosophiae* 4.pr.6), and her complaint (1355ff.) to St *Jerome (*Epistola adversus Jovinianum* 1.41–6).

In the absence of any specific evidence, it has often been supposed that *FranT* would have been written at roughly the same time as the tales of fragments III and IV: probably the early to mid-1390s. A parallel has been drawn between Dorigen's complaint and the list of virtuous women, also indebted to Jerome, which appears in the 'G' version (281ff.) of *LGWP* – a text regularly dated *c.* 1394. The manuscripts contain some significant textual variants, affecting both wording and line order. They also provide numerous glosses, mainly comprising references to Dorigen's complaint.

Further reading: Cooper (1996); Robert R. Edwards in Correale and Hamel (2002).

Freiris of Berwick, The see Scottish Chaucerians

French

Language spoken not only in *France but also by the aristocracy in England. During Chaucer's youth, French was used for all formal business within the royal households such as those in which he worked. It can, therefore, be assumed that he became a fluent speaker of the language. Since he was capable of translating *RR and of making sophisticated use of French sources (in poems such as *BD*) during the early stages of his career, he must also have acquired a sound reading knowledge of French while still young. Some of his earliest lyrics – which have not survived, but to which he may refer in *LGWP* (F.422–3/G.410–11) and *Ret* (X.1087) – could well have been written in French. Certainly the dominant models for such poems would have been the lyrics of French poets such as *Machaut. The results may well have been similar to the *'Ch' poems, which have been speculatively attributed to Chaucer. The fact that his surviving works are in English presumably reflects a decision to write in his native tongue rather than in French – a choice which would have been by no means obvious in the late 1360s or early 1370s. It is conspicuous that his slightly older contemporary John *Gower writes in Latin, French, and English. By the middle years of Chaucer's life, French was, however, losing ground to English as a language for the use of aristocratic and educated speakers in England. The simultaneous emergence of English as the normal literary language of England is a consequence of several things, not least Chaucer's own achievement as a poet.

Chaucer makes one significant allusion to French in his work. He states that the *Prioress speaks the language in a manner associated with her English nunnery and that she does not know the French of *Paris (*GP* I.124–6). This reflects the development in England of a dialect – descended from the speech of the Normans and often termed Anglo-Norman – which would, doubtless, have sounded provincial to someone familiar with Parisian French.

Friar

Pilgrim and teller in *CT*. The portrait of the Friar in *GP* (I.208ff.) is the longest of the series (at 62 lines). It has often been taken to complete a group of regular clegy, comprising also the *Prioress (118ff.) and the *Monk (165ff.). While there is a general consensus that these three portraits describe pilgrims who fail to fulfil the ideals of their calling, some commentators discern, in the progression from the Prioress to the Monk to the Friar, an increasingly overt negation of such values. *GP* provides no specific hint of the quarrel between the Friar and the *Summoner, which occurs in Fragment III, beginning in *WBP* (829ff.), and continuing in their own prologues and tales. The attacks of the Friar and the Summoner on each other do, however, allude to activities mentioned in their respective portraits. As part of this process, the Friar is depicted in the unflattering account of the friar *John in *SumT*. While the fact that only two pilgrims, the Friar and the Prioress, are given names in *GP* has often been noted, the significance of the Friar's name, Huberd, is a matter of debate. It has been taken to associate him with Hubert the kite, a cynical figure in *beast epic. While this remains conjectural, the portrait clearly reflects the influence of satire against the friars, especially that contained in the account of Faus Semblant in *RR* (11,223ff.). Commentators have related many of the particulars in the portrait to this tradition – including the Friar's worldliness, fine clothes, handsome appearance, smooth manners, and musical talent, and the implications concerning his sexual laxity, cynicism regarding confession, and preference for the company of the wealthy. Many have observed that, while the implications of this satire are serious, the tone of the portrait is genial.

Further reading: Andrew (1993); Mann (1973).

friars *see* John (3)

Friar's Prologue and Tale, The

Prologue and satirical exemplary tale from Fragment III of *CT*. *FrP* begins with an allusion to the enmity between the *Friar and the *Summoner. This had initially manifested itself at the end of *WBP* (III.829ff.), and now emerges once more, as the Friar states first that his tale will not emulate the learned observations of the *Wife of Bath, and then that he will tell a 'game' about a summoner. When the *Host intervenes, to request that he should be courteous, the Summoner interjects, expressing his own intention to respond in due course by telling a tale about a friar. Some commentators have taken this to indicate that the Friar and the Summoner are presented as having already known each other (which well may be implied with regard to the *Miller and the *Reeve: see *MilP* I.3136ff.). It has, however, generally been felt that their enmity suggests professional competition, arising from the kind of activities described in their respective portraits (*GP* I.208ff., 623ff.). In either case, the motivation for their tales has been made clear.

The Friar's intention to attack the Summoner remains apparent throughout his tale. During the early stages (III.1332–7), it provokes a brief interruption from the Summoner, which the Host deals with firmly; at the equivalent point in *SumT* (III.1761–3), the Friar is goaded into a similar interruption, to which the Host responds in the same way. Though the Friar's prospective description of his tale as a 'game' might have led one to expect a *fabliau, *FrT* proves to be a harshly satirical *exemplum, the analogues of which are moral exempla about greed and intention. The Friar sustains his attack on the Summoner through the presentation of a cynical but foolish summoner, who allows himself to be trapped by the devil, and thus damned. The devil is depicted as a yeoman (1379ff.) – arrayed, like the *Yeoman in *GP* (I.101ff.) as a hunter – though one whose prey is human. Much of the tale proceeds through dialogue between the summoner and the devil, in which the crudity of the former and the sophistication of the latter are emphasized. The devil clearly explains what he is and how he operates, as a shape-changer and hunter of human souls (1447ff.). He even demonstrates a kind of principle when he and the sum-moner hear a carter, temporarily exasperated as his cart gets stuck on a muddy road, consign his horses, cart, and load to the devil (1537ff.). While the summoner encourages the devil to take this literally, he declines to do so, since it was not intended. The following episode (1571ff.) describes how the widow (addressed as 'Mabely'), is provoked by the summoner's victimization, and con-signs him to the devil with unequivocal intent. While the immediate irony results from the exposure of the summoner's inability to understand and act upon the knowledge given to him by the devil, the tale generates various other ironic effects – among them the shifting significance of the term 'broother', by which the two of them address each other. Above all, *FrT* (like *PardT*) is told by a teller who appears (in this case from his portrait in *GP*) to be guilty of precisely the kind of unprincipled conduct that he exposes in his tale.

While *FrT* is emphatically paired with *SumT*, it also has links with *WBP* and *WBT* (see above). Some commentators maintain that the Friar parodies *WBT* as a riposte to the Wife's satire of friars in *FrT* – taking his shape-changer (the devil) as a parodic response to hers (the *hag). More generally, the theme of promises, undertakings, and intentions recurs throughout *CT* (most notably in *FranT*).

It has generally been assumed that the remainder of Fragment III was written at much the same time as *WBP* and *WBT* – that is, the early to mid-1390s. The text of *FrP* and *FrT* contains relatively few variants.

Further reading: Cooper (1996); Peter Nicholson in Correale and Hamel (2002).

Friday

Day associated with misfortune. An allusion to Friday as a day of misfortune occurs in *NPT* (VII.3341–52/B².4531–42). In *KnT* (I.1534–9) it is identified as a day unlike the rest of the week (also a traditional idea).

Frideswide, St

(*c.* 680–735)
Mercian princess and virgin saint. Since Frideswide was the patron saint of Oxford, it seems appropriate that John, the Oxford carpenter in *MilT*, should call upon her for help (I.3349).

Froissart, Jean

(*c.* 1333–*c.* 1404)
Poet and chronicler. During the 1360s, Froissart served as secretary to Queen *Philippa, wife of Edward III. Like her, he came from Hainault, and would have been a native French speaker. If, as seems very likely, Chaucer's wife was the daughter of Sir Paon de *Roet, who also came from Hainault, this may have given him a connection with a regional group which would have included Froissart. It is, in any case, clear that Chaucer was influenced in the early stages of his career by the courtly styles and forms of French poetry written by poets including Froissart and *Machaut. Two of Froissart's poems are particularly significant sources: *Le Paradys d'Amours* in *BD*, and *Le Temple d'Honneur* in *HF*.

Furies

The Eumenides, agents of the gods' vengeance in classical myth. Chaucer terms them both the Furies and the Erinyes ('Herynes', 'Herenus'). He refers to the Furies in two invocations in *Tr* (1.6–14, 4.22–8) – naming them as Megaera, Alecto ('Alete'), and Tisiphone ('Thesiphone') in the latter, but mentioning only Tisiphone in the former. Passing allusions to one or more of the Furies occur in several other works, including *Bo* (3.m.12.33–4), *LGW* (2252), and *FranT* (V.950). In *KnT* (I.2684–91), the death of *Arcite is caused by a 'furie infernal', sent by *Pluto at the request of *Saturn. A curious reference to *Pity as queen of the Furies appears in *Pity* (92).

Furnivall, Frederick J.

(1825–1910)
Chaucerian scholar. Furnivall was a teacher, man of letters, and radical philanthropist. His work on Chaucer is mainly associated with the *Chaucer Society, which he founded in December 1867. He was also involved in the foundation of several other societies, including the Early English Text Society (1864) and the Wiclif Society (1881). Through the auspices of the Chaucer Society, Furnivall printed a series of volumes, mainly comprising transcripts from manuscripts containing works by Chaucer, often arranged in parallel text format. These provided an invaluable source of material for the use of later editors, notably *Skeat. Furnivall was a great collaborator, and drew on the advice of various scholars (especially *Bradshaw), but took personal responsibility not only for the selection of the manuscripts used, but also for devising the format, proof-reading, and supervising the arrange-ments for printing the Chaucer Society's publications. His life and writings reveal a man of prodigious energy, genuine goodwill, and conspicuous modesty regarding his own work.

Further reading: Donald C. Baker in Ruggiers (1984).

G

Gaddesden *see* **John of Gaddesden; Galatea**
see **Pamphilus**

Galen

(*c.* 130–201)
Galen of Pergamum, Roman medical authority. He is named twice by Chaucer in combination with *Hippocrates: among the authors known to the *Physician (*GP* I.431), and as an example of a great authority on medicine (*BD* 572). Galen is also mentioned as a medical authority in *ParsT* (X.831).

Gamelyn, The Tale of see Cook's Prologue and Tale, The

Ganelon

Traitor from the *Song of Roland*. Allusions to Ganelon ('Genylon', etc.) as the person who betrayed Roland and *Oliver occur in *BD* (1121–3) and *MkT* (VII.2387–90/B².3577–80) – the latter with reference to the betrayal of *Pedro I of Castile. In *NPT* (VII.3227/B².4417) the fox is jestingly compared to Ganelon. The punishment of Ganelon (that of being torn apart by wild horses) is mentioned in *ShT* (VII.194/B².1384); an earlier comment (136/1326) may also allude to this.

Gascoigne, Thomas

(1403–58)
Theologian. Gascoigne's statement to the effect that Chaucer experienced a deathbed repentance – probably made on the basis of *Ret* – is included in Crow and Olson (1966: 547) and quoted by Pearsall (1992: 275), who also provides a translation.

Gaufred *see* **Geoffrey de Vinsauf; Gaunt, John of** *see* **John of Gaunt**

Gawain

Arthurian knight. There are two allusions to Gawain in Chaucer's work (*SqT* V.95, *Rom* 2209), both of which mention his reputation for courtesy. *See also*: **Fairy**.

General Prologue

Opening passage of *CT*. *GP* divides naturally into three sections of notably unequal length: an introduction (lines 1–42), the portraits (43–714), and the tale-telling agreement (715–858). While the celebrated opening description of spring (1–18) draws on traditions of nature poetry going back to classical literature, no particular source has been discovered. The formality of these lines soon gives way to an informal style which is sustained throughout the rest of *GP*. The opening has, however, served to suggest a potential tension between worldly and spiritual matters, which proves richly evocative as *CT* develops. Chaucer proceeds to specify an occasion, a place, and some individuals: a pilgrimage to *Canterbury; the *Tabard Inn, *Southwark; and a group of 29 pilgrims, which he himself joins. The idea of the (fictional) pilgrimage to Canterbury has been rapidly established.

The second part of *GP* comprises some 22 descriptions, normally referred to as 'portraits', ranging in length from 9 to 62 lines. Since one of the portraits (361–78) describes five *Guildsmen, this would make a total of 26 pilgrims, which increases to 30 if the nun and three priests accompanying the *Prioress (mentioned in 163–4) are included. The apparent disparity between this total and that of 29 pilgrims (specified earlier) has been much discussed, without any full consensus emerging. It is often related to the signs of possible and potential revision: the allusion to a group of rogues (542–4 – sometimes taken to indicate that the last five portraits were added after the original composition of *GP*); and the allusion to the Prioress's entourage (sometimes taken to indicate the intention to add portraits of pilgrims including the *Second Nun and the *Nun's Priest). The sequence of the portraits equates broadly, but not precisely, with a descending order of social rank: it is, for instance, clear that the *Sergeant of Law (309–30) would have enjoyed higher social status than the *Yeoman (101–17). Among the portraits, various implied pairings, contrasts, and groupings emerge – including the pairing of the *Summoner and the *Pardoner, the contrast between the *Merchant and the *Clerk, and the grouping of the Prioress, the *Friar, and the *Monk. The identification of the pilgrims as (typically supreme) examples of their particular professions reflects the influence of estates satire, which castigated the characteristic vices of each 'estate' or social group. Chaucer's technique is more subtle and elusive, and tends to avoid overt judgement. The variousness of the length and content of the portraits, the sophisticated manipulation of tone and viewpoint within them, and the numerous links between them and other parts of *CT* have been much discussed. From the very beginning of scholarly work on Chaucer, commentators show their awareness of the unusual density of allusion in these portraits – a quality which both tempts them to seek models for the pilgrims and challenges them to provide explication of particular allusions. (For examples, see entries on individual pilgrims.)

The final part of *GP* introduces the *Host and the idea of the story-telling contest, and serves as a link to the first tale, that of the *Knight. The Host entertains the pilgrims with great geniality and aplomb, and quickly secures their agreement to his proposal that they should take part in a tale-telling contest on the journey to Canterbury and back, in which he will act as manager and judge, and the prize of a supper at the Tabard will be offered to the winner. Critics have inferred both that he will profit from this arrangement and that he manipulates the draw to select the first teller. The pilgrims' acceptance of the Host's scheme is (of course) fundamental to the structure of *CT*. Since he proposes that they should each tell two tales on each journey, it creates the framework for a potentially massive set of tales (only a small proportion of which were ever written). In the process, the pilgrims become tellers, collaborators, and rivals, and the potential for the rich interplay of the tales and of the links between them is established.

It seems likely that *GP* was written fairly early in the evolution of *CT*. Though some commentators have suggested that it was later revised (see above), this hypothesis derives no support from the manuscripts, in which textual variants are relatively insignificant and few in number. The title is editorial. *See also*: **Canterbury Tales, The**.

Further reading: Andrew (1993); Cooper (1996); Mann (1973).

'gentilesse'

Nobility of birth or conduct. The concept of 'gentilesse' is cognate with 'gentil' – which can, likewise, denote either social status or principled behaviour. Sometimes the two are mingled in ways that elude precise definition ('nobility'). In *Gent*, Chaucer presents 'gentilesse' as a quality not guaranteed by high birth but reflected in decent and compassionate conduct. A similar view is asserted at length by the *hag in *WBT* (III.1109ff.), with specific reference to the values and behaviour of her new husband. The association of 'gentilesse' with appropriate demeanour and conduct in a love relationship recurs in several works, notably *Tr* (1.881, 2.662, 3.1414), *FranT* (V.754, 1524–8), and *SqT* (V.483, 505). In the exchange at the end of *SqT* (673ff.), the *Franklin's fulsome praise of the *Squire's 'gentilesse' is dismissed with some impatience by the *Host.

Gentilesse

Moral lyric of 21 lines. *Gent* survives in 10 manuscripts, and is attributed to Chaucer by *Shirley and also by Henry *Scogan, who incorporated it (with due acknowledgement) into a poem of his own (text in Skeat, 1897: 237ff.). The title was provided by Skeat. *Gent* is a *ballade in three *rhyme royal stanzas. In it, Chaucer maintains that the proof of true *'gentilesse' lies in conduct rather than in birth – an argument also presented in *WBT* (III.1109ff.). *Gent* is often included (with *Form Age, For, Truth*, and *Sted*) in a group of 'Boethian' lyrics, dealing with issues addressed in the *De consolatione philosophiae* of *Boethius. It draws on *Bo*, book 3 (p.6, m.6), and also echoes *RR and *Dante. *Gent* has usually been assigned to Chaucer's 'Boethian' period, the 1380s.

Further reading: Pace and David (1982); V.J. Scattergood in Minnis (1995).

Geoffrey of Monmouth

(*c*. 1100–*c*. 1154)
Welsh chronicler. Geoffrey was the author of the enormously successful *Historia regum Britanniae* ('History of the kings of Britain'), a largely fictional history of British kings from their mythical founder, *Brut, to the late seventh century. This is the earliest surviving work to offer an extensive account of king *Arthur. The inclusion of Geoffrey among the writers on *Troy named in *HF* (1470) reflects the mythical Trojan associations of the early British kings.

Geoffrey de Vinsauf

(fl. late 12th – early 13th centuries)
Authority on *rhetoric. Geoffrey de Vinsauf, who was probably English, wrote (around 1200) an influential verse manual on rhetoric, *Poetria Nova*

('The new poetry'). In *NPT* (VII.3347–54/B².4537–44), Chaucer parodies the celebrated apostrophe on the death of *Richard I in the *Poetria Nova* (375–6), referrring to its author as 'Gaufred, deere maister soverayn'. Another echo of lines from this work (43–5) – which compares the process of poetic composition to that of designing a house – occurs in *Tr* (1.1065–9).

Gernade *see* Granada

Gerveis

Blacksmith in *MilT*. Gerveis supplies *Absolon with a hot coulter (i.e. blade from a plough) to use as a weapon against *Nicholas (I.3760ff.).

Gilbertus Anglicus

(fl. mid-13th century)
English physician, associated with Montpellier. The inclusion of Gilbertus among the authorities known to the *Physician (*GP* I.434) reflects the success of his *Compendium Medicinae*, also known as the *Laurea Anglicana*.

Giles, St

(d. *c.* 710)
Hermit saint also known as Aegidius. Passing invocations of the name of this popular saint occur in *HF* (1183) and *CYT* (VIII.1185).

Gill *see* Robin; Girart d'Amiens *see* Squire's Introduction and Tale, The

Glascurion

(fl. 10th century?)
Welsh bard. Glascurion, mentioned in a passage on harpers in *HF* (1208), can probably be identified with a Welsh bard, brother of Morgan Hên, king of Glamorgan (see Benson, 1987: 986).

Gluttony

One of the *Seven Deadly Sins. Gluttony (which includes drunkenness) provides the subject of a passage in *PardT* (VI.477ff.) and a section of *ParsT* (X.818ff.). Allusions to it also occur in *SumT* (III.1915–17, 1927). All three texts identify Gluttony as a cause of the Fall.

Golden Legend, The see Legenda aurea

Goodelief

Wife of the *Host. 'Goodelief' has sometimes been interpreted as an epithet, 'goode lief', meaning 'sweetheart' (as in *WBP* III.431), but is normally taken to be a name. In *MkP* (VII.1891ff./B².3081ff.), the Host expresses regret that his wife has not been able to hear about the patient and peace-loving *Prudence in *Mel*, since she herself is a woman notably lacking in such qualities. Here, as in *MerE* (IV.2419ff.), he claims that his wife keeps him in a state of anxious subjection.

Gordon, Bernard (of) *see* Bernard of Gordon

Gotland

Island off the east coast of Sweden. Gotland is mentioned in *GP* (I.408), together with *Finisterre, as (respectively) the northern and southern limits of the coastal area known to the *Shipman.

Gower, John

(*c.* 1330–1408)
Trilingual poet and acquaintance of Chaucer. Gower came from a Kentish family of considerable means and developed a connection with the House of Lancaster. During the latter part of his life, he took up residence as a lay brother in the Priory of St Mary Overyes, *Southwark (not far from the *Tabard inn), and married one Agnes Groundolf.

Gower's tomb in St Saviour's church, Southwark (now Southwark cathedral) includes representations of three folio volumes, symbolizing his major works: the *Mirour de l'Omme*, the *Vox Clamantis*, and the *Confessio Amantis* (hereafter, *MO, VC,* and *CA*) – which were written in *French (more precisely,

Anglo-Norman), Latin, and English respectively. Though he wrote other poems, in all three languages, these three substantial works represent his essential output and claim to fame. *MO* and *VC* are serious moral works which deal with human frailty and the ills of society. By comparison, the *CA* is a less austere work, which one might suppose to have been more congenial to Chaucer. It uses the device of a lover's confession to Venus as a frame for a remarkably varied series of narratives, arranged into eight books, one loosely based on each of the *Seven Deadly Sins, and the eighth on the education of *Alexander the Great.

The earliest evidence of a connection between the two poets occurs in 1378, when Chaucer granted power of attorney jointly to Gower and a royal esquire, Richard Forester (see Crow and Olson, 1966: 54, 60). Two *Valentine day poems among Gower's *Cinkante balades* (nos 34 and 35) may reflect the influence of *PF*. The well-known dedication of *Tr* (5.1856–9) to 'moral Gower' (together with 'philosophical *Strode') probably alludes to the moral seriousness of *MO* and *VC*. It is, however, the relationship between Gower's work in *CA* and Chaucer's work, mainly in *CT* and *LGW*, which is particularly rich and interesting. This relationship is partly derived from shared stories; a comparison of *MLT* and *WBT* with Gower's tales of Constance and of Florent (*CA* 2.587ff., 1.1407ff.) will provide examples of the two poets' mutual indebtedness. Elsewhere, however, there are conspicuous differences between their handling of common material – as in the cases of the stories of Phoebus and the crow (compare *MancT* with *CA* 3.783ff.) and of Tereus (compare *LGW* 2228ff. with *CA* 5.5551ff.). The latter example may suggest that, when dealing with sexual deviance and cruelty, Chaucer was more restrained than Gower. If so, it may be related to the much-discussed passage in *MLIntro* (II.77ff.), which expresses a censorious view of writers who tell stories of incest, such as those of Canacee and Apollonius of Tyre – both of which appear in *CA* (3.143ff., 8.271ff.). Some scholars have related this to the fact that a passage in praise of Chaucer, contained in the first version of *CA* (8.2941ff.), is omitted from the second version, and have supposed that the two poets quarrelled over this issue. Whether or not any such disagreement ever occurred, it is clear that Chaucer knew Gower well, and was strongly influenced by his work.

Further reading: Fisher (1964).

Granada

Moorish kingdom in southern *Spain. Granada ('Gernade') is mentioned in *GP* (I.57) as the location of the siege of *Algeciras.

Granson, Oton de

(*c.* 1345–97)

Savoyard poet and knight. Chaucer acknowledges his indebtedness to Granson in *Ven* (82). While Granson may also be associated with Chaucer as a writer of poems celebrating St *Valentine's day, and echoes both *BD* and *PF* in his work, the most significant influence on his output of lyric and narrative poetry was *Machaut. Granson provided martial service in England under *Edward III and *Richard II, and was renowned for his courage.

Gratian *see Decretum*

Great Schism

Establishment of rival popes in Rome and Avignon. The Great Schism began after the election of Urban VI in 1379 and the establishment of Clement VII as a rival in Avignon the following year. It lasted until 1417 and caused a significant division throughout Europe – in which the pope in Rome was supported by countries including England and the pope in Avignon by countries including France. Though the Great Schism had no direct bearing on Chaucer's work, it served to intensify anti-papal sentiment, such as that expressed by *Wyclif.

Greenwich

Small town on the *Canterbury Way, about five miles from *London bridge. Greenwich is mentioned in *RvP* (I.3907), together with *Deptford. The added comment, 'ther many a shrewe [scoundrel] is inne!', may suggest that Greenwich had a dubious reputation at the time. It is also possible that Chaucer lived there from the late 1380s onwards, and that this constitutes a joke at his own expense.

Gregory, St

(*c.* 540–604)

Gregory the Great (Pope Gregory I), one of the four doctors of the early church (along with SS *Ambrose, *Augustine, and *Jerome). There are ten references to Gregory in *ParsT* (X.92, 214, 692), on a range of topics including penitence, hell, and various sins. He is cited similarly, on the patient acceptance of suffering, in *Mel* (VII.1497ff./B^2.2687ff.).

Grisilde

Long-suffering wife of *Walter in *ClT*. Grisilde is based on Griseldis in
Chaucer's main source, a story by *Petrarch. As a peasant woman chosen to
be the wife of a marquis, she comes to exemplify the qualities of obedience
and patience. The tale describes how Walter subjects Grisilde to a series of
tests – removing from her first her daughter and then her son (so that she
believes them to be dead, while they are being raised elsewhere), and then
pretending to repudiate her in favour of a younger and more appropriate
bride (unwittingly represented by their daughter). Though in the end
Griselde is reunited with her children and reconciled with her husband, she
remains memorable essentially for her superhuman patience in adversity.

Grosmont, Henry *see* Blanche; Grosvenor, Sir Robert *see* Scrope, Sir Richard

Guido delle Colonne

(fl. late 13th century)
Italian author. Guido delle Colonne (or de Columnis) translated *Le Roman de
Troie* of *Benoît de Sainte-Maure into Latin prose. This work, completed in
1287, was remarkably successful, and came to be regarded as an accurate
historical record of the Trojan war. Chaucer includes Guido among the writers
on *Troy mentioned in *HF* (1469), and acknowledges indebtedness to him
(for the story of *Jason and the Golden Fleece) in *Hypsipyle* (*LGW* 1396, 1464).
He also draws on Guido at the beginning of the subsequent *Medea* and (more
significantly) in *Tr* – though this remains unacknowledged in each case. The
influence of Guido in *Tr* cannot always be distinguished from that of Benoît,
despite the differing emphases of their two works. Guido provides a earnest
account of the conflict between the Trojans and the Greeks, and shows little
interest in human matters such as the love between *Troilus and Briseida
(forerunner of *Criseyde), which Benoît treats sympathetically. It was,
above all, a sense of the 'history' of Troy that Chaucer derived from Guido.

Guildsmen

Pilgrims in *GP*. The portrait of the Guildsmen (I.361ff.) precedes that of the
*Cook, the first line of whose portrait has been taken to suggest that he has
been employed by them for the duration of the pilgrimage. Two conspicuous
facts – that this is the only group portrait in *GP*, and that none of the

Guildsmen tells a tale – have been variously interpreted. Some commentators have speculated that the Guildsmen would have been omitted from a revised version of *GP*. Many have seen the lack of individualization between the members of the group as implying a contemptuous view of them, and have related this to the satire of self-importance which dominates the portrait. The selection of trades mentioned has generated some discussion. Commentators argue, first, that the omission of victualling trades from the group reflects the conflict between the victualling companies, which supported protectionism, and the non-victualling companies, which opposed it. They subsequently show more interest in the kind of guild implied by the fact that this is represented as having members from several different trades. It has generally been concluded that this indicates a parish guild (which would have been dedicated to the welfare of the various tradespeople of a particular parish) rather than a craft guild (which would have been restricted to the members of a particular trade).

Further reading: Andrew (1993); Mann (1973).

Guillaume de Lorris

(d. 1237)
French poet. Guillaume de Lorris wrote the first part of *RR.

Guillaume de St Amour

(d. 1272)
French writer. Guillaume expresses his opposition to the friars in his polemical and apocalyptic work *De periculis novissimorum temporum* ('On the perils of the most recent times'). His influence is reflected especially in the 'confession' of Faus Semblant in *RR (10,887ff.) – equivalent to that of *Fals-Semblant in *Rom* (5811ff.) – where Guillaume is cited (*RR* 11,483ff./*Rom* 6759ff.).

Guy of Warwick

Hero of romance. In *Th* (VII.897–902/B².2087–92) it is claimed that Sir *Thopas surpassed various heroes of romance, including Guy of Warwick and *Bevis of Hampton. These are both heroes of English romances translated from the Anglo-Norman and preserved in the *Auchinleck MS.

H

Haberdasher *see* **Guildsmen**

hag

Female protagonist of *WBT*. The hag – unnamed, but sometimes termed the 'loathly lady' (see III.1100) – provides the answer to the question on which the life of the knight depends: what do women most desire? In return, he has promised to grant her wish, and is appalled when she chooses to marry him. This presents her with the opportunity to complete his education, first by explaining the nature of true *'gentilesse', then by offering him a choice – between having her ugly but faithful or beautiful but possibly unfaithful. When he defers to her preference on this matter, his action undoes an enchantment, and the hag is transformed into a beautiful young lady (who promises also to be faithful).

Hailes

Hailes abbey, Gloucestershire. The Pardoner alludes (*PardT* VI.652), as an example of swearing, to an oath on the blood of Christ kept in a vial at Hailes abbey (which survives only as a ruin).

Haly

Medical authority. The Haly included among the authorities known to the *Physician (*GP* I.431) can be identified as either Haly Abbas or Haly filius Rodbon. Haly Abbas (d. 994) was a Persian who wrote a medical compendium, translated into Latin as the *Liber Regius*. Haly filius Rodbon (*c.* 998–*c.* 1067) lived in Cairo and was author of commentaries on authors including *Hippocrates and *Galen.

Hammond, Eleanor Prescott

(1866–1933)
Chaucerian scholar. Hammond is best known for her book, *Chaucer: A Bibliographical Manual* (1908), which provides admirably full and accurate information on the works of Chaucer.

Harbledown

Small town on the *Canterbury Way. Harbledown, two miles from *Canterbury, is the probable identity of 'Bobbe-up-and-doun' by the 'Blee' (Blean forest), mentioned in *MancP* (IX.2–3). Two other possible identifications have been proposed: see Benson (1987: 952).

Hasdrubal's wife

Celebrated suicide. Allusions to the story of the suicide of Hasdrubal's wife and children when the Romans seized *Carthage occur in *FranT* (V.1399–1400) and *NPT* (VII.3362–5/B^2.4552–5).

Hawes, Stephen *see* English Chaucerians; Hawley, John *see Maudelayne*; Hayles *see* Hailes

Hector

Trojan leader; son of *Priam and *Hecuba; brother of *Troilus. Despite his prominence as a great warrior and the eldest of the Trojan princes, Hector plays a relatively minor role in *Tr*. He is, however, portrayed positively: as a supporter of *Criseyde (1.105ff.), as someone opposed to exchanging her for *Antenor (4.176–82), and (repeatedly) as the only warrior to outshine Troilus (2.158, 740; 3.1775; 5.1803–4). Allusions to Hector's death occur in *Tr* (5.1548–54) and several other works, including *KnT* (I.2830–4) and *BD* (1064–6). The dream in which his wife, Andromache, foresees his death is mentioned in *NPT* (VII. 3141–8/B^2.4331–8).

Hecuba

Queen of *Troy; wife of *Priam; mother of *Troilus. Hecuba is mentioned briefly in *Tr* (5.12).

Helen

Helen of *Troy: the wife of Menelaus, abducted by *Paris. The role of Helen in *Tr* is slight but positive: she appears as a member of the social group to which the Trojan princes belong, offering kindly support to *Criseyde and to *Troilus (2.1625ff., 3.204ff.). Elsewhere in *Tr*, there are various references to her political significance in the Trojan war (e.g. 1.62, 4.1347, 5.890).

Passing allusions to Helen occur in several other works, including *MerT* (IV.1752–4), *MLIntro* (II.70), *BD* (331), and *PF* (291).

Helen, St

(*c*. 255–330)
Mother of the first Christian emperor, Constantine the Great. The traditional attribution to St Helen of the discovery of the cross on which Christ was crucified is reflected in an allusion at the end of *PardT* (VI.951).

Helicon

Mount Helicon, sacred to the *Muses. Helicon ('Elicon', etc.) is associated with the Muses in *HF* (522), *Anel* (17), and *Tr* (3.1809). The allusion in *HF* erroneously describes it as a 'welle' – possibly reflecting confusion with Aganippe, the fountain of inspiration at the foot of Helicon.

Héloïse

(*c*. 1098–1164)
French abbess; lover and wife of Abelard. The inclusion of Héloïse among the authors in *Jankin's *'book of wicked wives' (*WBP* III.677) reflects the anti-matrimonial sentiments expressed in her letters to Abelard (despite the fact that they had secretly married).

Hengwrt MS

Manuscript of *CT*. The Hengwrt MS (National Library of Wales MS Penarth 392 D) is probably the earliest surviving manuscript of *CT* – dating from shortly before or soon after Chaucer's death. Scholars generally accept that it and the *Ellesmere MS are the most authoritative manuscripts of *CT* and that they were written by the same scribe, recently identified as Adam *Pynkhurst. While the text in the Hengwrt MS may well be closer to what Chaucer actually wrote than that in any other manuscript, there are signs that it was compiled hastily: several texts (including *MerP*, *CYP*, and *CYT*) are missing, and the tale order is clearly unsatisfactory. For these reasons, it has seldom been used as a base text.

Henry IV

(1367–1413)

Henry of Bolingbroke, King of England 1399–1413. Henry was the son of *John of Gaunt and his first wife, *Blanche. In September 1398 he was banished by *Richard II for ten years, following a dispute with Thomas Mowbray, Duke of Norfolk. On the death of Gaunt in February 1399, Richard seized the Lancaster estates and titles, to which Henry was heir, and exiled him for life. Henry returned to England, seized power, and forced Richard to abdicate. After his accession on 30 September 1399, Henry renewed and supplemented the annuity which Chaucer had received from Richard. Chaucer's address to Henry IV in the *envoy to *Purse* may reflect a brief period of financial uncertainty between the termination of his annuity on the deposition of Richard II and its restoration by the new king. It is probable that Chaucer died just over a year after the accession of Henry IV.

Henry Grosmont *see* Blanche

Henryson, Robert

(d. before 1505)

Scottish poet. Henryson is perhaps the best of the poets who have been termed, somewhat disparagingly, the *'Scottish Chaucerians'. Despite the originality and variety of Henryson's work, two of his poems strongly reflect the influence of Chaucer. One of these, the story of the cock and the fox from his Aesopic collection, *The Moral Fabillis*, is indebted to *NPT*. The other, *The Testament of Cresseid*, engages with *Tr*, offering an alternative conclusion, in which Cresseid outlives Troilus, is rejected by Diomede, and eventually dies a leper. Though Henryson's version of the story can hardly be reconciled with Chaucer's, this bleak but splendid poem was printed along with *Tr* in editions of Chaucer from that of *Thynne until the end of the eighteenth century.

Hercules

Ancient Greek hero, son of *Jupiter and Alcmena. The story of the twelve labours of Hercules is related in *MkT* (VII.2095ff./B^2.3285ff.) and *Bo* (4.m.7.28ff.). The former also describes how he dies from wearing a poisoned shirt given to him by his wife *Deianira. In *LGW* (1451ff.) Hercules assists *Jason in his seduction of *Hypsipyle. Elsewhere, there are passing references to various aspects of Hercules, including his strength (*KnT* I.1943), his status as a hero (*MLT* II.200), several of the twelve labours (*Bo* 2.pr.6.69–70; 4.p.6.19–20), his relationship with Deianira (*WBP* III.725–6), and his association with *Alceste (*LGWP* F.515/G.503). In *Tr* (4.32), there is an allusion to the astrological sign Leo, identified with the Nemean lion slain by Hercules.

Hermengild

Woman who offers hospitality to *Custance in *MLT*. Hermengild is the wife of a 'constable', the warden of a royal castle. She and her husband are pagan Anglo-Saxons who welcome the shipwrecked Custance to their home, and are converted to Christianity by her (II.505ff.). Hermengild is murdered by a disappointed suitor of Custance, who is accused of the crime but then miraculously exonerated.

Herod

Biblical rulers of the Jews, Herod the Great (d. 4 AD) and Herod Antipas (d. 39). The three allusions to Herod ('Herodes') in Chaucer's work imply both individuals. In *MilT* (I.3384), *Absolon is said to have performed the part of Herod the Great in the *mystery plays (where he was represented as a ranting tyrant). In *PardT* (VI.488–91), the decision of Herod Antipas to order the death of *John the Baptist is attributed to the effects of drunkenness (for the possible source of this idea, see Benson, 1987: 907–8). Given its association with the murder of a child, the unspecific allusion in *PrT* (VII.574/B².1764) suggests Herod the Great, who ordered the 'slaughter of the innocents' (Matt. 2:16).

Heroides *see* Ovid; Herynes, Herenus *see* Furies

Hippocrates

(*c.* 460–*c.* 377 BC)
Hippocrates of Cos, ancient Greek physician. Chaucer echoes the opening of the *Aphorisms*, the best-known work of Hippocrates ('Ypocras') in the first line of *PF*. Hippocrates is named among the medical authorities known to the *Physician in *GP* (I.431) and (together with *Galen) as a great physician in *BD* (572).

Hippolyta

Wife of *Theseus and sister of *Emily in *KnT*. Hippolyta appears early in *KnT* (I.865ff.) as a brave and beautiful Amazon, queen of *Scythia, who has been first conquered by Theseus and has then married him. Her role in the remainder of the tale is slight. A view similar to that presented at the beginning of *KnT* appears (more briefly) in *Anel* (36–42).

Hippomedon *see* Seven Against Thebes

Hoccleve, Thomas

(*c.* 1367–1426)
English poet. Hoccleve made his living as a clerk in the office of the Privy Seal. As a poet, he was profoundly influenced by Chaucer. Hoccleve acknowledges this indebtedness with notable respect and affection, even arranging for a portrait of Chaucer to be inserted in a manuscript of his major work, *The Regement of Princes*. It has been suggested that he could have acted as the editor of the *Ellesmere MS. One of the two poems called *The *Plowman's Tale* (and presented as an addition to *CT*) was actually by Hoccleve.

Hogge of Ware *see* Cook

Holcot, Robert

(d. 1349)
English theologian. It has been suggested that Chaucer used material from Holcot's commentary on the Book of Wisdom in the long speech by *Chauntecleer in *NPT* (VII.2970ff./B².4160ff.) concerning the significance of dreams.

Holderness

District in Yorkshire to the east of Hull. Holderness, described as 'a mersshy contree', serves as the setting for *SumT* (III.1710).

Holofernes

General of *Nebuchadnezzar, killed by *Judith. The story of the success and renown of Holofernes ('Oloferne', 'Olofernus') and of his death, based on the

Apocryphal Old Testament Book of Judith, constitutes a brief 'tragedy' in *MkT* (VII.2551ff./B².3741ff.). Passing allusions to his death occur in *MLT* (II.939–42), *MerT* (IV.1366–8), and *Mel* (VII.1099/B².2289).

Homer

(*c.* 8th century BC)
Ancient Greek poet. Chaucer would have known the works attributed to Homer (the *Iliad* and the *Odyssey*) indirectly, through traditions regarding the Trojan war and the works of other writers. He refers to Homer (usually 'Omer') several times, most memorably as one of the great poets to whom he dedicates *Tr* (5.1792). Homer is also acknowledged as an authority on the Trojan war in *HF* (1464–80) and in *Tr* (1.146), and as the author of the story of *Penelope in *FranT* (V.1443). *Bo* (5.m.2) includes Chaucer's translation of a passage in which *Boethius refers to Homer and quotes from the *Iliad* (1.605).

Horace

(65–8 BC)
Quintus Horatius Flaccus, Roman poet. Chaucer draws on Horace's *Ars poetica* ('The art of poetry') in *Tr* (2.22–8, 1041–3; possibly 1.631–44, 2.1030–6), *MerT* (IV.1715–17), and *MancT* (IX.116–18). Less significant echoes of Horace's *Epistles* and the *Satires* have been detected in *Mel* (VII.1562/B².2752) and in *Bo* (5.p.3.132–5) respectively. The allusion to 'Etik' in *LGWP* (F.166) has been taken to signify either Horace (*Epistles* 1.18.9) or *Aristotle's *Ethics* (see note in Benson, 1987: 1062). Some scholars have argued that the name of *Lollius, the mysterious authority on the Trojan war and supposed source for *Tr*, is derived from a misreading of lines from Horace's *Epistles* (1.2.1–2).

Horaste

Notional rival to *Troilus for the love of *Criseyde in *Tr*. Horaste is an imaginary rival, invented by *Pandarus in order to put pressure on Criseyde at a crucial moment in *Tr* (3.778ff.). Chaucer created this character, deriving his name from that of Orestes in *Guido delle Colonne.

Horn

Hero of romance. The name of 'Horn child' appears in *Th* (VII.898/B².2088), among a group of heroes said to have been eclipsed by Sir *Thopas. Horn is the hero of two English romances, one of which survives in the *Auchinleck MS.

Host

Organizer of the tale-telling contest in *CT*. The Host appears for the first time towards the end of *GP* (I.747ff.), when the pilgrims spend the night at his inn, the *Tabard. He is described as a large, impressive man, and later (*CkP* I.4358) addressed as 'Herry Bailly', who has been identified with Harry Bailey, innkeeper and member of parliament for *Southwark in 1376 and 1378. The Host proposes that the pilgrims should take part in a tale-telling contest, in which the prize – a dinner at the Tabard on their return, paid for by everyone else – will be awarded for the best tale. He offers to accompany the pilgrims as the manager of the contest. In the links, he makes numerous interventions in this role – typically commenting on the tale which has just been told and inviting the next speaker to contribute. The first such intervention occurs in the first link, *MilP* (I.3109ff.), and shows how the Host's attempt to control the tale-telling sequence is challenged and undermined by the *Miller. Thereafter, his control over the process is only partial, and involves a good deal of negotiation. The tone of his comments varies, and appears generally to reflect a conservative view of social structures and roles – as, particularly, in his words to the *Reeve (*RvP* I.3899–908). While he can be abrupt and judgemental at moments like this, he is notably deferential to pilgrims such as the *Sergeant of Law and the *Prioress (*MLIntro* II.33–8; *ShT* VII.445–51/B^2.1635–41). He can demonstrate firmness and good judgement, as in his handling of the quarrel between the *Friar and the *Summoner (*WBP* III.850–53; *FrP* III.1286–1300; *FrT* 1334–7; *SumT* III.1762–3). His most decisive intervention is to interrupt Chaucer as he tells *Th* (VII.919ff./ B^2.2109ff.), with the observation that his 'drasty rymyng is nat worth a toord' (930/2120). A similarly scatological turn of phrase emerges in his aggressive response to the *Pardoner at the end of *PardT* (VI.946–55). There are repeated allusions to his tendency to jest and to swear (e.g. *MilP* I.3114; *PardIntro* VI.287; *ThP* VII.693/B^2.1883; *MancP* IX.4); the latter draws an expression of disapproval from the *Parson (*MLE* II.1170–1). The Host speaks in a mocking or disrespectful manner to several pilgrims, including the *Clerk (*ClP* IV.1ff.), the *Monk (*NPP* VII.2780ff./B^2.3970ff.), and Chaucer himself (*ThP* VII.693–704/B^2.1883–94). His exchanges with and concerning the *Cook (*CkP* I.4344ff.; *MancP* IX.4ff.) may suggest professional rivalry. The impression of manly assertiveness is qualified by his own admission that he goes in fear of his shrewish and aggressive wife, *Goodelief (*MerE* IV.2419ff.; *MkP* VII.1891ff./B².3081ff.).

Further reading: Andrew (1993).

House of Fame, The

*Dream vision on literary authority and reputation. *HF* is written in *octosyllabic couplets, which Chaucer handles with rather more assurance here than in *BD*. It alludes to his work in the customs (652–60), which began in 1374. These considerations, along with evidence of a widening range of literary allusion, especially to *Dante, has led scholars to date *HF* considerably later than *BD*, generally around 1378–80. Suggestions as to dating have sometimes reflected a wish to argue that the poem was written for a specific occasion – the most strongly supported of which has been the betrothal of *Richard II to *Anne of Bohemia (1381). This process is rendered uncertain by the incomplete state of *HF*, which breaks off at line 2158, just as 'a man of gret auctorite' is about to make a significant announcement, apparently concerning love. It remains uncertain whether the ending was lost in the early stages of transmission, or whether Chaucer failed to complete the poem – or perhaps chose not to provide a conventional ending for it.

Uncertainty characterizes both the theme and the structure of *HF*. The poem is, admittedly, divided into three books, each of which begins with a proem and invocation (those in books two and three apparently constituting the first invocations to the *Muses in English poetry); but the clarity this might seem to promise does not materialize. In the first book (lines 1–508), the dream vision is introduced by a proem on the interpretation of dreams and an invocation to the god of sleep (cf. *BD*). The dream itself – which takes place, for no apparent reason, on 10 December (63, 111) – transports the poet-narrator to a temple of glass, dedicated to *Venus. This serves as the setting for an account of the destruction of *Troy and the doomed love of *Dido and *Aeneas. Chaucer specifies his authorities here as *Virgil and *Ovid (378–9), whose respective approaches to the story of Dido and Aeneas differ significantly: while Virgil presents the departure of Aeneas for Rome as a triumph of duty over temptation, Ovid concentrates on the experience of Dido as woman betrayed by her lover. Support for the latter view may be implied by allusions to various other examples of male infidelity – of which the stories of Phyllis, Hypsipyle, Medea, and Ariadne, as well as that of Dido, are subsequently told by Chaucer in *LGW*. The first book ends with the narrator stepping outside and observing an *eagle in flight. In the second (509–1090), after a brief proem and invocation, he is seized by the eagle and carried far into the heavens. The eagle explains that he has been sent by *Jupiter to reward the poet – who, though not experienced as a lover, has served love through his poems – by taking him to the House of *Fame, where he can learn more about love. Meanwhile, the eagle offers him lengthy instruction on the nature of the universe and the workings of sound. Two passing allusions in this book provide fleeting impressions of Chaucer's personal life: his own observation (554ff.) that the eagle's first word to him ('Awak') reminds him of the voice of one he will not name (often assumed to be his wife), and the eagle's account (652–60) of how, after a hard day's work (presumably at the customs), he spends his evenings absorbed in books. The promised visit to the House of Fame takes place in the third book (1091–2158). This beautiful and elaborate building, placed on the precarious foundation of a rock of ice, provides the poet-narrator with glimpses of a dazzling variety of traditional stories and renowned individuals. These include a series of famous writers – among them *Homer, Virgil, Ovid, *Lucan, and *Statius – set upon a series of pillars. Fame herself is represented as a goddess who distributes good and ill repute to various petitioners in an entirely arbitrary manner. When asked by an unidentified individual whether he himself seeks fame, the poet-narrator responds, in a fascinating passage (1868ff.), by stating that he has no such desire, and seeks only 'tydynges' – for which purpose his guide directs him to the House of Rumour. This is a fantastic, labyrinthine structure, made of twigs and whirling around, to which all sounds from the earth, true or false, eventually make their way. Paradoxically, it is here that the 'man of gret auctoritee' was to make his announcement: thus the potential for this to be truly authoritative would seem to have been undermined by the context.

The entire poem, with its essential instability and elusiveness, presents a severe challenge to interpretation. While critics have expressed conspicuously divergent views, most would regard *HF* as a poem in which Chaucer explores the fundamental issues of literary authority, influence, and reputation. It is his most bookish poem, packed with allusions to stories, traditions, and individual writers. He was clearly influenced by the genre of mental or celestial travel, significant examples of which include *Dante's *Divine Comedy*, *Cicero's *Somnium Scipionis*, St *Paul's journey to the 'third heaven' (2 Cor. 12: 2–4), and the Book of *Revelation. The expectation that the journey will bring revelation – fundamental to all such narratives – is, however, plainly subverted in *HF*. Similarly, the eagle – based on Dante (*Purgatorio* 9.19ff.), whose representation there reflects the awe-inspiring associations of this bird with divine knowledge – becomes garrulous and mildly absurd in Chaucer's poem. For the concept of Fame, Chaucer is indebted to Virgil

(*Aeneid* 4.173ff.) and Ovid (*Metamorphoses* 12.39ff.). Some commentators have suggested that he also drew on the account of the house of *Fortune in the *Le Dit de la Panthère d'Amours* of Nicole de Margival (*c.* 1300), and on that of the temple of Honour in *Froissart's *Le Temple d'Honneur*.

HF is preserved in three manuscripts, of which two end at line 2158, the other at line 1843. With this exception, the variants in the manuscripts are not particularly significant. Caxton, who was apparently working from a manuscript which ended at line 2094, wrote a brief conclusion to the poem. *The Temple of Fame*, an early poem by *Pope, was inspired by the third book of *HF*.

Further reading: Minnis (1995); Windeatt (1982).

Huberd *see* Friar

Hugh of Lincoln, St

(d. 1255)
Boy martyr. Hugh of Lincoln – known as 'Little St Hugh' in order to distinguish him from the other saintly Hugh of Lincoln (d. 1200) – was a boy of nine, supposedly killed by members of the Jewish community. An allusion to him occurs at the end of *PrT* (VII.684–90/B.21874–80).

Hugolino *see* Ugolino

Hull

Port on the Humber estuary in Yorkshire. A passing allusion to Hull occurs in the portrait of the *Shipman (*GP* I.404).

Hundred Years' War

Conflict between England and *France, lasting intermittently from 1337 to 1453. The Hundred Years' War resulted from the claims of successive English kings to the throne of France. It was interrupted by various periods of peace, some of which were quite protracted. Chaucer had some direct personal experience of the war: in 1359–60, while still very young, he served in a campaign to northern France, during which he was captured and ransomed; he was also involved in some later expeditions. In 1377, he participated in peace negotiations at Montreuil-sur-Mer. While parts of his work appear to endorse the values of chivalric conflict, others – notably *Mel* – can be taken to suggest pacifist leanings.

husbands

Several unnamed characters in *CT*. The most memorable of these are, perhaps, the first four husbands of the *Wife of Bath – one of whom is, however, referred to in passing as Wilkin (*WBP* III.432).

Hypermnestra

Daughter of *Aegyptus and wife of *Lynceus. Hypermnestra ('Ypermystra', 'Ipermystre', etc.) is portrayed in the unfinished 'legend' about her (*LGW* 2562ff.) as a gentle and honest woman, who is horrified that her father should order her to kill Lynceus on their wedding night. When she warns Lynceus of the threat to his life, he flees, abandoning her to imprisonment. Passing references to the story of Hypermnestra occur in *MLIntro* (II.75) and *LGWP* (F.268/G.222).

Hypsipyle

Queen of Lemnos and abandoned lover of *Jason. *Hypsipyle and Medea* (*LGW* 1368ff.) tells the story of how Jason, with the assistance of *Hercules, seduces Hypsipyle ('Isiphile', 'Ysiphile', etc.) during the quest for the Golden Fleece, but later deserts her and their two children. Passing allusions to this story occur in *MLIntro* (II.67), *HF* (400), and *LGWP* (F.266/G.220).

I

Iarbas

Disappinted suitor of *Dido. Chaucer mentions the sorrow of Iarbas ('Yarbas') on hearing that Dido and *Aeneas have become lovers (*LGW* 1242–53).

Icarus

Figure of ancient Greek myth, son of *Dedalus. In *HF* (920) there is a passing allusion to the story of the flight of Icarus on wings made from feathers and wax – with which he flies too near the sun, so that the wax melts and he falls into the sea and drowns.

Idleness

Personified figure in *Rom*. Idleness (Oiseuse in *RR*) appears as a beautiful maiden who opens a door to admit the dreamer to the garden (*Rom* 531ff.). In the description of the temple of Venus in *KnT* (I.1940), Idleness is depicted as the porter in the dwelling of Venus. The section on *Sloth in *ParsT* (X.677ff.) includes an allusion to idleness (not personified) as 'the yate [gate] of alle harmes' (X.714).

illustrations *see Canterbury Tales, The*; Corpus Christi MS 61; Ellesmere MS

Innocent III

(1160–1216)

Pope and author. Before his election to the papacy in 1198, Innocent III wrote – as Lotario dei Segni – his influential work, *De miseria condicionis humane* ('On the wretchedness of the human condition'), also known as *De contemptu mundi* ('On contempt of the world'). This provides a grim account of the miseries of human conception and life, the illusory nature of wealth and pleasure, and the pains of hell. An allusion in *LGWP* (G.414–15) indicates that Chaucer made a translation of this work (apparently entitled 'Of the Wreched Engendrynge of Mankynde'). Chaucer's lost translation is normally dated *c.* 1390. *MLP* (II.99ff.) constitutes a free adaptation of a passage from *De miseria* (1.14). This work is also echoed at various points in *PardT* and cited in *Mel* (VII.1568–70/B².2758–60).

Ipocras *see* Hippocrates; Ipomedon *see* Seven Against Thebes

Ire

One of the *Seven Deadly Sins. A substantial section of *ParsT* (X.533ff.) deals with Ire (also termed Wrath) and the remedies for it. The forms of evil conduct described are notably varied, including such things as manslaughter, swearing, scorn, and japing. In *SumT* (III.1992ff.), the friar *John identifies Ire as one of the Seven Deadly Sins and addresses *Thomas on the subject at some length.

Isabella

(1389–1409)
Second wife of *Richard II. Isabella was the eldest surviving daughter of the French king Charles VI and his wife Isabella of Bavaria. Richard proposed marriage to Isabella, then a child of six, in 1395, following the death of his first wife, *Anne of Bohemia. The marriage took place in November 1396, and was linked to a peace treaty between England and *France. The notion that *Ros* was addressed to Isabella has not been widely supported. After Richard's death, Isabella married the poet Charles of Orléans, Count of Angoulème.

Isidore, St

(*c*. 560–636)
Archbishop of Seville; encyclopedist and writer on religious matters. Isidore was best known during the Middle Ages for his immensely successful etymological encyclopedia, the *Etymologiae* ('Etymologies'). Chaucer cites both this work and Isidore's *Sententiae* ('Aphorisms') in *ParsT* (X.551, 89 respectively).

Italian *see* Chaucer, Geoffrey; Italy

Italy

Country roughly equivalent to present-day Italy, but divided into numerous kingdoms and city-states. Chaucer's two visits to Italy, in 1372–73 and 1378, were of great importance to his development as a poet, since they brought him into contact with the works of *Dante, *Petrarch, and *Boccaccio. Most commentators assume that he had learned some Italian in his youth. His use of Italian sources demonstrates that, by his middle years, he had developed a sound reading knowledge of the language. Chaucer mentions ancient Italy as the destination of *Aeneas after the fall of *Troy in both *HF* (147, 187, etc.) and *Dido* (*LGW* 952, 1298, etc.). Several tales have more contemporary Italian settings: *ClT* in Lombardy, *MerT* in *Pavia, and the story of *Ugolino (*MkT* VII.2407ff./B^2.3597ff.) in *Pisa. Chaucer refers to several other regions and cities in Italy, with a diversity of connections, including Venice as a place from which fine gold coins originate (*HF* 1348), Florence as the home of Dante (*WBT* III.1125–6), and Lombardy as a region associated with tyranny. He also makes numerous allusions to *Rome, ranging in period from the ancient to the contemporary.

J

Jack Straw *see* **Straw, Jack; Jacobus de Voragine** *see* ***Legenda aurea*; James I, King of Scotland** *see* **Scottish Chaucerians**

James the Great, St

(d. 44)
Disciple, apostle, and martyr. According to tradition, the body of St James the Great was translated to Galicia in north-west Spain, where *Santiago de Compostella became a great centre of pilgrimage. His name is used in several oaths and exclamations, some of which appear to be formulaic – 'by that lord that called is Seint Jame' occurring in *RvT* (I.4264) and *WBP* (III.312), and 'by God and by Seint Jame' occurring in *FrT* (III.1443) and *ShT* (VII.355/B².1545).

James the Less, St

(fl. 1st century)
Apostle and supposed author of the Epistle of St James. This work is cited four times in *Mel* (VII.1119, 1517, 1676, 1869/B².2309, 2707, 2866, 3059) and once each in *ParsT* (X.349) and *ClT* (IV.1154), on topics including patience and wisdom.

Janicle

Father of *Grisilde in *ClT*. Janicle (also 'Janicula', as in *Petrarch) is introduced as the poorest man in his village (IV.204ff.), and represents, throughout the tale, the values of honest poverty which inform the background of Grisilde.

Jankin

Two characters in *CT*: (1) the fifth husband of the *Wife of Bath in *WBP*; (2) the squire of the lord of the manor in *SumT*. (1) Jankin in *WBP* is portrayed as a clerk in minor orders who marries a woman substantially older and wealthier than himself. The Wife of Bath describes him as her favourite husband – despite her resentment of his *'book of wicked wives', the violence with which he treats her, and the intensity of their struggle for dominance over each other. (2) Jankin appears at the end of *SumT* as the squire who provides the ingenious solution to the problem of dividing the fart.

The name Jankin is a diminutive of *John.

January

Knight of *Pavia and husband of *May in *MerT*. January is portrayed as a cynical and largely unappealing individual, who resolves at the age of sixty, after leading a dissolute life, to marry in order to provide himself with an heir. While his name tends to identify him with a stereotype – that of the old man, married to a young wife, and apt to become a cuckold (cf. *John in *MilT*) – he also has some distinctive features. The process by which he decides to marry and selects a bride shows him to be grossly insensitive and prone to self-delusion. While the former quality extends into January's treatment of his young wife (particularly in their sexual realtionship), he also shows concern both for her welfare and for that of his squire and (unknown to him) rival, *Damian, and makes notably generous provision for May in his will.

Jason

False lover of *Hypsipyle; false lover and husband of *Medea. Jason is repre-sented as the archetypal faithless male. During his quest for the Golden Fleece, he seduces and abandons Hypsipyle (*LGW* 1368ff.). He then becomes the lover of Medea, who helps him win the Golden Fleece, and marries him and bears him two children, only to be abandoned in her turn (*LGW* 1580ff.). The subsequent episode of the latter story, in which her betrayal by Jason leads Medea to kill her children, is mentioned in *MLIntro* (II.72–4) and *BD* (725–7). Allusions to Jason as a false lover also occur in *HF* (400–1), *SqT* (V.548–9), and *LGWP* (F.266/G.220).

Jealousy

Personification in *Rom*. Jealousy endeavours to protect the Rose from the lover by buiding a castle around the rose bush (*Rom* 3820ff.).

Jean de Meun

(d. 1305)
French poet. Jean de Meun wrote the final part of *RR*. He also produced a translation of the *De consolatione philosophiae* of *Boethius, which Chaucer used in the composition of *Bo*.

Jerome, St

(*c.* 341–420)
Translator of the *Bible into Latin; one of the four doctors of the early church (along with SS *Ambrose, *Augustine, and *Gregory). St Jerome is cited seven times in *ParsT*, on a range of topics including contrition, meekness, and lechery (e.g. X.159–60, 657, 933). A similar allusion, on idleness, occurs in *Mel* (VII.1595/B².2785). His well-known tract, *Epistola adversus Jovinianum* ('Letter against Jovinian'), in which he refutes the views of Jovinian on virginity, is cited in *LGWP* (G.281ff.) and included in *Jankin's *'book of wicked wives', mentioned in *WBP* (III.669ff.). Chaucer uses material from this work in several tales, including *FrT, SumT, MerT, FranT,* and *PardT*.

Jerusalem

The 'Holy City'. Jerusalem is mentioned in *GP* (I.463) as a pilgrimage site, which the *Wife of Bath has (remarkably) visited three times. She alludes to her return from one of these journeys in *WBP* (III.495). Jerusalem features in three stories, from Old Testament or Apocryphal sources, included among the *Monk's 'tragedies': those of *Nebuchadnezzar, *Belshazzar, and *Antiochus (*MkT* VII.2147, 2196, 2596/B².3337, 3386, 3786). The Parson refers twice to 'Jerusalem celestial', the New Jerusalem of Apocalypse (*ParsP* X.51; *ParsT* X.80). Passing allusions to Jerusalem (as an actual place) also occur in *ParsT* (X.589) and *Rom* (554).

Jesus *see* Christ

Jesus filius Sirach

(2nd century BC)
Author or compiler of the Apocryphal Old Testament book, Ecclesiasticus. Several references to Jesus filius Sirach (also 'Jhesus Syrak') occur in *MerT* (IV.2250) and *Mel* (VII.1045, 1059, etc./B².2235, 2249, etc.).

Joan of Kent

(1328–85)
Countess of Kent, wife of *Edward, Prince of Wales, and mother of *Richard II. Though Joan was regarded as a great beauty, by the time of her marriage to Edward in 1361 she was a widow with three children. This was not the only

reason for the match causing controversy. Edward and Joan were both grandchildren of Edward I, and were therefore related too closely to be married without papal dispensation. Joan had, moreover, previously been married twice – to William Montacute, Earl of Salisbury, and to Sir John Holland. The former marriage took place in 1347 and was dissolved in 1349 (on the grounds that Joan had previously exchanged vows with Holland); the latter ended with Holland's death in 1360. While it has often been suggested that Chaucer enjoyed the patronage of Joan, there is no evidence to support this attractive idea.

Job

Old Testament figure, typifying the patient acceptance of suffering. Consideration of the fear of hell in *ParsT* (X.175ff.) is based on an exegetical interpretation of a passage from the Book of Job (10.20–22). Allusions to Job as a model of patience or humility occur in *Mel* (VII.999–1000/B².2189–90), *ClT* (IV.932), and *FrT* (III.1491).

John

Four characters in *CT*: (1) the carpenter in *MilT*; (2) one of the scholars in *RvT*; (3) the friar in *SumT*; (4) the monk in *ShT*. (1) John in *MilT* is based on the conventional figure of the jealous old man with a wild young wife. Though gullible and easily duped by the clever and cynical scholar, *Nicholas, John emerges as a kindly man, devoted to his wife, *Alison. (2) John and his companion *Alan in *RvT* constitute a pair of Cambridge scholars who are cheated by the miller *Simkin and take their revenge on him. (3) The cynical and grasping friar in *SumT* is called John on one occasion (III.2171). His attempts to extract money for his order from the sick and wealthy *Thomas meet with a vulgar and comic reversal. (4) The monk in *ShT* is consistently termed 'daun [master] John'. Chaucer depicts him as a lecherous and opportunistic individual, who gains money and sexual favours from the merchant and his wife (respectively) through audacious trickery.

The *Nun's Priest is called 'sir John' on two occasions (*NPP* VII.2810, 2820/B².4000, 4010). This (and the third and fourth cases mentioned above) may reflect the conventional use of 'John' as the standard name for a priest. It is one of the names jestingly applied to the *Monk by the *Host (*MkP* VII.1929/B².3119), who also uses its diminutive, *Jankin, in a derisive reference to the *Parson (*MLE* II.1172).

John, St

(fl. 1st century)
Apostle; traditionally acknowledged as author of the Fourth Gospel, the Book of Revelation, and three Epistles. The Gospel and Revelation are cited and quoted several times in *ParsT* (e.g. X.349, 565, 687). Less explicit references to these texts and to St John as their author occur in *FrT* (III.1647), *PrT* (VII.582/B².1772), *HF* (1385), and *Rom* (e.g. 7167, 7178). The name of St John also appears, with varying degrees of significance, in oaths and invocations, in works including *SumT* (III.1800, 2252), *MLT* (II.1019), *Mars* (9), and *PF* (451). The allusion in *BD* (1319) does have a specific significance, since John would have been the name-saint of *John of Gaunt.

John the Baptist, St

(d. *c.* 30)
The precursor of *Christ. There are brief allusions to John as a hermit in *Rom* (6995–8) and to his death in *PardT* (VI.491).

John of Gaddesden

(*c.* 1280–1349)
English medical authority. John was a fellow of Merton College, Oxford, and author of a medical compendium, the *Rosa Anglica*. Among the medical authorities known to the *Physician (*GP* I.429–34), he is the nearest to a contemporary of Chaucer.

John of Gaunt

(1340–99)
Fourth son of *Edward III and *Philippa of Hainault; father of *Henry IV. John, who is generally known as 'Gaunt' from his place of birth (Ghent), became Earl of Richmond in 1342. He married *Blanche, younger daughter of Henry Grosmont, Duke of Lancaster, in 1359. At this point, since Henry had no son, Blanche and her childless sister, Maud, Countess of Leicester, were co-heirs to his estate. The death of Henry in 1361 was followed by the unexpected death of Maud in 1362. As a consequence, Gaunt inherited the vast Lancastrian estates, and became Earl of Leicester, Lincoln, and Derby, and Duke of Lancaster.

Blanche died in September 1368, having borne five children, of whom three survived, including the future Henry IV. Gaunt's second marriage, to *Constance (Constanza), daughter of *Pedro I of Castile, took place in September 1371. This union was motivated largely by dynastic ambitions – reflected in the fact that Gaunt styled himself 'King of Castile' for a considerable period (1372–88), and spent some years (1386–89) in Spain, trying to secure the crown. Though this proved unsuccessful, Catherine (Catalina), the only surviving child of his marriage with Constance, eventually married Enrique III of Castile. Gaunt's long relationship with Katherine *Swynford appears to have begun in the early 1370s, and by 1380 had produced four children, known as the Beauforts. After the death of Constance, Gaunt was able, belatedly, to marry Katherine in 1396, and thus to secure the legitimacy of their children (the eldest of whom, John, was the grandfather of Margaret Beaufort, mother of Henry VII). Gaunt died on 3 February 1399, and was buried beside Blanche.

Chaucer was connected with Gaunt in various ways. He wrote *BD* in response to the death of Blanche, who is clearly identified, along with Gaunt, in some mildly cryptic allusions (*BD* 948, 1318–19). While Chaucer's representation of the grief of the bereaved husband, the *Man in Black, plainly addresses the actual experience of Gaunt, the extent to which it is personalized remains a matter for interpretation. *BD* does not, however, include a dedication to Gaunt, and there is no firm evidence that he commissioned the poem. By comparison, the rewards provided by Gaunt both to the poet and to his wife, Philippa *Chaucer, are a matter of record (albeit incomplete): both received substantial annuities from him throughout much of their working lives. While those paid to Philippa were in recognition of her service in the household of Constance, the service provided by Chaucer himself would have been more diverse, and would have included a range of diplomatic activities. Gaunt's patronage was notably extended to their elder son, Thomas *Chaucer. While his generosity in this case has led to speculation that he was Thomas's actual father (and thus that he had an affair with Philippa Chaucer), this seems unlikely. In assessing Gaunt's patronage of the Chaucers, it is important to bear in mind his great wealth, power, and prominence in the court and in political life. The deaths of his three older brothers – William of Hatfield (b. 1338) as an infant, *Lionel of Antwerp in 1368, and *Edward, Prince of Wales, in 1376 – combined with the Lancaster inheritance greatly to enhance his status and influence. During the last years of his father's reign, the Prince of Wales was first absent in Aquitaine and then a dying man, which increased both Gaunt's duties and his opportunities. When his nephew, *Richard II, came to the throne,

Gaunt was, without question, the most powerful man in England next to the king. While his personal views and concerns are reflected in his controversial support for *Wyclif, his unpopularity with the citizens of London – expressed most vividly when his palace, the Savoy, was destroyed during the *Peasants' Revolt – resulted largely from his determined support for the young king and the royal power. It is notable that he died before his son deposed Richard, usurped the throne, and became Henry IV.

The temptation to speculate about the existence of a significant personal relationship between Chaucer and Gaunt has proved too much for some writers. Though it is almost certain that Philippa Chaucer and Katherine Swynford were sisters – and that Chaucer was thus married to the sister of Gaunt's long-term mistress, and became (relatively briefly and very belatedly) his brother-in-law – the extent to which this would have brought personal contact between them remains a matter of conjecture. Most disappointing of all, there is little evidence to suggest that Gaunt took any interest in Chaucer's poetry or provided patronage of him as a poet.

John of Sacrobosco *see* **Treatise on the Astrolabe, A**

John of Salisbury

(*c.* 1115–80)
Ecclesiastic and author. John's most significant work was the *Policraticus* ('The statesman's book'), a mirror for princes which includes a wealth of material gathered from classical sources. Indebtedness to the *Policraticus* has been detected throughout Chaucer's work. Examples include the material from *Macrobius, echoed in the opening of *HF*, which may have been based on *Policraticus* (2.15), and the story of *Stilboun in *PardT* (VI.603–20), which is clearly based on this work (1.5). Perhaps most interesting of all, Chaucer may have derived the intriguing name *Lollius from a misreading of lines from *Horace's *Epistles* (1.2.1–2), quoted by John of Salisbury (*Policraticus* 2.15).

John of Wales

(d. *c.* 1283)
Franciscan theologian and writer. It has been suggested that the immediate source for the material from the *De ira* of *Seneca, used in *SumT* (III.2017ff.), was John's *Communiloquium sive summa collationum* ('Handbook of common expressions or resumé of comparisons'). Commentators have also detected

the influence of this work in Chaucer's representation of the language of preaching, especially in *SumT* and *PardT*.

Joseph

Son of Jacob and Rachel (Old Testament). Allusions to Joseph as an interpreter of dreams (see Gen. 37–41) occur in *NPT* (VII.3130–5/B².4320–5) and *BD* (280–3). He is also mentioned twice in *ParsT* (X.443, 880) – in the latter case, with reference to his rejection of the advances of Potiphar's wife.

Joseph of Exeter

(fl. late 12th century)
Author of a Latin poem on the Trojan war. Joseph's *Frigii Daretis Ilias* ('Iliad of Dares Phrygius') is a poem of about 3600 lines in Latin hexameters, largely based on *Dares. While Joseph is not cited by Chaucer, the summary portraits of Troilus, Criseyde, and Diomede in the final book of *Tr* (5.799ff.) are based on his poem, the influence of which has also been detected in the catalogue of trees in *PF* (176–82).

Jove, Joves *see* Jupiter; Jovinian *see* Jerome, St

Judas

Judas Iscariot, apostle who betrayed Christ. Allusions to Judas as a figure of betrayal or treachery occur in *CYT* (VIII.1000–9), *ParsT* (X.616), and (with comic intent) *NPT* (VII.3227/B².4417). In *ParsT*, reference is also made to his objections when Mary Magdalene anoints the feet of Christ (X.502; see John 12.3–8) and the despair which leads him to suicide (X.696, 1015; see Matt. 27.5).

Judith

Protagonist of the Apocryphal Old Testament Book of Judith; slayer of *Holofernes. While the account of the death of Holofernes in *MkT* (VII.2567–74/B².3757–64) is not sympathetic to Judith, the brief allusion in *MLT* (II.939–42) attributes her courage to divine support. Allusions to her as an example of good counsel – in recognition of her having persuaded the relevant authorities to endorse her plan for freeing the people of Bethulia from Holofernes – occur in *MerT* (IV.1366–8) and *Mel* (VII.1099/B².2289).

Julian, St

St Julian the Hospitaller. Though probably mythical, St Julian had considerable currency during the Middle Ages, and was associated with hospitality
and travel. He is named in a general greeting in *HF* (1022). The allusion in *GP*
(I.340) is more specific, terming the Franklin 'Seint Julian ... in his contree' – a
compliment later echoed, with reference to Thomas *Chaucer in a poem by
*Lydgate ('On the Departing of Thomas Chaucer').

Julius *see* Ascanius

Julius Caesar

(*c.* 100–44 BC)
Gaius Julius Caesar, Roman general and statesman. Julius Caesar was
(erroneously) regarded in the Middle Ages as the first Roman emperor. The
account of his life and death in *MkT* (VII.2671ff./B^2.3861ff.) constitutes one
of the Monk's 'tragedies', and emphasizes both his triumph after his defeat
of *Pompey and the circumstances of his assassination in the Capitol.
Various allusions to his triumph, fame, and death occur elsewhere: see *HF*
1502; *KnT* I.2031; and *MLT* II.199, 400. In *Astr* (1.10) Chaucer associates
Julius Caesar with the month of July, even stating (erroneously) that he took
two days from February and put them into 'his month'.

Juno

Sovereign goddess; daughter of *Saturn, wife and sister of *Jupiter. Juno's
traditional concern for women and marriage is reflected in her response to
the prayers of *Alcione in *BD* (108ff.). This also informs (in varying degrees)
several passing allusions in other works (e.g. *LGW* 2249; *Tr* 4.1594). The
enmity of Juno toward *Thebes is taken by *Palamon and *Arcite in *KnT*
(I.1328–31, 1542ff.) to have caused their misfortune. An allusion to this enmity
occurs in *Anel* (51 – the explanatory note to which in Benson [1987: 992]
provides an account of its origins). Juno's opposition to Troy (which does
not feature significantly in *Tr*) is mentioned in *HF* (198–208, 461–5).

Jupiter

The supreme god of classical mythology; son of *Saturn, brother and
husband of *Juno. Chaucer refers to him indiscriminately as 'Jupiter' or

'Jove(s)'. He is represented as an omnipotent and (mostly) benign deity, notably in the 'first mover' speech of *Theseus in *KnT* (I.2987ff.), but also in several other works, especially *Tr*. In this capacity, both *Troilus and *Criseyde pray to him and appeal to him for help (e.g. 3.722–8, 1016–22; 4.1149–50; 5.957–9). He is associated with the destiny of the soul in *KnT* (I.2783–97) and *LGW* (1338–40). In *HF*, Jupiter both protects *Aeneas (212–38, 451–67) and permits the poet-narrator to visit the House of Fame (605ff.). He is described as the god of thunder in *HF* (608–9) and *Tr* (2.233). While he can be treated for the most part neutrally as a pagan god in these and some other texts (e.g. *MkT* VII.2744, 2752/B².3934, 3942), he is identified with idolatry elsewhere – especially in *SNT* (VIII.364–6, 413) and the 'palinode' of *Tr* (5.1852–3). Astrological or astronomical allusions to Jupiter occur in *MerT* (IV.2224) and *Astr* (2.12.24, 28, etc.), and an alchemical allusion in *CYT* (VIII.828).

Justinus

One of the brothers of *January in *MerT* (the other being *Placebo). When January consults his brothers regarding his prospective marriage (IV.1469ff.), the uncritical recommendation of Placebo is countered by Justinus, who advises caution. Though his name signifies 'the just one', his views appear pragmatic rather than just – and are (of course) rejected by January.

Juvenal

(*c.* 55–*c.* 140)
Decimus Iunius Iuvenalis, Roman poet. Chaucer cites Juvenal's *Satires*, which were well known during the Middle Ages, twice: in *Tr* (4.196–201), to the effect that people do not know what is best for them (echoing *Satires* 10.2), and in *WBT* (III.1192–4), to the effect that the poor need not fear robbery (echoing *Satires* 10.22). The latter also appears as a gloss in *Bo* (2.p.5.181–4).

K

Kayrrud

Home of *Arveragus in *FranT*. Kayrudd (V.808) has not been identified, but has been related to the Welsh 'caer rhudd' (red fort or town).

Kelmscott Chaucer *see* Morris, William

Kenelm, St

(d. 812 or 821)
Anglo-Saxon child saint. The legend of his death, foretold in a dream, is cited by *Chauntecleer in *NPT* (VII.3110–21./B².4300–11).

Kent

County in south-east England. Pilgrims on the *Canterbury Way passed through Kent as they travelled to *Canterbury, the county town. *Thomas à Becket is twice termed 'Seint Thomas of Kent' (*MilT* I.3291; *HF* 1131). Chaucer lived in Kent – possibly in *Greenwich – for a considerable period, and served the county in several adminstrative and representative capacities.

Kittredge, George Lyman *see* marriage debate

Knight

Pilgrim and teller in *CT*. The fact that the Knight is the first pilgrim described in *GP* (I.43ff.) has generally been taken to reflect his social pre-eminence in the company of pilgrims. It has often been supposed that this consideration leads the *Host to manipulate the draw for the tale-telling contest, ensuring that the Knight tells the first tale (see I.827ff.). The portrait in *GP* represents the Knight as a worthy and honourable man who has dedicated his life to chivalry, and conducts himself in a notably modest and restrained manner. It emphasizes his activity as a crusader (51–66), stating that he has partici-pated in a substantial series of campaigns which would have begun in the 1340s and continued into the 1380s. This long time-span has been understood to indicate that the Knight should be regarded as a man of mature years. While most commentators have concluded that the portrait could not be based on the activities of a single individual, some have suggested that Chaucer could be alluding here to the activities of several prominent contemporary crusaders. It has been observed that the Knight's campaigns do not include any from the *Hundred Years' War – which has sometimes been taken to imply Chaucer's disapproval of warfare between Christian nations. The portrait has been interpreted by a small minority as a satirical account of an unprincipled mercenary.

The Knight makes two significant interventions later in *CT* – resolving the unseemly quarrel between the Host and the *Pardoner at the end of *PardT* (VI.941ff.), and bringing to a conclusion the increasingly tedious series of 'tragedies' which comprise *MkT* (VII.2767ff./B^2.3957ff.). Each suggests the Knight's authority (and, arguably, his decency and good sense).

Further reading: Andrew (1993); Mann (1973).

knights

Several unnamed characters in *CT*, notably: (1) the male protagonist of *WBT*; (2) the giver of magical gifts in *SqT*; (3) the false accuser of *Custance in *MLT*.

Knight's Tale, The

Chivalric *romance; the first tale of *CT*. In this substantial and majestic poem, Chaucer introduces many of the central themes, issues, and devices which will recur throughout *CT* – including the themes of love, courtship, and marriage; the tension between public duties and private desires; questions of providence, destiny, and astrological influence; and the device of the love triangle. The potential for these initial explorations of such themes and motifs to provoke response and discussion is indicated immediately, in the following *MilP*. There *KnT* is treated explicitly as a statement by the *Knight – an impression encouraged by the emphatic presence of a narrative voice in the poem (see, for instance, I.875ff., 1347–54, 1881–6, 2206–8, 2919ff.). While the connections between teller and tale are relatively slight by comparison with some others (especially those involving the *Wife of Bath and the *Pardoner), the attribution to the aristocratic and widely travelled Knight of a courtly romance, dealing with love and conflict in a remote and exotic setting, seems broadly appropriate.

While the story is, at heart, that of a love triangle – in which the noble Theban cousins, *Palamon and *Arcite, compete for the love of *Emily, the sister of *Hippolyta, wife of duke *Theseus – its scale is more magnificent and its implications more profound than this might suggest. *KnT* comprises a series of memorable episodes and superb descriptions. These include the following: the appeal of the Theban *widows to Theseus for justice against *Creon (893ff.); the sequence in which Palamon and Arcite first catch sight of Emily and fall in love with her (1033ff.); their duel in the grove, interrupted by Theseus, accompanied by Hippolyta and Emily (1649ff.); the temples of *Venus, *Mars, and *Diana (1918ff.); the prayers of Palamon, Emily, and Arcite to Venus, Diana, and Mars respectively (2209ff.); the tournament to decide between the rival claims of Palamon and Arcite for the hand of Emily (2569ff.); the death and funeral of Arcite (2743ff.). The setting of the tale in ancient *Athens permits Chaucer to describe exotic buildings, artefacts, events, and customs, but does not account for the tale's reflective and philosophical character. This derives in part from Chaucer's handling of his main sources, the *Teseida* of *Boccaccio and the *De consolatione philosophiae* of *Boethius. The story of *KnT* is based on the former, which Chaucer radically modifies – substantially reducing its length (of nearly 10,000 lines), and creating a far more economical, balanced, and symmetrical narrative. He draws on Boethius for some material of crucial thematic significance, notably the complaints of Arcite and Palamon against the cruelty of Fortune (1235ff., 1303ff.), and the 'First Mover' speech of Theseus on the benign Providence which governs the world (2987ff.). These sources facilitate the composition of a poem which engages with the tensions between order and disorder, and balances the happy ending normal in romance with an acknowledgement of the bleaker aspects of life. The restoration of positive values in the concluding marriage of Palamon and Emily is, indeed, achieved only as a result of Arcite's misfortune and death. More generally, *KnT* emphasizes the violence of conflict – in warfare, as in the aristocratic rituals of the duel and the tournament – and the apparently arbitrary cruelties of life. The latter are powerfully realized through the treatment of the classical gods, who are represented mainly as malign astrological influences, both in their selfish bickering over the contest between Palamon and Arcite (2663ff.), and in the description of the three temples.

The influence of other sources is relatively slight. Several manuscripts include an epigraph from the *Thebaid* of *Statius (on the return of Theseus to Athens after defeating the Amazons), a longer version of which occurs in *Anel* (following line 21). Otherwise, indebtedness to sources is limited to particular echoes of various works, including *RR, *Ovid's *Metamorphoses*, and *Dante's *Divine Comedy*, as well as the *Thebaid*. The allusion in *LGWP* (F.420–1/G.408–9) to a poem by Chaucer on the story of Palamon and Arcite has been taken to indicate that an earlier version of *KnT* was written before Chaucer started work on *CT*, and later adapted to serve as a tale for the Knight. Since the only traces of this process occur in the early lines and the final line of *KnT* (875ff., especially 889–92, and 3108), it has generally been supposed that the modifications would have been relatively minor. The composition of the original poem has been tentatively dated in the early to mid-1380s (when Chaucer was working on *Bo* and *Tr*), that of its incorporation into *CT* to the late 1380s (during the early stages of this project).

The familiar division of *KnT* into four parts is based on the *Ellesmere MS alone. One couplet (2681–2), which offers a somewhat unsympathetic comment on Emily, is omitted from several manuscripts, including Ellesmere and *Hengwrt. Otherwise, the manuscripts contain relatively few variants of any great significance.

*Shakespeare drew on *KnT* both in *The Two Noble Kinsmen* (which he wrote in collaboration with Fletcher) and (less directly) in *A Midsummer Night's Dream*. *Dryden's poem, *Palamon and Arcite*, is a free translation of *KnT*.

Further reading: Cooper (1996); Havely (1980); Robert A. Pratt in Bryan and Dempster (1941).

Koran

Sacred book of Islam. Chaucer alludes to the Koran ('Alkaron') in *MLT* (II.330–3), where the Sultaness complains that her son's impending marriage to *Custance is against its laws, established by *Mohammed. Since the Koran is not mentioned at this juncture in *Trevet, the main source for *MLT*, it seems possible that Chaucer knew the twelfth-century Latin translation of the Koran by Robert of Ketton, though more likely that his knowledge was secondhand (possibly from *Mandeville's Travels*).

L

Lachesis *see* **Fates**; *Ladies, Book of XXV see* **Legend of Good Women, The**

Lak of Stedfastnesse

Moral lyric of 28 lines. *Sted* survives in 15 manuscript copies, and is attributed to Chaucer by John *Shirley. The title derives from the transcripts of the *Chaucer Society. *Sted* is a *ballade in four *rhyme royal stanzas, the last of which comprises an *envoy to *Richard II. According to Shirley, it was written in the final years of Chaucer's life (see Benson, 1987: 1085–6), which broadly coincided with the troubled final phase of Richard's reign. Some scholars have, therefore, dated the poem *c.* 1397–99, though others have associated it with Richard's loss of power in 1388–90, or dated it less specifically in the 1380s, on the basis of its connections with the 'Boethian' group of lyrics (*Form Age, For, Truth,* and *Gent*). *Sted* constitutes a finely-wrought complaint on the evils of the times – essentially conventional, but more overtly political than would be usual in Chaucer. While no particular source has been identified, echoes of writers including *Boethius, *Deschamps, *Machaut, and *Granson have been identified.

Further reading: Pace and David (1982); V.J. Scattergood in Minnis (1995).

Lamech

Old Testament bigamist. An allusion to Lamech as the first bigamist (see Gen. 4: 19–23) occurs in *WBP* (III.54). He thus becomes a model of male infidelity, as in *Anel* (148–54) and *SqT* (V.550–1).

Lancaster, Duchess of *see* Blanche; Lancaster, Duke of *see* John of Gaunt

Lancelot

Arthurian knight. Chaucer mentions Lancelot twice: in general terms, as an expert on courtly behaviour (*SqT* V.287), and, more specifically, as the protagonist of 'the book of Launcelot de Lake' (*NPT* VII.3212–13/B².4402–3) – the story of his love affair with Guinevere.

Lane, John *see Squire's Introduction and Tale, The*

Langland, William

(*c*. 1330–*c*. 1386)

English poet. Langland is generally believed to be the author of *Piers Plowman*, a long religious poem in *alliterative verse, composed in several versions between *c*. 1365 and *c*. 1385. Though allusions in this work indicate that Langland spent some time living in London, there is no evidence that he and Chaucer knew each other. Many commentators have, however, taken the description of the *Plowman in *GP* (I.529–41) to suggest that Chaucer had read *Piers Plowman*, at least in part.

Latin

The main language of learning in medieval Europe. It is generally supposed that Chaucer received a good education as a boy – perhaps at the almonry school attached to *St Paul's – and thus learned the rudiments of Latin. His use, as a writer, of Latin sources demonstrates a reasonable degree of competence in the language. Scholars have, however, established that, when translating from Latin, Chaucer tends to seek the assistance of a *French version of the text in question if one should be available – as in the case of *Jean de Meun's translation of the *De consolatione philosophiae* of *Boethius, which he consulted in the composition of *Bo*.

Allusions to Latin in Chaucer's works are normally concerned with learning, and often with the appearance or the lack of it. Whereas the *Summoner babbles meaningless Latin words when drunk (*GP* I.637–43), the *Shipman defines himself as non-Latinate (*MLE* II.1190). The *Pardoner speaks a few words in Latin, with the cynical intention of impressing a naive audience (*PardP* VI.341–6); *Chauntecleer uses a somewhat similar technique to patronise his wife (*NPT* VII.3163–6/B².4353–6). Chaucer mentions the limited Latin of two boys – the anonymous victim in *PrT* (VII.523–4) and his own son, Lewis *Chaucer (*Astr* Prologue 25–8). He identifies Latin as the language of sources (real or imaginary) in *Anel* (10) and *Tr* (2.14).

Latumyus

Exemplary figure mentioned in *WBP*. *Jankin's *'book of wicked wives' includes the story of a tree in the garden of Latumyus, on which his three wives have hanged themselves – prompting his friend Arrius to ask for a cutting from the tree (III.757–64). Chaucer's source for this story was the *Epistola Valerii* of Walter *Map.

Lechery

One of the *Seven Deadly Sins. A section of *ParsT* (X.836ff.) defines Lechery and prescribes remedies for it. Notable features of this discussion include the severe attitude to the dangers of sex within marriage and the recurring link between Lechery and *Gluttony (X.836, 861, 951). Allusions to a personification of Lechery occur in *Rom* (3909ff.).

legend

Biography of a saint or other person. Chaucer uses this term to signify both a *saint's life (as in *NPT* VII.3121/B^2.4311 and *SNP* VIII.25, 83) and, more broadly, a biography with moral implications (as in *WBP* III.742 and *CIT* IV.1212d). The Miller's allusion to the tale he is about to tell as a 'legende' (*MilP* I.3141) presumably constitutes an ironic application of the term. Chaucer's use of it in *LGW* may suggest that these stories could be seen as the secular equivalents of saints' lives.

Legend of Good Women, The

*Dream vision prologue followed by narratives about women unfortunate in love. *LGW* was composed in the decasyllabic couplet used by Chaucer for the bulk of *CT* – in which he had, apparently, already written *Palamon and Arcite*, the early version of *KnT* mentioned in *LGWP* (F.420–1/G.408–9). (*LGWP* also embodies a *ballade comprising three *rhyme royal stanzas: see F.249ff./G.302ff.) It has generally been supposed that Chaucer wrote *LGW* between *Tr* (to which there are several allusions in *LGWP*) and *CT* (which includes two allusions to *LGW*: see below). Thus a date of *c.* 1385–6 has often been proposed. *LGWP* exists in two versions, regularly designated F and G (signifying two manuscripts, respectively Bodleian Library MS Fairfax 16 and Cambridge University Library MS Gg.4.27). In F (496–7), *Alceste instructs the poet-narrator to present his poem, when complete, to the queen at *Eltham or *Sheen. Since the queen in question would be *Anne of Bohemia, who died in 1394, the omission of this instruction in G has generally been taken to indicate that it constitutes a version revised soon after her death. The same allusion probably lies behind *Lydgate's assertion, in the *Fall of Princes* (1.330–6), that *LGW* was written at the queen's request (a claim reiterated by *Speght). The fact that G also refers to two works not mentioned in F – the *Epistola adversus Jovinianum* of St *Jerome (281ff.) and Chaucer's lost translation of the *De miseria conditionis humane* of *Innocent III (414–15) – provides further support for the view that it is the later of the two versions.

LGW breaks off after 2723 lines, apparently towards the end of the ninth legend. It has not (as yet) proved possible to establish whether Chaucer left the work unfinished or wrote further legends which have not survived. The hypothesis that *LGW* was an unwelcome commission, and that Chaucer lost interest in the project and abandoned it, once commanded a good deal of support. This has, however, declined – partly on the basis of reconsideration of the evidence offered in *MLIntro* (II.60ff.) and *Ret* (X.1086). The former provides a lengthy account of *LGW*, specifying not only most of the legends which actually appear, but also eight more (on *Deianira, Hermione, Hero, *Helen of Troy, *Briseyde, Laodomia, *Penelope, and Alceste herself). The latter refers to the poem as 'the book of the XXV. Ladies'. It is mentioned in similar terms by Edward, Duke of York, in the preface to his translation of a French treatise on hunting, *The Master of Game* (c. 1413). Taken together, these allusions suggest that Chaucer may have written 25 legends, of which only nine have survived.

LGWP begins with a sententious observation, which encapsulates the need for experience to be augmented by authority, as preserved in 'olde bokes' (F/G.25). It proceeds to establish a Maytime garden setting, where devotion to the daisy is expressed. In this setting, the poet-narrator sleeps and has a dream in which he encounters the god of *Love and Alceste, who is identified with the daisy (F/G.40ff.). While the god of Love reprimands him for having written as an enemy of love in *Tr* and *Rom*, Alceste defends him, mentioning his praise of love in some other poems, but sets him, as a 'penance', to write a 'legende' of good women and the men who betrayed them, starting with *Cleopatra (F.475ff./G.465ff.). Almost incidentally, this passage offers a survey of Chaucer's works to date, which provides invaluable evidence regarding the chronology of his literary career (assuming that F represents a text written in c. 1385–86). It also identifies two lost works – *'Origenes upon the Maudeleyne' (F.428/G.418) and the translation from Innocent III, mentioned above (G.414–15).

The 'penance' specified by Alceste serves both to introduce the legends and to indicate their essential theme. The ballade (F.249ff./G.203ff.) had already identified several women who duly became the subjects of surviving legends (including Cleopatra, *Thisbe, and *Dido), and several who could have done so – some of whom (including Hero and Penelope) are named in

MLIntro (see above). Chaucer had previously told or alluded to several of these stories – notably those of Dido, *Medea, *Phyllis, and *Ariadne – in works such as *BD* and *HF*. It is, moreover, possible that he was writing the collection of stories later used in *MkT* at about the same time as *LGW*. None of these allusions, links, or parallels can, however, provide any hint as to the potential form or sequence of the legends: thus *Skeat's attractive theory that this would have culminated with a legend of Alceste remains conjectural.

The legends are distinctive in several ways. They characteristically praise women as wives and lovers, and censure the men who forsake or betray them. This sometimes necessitates a selective account, especially in the cases of Medea and *Philomela (both of whom were known as child-killers). The stories are, indeed, all from 'olde bokes', and – as a passing allusion in the G version of *LGWP* (299) observes – all concern pagan women. The allusion to *LGW* in *MLIntro* (II.61) as 'the Seintes Legende of Cupide' encourages comparison with the conventional *saint's life. Though there are parallels – such as the tendency for both groups of women to confront (male) authority, and to suffer for their convictions – it is notable that, whereas the saints express their devotion through virginity, the good women express theirs by being faithful wives and lovers. Interpretations of *LGW* have been conspicuously diverse – some commentators taking it as a genuine defence of women, others detecting varying degrees of satire, and a minority perceiving the entire work as covertly misogynistic.

LGW reflects the influence of several traditions and authors. For the praise of the daisy in the Prologue, Chaucer is indebted to such works as the two poems entitled *Le Dit de la Marguerite*, one by *Machaut, the other by *Froissart, and *Le Lay de Franchise* by *Deschamps. For the idea of the poet's repentance, he drew on Machaut's *Le Jugement dou Roy de Navarre*, which also alludes to stories of wronged women. The most significant influence in the legends is that of *Ovid's *Heroides* – as Chaucer himself implies in *MLIntro* (II.53–5). This provides the idea of the forsaken woman's letter of reproach to her unfaithful lover, reflected especially in the endings of *Dido* and *Ariadne* (*Heroides* 7 and 10 respectively), and constitutes the main source for *Phyllis* and *Hypermnestra* (*Heroides* 2 and 14 respectively). *Thisbe, Ariadne*, and *Philomela* are based on stories from Ovid's *Metamorphoses* (4:55ff., 8:6ff., and 6.424ff. respectively). Material from both the *Heroides* and the *Metamorphoses* is also used in *Hypsipyle and Medea* (*Heroides* 6 and 12; *Metamorphoses* 7.1ff.). The main source of *Lucrece* is Ovid's *Fasti* (2.685ff.). In *Dido*, the implications of the story drawn from *Virgil's *Aeneid* (books I–IV) are modified by the Ovidian ending. The influence of the *Ovide moralisé* has been detected in *Philomela*, and that of *Ceffi's translation of the *Heroides* in several legends, notably those of *Hypermnestra and Ariadne. *Hypsipyle and Medea* uses material from the *Historia destructionis Troiae* of *Guido della Colonne (1.1368ff.) – though with its characteristic anti-feminism removed. While no major source for *Cleopatra* has been found, it seems probable that Chaucer consulted the brief account in the *Speculum historiale* of *Vincent of Beauvais (6.5). The stories of Thisbe, Medea, *Lucrece, Ariadne, Philomela, and Phyllis are also told by *Gower (*Confessio Amantis* 3.1331ff., 5.3247ff., 7.4754ff., 5.5231ff., 5.5551ff., and 4.731ff. respectively).

LGW survives in 12 manuscripts and the early printed edition of *Thynne – all of which preserve incomplete or fragmentary texts. The revised version of *LGWP* is preserved only in Cambridge University Library MS Gg.4.27.

Further reading: Minnis (1995); Windeatt (1982).

Legenda aurea

Popular collection of sermon material. The *Legenda aurea* ('Golden legend') was a compilation of material for use in sermons, including saints' lives and information about feast days, organized in accordance with the liturgical year. It was collected by Jacobus de Voragine (d. 1298), and translated from Latin into several Middle English versions. Chaucer drew on the *Legenda aurea* for the life of St Cecilia in *SNT*.

Lenvoy de Chaucer a Bukton

Verse epistle of 32 lines. *Buk* survives in two manuscripts, one of which supplies its title. It is a *ballade, consisting of four eight-line stanzas, the last an *envoy. The stanza is that used in *MkT*; thus *Buk* lacks the refrain or repeated line of the strict ballade form. Like *Scog*, it is addressed by Chaucer to a friend, and suggests the existence of a circle of thoughtful and sophisticated individuals, who would appreciate his allusion to the views of the *Wife of Bath (29). Though the ostensible purpose of *Buk* is to advise the addressee against marriage, its tone suggests that this was not intended seriously. Two identifications for the addressee have been proposed: Sir Peter Bukton of *Holderness, Yorkshire (the setting of *SumT*) and (somewhat less likely) Sir Robert Bukton of Goosewold, Essex. While it appears that *Buk* has no specific sources, commentators have noted the general influence of epistolary verse by poets including *Ovid and *Deschamps. It is regularly assumed that Chaucer wrote *Buk* late in his career; if the allusion to Frisia (23) is specific, it would suggest a date of 1396 (for particulars, see Benson, 1987: 1087).

Further reading: Pace and David (1982); V.J. Scattergood in Minnis (1995).

Lenvoy de Chaucer a Scogan

Verse epistle of 49 lines. *Scog* survives in three manuscripts, from which the title has been derived. It is a somewhat free double *ballade, consisting of six *rhyme royal stanzas and an *envoy (a single rhyme royal stanza), and lacking the repeated rhyme and the refrain of the strict ballade form. *Scog*, like *Buk*, is addressed to a friend, almost certainly Henry *Scogan. The tone and content of the poem (again like those of *Buk*) imply an intimate circle who would understand the allusion to Scogan's blasphemy against the god of *Love and appreciate those to Chaucer's girth and his reluctant muse. It has often been supposed that the envoy, in which Chaucer asks Scogan to intercede on his behalf at court, turns this into something of a begging poem. *Scog* reflects much the same literary influences as *Buk*, and does not depend on a specific source. Commentators have agreed that it is a late poem; some attempt to identify the allusion to bad weather (14) with the actual conditions prevailing at particular times – most convincingly, the autumn of 1391 (see Benson, 1987: 1086).

Further reading: Pace and David (1982); V.J. Scattergood in Minnis (1995).

Lettow *see* Lithuania

Libra

Sign of the Zodiac. Libra features in the complex calculation of the time at the beginning of *ParsP* (X.1–12).

Lille, Alan of *see* Alan of Lille

Lionel of Antwerp

(1338–68)
Third son of *Edward III. Lionel became Earl of Ulster as a consequence of his marriage to *Elizabeth de Burgh in 1342, and later (1362) became Duke of Clarence. Chaucer was a member of his household in 1359–60 (and possibly for some time thereafter), and experienced military service under him in France (see Crow and Olson, 1966: 19–22). Between 1361 and 1366, Lionel visited Ireland several times as the king's viceroy, supervising the attempt to impose English rule. There is no evidence to suggest that Chaucer accompanied him on any of these visits. After the death of Elizabeth in 1363, Lionel

married Violante, daughter of Galeazzo Visconti, lord of *Pavia, but died in Italy shortly after his marriage.

Lithuania

Large kingdom, extending from the south of present-day Latvia to the Black Sea. The campaigns of the *Knight in Lithuania and *Russia, mentioned in *GP* (I.54–5), have been associated with the activities of the Teutonic Knights in *Prussia, and taken to be among the latest in his career. It has been noted that the Lithuanians were converted to Christianity in 1386.

Livia

A woman who poisons her husband, like Lucia. The stories of Livia and Lucia are included in *Jankin's *'book of wicked wives' (*WBP* III.747–56). While Livia poisons her husband, Drusus, deliberately (at the suggestion of her lover, Sejanus), Lucia poisons her husband, the poet Lucretius, inadvertently (by giving him a love potion).

Livy

(59 BC–17 AD)

Titus Livius, Roman historian. Chaucer retold two stories from Livy's history of Rome, *Ab urbe condita libri* ('Books concerning the foundation of the city') – those of *Virginia in *PhyT* and of *Lucrece in *LGW*. In each case, the evidence for direct use of Livy is slight. While Chaucer based *PhyT* mainly on the version of the story from Livy (3.44–50, 56–8) in *RR* (5589ff.), he based *Lucrece* mainly on *Ovid (*Fasti* 2.685ff.). He does, however, acknowledge Livy in both works (*PhyT* VI.1; *LGW* 1683), and mentions him again as an authority on Lucrece in *BD* (1082–4).

'loathly lady' *see* hag

Lollard

Term used to describe anyone sympathetic to radical reform of the church. Though this term was applied particularly to the followers of *Wyclif, it was used more loosely to indicate those endorsing a range of broadly radical opinion, opposed to various aspects of the established doctrine and organization of the church. While such debate and criticism was generally tolerated for much of Chaucer's lifetime, the prevailing mood became less tolerant towards the end of the century, and repressive action against the Lollards began in 1400 (the year of his death). The only use of the word in Chaucer's work occurs in *MLE* (II.1173), where the *Parson objects to the swearing of the *Host, who responds by contemptuously terming him a 'Lollere'. The description of the Parson in *GP* (I.477ff.) has often been taken to imply Lollard values, which Chaucer himself is sometimes assumed to have shared. *See also*: **Lollard Knights**.

Lollard Knights

Group of aristocrats with *Lollard sympathies. This group included Sir John *Clanvowe, Sir Lewis *Clifford, Sir John Montagu, and Sir Richard Stury. The surviving records indicate Chaucer's connections with these men, who shared his literary and intellectual interests.

Lollius

Supposed author of a work on the Trojan war. Since no such writer has been identified, Chaucer's three references to Lollius – one in *HF* (1468) and two in *Tr* (1.394, 5.1653) – constitute something of a mystery. In *HF*, Chaucer includes Lollius among a list of authorities on the Trojan war, the rest of whom are genuine. It has been suggested that this allusion reflects a misreading of lines in *Horace's *Epistles* (1.2.1–2) – possibly as quoted in *John of Salisbury's *Policraticus* (2.15) – which could be construed to suggest the existence of a poet called Lollius (see Benson, 1987: 1022). This can, however, hardly explain the references in *Tr*, where Chaucer twice acknowledges Lollius as his source – in each case at a juncture where he is following *Boccaccio. It has, therefore, generally been supposed that, while in *HF* Chaucer may mistakenly believe in the existence of Lollius as an authority on Troy, in *Tr* he deliberately uses the name to indicate a fictitious source.

London

Principal city of England; Chaucer's home for much of his life. In Chaucer's day, London was a walled city, extending to about one square mile. Its population has been estimated at around 50,000 – some five times that of any other city in England, but barely half that of *Paris. Travellers heading south – such as pilgrims on their way to *Canterbury or diplomats en route to France – would cross London bridge and then pass through *Southwark.

Chaucer was probably born and raised in his parents' house in Thames Street, just north of the river in Vintry ward. His job in the customs was located on the quayside, close to the Tower of London. Some of his other duties were based in *Westminster, a couple of miles to the west of the city. His work contains numerous allusions to London. The city and its environs provide settings in *CkT* and *CYT*. Several of his pilgrims have connections with the city or with nearby towns or institutions: the *Cook both with *Ware and with London itself (*CkP* I.4325, 4336; *MancP* IX.11), the *Sergeant of Law with the *Paryvs of *St Paul's cathedral (*GP* I.310), the *Manciple with the inns of court (*GP* I.567), the *Pardoner with *Rouncivale (*GP* I.670), and the *Prioress with *Stratford atte Bowe (*GP* I.125). Chaucer also alludes to various specific locations, both in London – such as Fish Street (*PardT* VI.564), Cheapside (*CkT* I.4377; *PardT* VI.564), Newgate prison (*CkT* I.4402), and the Tower (*MilT* I.3256) – and nearby – such as *Greenwich, *Deptford, *Eltham, *Sheene, and the *Watering of St Thomas.

A map of London in Chaucer's day is provided in Pearsall (1992: 20).

Love, god of

Cupid, the Roman god of love. Chaucer refers to this figure as 'Love', 'the god of Love', or 'Cupid(e)' (sometimes 'Cupido'). He appears in *LGWP* (F.210ff./G.141ff.) as a stern authority figure, whose censure of the poet-narrator for the unsympathetic treatment of love and women in *Tr* and *Rom* is qualified by the milder views of *Alceste. In *Scog*, Chaucer suggests that *Scogan has been guilty of similar 'blaspheme'. The portrayal of the god of Love in *Rom* is, of course, derived from *RR. In Fragment A, he appears as a handsome and courtly man, who takes an interest in the dreamer as someone who might fall in love (877ff.). Fragment B (which is almost certainly not by Chaucer) describes how the dreamer is struck by the arrows of the god of Love, and duly yields to him (1706ff.). Allusions to the god of Love (not always entirely distinct from the abstract concept he represents) occur in various works, including *BD, HF, PF, Tr, KnT*, and *FranT* (e.g. *BD* 766; *HF* 1489; *KnT* I.1785; *FranT* V.765). *Troilus utters several prayers to him – appealing for help, or expressing thanks or disappointment (e.g. *Tr* 1.421ff., 2.523ff., 3.1254ff., 4.288ff., 5.582ff.). When *Criseyde, in her letter from the Greek camp, addresses Troilus as 'Cupides sone' (5.1590), he has already cursed Cupid along with various other gods (5.207–8). Chaucer calls lovers 'love's servants' or 'love's folk'; thus the love poet can be envisaged as the servant of love's servants (see, e.g., *HF* 625, 645; *Tr* 1.15, 34, 48). He refers to Cupid as the son of *Venus, and to several of his traditional attributes, including blindness, wings, and arrows (e.g. *HF* 137–8; *PF* 212–13; *Tr* 3.1807–8).

Lover *see* **Roman de la Rose, Le; Romaunt of the Rose, The**

Loy, St

(*c.* 588–660)
St Eloi or Eligius, Bishop of Noyon. He had been a celebrated goldsmith before becoming a priest, and was the patron saint of goldsmiths, black-smiths, and farriers. There are two allusions to St Loy in Chaucer: the carter in *FrT* (III.1564) swears by him, and the 'gretteste ooth' of the *Prioress is said to be 'but by Seinte Loy' (*GP* I.120).

Lucan

(39–64)
Marcus Annaeus Lucanus, Roman poet. Lucan is one of the five classical poets named in the dedication at the end of *Tr* (5.1792). His *Pharsalia* (3.73–9), an epic on the civil war of 49–48 BC, is acknowledged by Chaucer as a source for material on *Julius Caesar in *MkT* (VII.2719/B².3909) and *MLT* (II.401). The allusion in *HF* (1497–1502) also associates him with the civil war. A brief citation of Lucan (*Pharsalia* 1.128) occurs in *Bo* (4.p.6.231).

Lucia *see* **Livia; Lucifer** *see* **Satan**

Lucrece

Virtuous and beautiful Roman woman, victim of an infamous rape. The well-known story, in which Lucrece (normally 'Lucresse') is raped by *Tarquinius and chooses to commit suicide rather than bring dishonour to herself, her husband, *Collatine, and her family, is related in *LGW* (1680ff.). This account represents Lucrece as an innocent victim of male lust and a model of wifely virtue, for whom St *Augustine felt compassion (1690). Passing allusions to the story occur in *LGWP* (F.257/G.211) and in *MLIntro* (II.62–3). Elsewhere, Lucrece is cited by *Dorigen in *FranT* (V.1405–8) as an example of a woman who chooses death rather than dishonour, and as a model of wifely nobility in *BD* (1082–3) and of steadfastness in *Anel* (81–2).

Lull, Ramón *see* *Canon's Yeoman's Prologue and Tale, The*; Lust *see* Lechery

Lybeaus Desconus

'The Fair Unknown', a hero of romance. In *Lybeaus Desconus*, a romance by Chaucer's contemporary Thomas Chester, this name is assumed by Guinglain, son of *Gawain. He is included (as 'Sir Lybeux') among a group of romance heroes, said in *Th* (VII.900/ B².2090) to have been surpassed by Sir *Thopas.

Lycurgus

King of *Thrace and father of *Phyllis. Lycurgus ('Lygurge', 'Ligurge') appears at the tournament in *KnT* (I.2128ff.) as an exotic figure, providing one hundred followers in support of *Palamon. He is mentioned briefly in *Phyllis* (*LGW* 2425).

Lydgate, John

(*c.* 1370–*c.* 1449)

English poet. Lydgate was a monk, attached to the Benedictine monastery at Bury St Edmunds (Suffolk). His works were strongly influenced by those of Chaucer – an indebtedness he respectfully acknowledges in several passages. One of these, in the Prologue to *The Fall of Princes* (1.274ff.), provides a survey of Chaucer's work which helps to confirm some aspects of the canon (such as the existence of two of the lost works, *The *Book of the Lion* and *Origenes upon the Maudeleyne*). Lydgate was a prolific poet, who developed a connection with Thomas *Chaucer and had several eminent patrons (including Henry V). His poem *The Siege of Thebes* is represented as an addition to *CT*, complete with a prologue. This serves as a link, describing the pilgrims' arrival in Canterbury and the beginning of the return journey, on which Lydgate's story of Thebes is the first tale. It opens with a description of spring, written in imitation of the opening of *GP*, but conspicuously lacking the subtlety and precision of the original. *See also*: **Julian, St.**

Lyeys *see* **Ayash**

Lynceus

Husband of *Hypermnestra. The unfinished *Hypermnestra* (*LGW* 2562ff.) describes how *Aegeus instructs his daughter, Hypermnestra, to murder her husband, Lynceus ('Lyno'), on their wedding night. When she warns him of the danger, he unworthily flees, leaving his loyal wife to her fate.

M

Mabely *see* **Friar's Prologue and Tale, The**; widows

Machaut, Guillaume de

(*c.* 1300–77)
French poet and composer. Machaut produced a large body of poetry, mainly about love, including over 400 lyrics, some of which he set to music. In these poems he used many of the standard forms of his day, such as the *ballade, rondeau, and virelay. His other works include several long 'dits amoureux' and a substantial verse chronicle about *Pierre de Lusignan (*Le Prise d'Alexandrie*). Machaut's poetry exercised a considerable influence on the next generation of French poets, *Froissart, *Deschamps, and *Granson. It also influenced Chaucer, especially in the earlier part of his career. This is evident not only in his lyrics, but also in works such as *BD* and *LGWP*. The indebtedness to Machaut in the latter two works is particularly significant: notably to *Le Jugement dou Roy de Behaigne* and *Le Dit de la Fonteinne Amoureuse* in *BD*, and to *Le Jugement dou Roy de Navarre* and *Le Dit de la Marguerite* in *LGWP*. It seems probable that Chaucer's lost work *The *Book of the Lion* would have been a translation or adaptation of Machaut's *Le Dit dou Lyon*.

Macrobius

(fl. early 5th century)
Author of a commentary on a work by *Cicero. Chaucer cites Macrobius as an authority on dreams in *PF* (109–12), *BD* (284–9), and *NPT* (VII.3122–6/B².4312–16). The work to which he refers – also mentioned in *Rom* (6–10) – is the lengthy commentary of Macrobius on the *Somnium Scipionis*, the brief closing part of *Cicero's *De re publica*. The *Somnium* describes a dream in which *Scipio the Younger receives information and advice from his late adoptive grandfather, *Scipio the Elder, on such matters as his own future, the nature of the universe, and the destination of the soul after death. Chaucer provides a summary of this encounter in *PF* (29ff.). The commentary of Macrobius (1.3) identifies five types of dream: *somnium* (enigmatic dream), *visio* (prophetic dream), *oraculum* (oracular dream), *insomnium* (nightmare), and *visum* (apparition). These categories – which are

not mutually exclusive – proved highly influential in the Middle Ages, and inform much of the poetry written in the *dream vision genre.

Maghfeld, Gilbert *see* Merchant; Makomete *see* Mohammed

Malyne

Daughter of *Simkin in *RvT*. Malyne is named only once (I.4236) – by *Alan, with whom she has just spent the night.

Man in Black

Figure representing *John of Gaunt in *BD*. In response to questions from the narrator, the Man in Black provides a lengthy and moving account of how he wooed and gained the love of his lady (who represents *Blanche, Duchess of Lancaster), stressing her beauty and good character, and his profound sense of loss at her untimely death. Since John of Gaunt would have been 28 when Blanche died in September 1368, some commentators have been troubled by the allusion to the age of the Man in Black as 24 (*BD* 455). It has normally been supposed that this inconsistency results from a scribal error (such as the writing of 'xxiv' for 'xxix' – a hypothesis which might be taken to suggest that *BD* was written a year after the death of Blanche).

Man of Law *see* Sergeant of Law

Man of Law's Introduction, Prologue, Tale, and Epilogue, The

Introduction, prologue, moral tale, and epilogue comprising the second fragment of *CT*. At the beginning of *MLIntro* (also known as *The Man of Law's Headlink*), the *Host comments on the passing of time, and invites the Man of Law – who was termed the *Sergeant of Law in *GP* (I.309) – to tell a tale. He responds by offering some prefatory remarks on Chaucer as a teller of tales. These have been taken to constitute a mixture of self-deprecation and self-praise on Chaucer's part, since they provide a somewhat grudging assessment of his poetic skills while comparing his work to that of *Ovid. The Man of Law's account concentrates on *LGW*, and is of particular interest in that it mentions some legends which do not form part of the surviving work (and which may, therefore, either have been written but lost, or else have been planned but not written). The fact that he ends his introductory observations by expressing his intention to tell a tale in prose (II.96), but proceeds to tell one in verse, has led commentators to suppose that Chaucer originally assigned a prose tale, probably *Mel*, to him. It has been suggested that some of the retrospective comments in *MLE* (1188–90) would seem more relevant to *Mel* than to *MLT*.

Several further issues and uncertainities arise from *MLE* (also known as *The Man of Law's Endlink*). While this passage survives in a majority of manuscripts, it is missing in some of the most authoritative, including *Ellesmere and *Hengwrt. Most of those in which it does appear identify the speaker of the final lines as the *Squire (1179), which is plainly inappropriate (in terms of tone and content). Others assign it to the *Summoner or (in one case) to the *Shipman. In all these manuscripts, the selection of the speaker is dictated by the identity of the following tale. In some modern editions, on the other hand, the decision to follow the single manuscript which here identifies the Shipman as the speaker reflects the theory that *ShT* was originally attributed to the *Wife of Bath. While this is based mainly on the opening of *ShT*, which appears to identify the teller with married women, it may be reinforced by the fact that the phrase 'my joly body', used by the speaker in *MLE* (1185), recurs in *ShT* (VII.423/B².1613). *MLE* also contains the Host's suggestion that the *Parson could be a *Lollard (1173). It has been suggested that Chaucer might well have had second thoughts about this, his only direct allusion to Lollardy – and might, therefore, have been inclined to delete the passage.

By comparison with such complexities and uncertainties, *MLP* and *MLT* seem relatively straightforward texts. They are both written in the *rhyme royal stanza. *MLP* consists of reflections on the evils of poverty, based on the *De miseria conditionis humane* of *Innocent III (a work of which Chaucer apparently wrote a translation, now lost). *MLT* is a substantial and carefully structured poem, which recounts the remarkable experiences of a virtuous heroine, *Custance, daughter of the *Emperor of Rome. These include two marriages (first to the *Sultan of Syria and then to king *Alla of Northumbria), plots against her by the mothers of both her husbands (the Sultaness, who kills her own son, and *Donegild, who is executed by hers), two unjust sentences of exile resulting in lonely and perilous voyages, and a final happy reunion with her (second) husband and her son, *Maurice. While such occurences are at first presented as resulting from random fate, they are increasingly related to a divinely-ordered providence. In this way, *MLT* has been seen to take up issues raised in *KnT* – though in specifically Christian terms. Thus, for instance, the account of the first voyage of exile endured by Custance alludes to the motif of the rudderless ship, traditionally associated with the ark (II.438ff.). More sensationally, the unnamed knight who has falsely accused Custance of murder, following her rejection of his love, is miraculously struck down at her trial (659ff.).

The events described in *MLT* reflect the influence of two genres, *romance and *saint's life, and, more specifically, two types of folk-tale: that of the princess exiled for refusing to marry her father, and that of the queen exiled for giving birth to a monster. Both of these tale-types influenced the main source, the Anglo-Norman chronicle of Nicholas *Trevet, in which the element of incest is omitted and the story presented as history. *Gower's version of the story (in *Confessio Amantis* 2.587ff.), also based on Trevet, was probably (but not certainly) written before Chaucer's – which it may, therefore, have influenced. While the relatively high proportion of moral and sententious comments in *MLT* has been taken by some critics to suggest the character of its teller (as portrayed in *GP* I.309ff.), the links between teller and tale are hardly close.

Several pieces of evidence help to establish an approximate date for the composition of these texts. In *MLIntro* (1ff.), the Host's observations concerning the time of year are based on the *Kalendarium* of *Nicholas of Lynn, which was written in 1386. The subsequent discussion of Chaucer's work (45ff.) refers to *LGW*, which is generally dated *c.* 1385–6. The comments on the stories of *Canacee and *Appollonius of Tyre (77ff.) have been taken to allude to Gower's *Confessio Amantis*. This work – which may, as has already been noted, constitute a source for *MLT* – was completed in 1390. The use of the *De miseria* (see above) would suggest much the same period: Chaucer's lost translation is mentioned in the G version of *LGWP* (*c.* 1394), but not in the F version (*c.* 1385–6). For these reasons, *MLT* (and the rest of the second fragment of *CT*) has generally been dated *c.* 1390–94.

The text of *MLT* is divided into three parts in a few manuscripts, including Ellesmere. Several manuscripts include Latin glosses which provide references for some of the learned and sententious comments. With these exceptions – and those regarding *MLE*, specified above – the text contains relatively few significant variants.

Further reading: Cooper (1996); Margaret Schlauch in Bryan and Dempster (1941).

Manciple

Pilgrim and teller in *CT*. The portrait of the Manciple in *GP* (I.567ff.) is included in a final group, regularly taken to comprise pilgrims of dubious honesty. It concentrates on the Manciple's professional skill, emphasizing that this enables him to get the better of his masters, despite their learning and eminence (573–85), without specifying how he does so. A broadly comparable skill is attributed to the *Reeve in the following portrait (587ff.); commentators have related both to satirical writing on dishonest officials. The Manciple would have been responsible for buying provisions for a 'temple' (i.e. inn of court), and it is (presumably) this involvement with the catering trade which gives him a potential connection with the *Cook, developed in *MancP*. It has generally been felt that the lack of physical description or personal touches in the portrait make the Manciple an inconspicuous and elusive figure. Some critics take this to be reflected both in his subsequent conduct (i.e. in *MancP*) and in the moral of his tale.

Further reading: Andrew (1993); Mann (1973).

Manciple's Prologue and Tale, The

Lively prologue and exemplary tale comprising Fragment IX of *CT*. *MancP* begins with an allusion to a small town, 'Bobbe-up-and-doun'; though some doubt remains as to whether this should be identified as *Harbledown, it does seem to indicate that the pilgrims are nearing *Canterbury. The *Host's intention that the *Cook should tell the next tale raises an interesting problem, since the Cook has already introduced and told a tale, albeit apparently incomplete (see I.4325ff.). Some commentators take *MancP* to imply that Chaucer intended to cancel this, the final sequence in Fragment I.

The remainder (and bulk) of *MancP* consists of an exchange between the *Manciple, the Cook, and the Host. In the course of this, the Manciple offers to relieve the Cook of his tale-telling duties – at first politely, but then with censorious comments on his drunken state, to which the Cook responds with speechless rage before falling from his horse. The ensuing observations of the Host clearly allude to professional rivalry between the Manciple and the Cook, similar to that which underlies two earlier quarrels – those between the *Miller and the *Reeve, and the *Friar and the *Summoner – and, indeed, to the tensions between himself and the Cook, reflected in *CkP*. The Manciple responds by claiming to have intended all in jest, and by offering wine to the Cook in order to mollify him. This elicits from the Host an expression of amusement that *Bacchus should thus turn 'ernest into game' (99–100) – an interesting echo of a formula first used at the end of *MilP* (I.3186).

In this case, the professional rivalry implied in the prologue does not extend into the following tale. *MancT* is a brief exemplary story about the faithlessness of women and the dangers of careless talk. The three protagonists – *Phoebus, his pet *crow, and his unnamed wife – are introduced at the outset. Phoebus appears as the flower of chivalry, an outstanding archer and singer, who has taught his crow, which is as white as a swan, to speak; it can also sing better than a nightingale. The emphatic allusion to Phoebus as a jealous husband (139–54) provides an early indication of the way in which the tale will develop. The remainder of the narrative is swift and stark – relating how the crow informs Phoebus of his wife's infidelity; how he quickly kills her, but then regrets his actions, suspecting (wrongly) that the crow has lied to him; and how he punishes the crow, depriving him of his speaking and singing voice, turning him black, and throwing him out. The story is interspersed with a good deal of comment. This includes a sequence of three exempla, implying that the faithless behaviour of women is compulsive (163ff.), and reflections on the relationship between deeds and the words that describe them (203ff.). The Manciple emerges as a narrator with crude and unprincipled views. He expresses the moral to his tale in notably reductive terms: if you know a man whose wife is unfaithful, do not tell him (309–13). This introduces a final passage (318ff.), purporting to represent the views of the Manciple's mother, and consisting of repetitious aphoristic advice to the effect that one should take note of the crow's fate and avoid careless talk. The emphasis throughout is on expediency rather than ethical conduct. *MancT* clearly takes up the themes developed earlier in *CT*, especially those of women and marriage. The advice against careless talk has been taken to anticipate the *Parson's rejection of tale-telling in *ParsP* (X.31ff.).

Despite the presence in it of a speaking crow, *MancT* is an exemplary tale which owes relatively little to the genre of the *beast fable. The ultimate source for the story of Phoebus and the crow was *Ovid's *Metamorphoses* (2.531ff.) – from which Chaucer's version does, however, differ significantly. Thus, for instance, Ovid's version concerns a raven (not a crow), who observes the behaviour of Phoebus' unfaithful mistress (not wife), who has a name (Coronis). Chaucer's allusions to the crow's skill in singing and speaking are not derived from Ovid or from any other known version of the story, such as those in the *Ovide moralisé* (2.2130ff.), *Machaut's *Le Livre de voir dit* (7773ff.), or *Gower's *Confessio Amantis* (3.768ff.). The sequence of three exempla (162ff.) is based on separate passages from *RR* (13941–58,

14039–52, 7761–6). The aphoristic material reflects the influence of Old Testament books including Psalms and Proverbs, and of collections maxims such as the *Distichs* of *Cato.

There is no firm evidence for dating the composition of *MancP* and *MancT*. While commentators used to assume that *MancT* was written relatively early, it has come to seem more likely that the prologue and tale were written together for *CT*, and therefore represent mature work. The manuscripts contains few significant variants. *MancT* is among the Chaucerian texts translated by *Wordsworth.

Further reading: Baker (1984); Cooper (1996); James A. Work in Bryan and Dempster (1941).

Mandeville's Travels

Well-known account of travel to the Holy Land and Asia. *Mandeville's Travels* was written *c.* 1357 in Anglo-Norman, and had been translated into several languages, including English, Latin, and French by 1400. It remains unclear how much, if any, of the account is based on the first-hand experience of the author, who claims to have been an English knight, but whose identity has never been established. Chaucer may well have used *Mandeville's Travels* for information on the East – as, for instance, in his allusion to the *Koran in *MLT* (II.332).

Manly, John Matthews

(1865–1940)
Chaucerian scholar and editor. Manly, who spent most of his career at the University of Chicago, is best known for two distinct types of scholarly activity: the pursuit of information about people known to Chaucer or mentioned in his work, and the classification and editing of the manuscripts of *CT*. His proposals regarding the former (some convincing, others not) are presented in his engaging book, *Some New Light on Chaucer* (1926). The fruits of the latter activity – which he pursued over many years with the assistance of Edith Rickert (1871–1938) – are contained in their vast eight-volume edition, *The Text of the Canterbury Tales Studied on the Basis of All Known Manuscripts* (1940). This mainly comprises an assessment of the manuscripts and a record of variant readings. Unfortunately, neither the methods

adopted by Manly and Rickert nor the system employed for recording information are entirely clear. Thus, while their edition remains a valuable source of data, it should be used with care.

Further reading: George Kane in Ruggiers (1984).

Manning, Katherine *see* Chaucer, Agnes (1)

manuscripts *see* Auchinleck MS; Corpus Christi MS 61; Ellesmere MS; Hengwrt MS

Map, Walter

(*c.* 1140–*c.* 1209)

Cleric and author. Walter Map wrote the Latin prose work, *Epistola Valerii ad Rufinum* ('The letter of Valerius to Rufinus'), in which Valerius (a figure representing the author) advises his friend Rufinus against marriage. This work is included in *Jankin's *'book of wicked wives' (*WBP* III.671). Its influence may be detected in the arguments offered by *Justinus in *MerT* (IV.1469ff.) against *January's plans to marry. Though Map originally wrote the *Epistola Valerii* as a discrete work, he later incorporated it into his miscellany, *De nugis curialium* ('On courtiers' trifles'). The passing allusion to 'Valerye' in *LGWP* (G.280) could signify either the *Epistola Valerii* or *Valerius Maximus.

March

Month of March. Though the reference to the 'droghte' of March in *GP* (I.2) has often been taken to represent a classical (and thus Mediterranean) tradition rather than the actual climate of England, some scholars have pointed out that a dry March (especially when followed by a wet April) was regarded as ideal by English writers on husbandry. In *Tr* (2.764–70), the mixture of cloud and sun in March is used as a simile for changing emotions. While an allusion to the idea that the world was created in March occurs in *NPT* (VII.3187–8/B^2.4377–8), allusions to March elsewhere (e.g. *WBP* III.546; *SumT* III.1782; *Astr* 1.10.13) tend to be mundane or factual.

Marcian *see* **Martianus Capella; Marcus Tullius** *see* **Cicero**

Marie de France *see* **Breton lai;** *Nun's Priest's Prologue, Tale, and Epilogue, The*

Mark Antony *see* **Antony**

marriage debate

Discussion of marriage (supposedly) conducted in *CT*. The notion that *CT* contains a debate about marriage was proposed by George Lyman Kittredge in an article published in 1912. Kittredge argued that the *Wife of Bath initiates a discussion of marriage in the prologue to her tale, that the *Clerk offers a riposte in his tale, that the *Merchant responds in his prologue and tale, and that the debate is concluded by the *Franklin, whose views on the subject represent those of Chaucer. This theory proved highly influential, and led to the notion of a 'marriage group', comprising the prologues and tales mentioned above. The main advantage of Kittredge's ideas was to draw attention to the way in which themes and issues are constantly articulated, challenged, and redefined during the course of *CT*. Their main disadvantage was to suggest that discussion of marriage is limited to the 'marriage group' – whereas it plainly occurs in various other tales (including *Mel* and *NPT*). Moreover, while links between *WBT*, *ClT*, *MerP*, and *MerT* are clearly present in the text, there is no textual basis for claiming that the views expressed by the Franklin are those of Chaucer himself.

marriage group *see* marriage debate

Mars

God of war and son of *Juno. Mars (also 'Marte') features in Chaucer's works most conspicuously as the 'god of armes' in *KnT*, where he is first depicted on the banner of *Theseus (I.975–7) and subsequently responds to *Arcite's appeal for victory over *Palamon (I.2367ff.). The latter takes place in the temple of Mars, described splendidly in a passage (I.1967ff.) based on *Boccaccio's *Teseida* (7.29–37). Mars also appears in a more human role, arguing with *Venus over which of their knights (Arcite or Palamon) should enjoy success (I.2438ff.) – a dimension which may be linked with his role as the disappointed lover of Venus in *Mars*. His gentler side may also be suggested in *LGWP* (F.533–4/G.521–2), where he provides the daisy with its red crown. Allusions to the dedication of Theseus to Mars occur in *LGW* (2109) and *Anel* (29–35) as well as in *KnT* (I.1682). His enmity (shared with Juno) toward *Thebes is mentioned in both *KnT* (I.1542ff.) and *Anel* (50–6). The name of Mars appears in invocations (e.g. *Tr* 3.22–8; *Anel* 1–7), in oaths (e.g. *Tr* 2.593; *KnT* I.1747), and among the pagan gods rejected at the end of *Tr* (5.1853). Mars is mentioned in several works as a planetary influence – on an individual, the *Wife of Bath (*WBP* III.603–20), and (less memorably) on events (*MLT* II.305; *Tr* 3.715–17). *Astr* contains various technical references to Mars.

Marte *see* Mars

Martianus Capella

(fl. late 5th century)
Author from Carthage. The *De nuptiis Philologiae et Mercurii* ('On the marriage of Philology and Mercury') of Martianus Capella ('Marcian') was a well-known textbook on the liberal arts, the allegorical preface to which described the union of Mercury (signifying eloquence) and Philogy (signifying knowledge). Allusions to this work occur in *HF* (985) and *MerT* (IV.1732–5).

Martinus Dumiensis

(d. 579)
Author and Bishop of Braga (Spain). His works, including *De moribus* ('On morals') were often attributed to *Seneca. Several such attributions in *Mel* (e.g. VII.1147, 1531, 1775–6/B².2337, 2721, 2965–6) are actually from this work: see notes in Benson (1987: 925–8).

Mary, St

Virgin Mary, mother of *Christ. Chaucer's devotional poem, *ABC*, comprises an elaborate prayer to the Virgin. Both of the female religious tellers in *CT*, the *Prioress and the *Second Nun, preface their tales with invocations to the Virgin (*PrP* VII.467ff./B².1657ff.; *SNT* VIII.29ff.). *PrT* constitutes a miracle of the Virgin, in which she places a 'greyn' on the tongue of the murdered boy, thus permitting him to sing a hymn in her praise. Both *ABC* (89–96) and *PrP* (VII.467–73/B².1657–63) refer to the symbolic association between the burning bush seen by *Moses and the maidenhood of the Virgin. Allusions to the Ave Maria occur in *ABC* (104) and *PrT* (VII.508/B².1698). In *MLT* (II.639–44, 841–54), *Custance prays to the Virgin in times of trouble. The name of the Virgin is invoked – both as 'Marie' and in formulae such as 'Cristes mooder' – in blessings and oaths at numerous junctures: e.g. *HF* (573), *FrT* (III.1604), *SumT* (III.1762), *MerT* (IV.1337), and *Th* (VII.784/B².1974).

Mary Magdalene, St

Follower of *Christ. The allusions to Mary Magdalene in *ParsT* associate her with chaste wives (X.947) and true confession (X.996), as well as interpreting the story of her washing the feet of Christ with her tears, drying them with her hair, and anointing them (X.502–4). *See also*: **Maudelayne; Origenes upon the Maudeleyne.**

Massahalla *see* **Treatise on the Astrolabe, A**

Maudelayne

The *Shipman's vessel. The *Maudelayne* (i.e. *Mary Magdalene) is mentioned at the end of the description of the Shipman in *GP* (I.410). It has been pointed out that a ship of this name appears in the custom-house returns for *Dartmouth in 1379 and 1386, and that its owner was John Hawley and its master (in 1386) Peter *Risshenden.

Maurice

Son of *Custance and *Alla in *MLT*. Though not developed as a character, Maurice is described as sharing his mother's (undeserved) banishment at sea, and as being duly reunited with his father. He may be identified with the historical Byzantine emperor Mauritius Flavius Tiberius (d. 602).

Maurus, St

(6th century)
Follower of St *Benedict. The allusion to him in *GP* (I.173) is normally taken to reflect the tradition that St Maurus was reponsible for introducing the Benedictine Rule into France.

Mawfield, Gilbert *see* **Merchant**

Maximian

(fl. early 6th century)
Latin poet. The desire for death expressed by the *old man in *PardT* (VI.727–36) is based on the first elegy of Maximian, which was much read as a school text and exists in several Middle English versions.

Maximus *see* **Cecilia, St;** *Second Nun's Prologue and Tale, The*

May

The month of May. May is associated with spring and love in various works, including *KnT* (I.1033–50, 1500–12), *FranT* (V.906–12), *Tr* (2.50ff.), and *Rom* (49ff.). Some scholars have suggested that 3rd May – indicated or implied in *KnT* (I.1462–4), *Tr* (2.50–6), and *NPT* (VII.3187–91/B^2.4277–81) – was a day of particular significance to love (see note in Benson, 1987: 832). The other specific dates mentioned by Chaucer – 1st May (*LGWP* F.108) and 6th May (*FranT* V.906) – do not appear to have any special significance. The epithet 'as fresh as May' (with variations) is applied to several individuals, including the *Squire (*GP* I.92), *Deianira (*MkT* VII.2120/B^2.3310), *Aurelius (*FranT* V.927–8), and *Diomede (*Tr* 5.844). An allusion to the idea of the perfected garden in which May lasts for ever occurs in *PF* (129–30).

May

Wife of *January in *MerT*. Chaucer represents May (also 'Mayus') as a beautiful but materialistic young woman. Her marriage to a relatively old (and equally worldly) husband brings her social and financial advantages, and the prospect of wealth and security after his death. May's name (like January's) supports the impression that she is based on a stereotype: that of the attractive and potentially promiscuous young wife married to a jealous older man (cf. *Alison in *MilT*). While May clearly deserves some sympathy – especially with regard to her husband's repulsive love-making – she proves cynical and manipulative, specious and deceitful in her dealings with January, and notably quick to accept the advances of his squire, *Damian.

Medea

Princess of Colchis and skilled enchantress; abandoned wife of *Jason. *Hypsipyle and Medea* (*LGW* 1368ff.) provides an account of Medea's relationship with Jason: how she uses her skills to help him win the Golden Fleece; how they secretly marry and abscond to Greece; and how Jason later leaves her and their children, to marry another woman. In the allusion to this version of the story in *MLIntro* (II.72–4) Chaucer adds that, after her betrayal by Jason, Medea kills her children. This is also mentioned in *BD* (725–7). Passing references to the story of Jason and Medea occur in *HF* (401) and *BD* (330), and to Medea as an enchantress associated with *Circe in *HF* (1271) and *KnT* (I.1944).

Megaera *see* Furies

Meleager

Son of the king of Calydon. Allusions to the well-known story of Meleager as the slayer of the Calydonian Boar occur in *Tr* (5.1464ff.) and *KnT* (I.2069–72) – the former with reference to the lineage of *Diomede (especially in 5.1513–15).

Melibee

Husband of *Prudence in *Mel*. Melibee (also 'Melibeus') is described as a wealthy young man, wronged by three enemies who break into his house, beating his wife and inflicting serious injuries on his daughter, *Sophie. His name signifies 'a man that drynketh hony'(VII.1410/B².2600) – that is, one who has enjoyed worldly goods and pleasures. The tale largely comprises a moral debate, through which Prudence persuades Melibee to forgive those who have wronged him.

Melibee, The Tale of

Moral tale in prose from Fragment VII (Group B²) of *CT*. *Mel* is introduced by a passage following the end of *Th* (VII.919ff./ B².2109ff.), sometimes termed *MelP* or *The Thopas-Melibee Link*. This begins with the interruption of *Th* by the *Host, who expresses a bluntly unflattering view of Chaucer's talents in 'rym' (as demonstrated in *Th*). Brushing aside Chaucer's complaint that he is being treated unfairly, the Host suggests that he could tell another tale in 'geeste' or prose (933–5/2123–5). The former may signify *alliterative verse (cf. *ParsP* X.43); be that as it may, Chaucer states that his second tale will be 'a litel thyng in prose' (937/2127). It is preceded by an apology, which discusses the relationship between words and meaning in tales and in the gospels, and appears to imply the existence of an earlier and shorter version of *Mel*.

If any such work ever existed, it has not survived. The tale, as told in *CT*, proves to be far from 'litel': *Mel* does, in fact, constitute a long prose treatise, which argues the case for peace and reconciliation rather than war and vengeance. Though it begins with an account of how three enemies of the rich and powerful *Melibee break into his house in his absence and attack his wife (*Prudence) and his daughter (*Sophie), it soon turns away from narrative to concentrate on the discussion of ethical matters. The crucial issue is whether Melibee should take revenge on his attackers, who have not only violated his property and potentially damaged his reputation, but have also beaten Prudence and inflicted serious injuries on Sophie. The discussion takes the form of a debate between wife and husband, in which Prudence gradually persuades Melibee that he should forgive his enemies. The process is dominated by Prudence, who successively warns Melibee against excessive grief (974ff./2164ff.), advises him to summon a council (1002ff./2192ff.), helps him to distinguish between the good and bad advice received on that occasion (1115ff./ 2305ff.), cajoles him into seeking reconciliation with his enemies (1671ff./2861ff.), persuades them to submit themselves to him (1726ff./2916ff.), and finally convinces him that he should forgive them (1769ff./2959ff.). In the process, she deals with several related issues, especially in the central part of the work – defending the advice of women against Melibee's anti-feminist views (1055ff./2245ff.), providing an interpretation of the causes of his misfortune (1355ff./2545ff.), and offering counsel on such matters as the legitimate use of wealth and the proper concern for reputation (1546ff./2736ff.). Both Prudence and Melibee support their views by quoting maxims and citing authorities. She, typically, answers his objections on a particular point before moving the argument on to the next topic on her agenda.

Mel is a fairly close translation of *Le Livre de Mellibee et Prudence* of *Renaud de Louens – which constitutes a much freer translation of the *Liber consolatis et consiliis* of *Albertanus of Brescia. Albertanus was writing in the mid-thirteenth century on personal and political ethics, offering advice on prudent conduct and supporting his views with a substantial collection of maxims. Chaucer's motives for translating Renaud's version of his work have been variously interpreted. *Mel* has been read both as a pacifist tract (sometimes in combination with *Th*) and as a work advising *Richard II to avoid internal strife (in which connection it might be related to *Sted*). Commentators have noted that, while the issues tackled in *Mel* are, for the most part, too general to encourage identification with specific historical events, Chaucer does omit an allusion in his source to Solomon's comments on the miseries of a land ruled by a child (Eccles. 10:16) – which would have been singularly tactless during the first part of Richard's reign. It has also been observed that the allegorical reading, apparently encouraged by some of Prudence's comments, seems problematic: in particular, if the three attackers signify the world, the flesh, and the devil (1420ff./2610ff.), then it would seem perverse to recommend reconcilation with them. With regard to this problem, it may be argued that the focus of *Mel* is emphatically ethical rather than spiritual, and that an overall allegorical reading is therefore inappropriate. More generally, interpretations of *Mel* as a component of *CT* have differed sharply. At one extreme, it has been envisaged as a parody of tedious moral treatises, possibly constituting Chaucer's revenge on the Host for his interruption of *Th*. At the other, it has been regarded as an entirely serious work, the thematic concerns of which are central to *CT*. Whatever the virtues of these various readings, it is clear that several themes and topics dealt with elsewhere in *CT* are considered in *Mel*. Thus, for instance, the praise of patience and the censure of covetousness (1500ff./2690ff., 1576ff./2766ff.) revisit topics previously explored (respectively) in *ClT* and in *PardP* and *PardT*, while the distrust of Fortune (1444ff./2634ff.) is reminiscent of *KnT* and anticipates *MkT*. Most notable of all, the comments on anti-feminist views and the advice of women (1055ff./2245ff.) take up issues central to the *marriage debate, soon to resurface in *NPT* (see, especially VII.3256–64/ B^2.4446–54), and include three striking echoes of *WBP* (1086–8/2276–8; cf. III.112, 278–80, 775–81) and one of *WBT* (1724–5/2914–15; cf. III.1230–5).

There is no particular evidence for dating *Mel*. The apparent allusion to an earlier version of the tale (see above) may suggest that it was written as an independent work and revised for inclusion in *CT*. It has often been supposed that Chaucer originally intended *Mel* for the *Sergeant of Law, who states in *MLIntro* (II.96) that he will 'speke in prose', but then tells a tale in verse. While the notion that *Mel* may reflect on the political circumstances of the reign of Richard II (see above) does not, in itself, provide any precise indication of its date, a brief insertion by Chaucer (1325–6/2515–16), including allusions to a king and a hart, has been taken to refer to Richard's adoption of the badge of the white hart in 1390. The manuscripts contain relatively few variants, but all lack three brief passages (1062–3/2252–3, 1433–4/2623–4, 1664/2854), which are required for the sense and were presumably lost early in the process of transmission. Modern editions normally supply the equivalent lines from the French version. The number of separate copies of *Mel* is exceeded only in the case of *ClT* and equalled only in that of *PrT*.

Further reading: Cooper (1996); William R. Askins in Correale and Hamel (2002).

Merchant

Pilgrim and teller in *CT*. The portrait of the Merchant in *GP* (I.270ff.) is placed between those of the *Friar and the *Clerk. Commentators have noted a pattern of parallels and contrasts, especially that of the Merchant's worldly acquisitiveness linking with the inappropriate worldliness of the Friar, and contrasting with the unworldliness of the Clerk. The potential connection with the teller of *MerT* has often seemed problematic – critics finding it hard to reconcile the dignified self-presentation in the portrait with the self-revelation of *MerP* and the bitterness of *MerT*. A crucial passage in the portrait (278–82) has been interpreted in conspicuously divergent ways: while some take this to signify involvement in shady dealings, others claim that such activities were legitimate; similarly, while some understand it to imply that the Merchant was in debt, others take the opposite view. Clearly, though the portrait reflects the influence of the satiric stereotype of the dishonest merchant, it functions in a more elusive manner. The references to the Merchant's Flemish hat (272) and to trade between *Middelburgh and *Orwell (276–7) have been taken to suggest that he could have been a merchant of the Staple, based in *Flanders. It has been noted that Orwell is close to Ipswich, where John *Chaucer, the poet's father, had family connections. The final observation – that the narrator does not know his name – has been interpreted, on the one hand, as a contemptuous dismissal and, on the other, as an invitation to speculate as to his identity. The latter leads to the suggestion that the portrait was based on Gilbert *Mawfield (or Maghfeld), from whom Chaucer borrowed money in the 1390s (see Crow and Olson, 1966: 500–3).

Further reading: Andrew (1993); Mann (1973).

merchant *see Shipman's Tale, The*

Merchant's Prologue, Tale, and Epilogue, The

Prologue, satirical comic tale, and epilogue from Fragment IV of *CT*. The opening line of *MerP* is plainly linked to the final line of *ClT*. In response to the sardonic recommendation that a wife should cause her husband misery, with which the *envoy of *ClT* closes, the *Merchant claims that his wife does precisely this. He asserts that, though they have been married for only two months, she has already proved herself a shrew, the very opposite of patient *Grisilde. When the *Host asks him to continue on the subject, the Merchant agrees, with the proviso that he will say no more about his own sorrow. Nonetheless, *MerT* has clearly been introduced as a riposte to *ClT* – and has thus often been regarded as part of the *'marriage debate'. It does, however, seem likely that the relationship between these two tales arose as a consequence of revision: *MerP* is missing from several manuscripts (including the *Hengwrt MS), and there are traces in the early part of *MerT* which suggest that it was originally assigned to a clerical teller (see IV.1322; cf. 1251, 1390). Various conjectural explanations of this evidence have been offered. Perhaps the most convincing is that *MerT* was originally written for the *Monk, and would have offered a riposte, in the form of a tale about the misbehaviour of a wife, to *ShT*, a tale about the misbehaviour of a monk, originally written for the *Wife of Bath.

While *MerP* thus provides ostensible motivation for *MerT*, it does so apparently without developing any suggestions from the portrait of the Merchant in *GP* (I.270ff.). Indeed, some commentators have perceived inconsistency between the formal and restrained pilgrim of *GP* and the assertive and sardonic speaker/teller in *MerP* and *MerT*. There has been general acknowledgement of the relentlessly negative quality of the tale – in which ideals, principles, and assumptions are repeatedly set up only to be undermined – though the essential effect and significance of this characteristic have been interpreted in various ways. Whereas the notion that the portrayal of *January expresses the Merchant's disgust with himself and his own marriage would seem unconvincing to most critics, it has been generally accepted that January's apparently limitless capacity for self-delusion lies at the heart of the tale. The central manifestation of this characteristic is (of course) his view of marriage, which leads him to regard his wife, *May, as a sex object, both before and after their wedding. His attitudes are reflected in numerous passages, including the accounts of his thoughts about May as a prospective bride (1577ff.) and of his repulsive love-making on their wedding night (1818ff.). On the positive side, he is represented as providing generously for May (1697–9, 2172–3) and expresses concern for the welfare of *Damian (1906ff.); but these seem relatively minor virtues. The temporary blindness from which he suffers towards the end of the tale clearly symbolizes the moral blindness which typifies his views and most of his conduct throughout. While it would seem natural to sympathize with the young wife

of a wilful and repellant old husband, May's own conduct serves to undermine any such response, as she repeatedly demonstrates her utter cynicism
and considerable powers of manipulation. The most memorable example of
this is, perhaps, the scene where she tearfully assures January of her devotion
to him while covertly signalling to her prospective lover, Damian, with
whom she will shortly be copulating (2185ff.). Values fare no better in other
parts of the tale. Thus, for instance, the two debates on marriage – between
*Justinus and *Placebo on the one hand (1617ff.) and *Pluto and *Proserpina
on the other (2237ff.) – both prove to be shams, reflecting cynical manipulation and the expression of prejudice rather than human sympathy and the
exercise of reason.

In his presentation of the nihilistic world of *MerT*, Chaucer uses and mingles
several genres – notably *exemplum, *romance, and *fabliau. The discussion
of marriage in the opening part of the poem displays the generalizing and
moralizing tendencies of exemplum (though the undermining of values
would, of course, be inappropriate in this genre). The account of the wedding
and the daily life of January and May draws on the manner, vocabulary, and
norms of romance – of which the (ostensibly) happy ending would also be
typical. The pear-tree episode reflects the essential characteristics of fabliau,
including trickery, sexual intrigue, and bluntness of expression. This generic
mingling, which involves style as well as content, produces some startling
juxtapositions, as when the romance motif of the garden of love becomes the
setting for the fabliau plot. These clearly contribute to the disconcerting effect
of the poem. Sources and analogues are, likewise, diverse. The discussion of
marriage draws on a range of materials similar to those used in the last part of
WBP, including *Jerome's *Epistola adversus Jovinianum*, the 'Golden book on
marriage' by *Theophrastus, and various biblical texts. It also echoes two
works by *Albertanus of Brescia, the *Liber de amore et dilectione Dei* and the *Liber
consolationis et consilii*. Numerous analogues of the pear-tree episode have been
discovered among continental fabliaux; the closest of these is an Italian prose
tale from the *Novellino*. Recent scholars have expressed doubt regarding the
previously accepted view that Chaucer was indebted in the early part of *MerT*
to Deschamps' *Le Miroir de Mariage*, on the grounds that it might not have
been available to him in time. They have, likewise, tended to reject the notion
that he was influenced by the account of the relationship between an old man
and a young woman in *Boccaccio's *Ameto*. In both cases, most of the ideas
involved are commonplace. *MerT* also reflects the more general influence of
RR (cited in connection with the garden in 2032), and contains echoes of the
marriage service and various biblical texts, especially the Song of Songs –
which January paraphrases in a cynically offensive manner (2138–48).

MerT is directly linked with *ClT* (see above), and has been associated through the theory of the 'marriage debate' with *WBP*, *WBT*, and *FranT*. Various aspects of the poem have suggested several other thematic connections. It provides a searching exploration of the motif of the old man with a young wife, which was first presented in *MilT*, and considered from a distinctive viewpoint in *WBP*. It also uses the more general motif of the love triangle, which occurs first in *KnT*, and recurs, with variations, in *MilT* and *FranT*. (In the latter, the rival, *Aurelius is a squire, like Damian, though there the likeness ends.) The role of Pluto and Proserpina echoes that of the gods in *KnT* – with some diminution, which could be regarded as parodic. At the end of the tale, the Host provides a notably limited response in *MerE*, revealing that he, too, has the misfortune to be married to a shrew (a revelation later developed in *MkP*). The division between *MerE*, which ends Fragment IV, and *SqIntro*, which begins Fragment V, is editorial.

The date at which *MerP* and *MerT* were written cannot be established with any precision. The signs of revision (see above) suggest that the tale was written first, possibly for the Monk, and later revised and assigned to the Merchant when the prologue was written. This process established a link with *ClT* and, by extension, with *WBP* and the rest of Fragment III. On this basis, composition in the early to mid-1390s would seem likely. The manuscripts contain several significant variants; some provide extensive glosses, mainly in the section on marriage.

Echoes of *MerT* have been detected in *Shakespeare's *A Midsummer Night's Dream*. *Pope composed a free translation, entitled *January and May*.

Further reading: Benson and Andersson (1971); Cooper (1996); Germaine Dempster in Bryan and Dempster (1941).

Merciles Beaute

Triple *roundel of 39 lines, uncertainly attributed to Chaucer. *MercB* survives in a single manuscript (Pepys 2006) and a seventeenth-century transcription. Though the manuscript does not attribute *MercB* to Chaucer, it does contain several undoubtedly genuine poems (e.g. *ABC*, *Truth*, and *Scog*). Most complete editions of Chaucer include *MercB* among poems of doubtful authenticity. The title occurs in the index to the manuscript. Since the refrains are indicated in the manuscript only by '&c.', the correct form of the poem is a matter of interpretation. The first two roundels conform to the courtly convention of the lover 'slain' by his lady, only for this to be rejected in the third. While *MercB* was clearly written in the courtly tradition associated with *Machaut and *Deschamps, the conventional nature of its contents makes the identification of sources and echoes difficult. A single line (27) does, however, correspond closely to one in a *ballade by the Duc de Berry, written in 1389. This helps to establish a date for the English poem if it borrows from the French; if (as seems more likely) the opposite is the case, then the date of *MercB* remains uncertain.

Further reading: Pace and David (1982); V.J. Scattergood in Minnis (1995).

Mercury

Son of Jupiter; winged messenger of the gods. Mercury delivers two significant messages in stories told by Chaucer – advising *Aeneas to leave *Dido (*LGW* 1295–1300; *HF* 427–32), and *Arcite to return to Athens (*KnT* I.1385–92). Allusions to his wings and his birth (in Arcadia), and to his role of guiding the spirits of the dead to Hades occur in *Bo* (4.m.3.16–23) and *Tr* (5.321–2, 1826–7) respectively. The alchemical significance of Mercury is expounded by the *Canon's Yeoman (*CYT* VIII.1431–40). His astrological associations are described by the *Wife of Bath (*WBP* III.697–705). Mercury appears in *Mars* (113–19, 144–7), under the name of 'Cilenius', as part of the poem's astronomical scheme. *See also*: **Martianus Capella**.

Metamorphoses *see* **Ovid**; metre *see* **decasyllable couplet**; **octosyllabic couplet**; **rhyme royal**

Midas

Wealthy but foolish king of Phrygia. Chaucer refers twice to the story of Midas from *Ovid's *Metamorphoses* (11.100ff.). In *WBT* (III.951ff.) he relates the last part of the episode concerning the ass's ears growing on Midas' head, with the modification that the person who reveals this shameful secret is his wife rather than (as in Ovid) his barber. In *Tr* (3.1387ff.) Midas is mentioned briefly as an example of covetousness – an allusion to the well-known episode of the 'golden touch'.

Middelburgh

Dutch port on the island of Walcheren. The trading interests of the *Merchant are doubtless reflected in his concern that the sea route between Middelburgh and *Orwell should be protectd from piracy (*GP* I.276–7).

Miller

Pilgrim and teller in *CT*. The portrait of the Miller comes towards the end of
GP (I.545ff.), the first in a sequence of five pilgrims of dubious morality. It
represents him as powerful, dishonest, potentially threatening, and noisily
gregarious. These qualities are introduced through description both of typifying conduct (such as telling crude stories or heaving doors off their hinges
or – somewhat bizarrely – battering them down with his head) and of vivid
details (his sword and buckler, and, most memorably, his mouth gaping like
a furnace and his nose with wide nostrils and a hairy wart). While some
commentators have taken such features of the description, together with its
use of animal imagery, to suggest that the Miller is a figure of evil, most
would take a less rigidly censorious view. The description has been related to
the medieval stereotype of the thieving miller, which is doubtless reflected
in experiences of the kind represented in *RvT*. Here, the *Reeve, having taken
offence at *MilP* and *MilT*, seeks to exact revenge on the Miller by portraying
him as *Simkin, the cheating miller of *Trumpington, who is finally bested
by the Cambridge scholars, *Alan and *John. There is, however, nothing else
to associate the Miller with the mill at Trumpington; furthermore, he is
given his own name, Robin (I.3129). Some have taken this to link him with
*Robin, the 'knave' of John the carpenter in *MilT* – who, notably, helps his
master to lift a door off its hinges (I.3465ff.). In *GP*, the opposition between
the Miller and the Reeve, developed subsequently, is latent in their sharply
differentiated physiques and natures – the latter encapsulated in the contrast
between the Reeve, lurking at the back of the group of pilgrims, and the
Miller, leading them on their way to the sound of his bagpipe.
  Further reading: Andrew (1993); Mann (1973).

miller *see Reeve's Prologue and Tale, The*; **Simkin**

Miller's Prologue and Tale, The

Lively prologue and comic tale from the first fragment of *CT*. *MilP* (I.3109ff.)
serves as a link between the first of the tales, *KnT*, and the following *MilT*; thus
it is sometimes termed *The Knight–Miller Link*. The importance of this brief
passage for *CT* as a whole can hardly be exaggerated. Here, between the first
two tales, Chaucer establishes the potential for dynamic interaction, not just
between tale and teller, but also between tale and fictional audience (the
pilgrims), between tellers, and between the tales themselves. The process
begins with the positive response of the other pilgrims, especially 'the gentils',
to *KnT*. The *Host then invites the *Monk to tell the next tale, but is interrupted

by the drunken *Miller, who insists that he should tell a tale to 'quite' (i.e. answer, repay) the first teller. While the Host reluctantly accepts this undermining of his authority as master of ceremonies, the *Reeve vehemently objects to the Miller's stated intention of telling 'a legende and a lyf' about a carpenter and his wife, and how a scholar made a fool of the carpenter. The Reeve complains that the tale will be scurrilous, and apparently fears that it will imply an identification between himself – described in *GP* (I.613–14) as having trained as a carpenter – and the carpenter in *MilT*. Though this objection is brushed aside by the Miller, it resurfaces in *RvP* and *RvT*, and becomes the motivating force behind the Reeve's telling of his tale. Chaucer ends *MilP* by offering, in his role as narrator, an apology for any possible offence which may be caused by the tales told by the 'cherles', including the Miller and the Reeve, but asserting that his readers are free to choose other tales – some of which are more elevated or improving – and requesting that they should 'nat maken ernest of game'. This apology may be related to a passage near the end of *GP* (I.725ff.), which has been compared to an apology by *Boccaccio in the *Decameron*.

MilP proves an apt and evocative introduction to *MilT*. The tale describes how the worldly and resourceful Oxford scholar, *Nicholas, seduces *Alison, the attractive young wife of the elderly carpenter, *John, in whose home he lodges. It is, however, far more complex and interesting than this brief summary might imply. The tone avoids smuttiness or immorality, suggesting rather an exuberant and, for the most part, genial amorality. Though basically simple, the plot is complicated both by the elaborate machinations of Nicholas and by the presence of a second would-be lover for Alison in the person of *Absolon, the effete and largely inept parish clerk. The tale is narrated briskly, though it does include some set-piece descriptions, notably of Alison (I.3233ff.). It is handled with consummate skill: at its climax, two plot elements, previously separated, are brought together, with apparent naturalness and to splendid effect. While the story as a whole and its recognizably separable plot elements – the 'misplaced kiss', the flood, and the branding – are typical of *fabliau as a genre, and analogues have been found in several individual fabliaux, neither the originality nor the vitality of *MilT* is in doubt. It might seem a typically Chaucerian paradox that an amoral comic tale should be liberally sprinkled with biblical echoes. These may serve to discourage simple judgements about 'ernest and game', and perhaps to encourage consideration of the implied, jestingly blasphemous allusion to the annunciation (which would identify John, Alison, and Nicholas with Joseph, Mary, and Gabriel). Throughout, the effect of *MilT* is dependent on a pattern of ironic allusion to the preceding *KnT*. Though the two stories share a basic plot element in the rivalry of two young men for the affections of one young woman, and perhaps in the distinction between a more pragmatic and a more idealistic lover, the essential relationship between *KnT* and *MilT* is one of contrast and parody. The elevated ideals of love are juxtaposed with the basic physical urgency of sex, a barely attainable and virtuous princess with the willingly promiscuous wife of a carpenter, remote locations and exotic accoutrements with familiar surroundings and everyday objects.

Textual variants are relatively few and minor. Though *MilP* and *MilT* cannot be dated with any exactness, they are generally taken to have been written fairly early in the composition of *CT*.

Further reading: Bennett (1974); Benson and Andersson (1971); Cooper (1996); Ross (1983).

Milton, John *see* Dryden, John; Minerva *see* Pallas Athene

Minos

King of *Crete. Minos is represented in *Ariadne* (*LGW* 1886ff.) as a conqueror and tyrant, who demands human victims from the defeated Athenians and feeds them to his monster, the *Minotaur, which is eventually killed by one of the intended victims, *Theseus. The opening line of *Ariadne* refers to Minos as 'juge infernal' – an allusion to his role as judge in the underworld, to which reference is also made in *Tr* (4.1188).

Minotaur

Monstrous creature (half bull, half man) fathered by the Cretan Bull on *Pasiphae. *Ariadne* (*LGW* 1886ff.) tells how the Minotaur, which had been fed on a diet of Athenian youths, was killed by *Theseus. In *KnT* (I.978–80), Theseus bears a pennon celebrating this victory. The role of *Dedalus, who constructed the Labyrinth in which the Minotaur was kept, is mentioned in *Bo* (3.p.12.156).

Mirth

Personification in *Rom*. Mirth, lord of the garden in *Rom* (600ff.), is a figure representing pleasure.

Mohammed

(*c*. 570–629)
The prophet of Islam. An allusion to the laws of Mohammed ('Makomete'), recorded in the *Koran, occurs in *MLT* (II.330–6).

Monk

Pilgrim and teller in *CT*. The portrait of the Monk in *GP* (I.165ff.) has generally been regarded as satirical. Its main emphases – the enjoyment of hunting, fine clothes, and good food, and the questioning of monastic principles and discipline – have been related to the tradition of satire against gluttonous, lax, and worldly monks. Opinion as to the tone of the portrait and the clarity or otherwise of its message has, however, varied widely – ranging respectively from genial worldliness to severe censure, and from complete clarity to ambiguity and elusiveness. Commentators have regularly pointed out that the rejection of monastic discipline as old-fashioned is attributed to the Monk himself and partly expressed in his own reported words, with which the narrator expresses agreement (173–88). It has sometimes been argued that Chaucer portrays the Monk as someone whose administrative potential and responsiblities have led to worldliness (165–72). A pattern of sexual innuendo, based on the association of hunting and lust, has been detected by many critics. Their views gain some support from *MkP* (VII.1924ff./B².3114ff.), where the *Host expresses somewhat mocking admiration for the Monk's splendid appearance, which he sees as implying both administrative ability and sexual prowess. The connections, if any, with *MkT* have seemed more tenuous. The portrait's particular emphasis on hunting the hare has led to the suggestion that it could be modelled on William de *Cloune, Abbott of Leicester, but this has attracted little support. The Monk has often been seen as one of a group of worldly regular clergy, also comprising the *Prioress and the *Friar. His apparent worldliness and self-indulgence has sometimes been contrasted to the somewhat ascetic dedication of the *Knight, who later interrupts his tale (*NPT* VII.2767–70/B².3957–60). Shortly afterwards (2792/3982), the *Host addresses him as 'daun Piers'.

Further reading: Andrew (1993); Mann (1973).

monks *see* John (4)

Monk's Prologue and Tale, The

Significant prologue followed by tale comprising a series of 'tragedies' from Fragment VII (Group B²) of *CT*. *MkP* begins with the *Host's response to the preceding tale, *Mel*. He expresses the wish that his wife, *Goodelief, could have heard about the patience of *Melibee's wife, *Prudence. He goes on to maintain that Goodelief incites him to violence and revenge, thus implicitly contrasting her behaviour with the peace and reconciliation advocated by

Prudence. The allusion to the potential reversal of traditional male and female roles between the cowardly Host and his aggressive wife (VII.1906–7/B².3096–7) provides a comic echo of *Mel*, where a husband comes to accept that his wife should take over the traditionally male role of adviser and decision-maker. There are striking parallels between the opening of *MkP* and the stanza at the end of *ClT* (IV.1212a–g), sometimes termed the 'Host stanza'. These have generally been taken to indicate that Chaucer cancelled what he had originally intended as an end-link to *ClT*, and revised the material for use in *MkP*.

The middle part of *MkP* (1924ff./3114ff.) describes how the Host invites the *Monk to tell the next tale. This involves fulsome but disrespectful praise of the Monk's worldly attributes and sexual potential, echoing and developing parts of his portrait in *GP* (I.165ff.). It also provides a reminder of the worldly monk, *John, in *ShT* – particularly when the Host speculates that the Monk's name could be 'daun John' (1929/3119). The allusion to the proximity of *Rochester (1926/3116) raises an entirely different issue. Observing that this comes after the allusion to *Sittingbourne (III.847), though Rochester would have been reached earlier on the route to *Canterbury, *Bradshaw advocated moving Fragment VII from the position it occupies in the manuscripts, and placing it after *MLT* (in which position it has usually been termed Group B²).

In the third and final part of *MkP* (1965ff./3155ff.), the Monk introduces his tale. He responds with conspicuous dignity to the Host's banter, making it clear that his intentions are entirely serious. Having alluded to the possibility of relating the life of St *Edward, he decides to tell a series of 'tragedies' – of which he states (perhaps with ominous implications for his tale) that he has a hundred in his cell. He proceeds to offer a definition of tragedy – which was not a familiar concept in the Middle Ages – stating that this constitutes a story of a man who falls from 'heigh degree' and 'endeth wrecchedly'.

The Monk completes this definition in the opening lines of his tale, adding that the victims of tragedy are brought low through the untrustworthy fickleness of *Fortune. At the end of the tale (2761–6/3951–6) he reiterates the essential features of the genre. *MkT* turns out to comprise a series of 'tragedies', related in an intricate eight-line stanza, rhyming ababbcbc (also used in *ABC*, *Form Age*, and *Buk*). While this stanza lends a certain air of formality to the proceedings, the individual stories are often told in a relatively direct and straightforward manner. Their subjects consist of seventeen individuals, sixteen men and one woman: seven from the Old Testament, Apocrypha, and Christian tradition (Lucifer [see *Satan], *Adam, *Samson, *Nebuchadnezzar, *Belshazzar, *Holofernes, and *Antiochus); six from classical history and myth (*Hercules, *Zenobia, *Nero, *Alexander, *Julius Caesar, and *Croesus); and four from the contemporary or near-contemporary world, sometimes termed the 'modern instances' (*Pedro of Castile, *Pierre de Lusignan, Bernabò *Visconti, and *Ugolino of Pisa). The stories are arranged in a predominantly chronological order, though the position of the 'modern instances' varies (see below), and the sequence is, in any case, not entirely consistent – a deficiency for which the Monk apologizes in advance (1984–90/3174–80). While the seventeen individuals comprise a notably varied assortment of the good, the bad, and the indifferent, each is envisaged as a victim of fate. Allusions to divine punishment occur in some cases – notably that of Antiochus (2615–22/3805–12) – but without any consistency. Some commentators have taken this lack of a coherent moral vision to reflect the Monk's worldliness.

It has generally been supposed that Chaucer modelled MkT on *Boccaccio's Latin prose work, De casibus virorum illustrium, the title of which appears as an epigraph to the tale in several manuscripts. This assumption does, however, require some qualification: though the two works have several stories in common – those of Adam, Samson, Zenobia, Nero, and Croesus (along with that of *Pompey, within the story of Julius Caesar) – in none of these does the version in the De casibus constitute the main source for that in MkT. Moreover, Boccaccio adopts a narrative procedure quite unlike Chaucer's (allowing each protagonist to tell his own story), and does not use the word tragedia. It seems likely that the overall concept of MkT also reflects the influence of a substantial and well-known passage in *RR (5829ff.), which includes an account of the goddess Fortune, mentions recent as well as traditional examples of those who have suffered from her fickleness, and provides the basis for the stories of Nero and Croesus. Other sources and influences are diverse. Chaucer was indebted to the De consolatione philosophiae of *Boethius for his concept of tragedy (see Bo 2.pr.2.67–72, which includes a gloss by *Trevet). It is notable that he refers to Tr (which was written around the time he was working on Bo) as a 'tragedye' (5.1786). The influence of Boethius may also be detected in the story of Hercules (cf. 4.m.7) – together, perhaps, with that of Ovid (Metamorphoses 9, Heroides 9). Several of the stories (including those of Samson, Nebuchadnezzar, Belshazzar, and Holofernes) are ultimately derived from the relevant sources in the Old Testament and the Apocrypha. In the story of Zenobia, Chaucer drew on Boccaccio's De claris mulieribus as well as his De casibus. The influence of the Speculum Historia of *Vincent of Beauvais has been detected in several stories, including those of Adam, Samson, and Julius Caesar. While the pathetic account of Ugolino is derived from *Dante's Inferno (33), it seems probable that those of the other 'modern instances' would have been based on oral reports rather than on written sources.

The four 'modern instances' have a significant bearing on arguments regarding the composition and revision of *MkT*. Though commentators have often assumed that the tale was written relatively early in Chaucer's career and subsequently revised for *CT*, probably with the composition of *MkP*, there is no firm evidence to support this view. In its final form, *MkT* could not have been written earlier than the beginning of 1386, since it reports the death of Bernabò, which occurred in December 1385. The tale does, however, show clear signs of revision. The 'modern instances' appear in two different positions: while a majority of manuscripts place them between the tales of Zenobia and Nero (2375–462/ 3565–652), the most authoritative place them at the end of the sequence. Recent editors adopt the former position, mainly because it allows the tale to end with the story of Croesus. The final stanza of this story provides comments which appear to reiterate and summarize the earlier definition of tragedy (see above), and are shortly echoed by the Host in the following *NPP* (VII.2782–3/B². 3972–3). They do, however, also suggest that the Monk may be in the process of drawing to a conclusion; thus the *Knight's interruption, which cuts off the tale, seems unnecessary. The alternative sequence, with the 'modern instances' at the end, would imply that the Monk resumes his series of tragedies after his general reflections on the story of Croesus. It makes the interruption more appropriate but weakens the link to the Host's words in *NPP*. A further small piece of evidence appears to support the hypothesis that this sequence results from revision (and is, therefore, the later of the two). While the manuscripts which place the 'modern instances' in the midst of the sequence describe Pedro's enemy as his 'bastard brother' (2378/3568), those which place them at the end term him simply 'brother' (the reading generally adopted by editors). It has been conjectured that this could represent a change made for political reasons after 1386, when reconciliation between the descendants of the two brothers was achieved through a marriage (between Pedro's granddaughter, a daughter of *John of Gaunt, and the grandson of his illegitimate brother).

By comparison with this textual crux, the omission of the story of Adam in three manuscripts (one of which, the *Hengwrt MS, added it later in the margin) seems relatively minor. While the manuscripts contain various headings, glosses, and notes to the stories, other textual variants are fairly insignificant. *MkT* is copied independently in two manuscripts, one of which combines it with *Mel*. See also: **Nun's Priest's Prologue, Tale, and Epilogue, The.**

Further reading: Thomas H. Bestul in Correale and Hamel (2002); Cooper (1996).

Montagu, Sir John *see* Lollard Knights

Morell, Revd Thomas

(1703–84)

Editor of Chaucer. Morell was a cleric and a fellow of King's College, Cambridge. In 1737 he published an edition of *GP* and *KnT*, together with modernized versions by various authors, including *Dryden. The main significance of this edition is that Morell collated several manuscripts in an attempt to establish a reliable text, thus anticipating the approach of *Tyrwhitt, the first truly scholarly editor of Chaucer.

Morpheus

God of sleep in *BD*. Following the instructions of *Juno, Morpheus recovers the body of the drowned *Ceyx, and appears in this guise to explain the circumstances of his death to his wife, *Alcione (135ff.).

Morris, Richard *see* Skeat, Revd Walter W.

Morris, William

(1834–96)

Craftsman and poet. Morris's admiration for Chaucer is reflected in several of his poems, notably *The Earthly Paradise* (1868–70). During the last few years of his life, Morris was working on a magnificent edition of Chaucer, which was intended to recreate the appearance of a lavish manuscript or early printed book. This exceptionally beautiful book – known as the Kelmscott Chaucer, after the name of Morris's press – contains 87 illustrations by Sir Edward Burne-Jones and borders designed by Morris. It appeared in 1896, a few months before Morris's death.

Moses

Founder of Israel in the Old Testament. The traditional interpretation of the burning bush, seen by Moses in Exodus (3:2), as a symbol of the maidenhood of the Virgin Mary is reflected in *ABC* (89–96) and *PrP* (VII.467–73/B².1657–63). Friar *John in *SumT* (III.1885–90) mentions how Moses fasts for forty days and nights on Mount Sinai (Exod. 34:28). A brief passage in *SqT* (V.247–51) associates Moses and *Solomon with magic. Passing allusions to Moses also occur in *ParsT* (X.195, 355–6).

Muses

Classical goddesses, patrons of the arts. The Muses were envisaged as nine sisters, each of whom was identified with a particular art form. Chaucer refers individually to three of them, each in an invocation: to Clio (muse of history) in *Tr* (2.8–14), to Calliope (heroic poetry) in *Tr* (3.45–9), and to Polyhymnia (sacred song) in *Anel* (15–20). Allusions to the Muses as a group occur in *MerT* (IV.1735) and *MLIntro* (II.92) – where they are termed 'Pierides' from their place of birth, Pieria (see note in Benson, 1987: 856). In *Bo* (1.p.1.44ff.), Lady *Philosophy dismisses the Muses, calling them strumpets. In *Scog* (38–9) Chaucer uses the striking image of his sleepy and rusting muse.

mystery plays

Biblical drama, composed in cycle form. Chaucer alludes to the representation in the mystery plays of *Pilate, *Herod, and *Noah in *MilP* and *MilT* (I.3124, 3384, 3538–43 respectively). A less specific allusion to attendance at performances of plays on religious subjects occurs in *WBP* (III.558).

N

Narcissus *see **Romaunt of the Rose, The***

Nature

Personification in *PF*. Nature is represented as a benign deity, presiding over the birds' parliament in *PF* (302ff.). The word 'nature' is sometimes capitalized elsewhere in editions of Chaucer (e.g. *GP* I.11; *PhyT* VI.9; *Tr* 4.251), to indicate a semi-personified figure.

Nebuchadnezzar

(*c*. 630–562 BC)
King of Babylon. The story of Nebuchadnezzar ('Nabugodonosor') from the Book of *Daniel is included among the 'tragedies' which comprise *MkT* (VII.2143ff./B^2.3333ff.). This account stresses the triumph, pride, and power of Nebuchadnezzar, his sudden transformation into someone who lives like a beast, and his later subservience to God's will. Daniel's advice to him is mentioned both here and in *ParsT* (X.126). There are also passing references to Nebuchadnezzar in the tragedy of Holofernes (*MkT* VII.2562/B^2.3752) and in *HF* (515).

Nero

(37–68)
Nero Claudius Caesar, infamous Roman emperor. The story of Nero in *MkT* (VII.2463ff./B^2.3653ff.), based mainly on *RR* (6183ff.), is told as the 'tragedy' of a man who falls from a position of great eminence. It mentions Nero's virtuous youth and the positive influence of his tutor *Seneca, but concentrates on his evil deeds – among them killing his brother and committing incest with his sister, causing the death of his mother by cutting open her womb, precipitating the suicide of Seneca, and burning Rome, thus causing the deaths of numerous senators. The story is also told and discussed at various junctures in *Bo* (2.m.6.1ff.; 3.m.4.1ff.; 3.p.5.47ff.). There are passing allusions to it in *KnT* (I.2032) and *NPT* (VII.3369–73/B^2.4559–63) – the former serious, the latter comic.

Nessus

Maker of the poisoned shirt which kills *Hercules in *MkT*. Chaucer describes how *Deianira gives Hercules the shirt without intending him any harm (VII.2119–34/B².3309–24), but does not mention that Nessus was a centaur, who poisoned the shirt with his dying blood after being fatally wounded by Hercules (see *Ovid, *Metamorphoses* 9.98ff.).

New Chaucer Society

Society for the promotion of Chaucerian scholarship. The New Chaucer Society was founded in 1978. It publishes a yearbook, *Studies in the Age of Chaucer*.

Newefangelnesse see Against Women Unconstant

Nicholas

Young male protagonist of *MilT*. Nicholas is an Oxford scholar who seduces *Alison, the attractive young wife of *John, the elderly carpenter with whom he lodges. Though Nicholas outwits John by means of ingenious plotting, he suffers a painful comic reversal at the hands of the effete *Absolon, his rival for the favours of Alison. It has been suggested that his name alludes to that of the astronomer *Nicholas of Lynne – which would be appropriate, given the apparent interest of Nicholas in astronomy (see *MilT* I.3209, 3449ff.).

Nicholas of Lynne

(fl. late 14th century)
Writer on astronomy. Nicholas was a Carmelite friar, based in Oxford. Chaucer cites him (along with John *Somer), in *Astr* (Prologue, 84–6), and uses his *Kalendarium* (1386) in the passages on the astronomical specification of time in *MLIntro* (II.1ff.) and *ParsP* (X.2ff.). *See also*: **Nicholas**.

Nicolas, Sir Nicholas Harris *see* **Chaucer, Geoffrey;**
Nicole de Margival *see* ***House of Fame, The***

Nigel of Longchamps

(fl. late 12th century)
Author, also known as Nigel Wireker. An allusion to Nigel's *Speculum Stultorum* ('The mirror of fools'), a popular *beast epic relating the comic adventures of Burnellus the ass, occurs in *NPT* (VII.3312–16/B².4502–6).

Noah

Old Testament patriarch. The allusions to Noah ('Noe') in *MilT* (I.3534ff.), made in connection with the supposed threat of a second Flood, reflect both the story of the Flood in Genesis (6–9) and the treatment of this story in the *mystery plays (see especially I.3538–43). Noah is also mentioned briefly in *ParsT* (X.766ff.).

Norfolk

County in East Anglia. The *Reeve is said to come from *Bawdeswell in Norfolk (*GP* I.619–20).

Northumberland

Anglo-Saxon kingdom of Northumbria, a setting in *MLT*. This is identified as the kingdom of *Alla (*MLT* II.575–81). The historical Ælla was, in fact, king only of Deira, the southern part of Northumbria – which was later combined with the more northerly kingdom of Bernicia, to form the (relatively) large and powerful kingdom of Northumbria.

Nun *see* Prioress; Second Nun

Nun's Priest

Pilgrim and teller in *CT*. While *GP* does not contain a portrait of the Nun's Priest, it is generally supposed that he can be regarded as one of the 'preestes thre', mentioned among the attendants of the *Prioress (I.163–4). It has been conjectured that Chaucer may have intended to add portraits of some or all of this group in due course. The *Host's brief description of the Nun's Priest, as a large, handsome man, who would have made a good lover if only he were secular, is contained in a passage which was probably cancelled (*NPE* VII.3447–62/B^2.4637–52). The status of this description is, therefore, doubtful.

Nun's Priest's Prologue, Tale, and Epilogue, The

Prologue, *beast fable, and epilogue from Fragment VII (Group B^2) of *CT*. *NPP* begins with the *Knight's interruption of the preceding *MkT*. The Knight shows considerable tact when he asks the *Monk to stop, suggesting that his audience has by now heard enough stories with unhappy endings, and would rather hear some that end happily. This view is endorsed by the *Host, who offers a bluntly unflattering assessment of the Monk's skills as a teller, echoes *MkT* (VII.2761–6/B^2.3951–6) in a disparaging manner, and states that it nearly bored him to sleep. His request that the Monk should tell another tale, perhaps about hunting, is met with a sullen refusal. The Host then turns to the *Nun's Priest, commenting jovially on his wretched horse – thus perhaps implying a contrast with the splendidly-mounted Monk (see I.168–72, 207) – and asking him to tell a merry tale. The Nun's Priest graciously agrees to do so.

Commentators have regarded this as a passage which draws attention, in the course of reflections on *MkT*, to issues concerning the function of literature, generic expectations, and audience response. It also raises textual issues, since *NPP* survives in two different forms, one significantly longer than the other. The longer version (the content of which is summarized above) survives in a majority of the manuscripts and is printed in virtually all editions. The shorter version omits some twenty lines (2771–90/3961–80) and attributes the interruption of the Monk to the Host. It seems likely that this constitutes an early draft, revised in a form represented by the longer version. The issue does, however, involve further complications: while the shorter version attributes the interruption to the Knight in some manuscripts, the longer version attributes it to the Host in others. Though the precise cause of these divergent readings remains a matter for conjecture, it is clear that they arose from the process of revision – evidence of which also occurs in *NPE*. This passage (3447–62/4637–52), which comprises the Host's (positive) response to *NPT* and includes his observations on the appearance of its teller, survives in only a relatively small number of manuscripts. Since there is no portrait of the Nun's Priest in *GP*, a description of him – even from a witness as unreliable as the Host – has seemed particularly appealing. It does, however, seem probable that Chaucer cancelled these lines when he wrote *MkP*, where the image of the 'trede-foul' (3451/4641) is applied to the Monk (1945/3135). Thus it remains uncertain whether this brief but striking description represents Chaucer's final intentions regarding the teller of *NPT*.

Whatever the uncertainties about its teller, the tale is among the most distinctive and captivating in *CT*. On the slight basis of a beast fable about a cock and a fox, Chaucer constructs an elaborate and sophisticated narrative, which engages with a wide range of issues. He exploits the potential, offered by this genre, for the animals simultaneously to represent human traits and display characteristics appropriate to their actual species. Thus *Chauntecleer can exemplify the intellectual confidence of an arrogant man, especially in his relationship with *Pertelote (e.g. 2970ff./4160ff., 3157–66/4347–56), while still behaving like a cock, notably with regard to the sexual mores and activities of the hen-coop and the farmyard (e.g. 2865–7/4055–7, 3177–8/ 4367–8). In the opening sequence, Chaucer establishes a contrast between the dullness of the human world, represented in the life of the poor and temperate widow, and the splendour of the animal world, in which her chickens, especially Chauntecleer and Pertelote, are described as aristocrats in all their colourful finery. Whereas the humans barely speak at all (see 3380–1/4570–1), the main animal protagonists, Chauntecleer, Pertelote, and *Russell the fox, are conspicuously articulate. This characteristic is evident especially in the two main episodes, the long debate between Chauntecleer and Pertelote on the significance of dreams (2908ff./4098ff.) and the attempt of Russell first to flatter and then to seize Chauntecleer (3282ff./4472ff.).

Commentators have considered *NPT* a stylistic triumph, pointing out that Chaucer uses a mock heroic style simultaneously to assert and to deflate the splendour of his protagonists and the significance of their actions and concerns. The moral comments offered by the narrator throughout the tale, and especially at the end (3438–46/4628–36), may seem specifically to encourage interpretation. *NPT* has, indeed, been interpreted in various ways – as, for instance, an allegory of the Fall or a sermon on moral awareness – but no such reading has seemed entirely convincing. It may, perhaps, be in the nature of this tale to offer various partial and (at times) competing views, none of which is unequivocally endorsed. In the process, it provides a mildly satirical comment on the view of tragedy expressed in *MkT* (3204–9/4394–9) and takes up several of the issues raised earlier in *CT*, especially those concerning gender. Thus, for instance, Chauntecleer's attitude to sex (3342–6/ 4532–6) would seem broadly to coincide with that of the *Wife of Bath, as expressed in *WBP*, while the narrator's tentative comment on women's advice (3252–62/4442–52) contradicts the views established in *Mel* (VII.1055ff./B².2245ff.,1724–5/2914–15) and *WBT* (III.1230–5).

The story of the cock and the fox, which lies at the heart of *NPT*, is ultimately derived from beast fable. Commentators have suggested that Chaucer may have known the version in the twelfth-century fables of Marie de France. The inclusion of this story in *beast epic – as an episode in the adventures of Renard the fox – is, however, of more immediate relevance. Chaucer's main source appears to have been a version of *Le Roman de Renart*, an anonymous French compilation dating from the late twelfth and early thirteenth centuries, which would have provided elements such as the prophetic dream and the originals of the main protagonists (Chantecler, Pinte, and Renart). The story also occurs in contemporary sermon collections. For the observations of Chauntecleer on the significance of dreams (including the exemplary stories), Chaucer drew on *Holcot's commentary on the apocryphal Book of Wisdom. The laxatives prescribed by Pertelote reflect material found in medical texts and encyclopedias. *NPT* contains allusions to various other stories, authorities, and works, including *Geoffrey de Vinsauf, the legend of St *Kenelm, *Physiologus, the fall of *Troy, and several books of the Old Testament.

Commentators have generally supposed that *NPT* was a written late in Chaucer's career, specifically for its current position in *CT*. If so, then the passing allusion to the *Peasants' Revolt of 1381 (3393–7/4583–7) would refer to an event some years in the past (which may help to explain its flippant tone). Other than a spurious couplet, the manuscripts contain few variants in the text of *NPT*. The substantial and significant variants in *NPP* and *NPE* are considered above. A free translation of *NPT*, entitled *The Cock and the Fox*, was written by *Dryden.

Further reading: Cooper (1996); Pearsall (1983); Edward Wheatley in Correale and Hamel (2002).

O

Octavian *see* **Augustus Caesar**

octosyllabic couplet

Form used by Chaucer in some of his early work. The octosyllabic couplet was widely used in French poetry (including *RR), and may well have seemed a natural choice for the translation of *Rom* and the composition of *BD* and *HF*. It is superseded in Chaucer's work by the longer and more flexible *decasyllabic couplet.

Odenathus *see* **Zenobia; Oenone** *see* **Paris**

old man

Two mysterious figures in *CT*: one in *PardT*, the other in *SNT*. In *PardT* (VI.711ff.) the old man is accosted by the three 'rioters', describes himself as someone who yearns for the end of his own life, and tells them where they can find *Death. In *SNT* (VIII.200–17), the old man questions Valerian at his baptism on matters of faith, appearing and disappearing without explanation.

Olifaunt, Sir *see* **Elephant, Sir**

Oliver

Heroic figure from the *Song of Roland*. Oliver is contrasted to the traitor *Ganelon in *BD* (1121–3) and *MkT* (VII.2387–90/B².3577–80). In the latter he is termed 'Charles Olyver' (i.e. 'Charlemagne's Oliver'), and distinguished from 'Genylon (i.e. Ganelon)-Olyver' – a reference to Oliver de Mauny who betrayed *Pedro I of Castile.

Origenes upon the Maudeleyne

Lost work by Chaucer. It has generally been supposed that the allusion to 'Origenes upon the Maudeleyne' in the list of Chaucer's works provided in *LGWP* (F.427–8/G.417–18) signifies a lost translation or adaptation of the popular Latin homily, *De Maria Magdalena*, which dated from the late twelfth or early thirteenth century, but was regularly attributed to the early theologian Origen (*c.* 185–*c.* 254). The statement that this work 'goon ys a gret while' has been taken to indicate that it was written early in Chaucer's career. *Lydgate cites it as a translation by Chaucer in *The Fall of Princes* (1.316–18).

Orion *see* Arion

Orléans

French city. Orléans features in *FranT* (V.1116ff.) as the location of a university and home of the clerk skilled in natural magic. The magician *Colle, mentioned in *HF* (1277–81), may have been associated with Orléans.

Orpheus

Legendary harper and poet. The story of Orpheus and Eurydice – derived from *Virgil's *Georgics* (4.454ff.) and *Ovid's *Metamorphoses* (10.1ff.) – is told in *Bo* (3.m.12) and mentioned in *Tr* (4.788–91). Allusions to Orpheus as a peerless musician occur in *BD* (569), *HF* (1201–3), and *MerT* (IV.1715–17).

Orwell

Formerly a port on the estuary of the river Orwell in Suffolk. The concern of the *Merchant regarding the protection of sea trade between Orwell and *Middelburgh is reported in *GP* (I.276–7).

Osney

Village in Oxfordshire, now a suburb of Oxford, mentioned in *MilT*. The absence of *John in Osney twice provides *Nicholas with opportunities for pursuing his amorous interest in *Alison. Subsequently, *Absolon is described as making enquiries in Osney regarding John's whereabouts.

Oswald *see* **Reeve; Oton de Granson** *see* **Granson, Oton de;
'ottava rima'** *see* **rhyme royal**

Ovid

(43 BC–17 AD)

Publius Ovidius Naso, Roman poet. Ovid's influence on Chaucer's work is
more substantial than that of any other classical author. It operates not only
directly but also indirectly – through commentaries, collections of extracts,
translations, versions (notably the *Ovide moralisé*), and the works of other
writers, themselves influenced by Ovid. In some passages, it has proved difficult to establish with any certainty whether the influence of Ovid is direct
or indirect. Chaucer refers to Ovid by name twenty times – most memorably
when he includes him among the poets to whom *Tr* is dedicated (5.1792).
On three occasions – all in *LGW* (725, 928, 2220) – Ovid is termed 'Naso'.

In *HF* (1486–96) Chaucer identifies Ovid specifically as a great love poet.
This reflects the fame of three works, the *Amores* ('Loves'), the *Ars amatoria*
('The art of love'), and the *Remedia amoris* ('Remedies for love'). It is not clear
whether Chaucer had any direct knowledge of the *Amores*. The influence of
the *Ars amatoria*, mentioned in *WBP* (III.680) as a component of *Jankin's
*'book of wicked wives', may well have been largely derived from other
authors and works, especially *RR*. Passing allusions to the *Remedia amoris*
occur in *BD* (568), *Mel* (VII.976/B².2166), and (probably) *GP* (I.475).

Chaucer's indebtedness to Ovid's *Heroides* ('Heroines') and *Metamorphoses*
('Transformations') is altogether more substantial. The *Heroides* consists
mainly of a series of letters from wronged or abandoned women to their
absent husbands or lovers. The influence of this concept is reflected in the
complaint of *Anelida (in *Anel*), in the letters of *Troilus and *Criseyde in *Tr*,
and (especially) throughout *LGW*. Various legends, including *Dido, Phyllis*,
and *Hypermnestra*, are partly based on the *Heroides*. It seems likely that the
same would have been true of several other legends, mentioned in *MLIntro*
(II.60ff.) and presumably either lost or never written, including those of
*Penelope and *Deianire. In *Hypermnestra* and *Ariadne* Chaucer appears to
draw on *Ceffi's translation of the *Heroides*. *Lucrece* is based on another of
Ovid's works, the *Fasti* ('Calendar'). Chaucer's indebtedness to Ovid's
Metamorphoses is even more ubiquitous than that to the *Heroides*. The
Metamorphoses comprises a collection of stories, which provide a rich source
of mythic material, on which Chaucer draws extensively. He uses this not
only for individual stories – such as those of *Ceyx and *Alcione in *BD*, of
*Phoebus and the *crow in *MancT*, of *Mars and *Venus in *Mars*, and of

*Thisbe, *Ariadne, and *Philomela in *LGW* – but also for a great range of mythic events, places, encounters, and relationships to which he alludes more briefly. These include the use of Ovid's palace of Fame as a model for the House of Rumour in *HF* (1924ff.), the adaptation of the story of *Midas and his ears in *WBT* (III.952ff.), and allusions to that of the Caledonian boar hunt in *Tr* (5.1464ff.) and in *KnT* (I.2069–72).

Ovide moralisé

French poem, based on *Ovid's *Metamorphoses*. The *Ovide moralisé* is a long poem, written in the early fourteenth century by an unknown Franciscan poet, who apparently set out to reconcile the *Metamorphoses* with Christian values and doctrine. It has been suggested that Chaucer drew on this work in *Philomela* (*LGW* 2228ff.).

Oxford

University town, setting for *MilT*. Oxford ('Oxenford[e]') is identified as the university of the *Clerk (*GP* 285, *ClP* IV.1) and of *Jankin (*WBP* III.527). By inference, it would also be that of *Nicholas in *MilT*. Critics have suggested that one of the ways in which *RvT* responds to *MilT* is by countering a tale set in Oxford with a tale set near *Cambridge. While no precise definition of the Oxford style of dancing – as demonstrated by *Absolon in *MilT* (I.3328–30) – has been established, the allusion has generally been interpreted as satirical. The various references to the latitude of Oxford in *Astr* (Prologue 10, 106; 2.22.6; 2.25.26–7) may indicate that Lewis *Chaucer was at school there. The claim made in some early biographies, to the effect that Chaucer himself was at university in Oxford, appears to have no basis in fact.

P

Padua

Italian city mentioned in *ClP*. The *Clerk claims to have learned his tale in Padua from *Petrarch himself (IV.26ff.). This allusion has led to speculation that Chaucer might have met Petrarch – who was living in Padua when Chaucer visited Italy in 1372–73, and to whom he is, indeed, indebted in *ClT*. It does, however, seem unlikely that a writer of Petrarch's status and self-importance would have taken any interest in an obscure young poet from England. Records indicate that it was not unusual for scholars from *Oxford to visit Padua in order to study.

Palamon

Theban prince in *KnT*. Palamon is based on Palemone in the *Teseida* of *Boccaccio. He and his cousin and brother in arms, *Arcite, are the two young male protagonists of *KnT*. After being captured and imprisoned by *Theseus, they become bitter rivals for the love of *Emily. Though the two cousins are portrayed as essentially alike, Palamon is, perhaps, represented as more reflective and gentler than Arcite – as may be suggested by their contrasting initial responses to falling in love (I.1070ff.) and by their respective devotion to *Venus and to *Mars.

Palamon and Arcite see Knight's Tale, The;
Palatye *see* Balat; Palladium *see* Pallas Athene

Pallas Athene

Goddess of wisdom. Chaucer normally calls this goddess 'Pallas', from her Greek name, Pallas Athene, but also uses her Roman name, Minerva. Allusions and appeals to her, some of them specifically associated with wisdom, occur in several works, including *Tr* (2.425–7, 1062–3; 5.977–8), *BD* (1072), *Anel* (5), and *PhyT* (VI.49). The religious festival in which the Trojans express their devotion to Pallas Athene before her image, the Palladium ('Palladion'), provides the occasion for *Troilus to fall in love with *Criseyde (*Tr* 1.148ff.). A brief passage in *Dido* (*LGW* 930–3) mentions that the wooden horse was offered to Minerva.

Pamphilus

Male protagonist of a poem about love. The *Pamphilus de Amore* is a Latin poetic dialogue, probably written in England during the late twelfth century, describing the love between Pamphilus and Galatea. While in *Mel* (VII.1556–61/B².2746–51) Chaucer cites this poem on the subject of wealth, in *FranT* (V.1109–12) he compares the conduct of *Aurelius to that of Pamphilus. The similarities between the sequence of events leading to the consummation of love in *Tr* with that in the *Pamphilus de Amore* have led to the suggestion that the latter may have had some (minor) influence on Chaucer's poem.

Pandarus

Friend of *Troilus and uncle of *Criseyde; go-between in *Tr*. Chaucer based Pandarus on Pandaro, the cousin of Criseida in *Boccaccio's *Il Filostrato*. He turns a youthful and rather callow nobleman into an engaging and distinctive character, presumably a good deal older, and a constant source of advice to both Troilus and Criseyde – comic, talkative, energetic, and manipulative. The discourse of Pandarus is full of worldly wisdom, often expressed in proverbial sayings. Though he has personally been a failure in love (like the narrator of *Tr*), he presents himself as an expert on the conduct of a successful affair, and pursues his role of go-between with great resourcefulness and determination. He emerges as a decidedly mixed character: while he is generally helpful, practical, good-humoured and self-deprecating, he also proves willing not only to cajole Criseyde but also to alarm her by inventing threats in order to persuade her to accept Troilus as her lover. Both aspects of Pandarus are evident in the long and memorable sequence leading up to the consummation scene (3.554ff.).

Pandion

King of *Athens, father of *Procne and *Philomela. In *Philomela* (*LGW* 2228ff.), Chaucer describes how Pandion's daughters are grievously wronged by *Tereus.

Panik

Countship in Italy. The sister of *Walter in *ClT* (IV.590) is described as the countess of Panik – a modified version of Panico in Chaucer's source, a story by *Petrarch.

Parcae *see* **Fates**

Pardoner

Pilgrim and teller in *CT*. The portrait of the Pardoner is the last of the series in *GP* (I.669ff.) and has often been contrasted with the first, that of the *Knight. Traditional interpretation would regard the Knight as a model of chivalry and ethical conduct, and the Pardoner as an epitome of evil and corruption – though both views have been challenged and qualified. If this link is only implicit, that with the *Summoner has a specific basis in the text (669–74). While the two of them are clearly represented here as companions, this notion does not recur later in *CT*; nor does the possible suggestion, in the allusion to their duet (672–4), of a homosexual relationship between them. The sexuality of the Pardoner does, however, receive further attention, direct and indirect, both in *GP* and elsewhere. The detailed description of his notably effeminate appearance (675–91) has been related to accounts of eunuchs in physiognomical texts, and has provided the basis for various interpretations of the Pardoner – as a natural eunuch, a spiritual eunuch, a hermaphrodite, and a homosexual. Some commentators have argued that the final line of this passage, with its acknowledgement of uncertainty, should encourage an open mind on the issue of the Pardoner's sexuality. The issue recurs, at least by implication, in his interruption of *WBP* (III.163ff.) – where he states that the comments of the *Wife of Bath on marriage are causing him to reconsider his intention to marry – and in the altercation at the end of *PardT* (VI.941ff.), which may suggest that the *Host perceives him as some kind of sexual deviant (cf. VI.318). Several other aspects of the portrait are developed later in *CT* – to a degree unparalleled in any case other than that of the Wife. This is, doubtless, related to the fact that she and the Pardoner are the only pilgrims who offer, in the prologues to their tales, lengthy and revealing accounts of their conduct and opinions. In the case of the Pardoner, the account of his false relics, and of how he uses these and his preaching skills to fleece simple people (694ff.) prove a rich basis for *PardP* and *PardT*. The statement in this passage, to the effect that he gains more in one day than a poor country parson gets in two months, has led some commentators to contrast him with the *Parson. More generally, the portrait has been related to satire on the corruption of pardoners and to contemporary disquiet about their conduct – some of which was specifically associated with *Rouncivale (670).

Further reading: Andrew (1993); Mann (1973).

Pardoner's Introduction, Prologue, and Tale, The

Introduction, confessional prologue, and exemplary tale from Fragment VI of *CT*. A link between *PardP* and the preceding *PhyT* is provided by *PardIntro*. Here, the *Host responds to the pathos of *PhyT*, maintaining that the gifts of fortune and of nature cause many deaths (VI.294–300). It has been suggested that, while the death of *Virginia in *PhyT* could be attributed to her beauty (a gift of nature), that of the three 'rioters' in *PardT* could be attributed to their discovery of the gold (a gift of fortune). There is, in any case, a clear pattern of parallel and contrast between *PhyT* and *PardT*: both are moral tales about death; but whereas one concerns the killing of an innocent victim, the other describes the self-destruction of three villains. The Host asks the *Physician for medicine to help him recover his equanimity before going on to request a comic tale from the *Pardoner, whom he addresses as 'thou beel amy' (318) – probably a disrespectful allusion to his effeminate appearance, as described in *GP* (I.675–91). The impression this has made is, presumably, also suggested in the response of the 'gentils' (cf. *MilP* I.3109–13), who assert that the Pardoner should not be allowed to tell a ribald tale. He agrees to think of 'some honest thyng' while drinking at a tavern.

The performance of the Pardoner in *PardP* and *PardT* proves simultaneously 'honest' and dishonest. He provides a powerful exemplary tale on the theme of greed as the root of all evil (*PardP* VI.334, 426), while clearly indicating that he is profoundly guilty of the vice he condemns (423–34). Throughout *PardP*, he appears to enjoy revealing the techniques he uses to fleece the simple people in his congregations. *PardT* is told as an *exemplum presented when he preaches, and comprises two contrasting elements: explication and narrative. The former consists of vivid description and exclamatory condemnation of the 'tavern sins' of drunkenness, gluttony, dicing, and swearing, supported by the citation of authorities and examples. The latter, by contrast, is notably spare and economical. It provides a chilling account of how the three 'rioters' set out to kill *Death, who has been killing their fellow revellers during an outbreak of the plague in *Flanders (692ff.). They show neither moral awareness nor understanding of what their objective might signify; motivated by greed, they end up by killing each other. Since they are clearly representative figures, it seems appropriate that they are not named. The only other significant figure in the story is the *old man, again unnamed, who tells them where they can find Death, in the form of a hoard of gold (760ff.). While the symbolic potential of his role has led to various specific interpretations, it seems probable that he remains an essentially ambiguous figure.

Commentators offer notably diverse interpretations of the Pardoner's motivation for revealing his own cynicism and fraudulence, taking this to reflect a contradictory urge to be honest, the desire to entertain, or the need for acceptance or approval. Readings of his apparent miscalculation at the end of the tale are also diverse: while some see his attempt to sell relics he has admitted to be false as a joke or a wild gamble, others suggest that he loses track of which audience he is addressing, as this changes from an imagined congregation to the actual audience of his fellow pilgrims. It is often supposed that his behaviour throughout indicates the effects of drink (following the allusions to drinking in a tavern: see above). The Host's vitriolic response when the Pardoner singles him out as a particularly sinful man has been seen as a symbolic castration, and sometimes taken to suggest discomfort with the Pardoner's sexuality. The role of the Knight in resolving the quarrel has seemed appropriate, given the social status and ethical conduct attributed to him in *GP* (I.43ff.).

PardP is generally regarded as a confessional prologue, like *WBP*. Commentators have observed that it reflects the influence of the confession of Faus Semblant in **RR* (11,065ff.) – equivalent to **Fals-Semblant in *Rom* (6082ff.). (It has been noted that some of the verbal echoes are closer to *Rom* than to *RR*.) The conduct of the Pardoner, especially in *PardP*, has been related to that of Fra Cipolla in **Boccaccio's *Decameron* (6.10). The fact that the Pardoner presents his tale as an exemplum in a sermon has led commentators to relate some aspects of the structure of *PardP* and *PardT* to the established conventions of sermon structure. Condemnation of the 'tavern sins' (see above), as in *PardP*, is a particularly common theme in sermon literature. Chaucer's treatment of this topic also draws on material from works including the *De miseria conditionis humane* of **Innocent III and the *Epistola adversus Jovinianum* of St **Jerome. The story told in *PardT* has its origins in folktale; while numerous analogues have been found, none is particularly close.

Commentators have normally assumed that *PardP* and *PardT* were written simultaneously, since they work so well together; it is, however, clear that the tale could stand alone. In the absence of any particular evidence regarding the date of composition, they are usually assigned to much the same period as the tales of fragments III, IV, and V: the early to mid-1390s. The manuscripts contain only minor variants and a few glosses.

Further reading: Cooper (1996); Mary Hamel in Correale and Hamel (2002).

Paris

Principal city of **France. Chaucer appears to have visited Paris several times on diplomatic business (see Crow and Olson, 1966: 44–53). He mentions Parisian **French in the portrait of the **Prioress (*GP* I.126). Other allusions to

Paris are made only in passing – as in *ShT* (VII.57, 332, 366/B².1247, 1522, 1556), *WBP* (III.678), and *Rom* (1654).

Paris

Lover of *Helen; brother of *Troilus. Chaucer establishes near the beginning of *Tr* (1.57–63) that the abduction of Helen by Paris caused the Trojan war. Otherwise, the significance of Paris in *Tr* seems slight (see 2.1447–9, 4.608–9), though his betrayal of Oenone, his previous love, is mentioned both here (1.653–65) and in *HF* (399). Passing allusions to Paris also occur in *BD* (331), *PF* (290), *SqT* (V.548), and *MerT* (IV.1754).

Parlement of Foules, The

*Dream vision on the nature and varieties of love. *PF* is generally acknowledged to be Chaucer's first poem composed entirely in the *rhyme royal stanza (a verse form he also used in part of *Anel*, which may well be earlier). Though most commentators would take *PF* to have been written after *HF*, both poems have sometimes been associated with the same event: the betrothal, in 1381, of Richard II to *Anne of Bohemia. This reading of *PF*, based on the last part of the poem (lines 365ff.), takes the formel eagle to represent Anne and the tercel eagles her three suitors (Richard II, Charles of France, and Friedrich of Meissen). This hypothesis is, however, weakened by the formel's reluctance to choose a mate, and the consequent postponement of her decision. It remains likely that *PF* was written in the early 1380s, possibly for a St *Valentine's day celebration.

While *PF* is clearly a poem about love, interpretation of its meaning has been varied. Such diversity of opinion comes as no great surprise, given the mingling of serious and comic material in the poem, and the conspicuously divergent kinds of love with which it engages. *PF* begins, like *BD*, with a narrator who has a dream based on a book – in this case, the *Somnium Scipionis* of *Cicero. The authority figure who emerges from this work, *Scipio the Elder (or Africanus), expresses a sternly ethical world view, stressing the insigificance of earthly glory, the immortality of the soul, and the importance of love for the common good (43ff.). He becomes the narrator's guide, escorting him to the gate of the garden of love, and (perhaps inappropriately for such a dignified person) pushing him through it when, confronted with an inscription about the positive and negative powers of love, he hesitates (120ff.). Within the garden, the narrator has two markedly different encounters: first with the temple of *Venus (211ff.), and then (at greater length) with the birds' parliament (295ff.). The former is a setting which portrays erotic love as a powerful but often destructive force, in a somewhat voyeuristic description. The latter respresents the urge to mate as a natural process, presided over by the authoritative but benign figure of the goddess *Nature. This context is, however, by no means free from tension: the impatience of the various groups of ordinary birds (worm fowl, seed fowl, and so on) with the protracted (and ultimately fruitless) courtship ritual of the aristocratic eagles reflects both their lack of refinement and their common sense, and leads to some splendid comic dialogue. Whether the tensions generated by this thinly disguised social satire are resolved when the birds sing their final celebratory song is a matter for interpretation. So are the broader issues of whether Chaucer implies that the various kinds of love explored in *PF* can be harmonized in some way, or that one of them should be seen as pre-eminent. Recent criticism has tended to regard *PF* as essentially open-minded and non-judgemental – as the comments of the narrator in the last stanza may suggest.

Though *PF* is a notably original and distinctive poem, Chaucer drew on several traditions and individual works in its composition. Near the opening, he summarizes material from Cicero's *Somnium Scipionis* (as preserved for the Middle Ages by *Macrobius). The inscription over the gateway to the garden echoes *Dante (*Inferno* 3.1–9). While the garden itself reflects the general influence of *RR, part of the description of the temple of Venus is more closely based on *Boccaccio's *Teseida* (7: 50–66). Chaucer derived the figure of Nature from the *De planctu naturae* of *Alan of Lille – a debt he duly acknowledges (*PF* 316–18). The themes and devices of the dream vision are significant throughout, as the frame of *PF* and the brief account of dream lore (99ff.) may suggest. Chaucer was also influenced by the genre of debate poetry, in which contradictory views are presented and discussed – and sometimes resolved. Such poems can involve birds, which are portrayed in accordance with characteristics traditionally ascribed to them in such works as bestiaries and encyclopedias. The use of traditional material does, however, not preclude genuine observation from nature: thus, for instance, Chaucer correctly identifies the hedge sparrow as the normal victim of the cuckoo (612). *PF* may also initiate a new tradition, that of poems for St Valentine's day. While the development of this idea is not entirely clear, it appears again in *Mars* and the doubtfully attributed *Compl d'Am*, in two poems by John *Gower, and in two by Oton de *Granson.

PF is preserved in 14 manuscripts (a relatively high number by comparison with *BD* and *HF*) and in an early edition printed by *Caxton. The text of the *roundel (680–92) reflects scribal confusion; the version of these lines printed in most modern editions is derived from *Skeat's reconstruction. Otherwise, textual variants are relatively insigificant. *Clanvowe's poem, *The Book of Cupid*, would seem to have been strongly influenced by *PF*.

Further reading: Minnis (1995); Windeatt (1982).

Parnassus

Mount Parnassus, sacred to the *Muses. Allusions to Parnassus ('Pernaso', 'Parnaso') – all in connection with the Muses – occur in *HF* (521), *Anel* (16), *Tr* (3.1810), and *FranP* (V.721).

Parson

Pilgrim and teller in *CT*. The portrait of the Parson in *GP* (I.477ff.) is placed between those of the *Wife of Bath (445ff.) and the *Plowman (529ff.). Commentators have regularly detected a contrast with the former's assertive individualism and a parallel with the quiet piety of the latter – subsequently termed his 'brother' (529). The Parson has also been contrasted with the other members of the clergy described in *GP*, all of whom appear to be worldly, and identified with a group of pilgrims regarded as ideal – in which he is normally joined by the *Knight, the Plowman, and (sometimes) the *Clerk. The portrait has frequently been related to anti-clerical satire; it has been noted that, by specifying the vices from which the Parson was free, Chaucer both defines his virtue and implies the vices of other priests (see 486–9, 498–518, 525–8). The ideal is, however, not without its contentious aspect: the Parson has often been described as a Wycliffite or *Lollard. Indeed, it was partly on the basis of this portrait that Chaucer was regarded in the sixteenth and seventeenth centuries as a writer who anticipated the Reformation. While the suggestion of some early commentators that the portrait was based on *Wyclif no longer attracts significant endorsement, a majority of their present-day successors would probably agree that it has a mildly Lollard air. This view derives subsequent support when the *Host twice refers to the Parson as a 'Lollere' (*MLE* II.1172–7). It has often been pointed out that, though the portrait provides an account of the Parson's way of life in his rural parish, including his characteristic behaviour and style of teaching, it does not mention his physical appearance. Some critics have detected a suggestion of his voice in the vividly aphoristic style of certain lines (especially 498–504). The portrait provided the basis for *Dryden's poem, *The Character of a Good Parson*.

Further reading: Andrew (1993); Mann (1973).

Parson's Prologue and Tale, The

Significant prologue (in verse) and pentitential tale (in prose) from Fragment X of *CT*. *ParsP* opens with a link to the preceding *MancT*, which might appear to indicate that fragments IX and X should be regarded as a single unit. The allusions to time in the two texts are, however, not entirely compatible: though the events described in *MancP* apparently occur during the morning (IX.16), by the time the *Manciple has finished his brief tale, it is already four in the afternoon (X.1–5). This could be taken to suggest that there was scope for inserting further tales between *MancT* and *ParsT*. Be that as it may, the *Host now plainly states that the *Parson is the only pilgrim who has not told a tale, and invites him to do so, in order to bring the series to a fitting conclusion (24–8).

While the *Parson consents, he rejects the Host's suggestion that he should relate a fable (29), going on to dismiss all 'swich wrecchednesse' (including both 'rym' and *alliterative verse) on the authority of St *Paul (31–47). He does, however, agree to tell a moral tale in prose, and, moreover, to show his audience the way of the 'parfit glorious pilgrymage' to 'Jerusalem celestial' (46–51). The implied transformation of the pilgrimage to Canterbury into a spiritual equivalent seems clear. Commentators have also perceived a connection between the warning about careless talk in the preceding *MancT*, the rejection of literary fiction here, and Chaucer's own apparent repudiation of all his own work other than that on explicitly moral topics in the following *Ret*.

ParsT proves to be less a tale, in the normal sense of the word, than a treatise, written in plain prose. It has been regarded as broadly appropriate to the Parson, whose commitment to the instruction of his parishioners is stressed in his portrait in *GP* (I.480–2, 527–8). While *ParsT* begins like a sermon, with a text – fittingly, one on the good way (Jer. 6:16) – it soon takes on the character of a treatise on the subject of penitence. This is identified as the means of combating sin, which can deflect a man or woman from 'the righte wey of Jerusalem celestial' (80) – the echo making a connection with the statement of the Parson's intentions in his prologue. The tale progresses in expository style, offering a series of relevant facts, including the meaning of penitence and its three essential components. The latter – contrition (regret for one's sins), confession (the actual process of confessing to a priest), and satisfaction (making amends and reparation) – provide the basic structure of the work. An account of contrition (127–315) is followed by the main body of the treatise, on confession (316–1028), and a brief passage on satisfaction (1029–75). The relative bulk of the central section reflects the fact that it provides a definition and discussion of each of the *Seven Deadly Sins in turn, together with the remedies appropriate to them. Though the style generally matches the seriousness of the subject matter, it is lightened by flashes of grotesque humour, by startling similes, and by brief but vivid descriptions of wicked or foolish conduct – as when the compulsive behaviour of an elderly lecher is compared to that of a dog which, when he passes a bush, 'though he may not pisse, yet wole he heve up his leg and make a contenaunce to pisse' (858). It is clear that many of the judgements offered could be applied in retrospect to the descriptions of the pilgrims or events in the tales. In the acount of *Pride, for example, the Parson censures such things as jangling like a mill, wishing to go to the offering before one's neighbour, and riding fine horses with costly bridles (406, 407, 432–3): plainly these comments, while essentially general, could provide specific assessments of details from the portraits of the *Miller, the *Wife of Bath, and the *Monk (see *GP* I.560, 449–52, 168–72). Similarly, the strange assertion of *January in *MerT* (IV.1839–40), to the effect that a man cannot sin with his wife any more than he can hurt himself with his own knife, is reversed – with better logic, but a notably bleak message – in *ParsT* (859). The judgements on matters associated with marriage, sex, and women are firm and conservative, without being extreme: certainly opinions such as those expressed by the Wife of Bath or *Chauntecleer on sex and marriage would get short shrift (see 852ff.). The effect is, however, by no means all negative: views articulated elsewhere in *CT* and endorsed here include the great value of patience, extolled particularly in *ClT* (see 654ff.), and the idea that conduct, not birth, provides the proof of true *'gentilesse', maintained especially in *WBT* (see 460–74).

The main sources of *ParsT* were identified long ago as the *Summa de poenitentia* of St *Raymund of Pennaforte and the *Summa vitiorum* of William *Peraldus – the former a penitential handbook, the latter a collection on the *Seven Deadly Sins. Both were written during the period following the Lateran Council of 1215, which stipulated that people should go to confession at least once a year. Chaucer was indebted to Pennaforte for material on penitence, contrition, and satisfaction (80–386, 958–1080), and to Peraldus for material on the sins (390–955). Recent scholarship has revealed that he probably used two redactions of Peraldus, known as the *Primo* and the *Quoniam*. He also seems to have consulted an anonymous work on the remedial virtues, the *Summa virtutum de remediis anime* ('Compendium on the virtues and remedies of the soul'). While the combination of material from these works has generally been attributed to Chaucer, it remains possible that he was using an unknown source in which this process had already taken place. *ParsT* is, naturally enough, full of references to authority – mainly biblical texts and the church fathers.

It seems virtually certain that *ParsP* was composed late in Chaucer's career. While there is no firm evidence for dating *ParsT*, its links to other parts of *CT* suggest that it may have been written at much the same time. The evidence of the manuscripts indicates that the divisions and headings in the text are partly authorial and partly scribal. The most authentic would seem to be those at lines 315–16 and 1028–9; as usual, the scribe of the *Ellesmere MS includes an abundance of divisions. Several scribes provide marginal glosses, identifying particular sins and authorities. Damage to the final leaves of various manuscripts has resulted in the loss of some of the text. The order of the last few lines of *ParsP* is altered, without manuscript support, in many editions: see Benson (1987: 956, 1134). Two separate copies of *ParsT* exist: in one it is accompanied by *Mel* and *Ret*; in the other it appears anonymously with some moral works.

Further reading: Cooper (1996); Richard Newhauser in Correale and Hamel (2002).

Parthonope *see* Seven Against Thebes

Parvys

The portico of *St Paul's cathedral, *London. The allusion to the Parvys in the portrait of the *Sergeant of Law (*GP* I.310) reflects its use as a place where lawyers met their clients. An allusion to the parvys of Notre Dame, *Paris, occurs in *Rom* (7108).

Pasiphae

Wife of *Minos, mother of the *Minotaur. Pasiphae is included in *Jankin's *'book of wicked wives' (*WBP* III.733–6), as someone guilty of 'horrible lust' (in mating with a bull).

Pasolini, Pier Paolo

(1922–75)
Director of the film, *The Canterbury Tales* (1972). This film, which was released in English and Italian versions, concentrates on the bawdy aspects of *CT*, using material based on *MerT, FrT, CkT, MilT, WBP, RvT, PardT, SumT,* and *SumP*. Pasolini himself appears as Chaucer.

Patience *see* Peace

Paul, St

(d. *c.* 65)

Apostle who brought Christianity to the Gentiles. The Epistles of St Paul had a profound influence on the development of Christian thought and doctrine. Chaucer's works contain many quotations from and allusions to them, some of which are specifically attributed to St Paul. Most of these attributions occur in *ParsT*, where St Paul is quoted or cited on a variety of topics and sins (e.g. X.162, 598, 651, 820). Elsewhere, the most notable allusions to him include those on vengeance in *Mel* (VII.989, 1291–3, 1440–3/B².2179, 2481–3, 2630–3), on gluttony in *PardT* (VI.521ff.), on virginity and marriage in *WBP* (III.73ff.), and on fruit and chaff in *ParsP* (IX.32–6) and *NPT* (VII.3441–3/B².4631–3).

Pavia

City in Lombardy, northern *Italy, the setting for *MerT*. This choice of setting could have some appropriateness, since Pavia was an important mercantile centre during the Middle Ages. Chaucer may have visited Pavia on his journey to Italy in 1372–73. He would doubtless have known it as the place where *Lionel of Antwerp died, and was probably aware that *Boethius was imprisoned and executed there. In *Rom* (1654) Pavia is mentioned, along with *Paris, as a pleasant place.

Peace

Personification, linked with Patience in *PF*. Dame Peace is described sitting with Dame Patience outside the temple of *Venus (*PF* 239–43).

Peasants' Revolt

Uprising in the summer of 1381. The decline in population following the *Black Death led to a shortage of labour and a loosening of traditional feudal obligations. Attempts by the authorities to restore ties of obligation and limit wages to earlier levels caused discontent and uprisings throughout Europe. The Peasants' Revolt of 1381 was also a response to the collection of the unpopular Poll Tax, which had first been imposed in 1377. Rebels from the south-east of England entered London, joined forces with dissidents there, and pillaged the city. Their targets included not only individuals identified with the government but also Flemings, who were regarded as having taken jobs away from local people. They killed numerous Flemings and several eminent men (including Simon Sudbury, Archbishop of Canterbury), and burnt the Savoy, the palace of *John of Gaunt, who was associated with the introduction of the Poll Tax. After the death of their leader, Wat Tyler, the rebels dispersed. Though reprisals against them were exacted, the Poll Tax was withdrawn and the loosening of traditional ties continued.

At this time Chaucer was living in an apartment in Aldgate, one of the gates through which the rebels entered London; as a crown employee, he could well have been in danger. Nonetheless, he makes only one unequivocal reference to the Peasants' Revolt in his work – the rather jocular allusion to the followers of the rebel leader, Jack *Straw, in *NPT* (VII.3394–6/ B².4584–6). Two other comments – in *Tr* 4.183–4 and *KnT* I.2459 – are sometimes taken as passing allusions to the Peasants' Revolt. Some commentators have expressed surprise that, within a few years of this event, Chaucer should have expressed an apparently positive view of a contented peasant in his portrait of the *Plowman (*GP* I.529–41).

Pedmark *see* Penmark

Pedro I

(d. 1369)
King of Castile, known as 'Pedro the Cruel'. A brief account of Pedro's death at the hands of his half-brother, Enrique (Henry), Count of Trastamare, constitutes one of the Monk's 'tragedies' (*MkT* VII.2375ff./ B².3565ff.). Chaucer would have known a good deal about Pedro, who had been supported by *Edward the Black Prince at the battle of Najera in 1367. His wife, Philippa *Chaucer, was attached for some time to the household of Pedro's daughter, *Constance, the second wife of *John of Gaunt. It has been suggested that Chaucer's journey to Spain in 1366 may have involved diplomatic business with the court of Pedro.

Pelias

Ruler of *Thessaly and father of *Jason. At the beginning of *Hypsipyle* (*LGW* 1396ff.), Chaucer describes how Pelias ('Pelleus') fears competition from Jason, and sends him away on the Quest of the Golden Fleece.

Penelope

Wife of *Ulysses. Allusions to Penelope as an example of a good and faithful wife occur in *BD* (1081), *Anel* (82), *Tr* (5.1778), *LGWP* (F.252–3; G.206–7), *MLIntro* (II.75), and *FranT* (V.1443–4).

Penmarch

Village in Brittany, near the home of *Arveragus in *FranT*. A passing allusion to Penmarch ('Pedmark') occurs early in *FranT* (V.801).

Pennafort, St Raymund of *see* Raymund of Pennafort, St; pentameter *see* decasyllabic couplet

Peraldus, William

(*c.* 1200–*c.* 1260)
French Dominican, author of theological works. His *Summa vitiorum* ('Compendium of the sins'), written around 1236, was a substantial collection of material on the *Seven Deadly Sins. In *ParsT*, Chaucer was indebted to this work and two redactions of it, apparently written in England, and known (from their first lines) as the *Primo* and the *Quoniam*.

Perkin

Male protagonist of *CkT*. In this fragmentary tale, the apprentice victualler Perkin is given the nickname 'Revelour' and described as a lively and amoral young man, excessively fond of dancing, gambling, and pursuing women.

Perotheus *see* Pirithous; Perrers, Alice *see* Edward III

Persius

(34–62 AD)
Latin poet. The Franklin's statement (*FranP* V.721), to the effect that he has never slept on Mount *Parnassus, appears to echo the satires of Persius (Prologue 1–3). In the absence of any other evidence of Chaucer's familiarity

with the work of Persius, it seems probable that the allusion was derived from another source.

Pertelote

Hen and female protagonist in *NPT*. Pertelote is based on Pinte in the *beast epic, *Le Roman de Renart*. Chaucer represents her as the favourite 'wife' of *Chauntecleer, and describes her in terms appropriate to a courtly lady. In debate with Chauntecleer, she shows both considerable tenacity and a notably practical turn of mind.

Peter, St

(d. *c.* 64)
Leader of the Apostles. Various statements by St Peter, both from his epistles and from Acts, are quoted or cited in *ParsT* – one of them, on salvation through the name of Jesus Christ (Acts 4: 12), twice (X.287, 597–8). He is quoted, similarly, on the patience of Jesus, in *Mel* (VII.1501–4/B².2691–4). Elsewhere, St Peter is mentioned as an apostle and patron of the papacy, and his name appears in various oaths and exclamations. There are also two more unusual allusions: to St Peter's sister (possibly with reference to a popular charm) in *MilT* (I.3486), and to a shred from the sail of his boat (among the *Pardoner's dubious relics) in *GP* (I.696–8).

Peter of Cyprus *see* Pierre de Lusignan

Peter of Riga

(*c.* 1140–1209)
French author. The *Aurora* of Peter of Riga (also known as Petrus de Riga) was a Latin verse paraphrase of parts of the Bible, accompanied by a commentary. Chaucer cites it in *BD* (1155–70) on the origins of music (with reference to Gen. 4: 21).

Peter of Spain *see* Pedro I

Petrarch, Francesco

(1304–74)
Francesco Petrarch (or Petrarca), Italian writer. Chaucer makes three references to Petrarch: in *ClP* (IV.26ff.), *ClT* (IV.1147–8), and *MkT*

(VII.2325–6/B². 3515–16). In the first of these, the *Clerk states that he will tell a tale which he learnt in *Padua from 'Frounceys Petrak, the lauriat poete'. Though Chaucer visited this part of *Italy in 1378, it seems unlikely that he would have met Petrarch; he did, however, clearly come into contact with Petrarch's work. The indebtedness acknowledged at the end of *ClT* is appropriate, since Chaucer based his tale on Petrarch's version (in Latin prose) of a story from *Boccaccio's *Decameron*. The third of these references, in *MkT*, suggests that Chaucer derived the 'tragedy' of Zenobia from Petrarch, though it was, in fact, based on two works by Boccaccio (the *De claris mulieribus* and the *De claris virorum illustrium*). Chaucer's other notable borrowing from Petrarch also involves a misleading attribution. Despite the preceding reference to *Lollius as a source, the 'Canticus Troili' in the first book of *Tr* (1.400ff.) is closely based on Petrarch's sonnet 132, and probably constitutes the first English version of a sonnet by Petrarch.

The allusion in *ClP* clearly indicates Chaucer's awareness that Petrarch had been crowned poet laureate. Commentators have taken this to be particularly significant as an indication of the rising status of vernacular poetry, and have related it both to the assertions of *Dante on the subject and to Chaucer's sense of his own status as a poet – suggested, for instance, in *HF* and at the end of *Tr* (5.1786–98).

Petrus Alfonsus

(1062–1110)
Spanish author. Petrus Alfonsus ('Piers/Peter Alfonce') was a Jew who converted to Christianity. His Latin compilation, *Disciplina clericalis* ('Clerical instruction') is cited five times in *Mel* (VII.1053, 1189, 1218, 1308–12, 1566–7/B². 2243, 2379, 2408, 2498–502, 2756–7), on the dangers of various kinds of behaviour, including hasty actions and befriending strangers.

Petrus de Riga *see* Peter of Riga

Phaedra

Daughter of *Minos and sister of *Ariadne. In *Ariadne* (*LGW* 1886ff.), Phaedra is credited with devising the means by which *Theseus defeats the *Minotaur. Chaucer does not specify Phaedra's role in the subsequent part of the story, where Theseus abandons Ariadne for her (because she is more beautiful than her sister). She is also mentioned in the summary of the story in *HF* (405ff.).

Phaethon

Son of *Apollo. The story of the formation of the Milky Way, derived from *Ovid's *Metamorphoses* (2.31ff.), is summarized in *HF* (935ff.) and mentioned in *Tr* (5.663–5). This tells how Phaethon ('Pheton') loses control of the sun-chariot, which Apollo has allowed him to drive, creating a huge scar in the sky.

Phania *see* Croesus

Pharaoh

Old Testament king of Egypt. Allusions to various aspects of the dream of Pharaoh (Gen. 41), and the service of *Joseph, particularly in interpreting the dream, occur in *BD* (280–3), *HF* (516), *NPT* (VII.3133–5/B².4323–5), and *ParsT* (X.443).

Philippa of Hainault

(1314–69)
Wife of *Edward III. Philippa, the daughter of William I, Count of Hainault, married Edward in 1328. Between 1330 and 1355, she bore him 12 children, nine of whom survived infancy. She died on 15 August 1369 and was buried in Westminster Abbey. Philippa was regarded with love and respect, and was devoted to her husband, whose conduct and mental state deteriorated markedly after her death. Records indicate that Chaucer's wife, Philippa *Chaucer – who had her own connection with Hainault if, as seems almost certain, she was the daughter of Sir Paon de *Roet – served as a lady of the queen's household for many years (see Crow and Olson, 1966: 67–85).

Philomela

Daughter of *Pandion and sister of *Procne; victim of *Tereus. *Philomela* (*LGW* 2228ff.) tells the horrifying story of how Tereus first rapes Philomela ('Philomene'), his sister-in-law, and then imprisons her secretly and cuts out her tongue to prevent her from reporting his crime. She is represented as a beautiful and innocent victim, who eventually proves resourceful enough to overcome the consequences of her mutilation by representing her suffering in a tapestry.

Philostrate *see* Arcite

Philosophy

Lady Philosophy, personification of wisdom and knowledge in *Bo*. She acts as the instructor of *Boethius and opposes the values of *Fortune. Chaucer also mentions this Boethian personification of philosophy in *HF* (972ff.) and *Rom* (5659ff.). Elsewhere, he uses the word less specifically, to denote a formal system of thought or learning in general (e.g. *RvT* I.4050, *ClP* IV.34).

Phoebus

God of the sun. Chaucer identifies this god by both the Greek name, Phoebus, and (rather less frequently) the Roman name Apollo. In *MancT*, Phoebus is portrayed as a chivalrous and talented man, who kills his wife when a loquacious *crow informs him of her infidelity. In *Mars*, he appears a slow and threatening figure, who brings about the end of the love affair between *Venus and *Mars. There are numerous allusions to this god, addressed mainly as Apollo, in *Tr* (e.g. 2.843, 3.540–6, 3.726–8), including several which refer to *Calchas' prophecy of the fall of *Troy (e.g. 1.64–77, 4.113–26). Apollo is among the gods dismissed in the 'palinode' of *Tr* (5.1853). In *FranT* (V.1031ff.), the prayer of *Aurelius to this god uses both of his names. Neither is used in the brief account of the story of *Phaeton (termed 'the sonnes sone') and his mishandling of the sun-chariot in *HF* (935ff.). Astrological and astronomical allusions are mainly to Phoebus (e.g. *Bo* 1.m.6.1–7; *Tr* 2.50–60; *FranT* V.1245–9), though both names are used in *SqT* (V.48–51, 263–5, 671). Phoebus regularly serves as an epithet for the sun (e.g. *Tr* 3.1495; *PhyT* VI.37–8; *MkT* VII.2745–6, 2753–4/B².3935–6, 3943–4). Passing allusions include those to Phoebus in *LGW* (986, 1206) and those to Apollo in *HF* (1091–3, 1232).

Phyllis

Daughter of *Lycurgus, king of *Thrace; abandoned lover of *Demophoön. *Phyllis* (*LGW* 2394ff.) describes how she offers hospitality to Demophoön, whose ship has been driven ashore in Thrace, and then falls in love with him. She is represented as a victim of male faithlessness, as Demophoön leaves for home and breaks his promise to return and marry her. The legend concludes with a letter in which Phyllis expresses her sense of betrayal before hanging herself. A summary of the story occurs in *HF* (388–96), passing allusions to it in *BD* (728–31), *MLIntro* (II.65), and *LGWP* (F.264; G.218).

Physician

Pilgrim and teller in *CT*. The portrait in *GP* (I.411ff.) consists mainly of praise for the Physician's professional skill and learning. Commentators have been divided as to how this should be interpreted – some envisaging the Physician as an outstanding practitioner and some as a quack, while others regard the account as ambiguous or ambivalent. Several models for the portrait have been proposed, but none of these identifications has seemed particularly compelling. The clear implications of sharp practice, pragmatism, and aquisitiveness – in the allusions to the Physician's mutually beneficial arrangement with the apothecaries (425–8), and to the profit he has made from the plague, his tight-fistedness, and his love of gold (441–4) – are regularly noted, and sometimes associated with his lack of interest in the Bible (438). Since many commentators take the portrait to be satirical, it has often been related to the traditional satire of physicians, which represents them as greedy, unscrupulous charlatans, and associates them with lawyers. While the latter connection has sometimes led to suggestions of a link between the Physician and the *Sergeant of Law, their portraits in *GP* are not overtly linked. Nor is there any direct connection between the Physician and *PhyT*, though some commentators have felt that the tale demonstrates a lack of moral sensibility which they consider appropriate to its teller.

Further reading: Andrew (1993); Mann (1973).

Physician's Tale, The

Moral tale from Fragment VI of *CT*. The sixth fragment opens with *PhyT*, which has no prologue or introduction: indeed (somewhat as in the case of *ShT*), its teller is not identified until the retrospective comments of the *Host (*PardIntro* VI.287ff.) – and, even then, only by implication. *PardIntro* serves to link *PhyT* with the prologue and tale of the next teller, the *Pardoner. Since Fragment VI closes with the altercation following *PardT* (and without any indication of who the next teller will be), it can be placed in several positions – as it has been, both in manuscripts and editions. The sequence of fragments from V to VI to VII, preserved in several manuscripts (including the authoritative *Ellesmere MS) does, however, gain favour with commentators and editors during the twentieth century. Its effect on *PhyT* is to suggest a potential connection with the final tale of Fragment V, *FranT* – and, particularly, with the examples of suffering women specified in the complaint of *Dorigen (V.1355ff.).

PhyT focuses on the death of the innocent fourteen-year-old girl, *Virginia. This serves to associate it with tales which describe the suffering of innocent women – *MLT, ClT,* and *SNT* – and with the account of the murder of the seven-year-old boy in *PrT*. The link with these tales does, however, not extend to the form of *PhyT*: while they are composed in the *rhyme royal stanza (which Chaucer uses in *CT* almost exclusively for moral and religious poems), it is written in the normal *decasyllabic couplet. In generic terms, *PhyT* proves more difficult to define than the reader might expect. Its content and manner suggest, from the outset, that it will develop into an *exemplum, illustrating a vice to be avoided or a virtue to be emulated. In the end, this can hardly be the case: the death of Virginia is caused by a combination of her own beauty, the moral rigour of her father (*Virginius), and the wickedness of the judge (*Apius) and his stooge (Claudius). The conduct of Virginius, who kills his own daughter in order to preserve her virginity, can plainly not be set up as a model for emulation outside of a fictional setting in the pagan ancient world. The conduct of Virginia is entirely blameless; her death cannot, therefore, be seen as an example of vice or negligence to be avoided. Thus the lengthy passage (VI.72ff.) warning governesses and parents to take particular care of the girls in their charge does not seem particularly relevant. While some commentators have taken this, together with the bland acceptance of the conduct of Virginius, to imply ineptitude on the part of the teller, there would appear to be no warrant for such a reading in the text, where the teller's presence is minimal (see above). It might well be concluded that the Host shows unusually acute judgement when he interprets *PhyT* as a tale of pathos (*PardIntro* VI.287ff.). Comparison of Chaucer's version of the story with his source, a passage from *RR (5589ff.), shows him emphasizing and developing precisely this aspect of the narrative. His allusion to *Livy (VI.1) is, incidentally, derived from *RR*.

The tenuous nature of the link between *PhyT* and the pilgrimage framework has led to the supposition that it may not have been originally composed for *CT*. The passage on the conduct of governesses has sometimes been taken as an allusion to a scandal of 1386, when Elizabeth, daughter of *John of Gaunt, eloped (which would have implicated her governess, Katherine *Swynford). *PhyT* does not reflect the influence of Gower's version of the story (*Confessio Amantis* 7.5131ff.), which appeared in 1390. A date of *c.* 1386–90 has, therefore, sometimes been suggested for its composition. The manuscripts contain several significant variants and a few spurious lines.

Further reading: Cooper (1996); Corsa (1987); Edgar F. Shannon in Bryan and Dempster (1941).

Physiologus

Legendary author of a bestiary. The allusion to Physiologus (signifying 'the naturalist') in *NPT* (VII.3270–2/B².4460–2) concerns the quality of the singing voice of the mermaid. The work attributed to Physiologus – and also itself known by this name – contains moralized accounts of a wide range of creatures, real and imaginary.

Picardy *see* Flanders

Pierre de Lusignan

(d. 1369)
King of Cyprus. A brief account of the assassination of Pierre de Lusignan ('Petro') is included among the 'tragedies' of *MkT* (VII.2391–8/B².3581–8). Pierre would have been known at the English court, and was involved in several of the campaigns mentioned in the description of the *Knight (GP* I.51–66), including those against *Alexandria, *Atalia, and *Ayash.

Piers *see* Monk; Piers Alfonce *see* Petrus Alphonsus; *Piers Plowman see* Langland, William

Pilate

(fl. 1st century)
Judge who sentenced *Christ to crucifixion. The allusion to the 'Pilates voys' of the *Miller (*MilP* I.3124) reflects the representation in the *mystery plays of Pilate as a loud and irascible figure.

Pinkhurst, Adam *see* Pynkhurst, Adam

Pirithous

Friend of *Theseus in *KnT*. It is at the request of Pirithous ('Perotheus') that Theseus releases *Arcite from prison (I.1189ff.).

Pisa

City in north-west Italy, setting for the story of *Ugolino in *MkT*.

Pity

Personification in *Pity* and *Rom*. Pity specifically personifies the sympathy shown by a lady to a prospective lover (as in *Pity* 1ff.; *Rom* 3543ff.). The allusion to her as queen of the *Furies (in *Pity* 92) has generated considerable debate: see Benson (1987: 1078).

Placebo

One of the brothers of *January in *MerT* (the other being *Justinus). When January seeks the advice of his brothers regarding marriage (IV.1469ff.), Placebo speaks – in an uncritical and sycophantic manner – in favour of marriage, especially that of an old man and a young woman. His name, meaning 'I shall please', appears to suggest flattery both here and in Chaucer's other allusions to it (*SumT* III.2075; *ParsT* X.617).

plague *see* Black Death

Plato

(*c.* 429–347 BC)
Ancient Greek philosopher. All of Plato's works were written as dialogues. Though only one, the *Timaeus*, was well known during the Middle Ages (through a fourth-century Latin translation), the influence of his ideas and his use of the dialogue form was ubiquitous. It reached Chaucer especially through the *De consolatione philosophiae* of *Boethius. Thus it comes as no surprise that the bulk of Chaucer's citations of Plato occur in *Bo* (his translation of this work) – nor that Dame *Philosophy refers to Plato as her disciple (*Bo* 3.p.9.189–95). He is cited and quoted on a range of subjects, including the value of wisdom (*Bo* 1.p.4.26–39), learning and memory (3.m.11.43–7; p.12.1–8), and the congruence between things and the words used to describe them (3.p.12.200–7). This last topic appears in the form of an adage (see Whiting [1968] W.645), and recurs in *GP* (I.741–2) and *MancT* (IX.207–8). *CYT* (VIII.1448ff.) reports a dialogue between Plato and a disciple, derived from an alchemical work by *Senior. Passing allusions to Plato as an authority on sound and on cosmology occur in *HF* (759, 931).

Pleyndamour

'Full of Love', supposedly a hero of romance. Pleyndamour, included among the romance heroes said in *Th* (VII.900/B².2090) to have been surpassed by Sir *Thopas, has not been identified. While his name has been compared to that of Sir Playne de Amoris in Malory's *Morte Darthur*, it may have been invented by Chaucer.

Plowman

Pilgrim in *CT*. The portrait of the Plowman in *GP* (I.529–41) follows that of the *Parson. While the reference to him as the Parson's 'brother' (529) has usually been understood literally, some commentators have taken it metaphorically (to mean 'fellow Christian'). The portrait has regularly been identified as an account of an estates ideal. Thus it has been linked not only with that of the Parson but also with that of the *Knight – the three of them (supposedly) combining to represent the traditional concept of those who fight, those who pray, and those who labour. The emphasis of the portrait is, clearly, on hard work, simple piety, and the acceptance of a modest position in life. Commentators have often expressed surprise that Chaucer should have offered such a positive view of a labouring man relatively soon after the *Peasants' Revolt. Many associate the portrait with the figure of Piers Plowman in *Langland's great poem, and read it allegorically. Others have found it lifeless, and detect in it a patrician view of rural life, from which hardship and suffering have been omitted. While Chaucer did not write a tale for the Plowman, two different works were later represented as *The *Plowman's Tale*.

Further reading: Andrew (1993); Mann (1973).

Plowman's Tale, The

Two tales added to *CT*. The two apocryphal tales which have been attributed to the *Plowman are entirely different. (1) In a single manuscript (Christ Church Oxford MS 152), the Plowman tells a Miracle of the Virgin, originally written by *Hoccleve. This poem (105 lines) describes how the Virgin rewards a young monk for his devotion to her, and is preceded by a prologue (35 lines) in which the Plowman introduces his tale. Both are composed in *rhyme royal stanzas. (2) A Lollard poem of 1328 lines is attributed to the Plowman in the second edition of *Thynne (1542), and retained by subsequent editors until *Tyrwhitt, who excludes it from his edition (1775).

Though this poem purports to consist of a debate between the Griffon and the Pelican, representing the established church and poor Lollards respectively, it actually constitutes a piece of anti-clerical polemic, which grants the Griffon few lines and no credibility. It is preceded by a 52-line pro-logue, describing how the Plowman leaves his home during the summer, joins the pilgrims in Canterbury, and is invited by the Host to tell a tale. This may have been written when the poem was adapted for *CT*. Both prologue and tale are composed in an eight-line stanza similar to that used in *MkT* (though with some slight variations to the rhyme scheme).

   Further reading: (1) Bowers (1992); (2) Dean (1991), Skeat (1897).

Pluto

Roman god of the underworld. In *MerT* (IV.2225ff.), Pluto and his wife *Proserpina discuss the conduct of *January and *May in relation to gender stereotypes. Pluto's arguments are in the tradition of *anti-feminist writing, and he brings matters to a head by restoring the sight of January (who had become blind) while his wife is deceiving him. He is described in *MerT* (IV.2038–41, 2225ff.) as the king of *Fairy – signifying the classical under-world, with which passing allusions associate him in various works, includ-ing *HF* (1510–12), *Tr* (3.592–3), and *FranT* (V.1074–5). In *KnT* (I.2684–91), Pluto sends, at the request of *Saturn, a 'furie infernal', which causes *Arcite to be thrown from his startled horse and fatally injured.

Poliphete

Supposed enemy of *Criseyde in *Tr*. *Pandarus invents the story of Poliphete's enmity in order to make Criseyde feel vulnerable and in need of the protection of *Troilus (2.1467ff.) – and thus more likely to accept him as a lover. There is no equivalent figure in any of the major sources of *Tr*.

Polyhymnia *see* Muses; Polynices, Polymyte(s) *see* Seven Against Thebes; Polyphemus *see* Ulysses

Polyxena

Daughter of *Priam. The story of Polyxena's unfortunate love for *Achilles – who waged war against her people and killed her brothers *Hector and

*Troilus – underlies the allusions in *BD* (1064–71) and *LGWP* (F.258/G.212). While the former refers specifically to the death of Achilles as he attempts to marry Polyxena, the latter may suggest her sacrificial death on his tomb. She is also mentioned briefly in *Tr* (1.455, 3.409).

Pompey

(106–48 BC)
Gnaeus Pompeius Magnus (Pompey the Great), Roman statesman and general. The defeat of Pompey by *Julius Caesar is mentioned in *MkT* (VII.2679–94/B².3869–84). (Chaucer incorrectly states here that Pompey was Caesar's father-in-law, whereas he was actually his son-in-law.) They are linked again in the allusions in *HF* (1497–506) and *MLT* (II.199) – the first to their fame, the second to the astrological prediction of their deaths.

Pope, Alexander

(1688–1744)
Poet; translator of works by Chaucer. During the first phase of his career (*c.* 1704–11), Pope produced two translations from *CT, January and May* (a version of *MerT*) and *The Wife of Bath Her Prologue*. He recreated both works in his own poetic idiom, expurgating and somewhat abbreviating Chaucer's poems. During the same period, Pope also wrote two imitations of Chaucer – one very slight, the other an interesting and impressive poem, *The Temple of Fame*, inspired by the third book of *HF*.

Poperinghe *see* Flanders; Portia *see* Brutus (2); portraits *see* Chaucer, Geoffrey

Priam

King of *Troy; husband of *Hecuba; father of *Hector and *Troilus. Priam is mentioned several times in *Tr*, most notably in connection with the exchange of *Criseyde for *Antenor (4.139–44), but remains a shadowy figure. The brief accounts of the fall of Troy in *BD* (326ff.), *HF* (151ff.), and *Dido* (*LGW* 930ff.) all refer to Priam (and, in the latter two cases, specifically to his death). The most striking allusion to this tragic event is, however, a comic one – that in *NPT* (VII.3355–61/B².4545–51).

Priapus

Greek god of fertility and gardens. In *PF* (253–6), Priapus appears as a phallic god, with specific reference to a story from *Ovid's *Fasti* (1.415ff.), which tells how his lustful approach to the nymph Lotis is interrupted by the braying of an ass. A more decorous allusion to his association with gardens occurs in *MerT* (IV.2034–7).

Pride

One of the *Seven Deadly Sins. A section of *ParsT* (X.390ff.) considers Pride, which is described as the root of all sin. This account emphasizes pride in immodest clothing, extravagance, personal accomplishments, and social standing.

priest *see* canon

printed editions *see* Caxton, William; Pynson, Richard; Thynne, William; Stow, John; Speght, Thomas; Morell, Revd Thomas; Urry, John; Tyrwhitt, Thomas; Wright, Thomas; Furnivall, Frederick J.; Morris, William; Skeat, Revd Walter W.; Root, Robert Kilburn; Robinson, F.N.; Manly, John Matthews

Prioress

Pilgrim and teller in *CT*. The portrait of the Prioress in *GP* (I.118ff.) has attracted a great deal of critical attention. During the early years of the twentieth century, commentators took its concentration on appearance and manners rather than spiritual issues to suggest a gently ironic view of the Prioress's values. They pointed out that the portrait alludes to infringements of monastic rules regarding such matters as dress, jewellery, and the keeping of pets (146–62), which are mentioned both in satire and in the records of visitations to nunneries. Some later critics take a more censorious view, reading the portrait as a harshly satirical account of pretence and worldliness. While assessments of its tone and outlook continue to range between mild irony and harsh satire, commentators tend to agree that it implies a certain shallowness, comprising an inappropriate concern with matters of the world and an inadequate commitment to those of the spirit. The Prioress's

name, Eglentyne (121), has generally been regarded as more appropriate to a
heroine of *romance than to a nun. The allusion to *Stratford atte Bowe
(125), which signifies the Benedictine nunnery of St Leonard's, Bromley, has
led to the suggestion that the Prioress might have been modelled on the contemporary head of this house, Mary Suharde or Syward (about whom little is
known). Commentators have regularly contrasted the primness and delicacy
of the Prioress with the more robust qualities of the *Wife of Bath, the only
other female pilgrim described at length. The portraits of the Prioress, the
*Monk, and the *Friar are often interpreted as a group of regular clergy, all of
whom fail to live up to the values they profess. The lines immediately following the portrait (163–4) refer to those attending on the Prioress, and are
sometimes taken to suggest that Chaucer might have intended to add portraits of several more pilgrims, including the *Nun's Priest and the *Second
Nun. *See also*: ***Prioress's Prologue and Tale, The***.

Further reading: Andrew (1993); Mann (1973).

Prioress's Prologue and Tale, The

Prologue and religious tale from Fragment VII (Group B²) of *CT*. The
prologue and tale of the *Prioress are linked to the preceding tale – that of
the *Shipman – by a brief passage (VII.435–52/B².1625–42). Here the *Host
interprets *ShT* as a warning about the dangers of hospitality (echoing the
*Cook's interpretation of *RvT* in *CkP*), before proceeding to ask the Prioress
to tell a tale. The formal courtesy of his address to the Prioress offers a
striking contrast to the jesting familiarity of his words to the Shipman.

The tone of the Prioress in *PrP* is also formal, and conspicuously pious.
Both *PrP* and *PrT* are written in the *rhyme royal stanza. *PrP* is a superb invocation to the Virgin *Mary – and thus an appropriate introduction to *PrT*,
which concerns a miracle performed by the Virgin. Miracles of the Virgin
constitute a late medieval genre, related to the *saint's life and characterized
by piety and sensationalism. Analogues to the story told in *PrT* – that of a
Christian boy killed by Jews for singing a hymn to the Virgin – have been
assigned to three groups. These differ in various ways, notably the ending:
while stories in two groups describe how the Virgin brings the murdered boy
back to life, those in the third group (to which *PrT* belongs) relate how her
miraculous intervention at his funeral brings revelation but does not restore
his life. Chaucer's version has several unique features, which may reflect
either an unknown source or his own modifications to the story. The most
significant of these are the emphatically liturgical quality of *PrT*, the severity
with which the Jews are punished for their crime (628–34/1818–24), and the

'greyn' laid on the boy's tongue by the Virgin (656ff./1846ff.) and removed by the abbott at his funeral. The liturgical element is established in *PrP*, which echoes the Little Office of the Virgin and the Mass of the Holy Innocents. It has been pointed out that, in the latter, grain serves as a symbol for the soul (freed from the chaff of the body), which might suggest the significance of the 'greyn' in *PrT*. Chaucer also draws on St Bernard's hymn to the Virgin from *Dante's *Paradiso* (33.16–21) in *PrP* (474–80/1664–70) – as he does in *SNP* (VIII.50–6).

While *PrP* has been recognized as one of Chaucer's finest passages of religious poetry, several aspects of *PrT* have proved challenging and contentious: its sentimentality, its cruelty, and, above all, its anti-Semitism. Commentators have felt particularly reluctant to attribute the views expressed and the values implied in the tale directly to Chaucer. Some have found it expedient to blame the teller for the unpalatable aspects of the tale, and to interpret *PrT* as a satirical exposure of the Prioress. A qualified version of this reading – in which such aspects of the tale are taken to reflect both the limitations of its genre and the shallowness of its teller – has come to seem more convincing. Hostility to the enemies of Christianity is fundamental to all such stories; a partial parallel may be found in the treatment of Muslims in *MLT*. While many modern readers will remain uncomfortable with the anti-Semitism of *PrT*, it may be worth noting both that the Jews are remote figures, living in an unnamed Asian city (488/1678), and that English people during the late Middle Ages would not normally have had any contact with Jews, following their expulsion from England in 1290. The account of the seven-year-old boy and his mother (a widow) in the first part of the poem is conspicuously sentimental. This does, however, change towards the end, when, through the miracle of the Virgin, the boy becomes a figure who speaks with the authority of divine knowledge. Even so, it has generally been felt that the treatment of the suffering of the innocent in *PrT* lacks the complexity and subtlety generated by this theme elsewhere, notably in *ClT*.

There is no specific evidence to date the composition of *PrT*. A hypothesis to the effect that it was written for a visit of *Richard II to Lincoln in 1387 has not attracted widespread support. It is normally assumed that *PrP* and *PrT* were written together, probably for *CT*. Both contain the words 'quod she' (454/1644, 581/1771), indicating a female speaker. A passing comment on the conduct of monks (642–3/1832) has been taken to refer to *ShT*, though it could also apply to the portrait of the *Monk in *GP* (I.165ff.), or to monks in general. Relatively few significant variants appear in the manuscripts, several of which contain a small number of glosses. The number of separate copies of *PrT* is exceeded only in the case of *ClT* and equalled only in that of *Mel*. *Wordsworth wrote a translation of *PrT*.

Further reading: Boyd (1987); Carlton Brown in Bryan and Dempster (1941); Cooper (1996).

Procne

Daughter of *Pandion, sister of *Philomela, and wronged wife of *Tereus. *Philomela* (*LGW* 2228ff.) relates how Procne ('Pro[i]gne') initiates a visit from her sister, Philomela, who is then raped by her husband Tereus. It goes on to describe how Tereus imprisons his victim secretly and cuts out her tongue in order to ensure than she cannot report his crime, but how she communicates the essential facts to her sister by depicting them in a tapestry. The gruesome end to the story as told by Ovid (*Metamorphoses* 6.424ff.) and Gower (*Confessio Amantis* 5.5551ff.) – in which Procne takes revenge by killing her son Itys and feeding his body to her husband – is omitted by Chaucer. An allusion to another aspect of the Ovidian ending, in which Procne is transformed into a swallow (and Philomela into a nightingale), occurs in *Tr* (2.64ff.).

Proserpina

Wife of *Pluto. In *MerT* (IV.2038–41, 2225ff.), Proserpina appears as the queen of *Fairy, the classical underworld. The well-known story of how Pluto seized her and carried her off to the underworld is mentioned briefly (2229–33). Pluto and Proserpina engage in a debate on gender, occasioned by the behaviour of *January and *May, in which she defends women against the anti-feminist arguments of her husband, and undertakes to provide May with the words to extricate herself from a compromising situation (2316–17). Passing allusions to Proserpina occur in *HF* (1507–12) and *Tr* (4.473–4).

Proverbs

Poem of eight lines, uncertainly attributed to Chaucer. *Prov* survives in four manuscripts, two of which specify Chaucer as its author. This attribution has been doubted for two reasons: the lack of support from *Shirley, and the presence of a non-Chaucerian rhyme ('compas'/'embrace'). The title is editorial. *Prov* consists of two quatrains, each of which poses a question in the first two lines and answers it with a proverb in the second two. The proverbs correspond to Whiting (1968) H.305 and M.774 – of which the latter also appears in a poem by *Deschamps and in *Mel* (VII.1214–15/B².2404–5). Some scholars have taken *Prov* to be a fragment of a longer poem. There is no evidence for dating.

Further reading: Pace and David (1982); V.J. Scattergood in Minnis (1995).

Pruce *see* Prussia

Prudence

Wife of *Melibee in *Mel*. The opening of the tale describes how three enemies of Melibee break into his house and attack Prudence and her daughter, *Sophie. The remainder consists largely of a moral debate, through which Prudence persuades her husband to be reconciled with his enemies and forgive them. In the process, her intellectual and moral superiority to Melibee become evident, though the values she advocates reflect ethical rather than spiritual concerns.

Prussia

Region on the Baltic coast, to the east of the Vistula. The service of the *Knight in Prussia, mentioned in *GP* (I.52–4), has been associated with the activities of the Teutonic Knights (who were based in Prussia), and taken to be among the latest of his campaigns. Passing allusions to a Prussian shield and to Prussia as a remote country occur in *KnT* (I.2122) and *BD* (1025) respectively.

Ptolemy

(*c.* 90–168)
Egyptian astonomer. The great treatise of Ptolemy ('Ptholome[e]', 'Tholome') on astronomy, the *Almagest*, is included among the books owned by *Nicholas in *MilT* (I.3208). While Chaucer cites the *Almagest* correctly in *Bo* (2.p.7.34), his citations in *WBP* (III.180–3, 323–7) are of proverbial sayings added as a preface to the Latin translation by Gerard of Cremona: see note in Benson (1987: 867).

Publilius Syrus

(fl. 1st century)
Roman author. His collection of maxims, known as the *Sententiae* ('Maxims'), was often attributed to *Seneca during the Middle Ages. Several such

citations in *Mel* (e.g. VII.1185, 1320, 1488, 1859/B^2.2375, 2510, 2678, 3049) are actually from this work: see notes in Benson (1987: 925–8).

Pynchbeck, Thomas

(fl. late 14th century)
Eminent lawyer. The notion that the portrait of the *Sergeant of Law in *GP* (I.309ff.) may have been modelled on Thomas Pynchbeck was proposed by *Manly (1926: 147–57), partly on the basis of the word 'pynche' (326), which he takes as wordplay. Manly later (1928: 517–18) reiterates the case, adding that when Chaucer was prosecuted for debt in 1388, one of the relevant writs was signed by Pynchbeck (see Crow and Olson, 1966: 386).

Pynkhurst, Adam

(fl. late 14th–early 15th centuries)
Chaucer's scribe. Recent research has identified the scribe who is mentioned in *Adam* and was responsible for both the *Ellesmere MS and the *Hengwrt MS as Adam Pynkhurst.

Pynson, Richard

(d. 1530)
Early printer of Chaucer's work. Pynson, who came from Normandy, published a reprint of *Caxton's second edition of *CT* in 1492. He was the first publisher to attempt a collected edition of Chaucer. This work, based mainly on Caxton, was published in 1526, and consists of three volumes, the second of which includes several pieces not by Chaucer.

Pyramus

Noble Babylonian youth, in love with *Thisbe. In *Thisbe* (*LGW* 706ff.), Pyramus is represented as a 'trewe and kynde' lover (921), and thus an exception to the male norm. He is also mentioned briefly in *MerT* (IV.2128) and *PF* (289).

Pyrrhus

Son of *Achilles. Allusions to the role of Pyrrhus ('Pirrus') in the sack of *Troy – at which he killed king *Priam – occur in *HF* (157–61), *NPT* (VII.3355–61/ B^2.4545–51), and *MLT* (II.288–9).

R

Ram *see* **Aries; Ravenstone, William** *see* **St Paul's**

Raymund of Pennaforte, St

(*c.* 1180–*c.* 1275)
Spanish canonist and theologian. Chaucer was indebted in *ParsT* to St Raymund's *Summa de poenitentia* ('Compendium concerning penance'), an influential work written in the 1220s.

Razis *see* **Rhazes**

Reason

Personification in *Rom*. Reason is represented as the mother of *Shame (*Rom* 3031ff.) and a model of moderation opposed to the excesses of passionate love (3189ff.). The allusion of *Nature to Reason in *PF* (632) may reflect the influence of the *Anticlaudianus* of *Alan of Lille, in which Ratio ('Reason') acts as an adviser to Natura.

Reeve

Pilgrim and teller in *CT*. The portrait of the Reeve in *GP* is placed third in the final sequence of five rather suspect individuals (I.587ff.). It opens by describing him as a thin, 'colerik' man, very closely shaven, with hair cropped like a priest's. An echo of this last point occurs at the end of the portrait, where, in a passage which provides some further description of the Reeve's physical appearance (615–22), his clothing is compared to that of a friar. This passage also mentions (among other things) that he wears a rusty sword, rides a good dappled horse named *Scot, and comes from *Bawdeswell in Norfolk. On the basis of this specific localization, some scholars have attempted to construct a pattern of contemporary allusion in the portrait – with somewhat unconvincing results. The central part of the portrait (593–614) concerns the Reeve's professional life. While praising his great skill as a farm manager, it strongly implies that he has gained substantially by stealing from his lord, and observes that the estate workers live in mortal fear of him. This part of the portrait draws on traditional satire against corrupt and dishonest officials. It does, however, conclude with a notable characteristic, entirely independent of such traditions, in the statement that the Reeve learned the trade of carpenter in his youth (613–14). This later assumes particular significance in the quarrel between the Reeve and the *Miller, which takes place in *MilP* and *RvP*; it also provides the motivation underlying *RvT*. In the process, the Miller and the Reeve are supplied with names: respectively, Robin and Oswald. The potential for disharmony between these two individuals, which may well suggest professional rivalry, is clearly reflected in the emphatic contrast between their portraits. These describe, on the one hand, a burly, aggressive, gregarious man who leads the company on its way, and, on the other, a slight, sinister, calculating individual, who lurks at the rear of the group.

Further reading: Andrew (1993); Mann (1973).

Reeve's Prologue and Tale, The

Confessional prologue and comic tale from the first fragment of *CT*. *RvP* begins, like *MilP*, with the reactions of the fictional audience to the preceding tale. All the pilgrims respond with good humour to *MilT*, except for the Reeve, who takes it as a personal insult on the part of the *Miller. He does so on the assumption of an implied identification between the carpenter *John, the cuckolded husband in *MilT*, and himself – based on his having trained as a carpenter in his youth (see *GP* I.613–14). This response, which was foreshadowed in *MilP* (I.3136ff.), leads the Reeve to introduce his own tale as one in which he will exact revenge (I.3864–6, 3909–20). His prologue also has a confessional aspect: he describes himself as an old man, still prone to lust though now impotent, and holds forth somewhat tendentiously on the ageing process. This aspect of his prologue receives short shrift from the *Host, who asserts that it is inappropriate for a reeve to preach (3899–908).

In his tale, the Reeve appears to have been as good as his word: *RvT* reflects throughout the intention to take revenge on the Miller. It describes how a thieving miller, *Simkin, cheats two *Cambridge scholars, *Alan and *John, and how they exact revenge by sleeping (respectively) with his daughter (Malyne) and his (unnamed) wife. The tale begins with some notably specific scene-setting – at the mill in *Trumpington, near Cambridge – followed by a satirical account of the absurd social pretensions of Simkin and his wife. The dishonest and violent Simkin is closely modelled on the Miller, as described in *GP* (I.545ff.). Moreover, *RvT* contains striking parallels and contrasts with *MilT* – most notably, responding to a tale set in Oxford with one set near

Cambridge, and capping its account of how a scholar seduces a carpenter's wife by describing how two scholars seduce a miller's wife and daughter. While the two poems are broadly similar in style, tone, and narrative technique, some of the minor differences between them are significant. The story of *RvT* moves even more swiftly and economically than that of *MilT*, and its tone, though similarly frank, seems darker because of the constant emphasis on revenge. The essential nature and pattern of the story, and its adroit manipulation of plot elements are, like those in *MilT*, typical of *fabliau. Several analogues have been discovered, one of which, the thirteenth-century French fabliau, *Le meunier et les. II. clers* ('The miller and the two clerks'), contains most of the basic plot elements of *RvT*. The proverbial and sententious ending to the tale (I.4313–24), while possibly suggesting the teller's tendency to 'preach' (as in his prologue), stresses common sense rather than moral insight, and, doubtless, serves mainly to express the Reeve's conviction that he has now taken his revenge on the Miller.

One of the distinctive aspects of *RvT* is Chaucer's use of dialect words and forms such as 'boes', 'howgates', and 'swa' (for 'must', 'how', and 'so' – all from the dialogue in 4026–39) to represent the northern speech of Alan and John. Some scribes attempt to normalize such words and forms; otherwise, the manuscripts contain few variants of any great significance. It has generally been supposed that *RvP* and *RvT* would have been written at much the same time as *MilP* and *MilT*.

Further reading: Peter G. Beidler in Correale and Hamel (2002); Bennett (1974); Benson and Andersson (1971); Cooper (1996).

Renaud de Louens

(fl. mid-14th century)
French writer. *Mel* is a close translation of the French prose *Livre de Mellibee et Prudence* of Renaud de Louens, written in 1337. This constitutes a free and somewhat condensed translation of the *Liber consolationis et consilii* of *Albertanus of Brescia.

Retraction, Chaucer's

Brief conclusion to *CT*. In *Ret* (X.1081–92), which follows the end of *ParsT*, Chaucer appears to revoke the more worldly of his works, while thanking God for those conducive to morality. Responses have been various: while some commentators take *Ret* literally, others interpret it as part of the fiction of *CT*. It probably provided the basis on which the fifteenth-century theologian

Thomas *Gascoigne asserted that Chaucer underwent a deathbed repentance. Many critics have related *Ret* to the palinode at the end of *Tr*. Several point out that recantations by writers towards the end of their lives are not uncommon, and may even be regarded as conventional. It is notable that *Ret* follows directly from the end of *ParsT*, and that Chaucer appears to take up the penitential message and apply it to his own life and work as a writer. In the process, he names a number of his own works, though his survey of those deemed worldly is conspicuously more detailed than that of those considered moral. The incompleteness of the list tends to compromise any notion that Chaucer could here be attempting to establish a canon. Various commentators have observed the implicit relationship of *Ret* to the final part of *CT*, with its progression from the *Manciple's warning against careless talk in *MancT*, to the *Parson's dismissal of fiction in *ParsP*, to Chaucer's apparent rejection of much of his own work here.

Ret occurs in all the manuscripts which are complete at this point. Most of these provide an appropriate heading.

Further reading: Cooper (1996).

Rhazes

(*c.* 850–923/4)
Persian writer on medicine. The inclusion of Rhazes among the authorities known to the *Physician (*GP* I.432) reflects his authorship of a medical encyclopedia, the Latin translation of which was called the *Colliget*.

rhyme royal

Stanza form used by Chaucer in various poems. The rhyme royal stanza consists of seven decasyllabic lines, rhyming ababbcc. Chaucer appears to have adopted it from French poetry, and uses it in many of his lyrics (including *Pity, Mars, Truth, Gent,* and *Purse*). The contribution of the rhyme royal form to Chaucer's narrative poetry is, however, far more substantial. In this connection, it has been related to the 'ottava rima' stanza used by *Boccaccio, which rhymes ababbcbc: thus a rhyme royal stanza is like an 'ottava rima' stanza with its seventh line omitted. While Chaucer's first experiment with rhyme royal in a narrative poem may well occur in *Anel*, it is in *PF* that the potential for this form to make a significant contribution to the coherence of his work becomes apparent. Chaucer goes on to develop the rhyme royal form in *Tr*, where it becomes a remarkably flexible, subtle, and powerful medium. In *CT*, he generally reserves it for prologues and tales on moral and religious themes (*MLP, MLT, CIT, PrP, PrT, SNP*, and *SNT*), though it also appears in *ThP*.

Richard I

(1157–99)
Richard Lionheart, King of England 1189–99. In *NPT* (VII.3347–52/ B².4537–42) Chaucer makes a parodic allusion to the celebrated lamentation on the death of Richard I by *Geoffrey de Vinsauf (*Poetria Nova* 375–6).

Richard II

(1367–1400)
Richard of Bordeaux, King of England 1377–99. Richard, the younger son of *Edward, Prince of Wales, and *Joan of Kent, was born in Bordeaux on 6 January 1367. He succeeded to the throne at the age of ten, on the death of his grandfather, *Edward III, as a consequence of the prior deaths of his father, Edward, Prince of Wales (in 1376) and of his elder brother (also named Edward, in 1371). On 14 January 1382 he married *Anne of Bohemia, who died, childless, in 1394. Richard proceeded to marry the seven-year-old French princess *Isabella in November 1396, simultaneously signing a treaty which resulted in 28 years of peace between England and France. After a decline into despotism, he was deposed in 1399 by his cousin Henry of Lancaster (son of *John of Gaunt), who assumed the throne as *Henry IV. Though it is known that Richard died shortly afterwards, the precise date and manner of his death are uncertain. Henry IV had him buried at King's Langley (Hertfordshire). His remains were subsequently moved by Henry V to the tomb in Westminster Abbey which Richard had built for Anne.

Throughout Richard's reign, Chaucer was in the royal service and was paid annuities for his work, which included journeys overseas on diplomatic business. While *PF* may allude to the negotiations which preceded his marriage to Anne, the only direct reference to Richard in Chaucer's work occurs in the *envoy to *Sted* (22–3), where the king is exhorted to behave with honour and rule well.

Richesse

Personification of generosity in *Rom*. Richesse appears as a lady accompanying the god of *Love in *Rom* (1033ff.), dressed in an extremely opulent manner (1071ff.). In *PF* (261–2), she serves as porter in the temple of Venus.

Rickert, Edith *see* **Manly, John Matthews; rime royal**
see **rhyme royal; 'rioters'** *see Pardoner's Introduction,*
Prologue, and Tale, The

Risshenden, Peter

(fl. late 14th century)
Possible model for the *Shipman. Risshenden is recorded in 1386 as the master of a *Dartmouth vessel, the *Maudelayne*, which was involved in actions
of dubious legality in 1391. Since both the name and the home port of this
ship are mentioned in the portrait of the Shipman in *GP* (I.388ff.), some
commentators have concluded that this is based on Risshenden.

Riverside Chaucer, The see Robinson, F.N.

Robin

Servant of *John in *MilT*. When *Nicholas is apparently overcome by the
effects of excessive study, John instructs Robin to gain access to his room by
lifting the door off its hinges (I.3448ff.). It has been noted that Robin shares
with the *Miller not only his name (see *MilP* I.3129) but also this facility with
doors (see *GP* I.550). By contrast, Gill – the name of John's maidservant,
mentioned in passing (I.3556) – has no particular resonance.

Robinson, F.N.

(1872–1967)
Editor of Chaucer. Robinson spent his career at Harvard University,
dedicating much of it to producing what was to become the standard edition
of Chaucer's works. This was commissioned as early as 1904, but did not
appear until 1933. In an octavo volume of some 1133 pages, it provided a
reliable text of the complete works (despite the somewhat misleading title,
The Poetical Works of Chaucer), supported by introductory material, textual
and explanatory notes, a bibliography, a glossary, and an index of proper
names. As an editor, Robinson was conservative but not doctrinaire. He
selected his base texts with care, and edited them in the light of evidence
from other manuscripts. In cases where numerous manuscripts exist, he was
selective in his collation: thus, in the (admitttedly extreme) case of *CT*, he
collated only ten manuscripts. Robinson lightly modernized the orthography

of his texts. He provided selective textual notes, substantial headnotes and explanatory notes, and a relatively succinct glossary. A second edition appeared in 1957, with a more appropriate title (*The Works of Geoffrey Chaucer*), a larger format, minor revisions to the text, and some updating of the explanatory notes. Thirty years later, a more radical revision appeared, with a new title, *The Riverside Chaucer*. This was prepared by a team of editors under the general editorship of Larry D. Benson. Alterations to the text are relatively few and insignificant. Despite other, more conspicuous, changes – including new headnotes and explanatory notes, the addition of glosses at the foot of each page of text, and the expansion of the textual notes and glossary – this remains, recognizably, a revised version of Robinson's edition.

Further reading: George F. Reinecke in Ruggiers (1984).

Rochester

Town on the *Canterbury Way, about 30 miles from *London bridge. Rochester is mentioned in *MkP* (VII.1926/B^2.3116). This allusion comes after that to *Sittingbourne (*WBP* III.847), which is, in fact, some ten miles further along the road. To rectify this apparent anomaly, *Bradshaw proposed a modification to the order of the fragments of *CT*.

Roet, Katherine *see* Swynford, Katherine

Roet, Sir Paon de

(fl. early–mid-14th century)
Probably the father of Philippa *Chaucer. Sir Paon (or Payne) de Roet was a knight from Hainault who came to England in the entourage of *Philippa of Hainault. The youngest of his three daughters became Katherine *Swynford, the third wife of *John of Gaunt. His second daughter, Philippa, is generally identified with Philippa Chaucer, the poet's wife.

Roet, Philippa *see* Chaucer, Philippa; Roger *see* Ugolino; Roger of Ware *see* Cook

Roman de la Rose, Le

French poem by Guillaume de Lorris and *Jean de Meun. The first part of *RR*, which consists of just over 4000 lines, was composed by Guillaume de Lorris around 1235. About forty years later, Jean de Meun wrote a much longer continuation, amounting to nearly 18,000 lines. *RR* is a dream vision, in which the dreamer, Amant (the Lover) falls in love with the Rose. He clearly represents the aristocratic male lover, while she represents the aristocratic lady as love object. The poem offers a searching account of his desires, and the various impediments to their fulfilment, making use of allegorical figures such as Bel Acueil and Daunger (signifying, respectively, the warmth of a lady's response to a prospective lover and her reticence, based on concern for her good name). While *RR* as a whole provides a detailed analysis of the nature and experiences of love, the two parts are quite different in tone and manner: the courtliness and idealism of the relatively brief opening section contrasts sharply with the satire, cynicism, and scholarly display of the far longer continuation. Indeed, the challenging views expressed by Jean de Meun caused a good deal of controversy. The most significant sources of this poem are *Ovid's *Ars amatoria* and *Metamorphoses*, the *De consolatione philosophiae* of *Boethius, and the *De planctu naturae* and *Anticlaudianus* of *Alan of Lille. *RR* came to be the most widely read and influential secular poem of the late Middle Ages.

The influence of *RR* on Chaucer's work was profound. It is reflected in his use of the *dream vision concerning love (especially in *BD, PF,* and *LGWP*), in various descriptions of gardens and of spring (such as those in *BD* and *MerT*), and in a great variety of stories, allusions, and examples (among them the story of *Virginia in *PhyT* and the treatment of *Fortune in *MkT*). While Chaucer shows relatively little interest in the personification allegory employed throughout *RR*, he draws extensively on Jean de Meun's satirical accounts of women, marriage, and clerical hypocrisy in various parts of *CT*, including *GP, WBP,* and *MerT*.

Allusions to the effect that Chaucer translated *RR* occur both in *LGWP* and in works by *Deschamps and *Lydgate. It is probable that this translation should be identified with *Rom*, a fragmentary version amounting to less than 8000 lines.

Further reading: Dahlberg (1971); Langlois (1914–24).

Roman de Thèbes, Le

French poem. *Le Roman de Thèbes* is a poem based on the *Thebaid* of *Statius, written by an anonymous Norman poet in the mid-twelfth century. Some scholars have associated the 'romaunce' on the siege of *Thebes, read to *Criseyde in *Tr* (2.78ff.) with this poem (see Benson, 1987: 1031–2).

Roman de Troie, Le *see* Benoît de Sainte-Maure

Roman de Troyle et de Criseida, Le

French translation of *Boccaccio's Il Filostrato*. This is a literal prose translation, apparently written by Beauvau of Anjou in the early fifteenth century. The hypothesis that it was written in the 1380s and used by Chaucer in the composition of *Tr* no longer commands support.

romance

Serious work of considerable length, typically involving love and conflict. Though the term 'romance' is notoriously elusive of definition, it remains indispensible. It originally signified a work written in the vernacular, but has come to be used as a broad generic term, encompassing a great range of predominately secular narrative works in verse and prose. These tend to share some general characteristics. The stories they tell are usually set in the past, often in exotic locations, and are concerned with idealized and codified versions of love and conflict. They relate the fictional experiences – often extemely unlikely, sometimes mysterious or magical – of conspicuously aristocratic and stereotypical protagonists. Most, but not all, have happy endings. When romances achieve subtle or sophisticated effects, these usually derive from the exploration of themes and ideas rather than that of character. Initially (in the twelfth century), they were written for a courtly audience, but this grew progressively wider, and had become quite mixed by the late fourteenth century.

Several of Chaucer's works may be defined as romances: *Tr, KnT, WBT, SqT, FranT*, and *Th*. The notable diversity of these poems reflects the great variety of romance as a genre. *Tr* demonstrates the potential of romance to deal both with highly significant quasi-historical events and with the experience and implications of love and loss. In *KnT*, Chaucer brings a striking philosophical dimension to a historical and chivalric romance, ostensibly about a love triangle. While *WBT* is Chaucer's only Arthurian romance, its most memorable qualities serve to associate it with folktale and fairytale. *SqT* illustrates the propensity of chivalric romance to become episodic and shapeless. The opposite qualities are reflected in *FranT*, which is defined specifically as a *Breton lai (a subdivision of romance). Finally, in *Th*, Chaucer provides a burlesque version of the popular 'tail-rhyme' romances. The influence of romance as a genre is reflected in various aspects of some other works by Chaucer. These include the exotic adventures of *Custance in *MLT*, the happy ending (after many trials and tribulations) in *ClT*, and some features of style in *MerT*.

Romaunt of the Rose, The

Fragmentary translation of *RR, attributed in part to Chaucer. *Rom* survives in a unique manuscript, University of Glasgow MS Hunter 409 (formerly Hunterian Museum, Glasgow, MS V. 3. 7). Since the first page of this manuscript is missing, there is no means of establishing whether it contained an attribution to Chaucer. The earliest edition to make such an attribution was that of *Thynne (1532), in which the text of *Rom* was based on the Glasgow manuscript.

Rom is the sole extant translation of *RR* in Middle English, and renders only about one third of the original. Since the end of the nineteenth century, scholars have recognized that it consists of three fragments, though there is no sign of this in the manuscript. The fragments have been termed A, B, and C. Fragment A (*Rom* 1–1705) is a close translation of the opening of *RR*, which could well have been written by Chaucer, though it contains some uncharacteristic rhymes. Fragment B (*Rom* 1706–5810) comprises a far freer translation, in which the use of northern dialect forms indicates that Chaucer was not the author. Fragment C (*Rom* 5811–7692) is, like A, a close translation in the Chaucerian manner; the presence of a relatively high proportion of uncharacteristic rhymes has, however, led most scholars to doubt that it was written by Chaucer. While fragments A and B provide a rendition of the whole of Guillaume de Lorris's part of *RR* and the opening of Jean de Meun's continuation (*RR* 1–5810), fragment C translates a passage from much later in the poem (*RR* 10,679–12,360). Fragment A recounts the beginning of the dream, and how the Lover enters the garden, meets the beautiful aristocratic people dancing and flirting there, and sees the rose bush reflected in the well of Narcissus. Fragment B describes how the Lover is struck by the arrows of the god of *Love and falls in love with the Rose. It goes on to provide an account of his pursuit of love, in which he is helped by some figures (including *Bialacoil) and impeded by others (especially *Danger), *Jealousy attempts to protect the Rose from him by building a castle around the rose bush, and *Reason advises him that subjection to passionate love is folly. Fragment C consists mainly of the 'confession' of *Fals-Semblant, with its harsh anti-clerical satire.

The most significant evidence that Chaucer wrote a translation of *RR* comes from his own work. In *LGWP* (F.327ff./G.253ff.) he describes how the god of *Love remonstrates with him over the views on women expressed in

Tr and in his translation of *RR*. This could be taken to impy that Chaucer made a complete translation of *RR* (as he did, for instance, of *Bo*). It would clearly suggest that his translation would have included some of Jean de Meun's satirical material on women, none of which appears in the passages rendered in *Rom*. Allusions to Chaucer as a translator of *RR* also occur in the works of *Deschamps (ballade 285) and of *Lydgate (*Fall of Princes* 1.301–8).

On the basis of this evidence, it has been generally accepted that Chaucer wrote a translation of *RR*, probably during the early stages of his career. Whether or not this would have been complete is a matter of conjecture, though there are reasons to suppose that it would have included a significant body of material from Jean de Meun's continuation of *RR*. How this relates to the surviving fragments of *Rom* seems less clear. Most commentators accept Fragment A as Chaucer's work, firmly reject Fragment B, and incline to reject Fragment C.

Further reading: Dahlberg (1999).

Rome

Centre of the Roman empire; greatest city of medieval *Italy; centre of western Christianity. Ancient Rome is the setting for several works, including *Lucrece* (*LGW* 1680ff.), the 'tragedies' of *Nero and of *Julius Caesar (*MkT* VII.2463ff, 2671ff./B^2.3653ff., 3861ff.), and the story of St *Cecilia (*SNT* VIII.120ff.). Various allusions to Rome during the time of *Boethius (d. 524) occur in *Bo* (e.g. 1.p4.168–72, 240–4; 2.p.7.59–72). In *MLT*, *Custance begins and ends her life in Rome – literally that of the late sixth century. The Rome of Chaucer's day is mentioned as the seat of the papal court (*GP* I.671, 687; cf. *ClT* IV.737) and as one of the pilgrimage sites visited by the *Wife of Bath (*GP* I.465). Passing allusions to Rome – in the context of various periods and associations – occur in several other works, including *NPT* (VII.3369–73/ B^2.4559–63), *SqT* (V.231), *BD* (1063), *HF* (1930), and *Tr* (2.36).

Root, Robert Kilburn

(1877–1950)
Chaucerian scholar and editor. Root, who had a long career at Princeton University, is best known for his edition of *Tr* (1926). At the time of its publication, this was remarkable for the fact that it was based on evidence from all known manuscripts. The way in which Root interpreted such evidence was, however, contentious. His views on the text of *Tr* – in brief, that Chaucer revised it twice – had already been expounded in his book,

The Textual Tradition of Chaucer's Troilus (1916). This theory informs all his editorial decisions, and (in the view of most scholars) compromises his text. Root's explanatory notes, on the other hand, are excellent.

Further reading: Ralph Hanna III in Ruggiers (1984).

Rose *see* **Roman de la Rose, Le; Romaunt of the Rose, The**

Rosemounde, To

*Ballade of 24 lines. *Ros* survives in a single manuscript, which also contains *Tr*. It is followed by a colophon, consisting of the words 'tregentil' and 'chaucer', separated by horizontal and vertical dashes (reproduced in some editions, including Benson, 1987: 649). The same two words appear in the (fuller) colophon at the end of *Tr*. It has been suggested that Tregentil may be the name of a scribe. *Ros* was first published in 1891 by *Skeat, who provided the title. It constitutes a strict ballade in three eight-line stanzas, without an *envoy. Though it offers the conventional praise of the disappointed lover for the unattainable lady, the traditional courtly hyperbole is undercut by humour throughout; as a consequence, some commentators find the tone elusive. No specific source for *Ros* has been discovered. Suggested dates for its composition range from early to late in Chaucer's career. The hypothesis that it was written to mark the arrival in London of the French princess *Isabella, a child of seven who was to become the second wife of *Richard II, has attracted little support.

Further reading: Pace and David (1982); V.J. Scattergood in Minnis (1995).

Rouncivale

Hospital of St Mary Roncevall in Charing Cross, to the west of *London. In *GP* (I.670) the *Pardoner is represented as belonging to this establishment, which was a subsidiary cell of the priory of the canons regular of St Augustine in Roncesvalles, Navarre. Scholars have established that 'Rouncivale' was associated with the distribution of dubious pardons.

roundel

Form used in lyric poetry. The roundel is a form derived from French courtly poetry. It uses only two rhymes, varies in length from eight to fourteen lines, and is characterized by the repetition of one or more lines to create a refrain.

Chaucer identifies the song sung by the birds at the end of *PF* (680–92) as a roundel (675). The only other possible example of this form in his work is the dubiously attributed *MercB*, which takes the form of a triple roundel.

Ruce *see* Russia

Rufus

(fl. early 1st century AD)
Rufus of Ephesus, Greek writer on medicine. The inclusion of Rufus among the authorities known to the *Physician (*GP* I.430) reflects the eminence of his works, especially a treatise on anatomy.

Ruiz, Juan

(*c.* 1283–*c.* 1350)
Spanish poet. Juan Ruiz was the archpriest of Hita and author of a long narrative poem, the *Libro de Buen Amor* ('Book of Good Love'). Since this work has some similarities with *CT* (notably the use of a great variety of genres), some scholars have speculated that Chaucer may have come into contact with it during his visit to *Spain in 1366.

Russell

The fox in *NPT*. Russell, the wily fox who assails *Chauntecleer, is based on Renart in the *beast epic, *Le Roman de Renart*. Chaucer names him 'daun Russell' only once in *NPT* (VII.3334/B².4524). 'Russell' suggests a reddish hue; the title 'daun' (derived from the Latin *dominus*) usually signifies a learned man, and is here used in jest.

Russia

Region approximating to the western part of the present-day Russian Federation. The service of the *Knight in Russia and *Lithuania, mentioned in *GP* (I.54–5), has been associated with the activities of the Teutonic Knights in *Prussia, and assumed to have occurred during some of his most recent campaigns.

S

Saint-Denis

Town six miles north of Paris, setting for *ShT*.

St James *see* Santiago de Compostella; St Leonard's, Bromley *see* Stratford atte Bowe

St Paul's

London's cathedral. Old St Paul's cathedral was destroyed in the Great Fire of London (1666). The engravings of the Czech artist Wenceslaus Holler, executed in the mid-seventeenth century, indicate that it was an impressive gothic cathedral. Both the Duchess *Blanche and *John of Gaunt had been buried there. Scholars have speculated that Chaucer may have been educated as a boy at the almonry school attached to the cathedral, which was close to his parents' home in Thames Street. Records indicate that in 1358 the school was left a fine collection of books by its late master (almoner), William Ravenstone, which included works by authors such as *Ovid, *Virgil, and *Statius.

Chaucer mentions St Paul's twice in *GP* – referring to its portico (the *Parvys) where lawyers met (I.310), and to the deplorable practice of priests who left their own parishes to become chantry priests in the cathedral (I.509). In *MilT* (I.3318) he alludes to a pair of shoes, decorated with a design based on one of the cathedral's windows (probably a rose window).

Saints Legend of Cupid see Legend of Good Women, The

saint's life

Biography of a saint. Many saints' lives, in both verse and prose, were written during the Middle Ages. Most of these are fairly brief works, which follow their subjects from birth to death, emphasizing marvellous or miraculous occurrences, and reaching a climax in the account of the saint's martyrdom. They were often gathered into collections such as the *Legenda* *aurea*. Though the saint's life is specifically a religious genre, it has a good deal in common with the secular genre of *romance: indeed, some romances constitute biographies of an exceptionally admirable eponymous hero, such as *Bevis of Hampton or *Guy of Warwick. Chaucer wrote a single saint's life, that of St *Cecilia, in *SNT* – which may be described, quite simply, as the supreme example of the genre in Middle English. The influence of the saint's life is apparent elsewhere in Chaucer's work, notably in *MLT* and *CIT*, and in his use of the term *legend, especially in *LGW*.

Saluzzo

Town and region in western *Italy, setting for *CIT*. Chaucer may have passed through Saluzzo ('Saluce[s]') during his visit to Italy in 1372–73.

Samson

Old Testament hero. The story of Samson ('Sampso[u]n'), based on the Book of Judges (13–16), constitutes one of the 'tragedies' in *MkT* (VII.2015ff./ B^2.3205ff.). This account emphasizes Samson's strength and martial prowess, his betrayal by *Delilah, and his destruction of the temple. The *Pardoner, in his account of drunkenness (*PardT* VI.549ff.), observes that the drunkard's cry of 'Sampsoun, Sampsoun' is inappropriate, since Samson did not drink wine – a point also made in *MkT* (2055/3245). Passing allusions to various aspects of the story of Samson occur in several works: to his death in *KnT* (I.2466) and *MLT* (II.201), to his betrayal by Delilah in *BD* (738–9) and *WBP* (III.721–3), and to his strength in *ParsT* (X.955).

Santiago de Compostella

Pilgrimage site in Galicia, north-west Spain. The tradition that the body of St *James the Great was miraculously translated to Galicia led to the development of Santiago de Compostella as an important centre of pilgrimage. It is mentioned in *GP* (I.466) among the places of pilgrimage to which the Wife of Bath had travelled. Some scholars have suggested that Chaucer may have visited this site during his journey to Spain in 1366.

Saraï

Saraï Berké, town near Volgograd in the present-day Russian Federation. 'Sarray' is mentioned as the location of the court of *Cambyuskan in *SqT* (V.9, 46). For further information, see Magoun (1961: 138–9).

Sarpedon

King of Licia and supporter of Troy in *Tr*. Troilus and Pandarus spend some time staying at the house of Sarpedon in the final book of *Tr* (5.400ff.).

Sarray *see* Saraï; Satalye *see* Atalia

Satan

The devil. The story of the fall of the angel Lucifer, who thus becomes the devil Satan, constitutes the first of the 'tragedies' in *MkT* (VII.1999–2006/B².3189–96), and is also mentioned in *ParsT* (X.895). In *SumP* (III.1675ff.), the *Summoner describes a dream of hell in which friars have their nest beneath Satan's tail. The role of Satan as a tempter and causer of trouble and sorrow is emphasized in *MLT* (II.365–72, 582–8, 596–602) and *PrT* (VII.558–64/B².1748–54). Other allusions to Satan occur in *FrT* (III.1524–30, 1655), *MLT* (II.633–4), and *MilT* (I.3750).

Saturn

Roman god of time, associated with malign planetary influence. Saturn features most significantly in *KnT* (I.2438ff.), where he resolves a dispute between *Venus and *Mars (as to whether *Palamon or *Arcite should prevail). He describes his influence in a chilling and powerful speech (2453ff.), and arranges the incident which causes the death of Arcite (2684–91). Both Arcite and Palamon have previously expressed the view that Saturn is at least partly responsible for their initial misfortune (1086–90, 1328–33). Allusions to his negative influence at the birth of *Troilus and of *Hypermnestra occur in *Tr* (3.715–21) and *LGW* (2596–9) respectively. In *Tr*, he is also associated with bad weather (3.624–8). Among several (otherwise neutral) references in *Astr*, one terms Saturn a 'wicked' planet (2.4.35).

Schism *see* Great Schism

scholars

Several unnamed characters in *CT*, notably the brother of *Aurelius and the 'clerk' of *Orléans in *FranT*. *See also*: **Alan; Clerk; Jankin (1); John (2); Nicholas.**

Scipio the Elder

(236–183 BC)
Publius Cornelius Scipio Africanus, Roman general and statesman. In *Cicero's *Somnium Scipionis*, he appears in a dream to offer advice to his adoptive grandson, *Scipio the Younger – an encounter summarized in *PF* (29ff.), where Chaucer calls him 'African'. The commentary of *Macrobius on the *Somnium Scipionis* was a significant influence in Chaucer's work.

Scipio the Younger

(184/5–129 BC)
Publius Cornelius Scipio Aemilianus, Roman general and statesman. Allusions to the dream of Scipio (also 'Scipio[u]n', 'Cipioun'), in which he receives advice from his late adoptive grandfather, *Scipio the Elder, occur in *BD* (285–8), *HF* (514, 916), *NPT* (VII.3122–6/B^2.4312–16), and *Rom* (10). An account of their meeting – described in *Cicero's *Somnium Scipionis*, and discussed at length in the influential commentary of *Macrobius – is provided in *PF* (29ff.).

Scogan, Henry

(*c.* 1360–1407)
Probable addressee of *Scog*. Henry Scogan was an esquire in the household of *Richard II and became tutor to the sons of *Henry IV. In his *Moral Balade* (text in Skeat, 1897: 237–44), he refers to Chaucer as 'my mayster', and quotes the whole of *Gent*.

Scot

The *Reeve's horse. Of the various horses mentioned in *GP*, this is the only one to be given a name (I.615–16) – as well as being further particularized as 'pomely [i.e. dapple] grey' and a 'stot' (a term regularly used for work horses in manorial records). It has been established that Scot was a common name for farm horses, as its recurrence in *FrT* (III.1543) may suggest.

Scottish Chaucerians

Scottish poets influenced by Chaucer. Commentators have come, increasingly, to regard the term 'Scottish Chaucerians' as unsatisfactory, since it tends to underestimate the variety and quality of the work of these poets and to exaggerate their dependence on Chaucer. With this proviso, however, it remains a useful means of indicating a group of poets including Robert *Henryson, King James I of Scotland, William Dunbar, Gavin Douglas, and the anonymous author of *The Freiris of Berwick*.

The Kingis Quair (i.e. little book), probably written by King James I of Scotland (1396–1437) derives various ideas from Chaucer, notably that of the sleepless narrator who reads a book – in this case the *De consolatione philosophiae* of *Boethius – which later informs a significant dream (cf. *BD*). The poem echoes several of Chaucer's works, including *PF, Tr,* and *KnT*. Dunbar (*c.* 1460–*c.* 1513) produced a varied body of poetry, some of which reflects Chaucerian influence. He praises Chaucer as a model of eloquence in *The Goldyn Targe* (253–61), and draws on several of his works, notably *WBP* and *MerT* in *The Tretis of the Tua Mariit Wemen and the Wedo* and *PF* in *The Thrissill and the Rois*. Gavin Douglas (*c.* 1476–1522) based his poem *The Palice of Honour* on *HF*. In the Prologue (339ff.) to his fine translation of Virgil's *Aeneid*, the *Eneados*, he praises Chaucer but objects to the portrayal of *Aeneas (in *LGW* 924ff.) as the man who betrayed *Dido. *The Freirs of Berwick* is a *fabliau, clearly indebted to *CT*.

Scrope, Sir Richard

(*c.* 1327–1403)
Party to a chivalric dispute, in relation to which Chaucer provided evidence. The dispute between Sir Richard Scrope and Sir Robert Grosvenor concerned the right to bear a certain coat of arms, and was the subject of proceedings in the High Court of Chivalry between 1385 and 1390 (see Crow and Olson, 1966: 370–4). The case was finally decided in favour of Scrope, for whom Chaucer had given evidence in October 1386. This is of interest mainly with reference to the dating of Chaucer's birth, which remains a matter of some uncertainty. In his evidence Chaucer describes his age as 'forty years and more' and states that he had first borne arms in the king's service 27 years previously. Since the latter event suggests that in 1359 he was at least 16 and his own description of his age implies something closer to 40 than to 50, the two statements combine to provide support for an estimated date of birth in the early 1340s.

Scythia

Mythical country of the Amazons. In *KnT* (I.865ff.) and *Anel* (22ff.), *Theseus is described as having conquered Scythia ('Scithia', 'Cithia', etc.) – also termed 'Femenye' in *KnT* (866, 877) – and married its queen, *Hippolyta.

Second Nun

Pilgrim and teller in *CT*. There is no portrait of the Second Nun in *GP*. It has generally been supposed that she can be identified with the nun mentioned as an attendant on the *Prioress (I.163–4). She would thus be a member of the Prioress's entourage, like the *Nun's Priest (though, unlike him, she does not have an exchange with the *Host in connection with her tale).

Second Nun's Prologue and Tale, The

Prologue and *saint's life from Fragment VIII of *CT*. Fragment VIII begins with *SNP*, and also comprises *SNT, CYP*, and *CYT*. Though neither the speaker of *SNP* nor the teller of *SNT* is identified in the text, all the manuscripts provide headings which assign these works to the *Second Nun. The comments of the author, apparently made as a writer addressing an audience of readers (VIII.78–84), has been taken to indicate that this prologue and tale were never fully integrated into the pilgrimage framework – though a link to *CYP* does occur in due course (554). The allusion to the narrator as an 'unworthy sone of Eve' (62) could suggest that the tale was once intended for a male teller, but has also been explained as a liturgical formula.

It has generally been felt that the life of St *Cecilia seems an appropriate tale to be told by a nun – albeit one about whom no further information is forthcoming. Both the prologue and the tale are composed in the *rhyme royal stanza. *SNP* comprises three main sections, indicated by headings in several manuscripts: a passage on the perils of idleness (1ff.), an invocation to the Virgin *Mary (29ff.), and an account of the various meanings of Cecilia's name (85ff.). Commentators have linked the threefold division both with the symbolic 'threes' associated with the Virgin in the invocation (including maid, mother, and daughter, and mercy, goodness, and pity) and with patterns of three in the tale – including the three male converts, Valerius, Tiburce, and Maximus, and the three blows struck at Cecilia, after which she survives three days, with her neck virtually severed (526ff.). The tale has regularly been described as the finest saint's life in Middle English. It is typical of the genre, particularly when concerned with a virgin martyr, that the absolute faith of the protagonist should be set against both civil authority and social norms – the former represented by Almachius, the latter by marriage. Almachius, prefect of *Rome (the setting for the tale) proves a ruthless enemy to the Christians; his willingness to kill Cecilia and her converts matches their willingness to be martyred (358ff.). Though Cecilia does not refuse to marry Valerius, she informs him on their wedding night of her determination to remain a virgin, warning him that her guardian angel will kill him if he makes any attempt on her virginity (141ff.). The inability of Valerius to see this angel until after his baptism reflects the contrast between physical and spiritual sight, and conforms, more generally, to the opposition between worldly and spiritual values. In this conflict, Cecilia is supported by the pope, *Urban I, who appears as a saintly old man, and consecrates her house as a church after her death. While *SNT* responds to several of the ongoing debates of *CT*, its most notable contributions are, perhaps, Cecilia's uncompromising view of sex in marriage and her status as a woman of singular authority. Echoes of several other themes and motifs occur shortly in *CYT*.

It has been known for many years that the final section of *SNP* (85–119) and roughly the first half of *SNT* (120–348) are based on the life of St Cecilia in the *Legenda aurea*. While the source for the second half of *SNT* (349ff.) has proved elusive, it now seems probable that Chaucer was indebted to an anonymous liturgical version of the story, associated with the Roman curia and the Franciscans. Liturgical influences are, likewise, significant in the invocation to the Virgin in *SNP* (29ff.), which reflects the influence of hymns from the Hours of the Virgin. Chaucer also draws on the prayer of St Bernard in *Dante's *Paradiso* (33) – here, as in *PrP* (VII.474–80/B².1664–70).

Commentators have generally assumed that *SNP* and *SNT* were composed at the same time. The inclusion of a life of St Cecilia among the works by Chaucer mentioned in *LGWP* (F.426/G.416) has been taken to suggest that *SNT* was written before *c.* 1386 and later incorporated into *CT*. The use of Dante in *SNP* would seem to indicate that it could not have been written before Chaucer's first journey to Italy in 1372–73. A date between the mid-1370s and the early 1380s would, therefore, seem probable. The manuscripts contain few significant textual variations. *SNT* is copied as a discrete work in two manuscripts.

Further reading: Cooper (1996); Sherry L. Reames in Correale and Hamel (2002).

Semiramis

Mythical queen of Assyria, infamous for her ruthlessness and promiscuity. Semiramis ('Semyrame/is/us') is acknowledged at the beginning of *Thisbe* (*LGW* 707) as the builder of *Babylon. In *MLT* (II.359), the wicked Sultaness (mother of the *Sultan of Syria) is termed 'Semyrame the secounde'. Semiramis is also mentioned briefly in *PF* (288).

Seneca

(*c.* 4 BC–65 AD)
Lucius Annaeus Seneca (Seneca the Younger), philosopher and statesman. In *MkT* (VII.2495ff./B².3685ff.), Chaucer describes how Seneca acted as tutor to *Nero, but fell from favour and was forced to commit suicide. An allusion to these events occurs in *Bo* (3.p.5.47–56). During the Middle Ages, Seneca's name was associated especially with maxims. This is reflected in Chaucer's work, in which many such sententious commonplaces are attributed to Seneca. Most of these quotations and citations are derived from Chaucer's immediate sources, and many are not based on Seneca's genuine works. They are most numerous in *Mel* (e.g. VII.984–5, 1147, 1320–1, 1531, 1859/B². 2174–5, 2337, 2510–11, 2721, 3049) – where they can mainly be traced back to *Publilius Syrus and *Martinus Dumiensis. Similar allusions occur elsewhere in *CT* (but not in Chaucer's other works): see, for instance, *MerT* (IV.1375–6, 1523–5, 1567), *WBT* (III.1168, 1183–4), *PardT* (VI.492–7), *MancT* (IX.345). The account of anger in *SumT* (III.2017ff.) draws on stories from Seneca's *De ira* ('On anger'), which Chaucer probably derived from *John of Wales.

Senior

(fl. 10th century)
Senior Zadith, writer on alchemy. Senior was the author of a commentary, originally written in Arabic, the Latin translation of which was known as the *Tabula Chimica* ('The chemical table'). Chaucer acknowledges his indebtedness to this work for the dialogue between *Plato and a disciple in *CYT* (VIII.1448ff.).

Serapion

(fl. early 12th century)
Serapion the Younger, medical authority. During the Middle Ages there were three writers on medical topics called Serapion. Thus the identity of the authority of this name, included in *GP* (I.432) among those whose work was known to the *Physician, cannot be entirely certain. Commentators have, however, generally supposed that the allusion would be to Serapion the Younger, who wrote a work on medical 'simples' in Arabic, the Latin translation of which achieved considerable success. *See also*: **Damascien**.

Sercambi, Giovanni *see Canterbury Tales, The*

Sergeant of Law

Pilgrim and teller in *CT*. The portrait of the Sergeant of Law in *GP* (I.309ff.) follows that of the *Clerk and precedes that of the *Franklin. The juxtaposition with the Clerk has generally been taken to imply a contrast between unworldliness and worldliness: between a poor man, dedicated to the service of others, and a rich one, concerned to further his own ends. Some commentators have supposed that the first line of the Franklin's portrait (331) indicates a specific connection between him and the Sergeant. In the absence of any further comment, this has sometimes been understood to imply a shared interest in professional life. The overwhelming emphasis of the Sergeant's portrait is, indeed, on his professional skill. Historical information about sergeants – who were very few in number and extremely senior members of the legal profession – has been used to confirm the impression of the portrait. It has been suggested that this was based on an individual, Thomas *Pynchbeck, and, moreover, that Chaucer had reasons for disliking him. While commentators acknowledge that the Sergeant is not directly accused of the vices traditionally associated with lawyers, such as greed and corruption, a majority would detect subtle satire in the portrait. This centres on two implications: that he uses his skills to bend the law to his own advantage (especially 318–20, 325–6), and that his appearance is deceptive (313, 321–2, 328–30). When the Sergeant emerges as a teller, he is termed the Man of Law. The connections between teller and tale seem relatively slight – though some critics perceive such qualities as complacency and pomposity in *MLT*, and relate this to the portrait.

Further reading: Andrew (1993); Mann (1973).

Seven Against Thebes

Seven heroes who attempt to seize *Thebes. This story concerns the sons of Oedipus, Ethiocles and Polynices ('Polymyte[s]'). When Ethiocles breaks the agreement that each should reign in Thebes for alternate years, Polynices attempts to seize the throne, with the support of six others – Adrastus, *Amphiaraus, *Capaneus, Hippomedon ('Ipomedon', 'Ypomedon'), Parthonope, and *Tydeus: together, the 'Seven Against Thebes'. After their efforts have ended in failure and all but Adrastus have been killed, the throne is seized by *Creon, who refuses to permit the burial of the dead heroes. The story, as told in the *Thebaid* of *Statius and in Le *Roman de*

Thèbes, is apparently the subject of the romance read to *Criseyde in *Tr* (2.78ff.). *Cassandra subsequently (5.1485ff.) provides a summary of it with particular reference to the lineage of *Diomede (son of Tydeus). Significant allusions to this story occur in *KnT* (I.893ff.) – where the widows of the unburied heroes petition *Theseus for action against Creon (which he duly provides) – and in *Anel* (50ff.).

Seven Deadly Sins

Traditional categories of sin. The substantial section of *ParsT* (X.387ff.) which defines and describes the sins is based on this concept, and deals in turn with *Pride, *Envy, *Ire, *Sloth, *Avarice, *Gluttony, and *Lechery.

Seys *see* Ceyx

Shakespeare, William

(1564–1616)
Playwright and poet. Chaucer is named in Shakespeare's works only once, in *The Two Noble Kinsmen* (Prologue 13) – a play written by Shakespeare in collaboration with John Fletcher (1579–1625). Though quite closely based on *KnT*, this play compresses the chronology of the story, introduces some new elements (such as the love of the gaoler's daughter for Palamon), and makes some significant changes (especially the threat of death to the loser of the tournament). Shakespeare also makes significant use of Chaucer's work in *Troilus and Cressida*, which draws on a range of literary and quasi-historical materials including *Tr*. His version of the story differs markedly from Chaucer's, both in tone and in emphasis: it comprises a bitterly satirical account of political corruption and false values, in which the main characters of the love story are shallow and contemptible. *Dryden wrote a radically revised version of this play, *Troilus and Cressida: Or, Truth Found Too Late* (1679), in which he attempted to streamline the plot and devise a positive ending (even going so far as to exonerate Cressida) – but with singularly unconvincing results.

The same two works by Chaucer are influential in two further plays. *Romeo and Juliet* may be associated with *Tr* in several ways, including its essential subject (ill-fated love) and its emphatic linking of love with death. There are, moreover, notable parallels between the two pairs of lovers (in each case a man inclined to hyperbole and a more down-to-earth woman), and between

Juliet's nurse and *Pandarus. In *A Midsummer Night's Dream*, the setting in Athens and the characters of Theseus and Hippolyta appear to be derived from *KnT*. It has also been suggested that the quarrel between Oberon and Titania may be based on that between *Pluto and *Proserpina in *MerT*.

Otherwise, parallels to Chaucer in Shakespeare's work comprise numerous echoes and allusions (both thematic and verbal), in which direct indebtedness is often difficult to establish. Examples include the dismissal of the lovers at the end of *Love's Labours Lost*, which may echo the delay imposed at the end of *PF*, the theme of love and friendship in *The Two Gentlemen of Verona*, which may reflect the influence of *KnT*, and several particulars in *The Rape of Lucrece*, which may be derived from *LGW*.

Shame

Personification in *Rom*. Shame is the daughter of *Reason and one of the guardians of the Rose, along with *Danger and *Wicked Tongue (*Rom* 3015ff.).

Sheen

Royal manor in present-day Richmond (approximately 15 miles west of central London). Sheen is specified by *Alceste in *LGWP* (F.497), along with *Eltham, as a place where Chaucer might present *LGW* to the queen (*Anne of Bohemia). The removal of this reference in the revised version of the prologue (G) has normally been taken to indicate that it was written after the death of Anne in 1394. She had, in fact, died at Sheen, the demolition of which the king (*Richard II) ordered as a mark of respect.

Shipman

Pilgrim and teller in *CT*. The portrait of the Shipman in *GP* (I.388ff.) emphasizes his outstanding knowledge, skill, and courage as a sailor and the master of a ship. It also mentions, without overt censure, two dubious aspects of his conduct: that he steals from cargoes of wine in his custody (396–7); and that, when involved in fighting, he throws his prisoners overboard (399–400). The latter, which suggests involvement in piracy, has been related to the concern of the *Merchant that the seas should be kept safe for trade (276–7). On the basis of the allusions to *Dartmouth as the Shipman's probable home port (389), and to the *Maudelayne* as the name of his ship (410), it has been argued that he was modelled on Peter *Risshenden, the contemporary master of an appropriately-named Dartmouth vessel. Records indicating that this ship had been involved in piracy have been taken to strengthen the case. The portrait has also been related to the broadly similar treatment of sailors in satirical literature, though this is a comparatively minor tradition.

Further reading: Andrew (1993); Mann (1973).

Shipman's Tale, The

Comic tale from Fragment VII (Group B^2) of *CT*. The seventh fragment opens with *ShT*, which thus follows *PardT*, the final tale of Fragment VI in the *Ellesmere order (though not in the *Chaucer Society order). Some manuscripts include a link, clearly not the work of Chaucer, between *PardT* and *ShT*. The two tales do have some features in common: they both allude to *Flanders (*Bruges in the case of *ShT*) and share several themes, such as money and trickery. *ShT* (like *PhyT*) has no prologue, and the *Shipman emerges as its teller only after the event, in comments by the *Host (VII.435ff./B^2.1625ff.). There is a good deal of evidence to suggest that it was initially written for a female teller, notably a pattern of allusions and implications in its opening and closing lines (1–19, 433–4/1191–1209, 1623–4). Since these appear to identify the teller as a married woman, and have some qualities in common with *WBP* and *WBT*, it has generally been supposed that Chaucer originally intended *ShT* for the *Wife of Bath. A more elaborate version of this theory postulates that the Wife would have told what became *ShT*, a tale about the trickery of a monk, in response to what became *MerT*, a tale about the trickery of a wife, told by its putative original teller, the *Monk. Be that as it may, the links between *ShT* and the Shipman, as described in *GP* (I.388ff.) seem particularly tenuous.

ShT is, in many ways, a typical *fabliau – with its fast-moving, uncluttered plot, its focus on sex and trickery, and its worldly, cynical tone. It takes an entirely amoral view of human relationships, plainly equating sex with money. The tale's three protagonists are rapidly sketched: the wealthy, good-natured, trusting merchant; his beautiful, extravagant, promiscuous wife; and the handsome, worldly, and resourceful monk, *John. The fact that only the last of these is named (and even he is given the most conventional of names) suggests that they are essentially typical figures. Wordplay reinforces the identification of money and sex, most memorably in the wife's final reference to her 'taille' (416/1606) – which signifies 'tally' while clearly implying a second, explicitly sexual, meaning. Though it does not form part of what has been termed the *marriage debate, *ShT* plainly contributes to the more general discussion of marriage in *CT*, and, like several other tales (including *KnT, MerT, FranT*, and *MancT*), features a version of the love triangle. The way in which the cynicism and worldliness of the monk and the wife undermine values and the words that express them may seem reminiscent especially of *MerT*.

No specific source for *ShT* has been found, though commentators have speculated, mainly because of the setting in France, that it may be based on a French fabliau. Various analogues have been identified among fabliaux conforming broadly to the folktale type known as 'the lover's gift regained'. While none of these is particularly close – none, for instance, allowing the wife to keep her ill-gotten gains, as Chaucer does – the closest seems to be a tale from *Boccaccio's Decameron (8.1), the eighth day of which has trickery for its theme. The following tale (8.2) constitutes another version of the same story.

While it seems probable that Chaucer wrote *ShT* for *CT*, not least because of the allusion to a teller near the beginning (23/1213), there is no specific evidence for dating the composition of the tale. Commentators have considered it likely that the tales of Fragment VII were written at various times, and brought together relatively late in the composition of *CT*. The manuscripts contain few significant variants in the text of *ShT*.

Further reading: Benson and Andersson (1971); Cooper (1996); John W. Spargo in Bryan and Dempster (1941).

Shirley, John

(*c.* 1366–1456)
Scribe and book collector. Shirley's involvement in the compilation and dissemination of manuscripts in London during the late fourteenth and early fifteenth centuries makes him an important witness regarding authorship in several cases where poems are ascribed to Chaucer on the basis of incomplete or uncertain evidence (e.g. *Bal Comp* and *Proverbs*). In some other cases, he provides significant information regarding the patterns of allusion in a poem or the circumstances of its composition, though this is not always entirely reliable (e.g. *Mars, Ven, Truth*, and *Purse*).

Shuchirch, William *see Canon's Yeoman's Prologue and Tale, The*

Sibyl

Prophetess of Cumae (near Naples). In *HF* (439ff.), Chaucer describes how Sibyl leads *Aeneas through Hades in search of the spirit of his father,

*Anchises. The name is also applied (in the general sense of 'prophetess') to *Cassandra in *Tr* (5.1450).

Sidyngborne *see* Sittingbourne

Simkin

Thieving miller of *Trumpington in *RvT*. The scathing portrayal of Simkin – as a dishonest, violent man with ludicrous social pretensions – is represented as constituting retaliation by the *Reeve against the *Miller. In *RvT*, Simkin cheats the two *Cambridge scholars, *Alan and *John, who then take revenge by sleeping (respectively) with his daughter (*Malyne) and his (unnamed) wife. His name is a diminutive of Simon. While the narrator always terms him Simkin, the scholars call him Simon ('Symond'), and his wife uses both forms (see *RvT* I.4022–6, 4288–91).

Sinon

Greek warrior associated with the Trojan horse. Sinon plays a crucial role in the fall of *Troy, first persuading *Priam to allow the wooden horse into the city, and then releasing the men concealed inside. Allusions to his trickery and its drastic consequences occur in *HF* (151–6), *LGW* (930–3), *SqT* (V.209–10), and *NPT* (VII.3228–9/B².4418–19), but not in *Tr*.

Sir Gawain and the Green Knight see Squire's Introduction and Tale, The

Sittingbourne

Small town on the *Canterbury Way, about 40 miles from *London bridge. Sittingbourne is mentioned in *WBP* (III.847). This allusion occurs before that to *Rochester (*MkP* VII.1926/B².3116), which is, in fact, closer to London. A solution to this apparent anomaly was proposed by *Bradshaw.

Skeat, Revd Walter W.

(1835–1912)
Editor of Chaucer. When ill health caused Skeat to retire at the age of 28 from his position as a Church of England rector, he returned to Christ's

College, Cambridge, where he had been an undergraduate, and became a lecturer in mathematics. In 1878 he was appointed to the Bosworth Professorship of Anglo-Saxon. For many years he acted as an assistant to *Bradshaw, who was working on a major edition of Chaucer. On Bradshaw's death in 1886, Skeat took over the project, which led to the publication in 1894 of the first truly scholarly complete works of Chaucer. This edition appeared in six volumes, and was followed three years later by a companion volume, containing 'Chaucerian and other pieces' – many of which had previously been attributed to Chaucer. The significance of Skeat's edition can hardly be exaggerated. For the first time the whole of Chaucer's work was available to readers in a scholarly text, free from spuriously attributed works, and supported by substantial explanatory notes and an excellent glossary. Skeat made extensive use of the transcripts published, under the direction of *Furnivall, by the *Chaucer Society. From these he selected a base text and conducted most of his collations. He was indebted not only to the help and support of Bradshaw and Furnivall, but also to the work of several other scholars – notably *Tyrwhitt, the most scholarly of the earlier editors of Chaucer, and Richard Morris (1833–94), one of the founding editors of the Early English Text Society, who published editions of various texts by Chaucer and other medieval writers. Skeat drew extensively on the work of such scholars – which is often absorbed into his explanatory notes without acknowledgement. His edition has various flaws and limitations: he slightly regularizes his text, collates only selectively, and does not record variants consistently. Nonetheless, his contribution to the development of the editing of Chaucer is outstanding.

Further reading: A.S.G. Edwards in Ruggiers (1984).

Skelton, John *see* English Chaucerians

Sloth

One of the *Seven Deadly Sins. A section of *ParsT* (X.677ff.) deals with Sloth (also termed 'Accidie') and the remedies for it.

Socrates

(469–399 BC)
Greek philosopher. Lady *Philosophy describes Socrates as *Plato's master and refers to the injustice of his death by poisoning (*Bo* 1.p.3.26ff.). He is associated in *For* (17–22) and *BD* (717–19) with indifference to *Fortune.

The contemptuous treatment of him by his wife, *Xantippe, is mentioned in *WBP* (III.727–32). Passing allusions to the thought of Socrates and to the foretelling of his death occur in *Bo* (1.p.4.157–62) and *MLT* (II.201) respectively.

Soler Hall

Cambridge college mentioned in *RvT*. The two scholars, *Alan and *John, are said to belong to Soler Hall (I.3989–90). This has been taken to signify King's Hall, which was later merged with Trinity College. See Bennett (1974: 94ff.).

Solomon

Old Testament king of Israel; supposed author of the books of Proverbs and Ecclesiastes. The association of Solomon ('Salomon') with wisdom is reflected in numerous quotations from and citations of him in *Mel* (e.g. VII.1003, 1178–9, 1512–16, 1578–80, 1589–91/B².2193, 2368–9, 2702–6, 2768–70, 2779–81). They concern a range of topics – including good counsel, patience, wealth, flattery, and idleness – and often involve quotations from Proverbs, Ecclesiasticus, or Ecclesiastes. Solomon is also quoted and cited in *ParsT* (e.g. X.127, 614, 688), on topics including penitence, flattery, and sloth. In *MerT* (IV.2237ff.), *Pluto and *Proserpina debate Solomon's assertion to the effect that he found one wise man in a thousand but no wise woman (Eccles. 7: 28). While Pluto cites Solomon as a great authority, Proserpina dismisses him as a lecherous idolator. His association with lechery is also significant in *WBP* (III.35–43) – where the *Wife of Bath points out that he enjoyed sexual relations with many wives – and in *KnT* (I.1942). The anti-feminist aspects of Proverbs are reflected in the inclusion of extracts from it in *Jankin's *'book of wicked wives' (*WBP* III.679). A single allusion, in *SqT* (IV.247–51), associates Solomon and *Moses with magic. Passing allusions to Solomon as a source of wisdom occur in *MilT* (I.3529–30), *CkP* (I.4330–1), *ClP* (IV.6), *CYT* (VIII.961), *MancT* (IX.314–15, 344), and *Rom* (6529–43).

Somer, John

(fl. late 14th century)
Writer on astronomy. John Somer, a Franciscan friar based in Oxford, was the author of the *Kalendarium* (1380). He is cited by Chaucer, along with *Nicholas of Lynn, in *Astr* (Prologue, 84–6).

Somnium Scipionis *see* **Cicero; Macrobius; Scipio the Elder; Scipio the Younger**

Sophie

Daughter of *Melibee and *Prudence in *Mel*. Sophie suffers serious injuries when Melibee's enemies attack his house. Her name was apparently supplied by Chaucer, since it does not appear in the main source (by *Renaud de Louens) or its Latin original (by *Albertanus of Brescia).

Southwark

Small town situated at the southern end of *London bridge. The road south from London took travellers through Southwark, where the *Tabard inn was located. It is here that the pilgrims meet at the beginning of their journey to *Canterbury (*GP* I.19ff.).

Spain

Country roughly equivalent to present-day Spain, but divided into several kingdoms. In the late Middle Ages, the Iberian peninsula consisted of five kingdoms: Castile (also known as Castile and Leon), which occupied the bulk of the territory; Portugal (roughly equivalent to present-day Portugal); Aragon in the east; and two small kingdoms, French-ruled Navarre in the north and Moorish Granada in the south. Chaucer's visit to Spain in 1366 may have been associated with a pilgrimage to *Santiago de Compostella or with a diplomatic mission involving *Pedro I of Castile. After his (second) marriage, to Pedro's daughter *Constance (Costanza), *John of Gaunt termed himself King of Castile. Chaucer makes several allusions to Spain in his work, notably to its mountainous scenery in *HF* (1116–17) and to its coastline in the portrait of the *Shipman (*GP* I.388ff.).

Speculum Stultorum *see* **Nigel of Longchamps**

Speght, Thomas

(b. *c.* 1550)
Early editor of Chaucer. Speght was a schoolmaster and canon of Ely cathedral, whose first edition of Chaucer's works appeared in 1598. This was

based on the edition of John *Stow – itself an augmented version of that of William *Thynne. It does, however, have several significant features: a life of Chaucer, substantially indebted to the researches of Stow, in the introduction; various forms of annotation, including brief comments on each work; and a glossary of some 2000 words. Following the suggestions of Francis *Thynne, Speght produced a second edition in 1602. Modifications included some textual emendations and the addition of basic etymologies to the glossary. More significantly, it adds the text of Chaucer's *ABC*. This edition was reprinted, with minor alterations, in 1687. Speght's edition would have been used by writers including Milton, Dryden, and Pope. It is notable especially for being the first edition with a glossary and annotation, and for providing a life of Chaucer which remained standard until the mid-nineteenth century.

Further reading: Derek Pearsall in Ruggiers (1984).

Spenser, Edmund

(*c.* 1552–99)
Poet. In Spenser's first major work, *The Shepheardes Calender*, the figure of Colin Clout, who represents the poet, states that he learned his craft from Tityrus, who represents Chaucer, and offers a lament for his death (*June* 81–96). This work contains numerous reminiscences of Chaucer, notably that of the poet's address to his 'litel book' in *Tr* (5.1786–92), which is echoed twice: in the prefatory verses ('To his booke') and in the epilogue. The prefatory letter, addressed by 'E.K.' (Edward Kirke) to Gabriel Harvey, opens with another allusion to *Tr* (1.809), and compares Chaucer to Virgil. In his great work, *The Faerie Queene* (4.2.32ff.), Spenser completes the story left untold when the Franklin interrupts *SqT* (V.673ff.), referring to Chaucer as a 'well of English vndefyled'. Later, in the 'Mutability Cantos' (7.7.9), Spenser alludes to *PF* and terms Chaucer 'the pure well head of Poesie'. The notion of Spenser as the literary heir to Chaucer was often repeated, notably by *Dryden.

Spurgeon, Caroline F.E.

(1869–1942)
Chaucerian scholar. Spurgeon is best known for her book, *Five Hundred Years of Chaucer Criticism and Allusion, 1357–1900*, which appeared in fascicle form between 1908 and 1917, and was printed in three volumes in 1925. This provides a substantial collection of allusions to Chaucer in English, arranged in

chronological order, followed by appendices containing equivalent collections in French and in German.

Squire

Pilgrim and teller in *CT*. The portrait of the Squire in *GP* (I.79ff.) follows that of his father, the *Knight. Commentators have stressed the contrasts between the two of them: while the first is presented as a notably restrained crusader, dressed in rusty armour, with an extensive record of campaigning in distant lands, the latter appears as a lively young man, wearing bright, fashionable clothes, who has been motivated by love to take part in a single campaign relatively near at hand. They do, however, regularly point out that, while the portrait emphasizes the typical interests of youthful aristocratic males – such as riding, jousting, singing, and love – it ends by emphasizing the Squire's proper fulfilment of his duties to his father. Several commentators have suggested, mainly on the basis of the allusion to the Squire's efforts at writing love songs (95), that the portrait reflects Chaucer's memories of his own youth. Those who perceive negative connotations have tended to define these by reference to the censure of extreme fashion in moral and satirical writing, though some have drawn attention to contemporary criticism of the campaign in *Flanders on which the Squire has served, asserting that this was not only unsuccessful but also sordid. It has been suggested that the portraits of the Knight and the *Yeoman were written before that of the Squire, which was later inserted between them, thus causing some uncertainty regarding the referent of 'he' at the beginning of the portrait of the Yeoman (101).

Further reading: Andrew (1993); Mann (1973).

Squire's Introduction and Tale, The

Brief introduction and chivalric *romance from Fragment V of *CT*. Fragment V opens with a request from the *Host that the *Squire should tell a tale of love. The Host's assumption that the Squire would be an expert on this subject (V.2–3) presumably reflects the impression created by his appearance and conduct, as described in *GP* (I.79ff.). The division between *MerE* (which completes Fragment IV) and *SqIntro* is editorial: in the manuscripts that contain them, they appear as a single unit (sometimes termed *The Squire's Prologue*). Many commentators have concluded that this passage was written to link fragments IV and V, and have suggested that, after experimentation with various sequences (evidence of which survives in several manuscripts),

Chaucer settled on the sequence familiar from most modern editions: *ClT – MerT – SqT – FranT*. This actually appears in relatively few manuscripts, though these do include the authoritative *Ellesmere MS.

The ending of *SqT* raises a quite different issue. The narrative breaks off immediately after its teller has offered a summary of the further episodes he has in mind (651–70), and just as he is embarking on a new section of his tale. While it remains possible that Chaucer intended to complete *SqT*, most commentators would accept that the *Franklin interrupts the tale – much as the *Knight later interrupts *MkT* (see VII.2767ff./B².3957ff.) – because the further episodes proposed by the Squire suggest that his narrative will be excessively long. The next passage (673ff.) thus becomes a polite subterfuge on the part of the Franklin, who praises the Squire's eloquence and *'gentilesse', stating that his own son would have much to learn from him. The Host's intervention (695–8, 702) shows irritation with the Franklin's talk of 'gentilesse', but nominates him as the next teller – thus, in effect, endorsing his interruption of the Squire.

This interpretation has sometimes been extended to one in which the content and manner of the tale are taken to satirize the teller. While most critics would regard such a view as somewhat overstated, it does address several significant issues: not only the interruption of the tale, but also its characteristic hyperbole and notable lack of coherence. Having undertaken to tell a tale of love, the Squire begins by describing a birthday feast at the exotic court of the Tartar king *Cambyuskan, on which occasion he and his daughter *Canacee are presented with magical gifts by a visiting knight. The most intriguing of these is a flying horse made of brass (given to the king); the most relevant proves, however, to be a ring, given to Canacee, which empowers its wearer to understand the language of birds. The second part of the tale (347ff.) relates how Canacee, wearing her ring, goes for a walk in the woods, overhears the lament of a (female) falcon wronged in love, and offers her comfort. The link between the two parts of the tale is, plainly, tenuous: the first comprises an account of marvels, the second a lover's lament. The Squire's summary of the other stories he intends to tell suggests that his tale would be not only long but also rambling. These are qualities typical of the interlaced romance, a well-known form which Chaucer appears to be gently satirizing. It may also seem appropriate that the Squire, described in *GP* (I.82) as a young man, tells a tale which lacks the formal control attributed to some other tellers, including the Franklin. *SqT* and *FranT* do, nonetheless, share some significant characteristics, notably their interest in magic, idealism, and 'gentilesse'. The portrayal of Canacee is, indeed, so positive that it would be difficult to envisage how the tale could go on to provide an account of the incestuous relationship with which she was associated – as the Squire's summary (667–9) may suggest it will. Some commentators have seen this as an additional reason why Chaucer might have been reluctant to complete the tale, noting the disapproval of stories such as that of Canacee's incest, expressed in *MLIntro* (II.77ff.).

Though Chaucer appears to suggest that *SqT* is based on a source (V.67–72, 655), none has been discovered. Various analogues for the first part of the tale have been identified, especially for the magical gifts. The most significant of these are two, conspicuously similar, late thirteenth-century French romances, the *Meliacin* of Girart d'Amiens and the *Cleomadés* of Adenet le Roi. It has been suggested that the account of the arrival of the visiting knight (89ff.) – combined, as it is, with an allusion to *Gawain – could indicate that Chaucer knew the great fourteenth-century English romance, *Sir Gawain and the Green Knight*. While the influence of oriental tales and accounts of travel in the orient would seem apparent throughout the first part, the precise source of these remains uncertain. The most striking parallels to the second part of the tale come from Chaucer's own works: the lament of *Anelida in *Anel* (211ff.) and the wooing of the eagles in *PF* (414ff.).

There is no direct evidence for dating *SqT*, though its links with the other tales of fragments IV and V would suggest composition in the early to mid-1390s. The text contains few significant variants. *SqT* is regularly divided into two parts (at 346–7); the beginning of the embryonic third part (671–2) is missing from some manuscripts. Continuations of the tale were written by *Spenser in *The Faerie Queene* (4.2.32ff.) and by the early seventeenth-century poet John Lane (see Spurgeon, 1925: 1.189). Neither has much in common with the original.

Further reading: Baker (1990); Cooper (1996); Vincent DiMarco in Correale and Hamel (2002).

squires *see* **Aurelius; Damien; Jankin (2)**

Statius

(*c*. 50–*c*. 96)
Publius Papinus Statius, Roman poet. Statius ('Stace') was the author of the *Thebaid*, an epic in twelve books which tells the story of the *Seven Against Thebes, and the *Achilleid*, an unfinished epic on the deeds of *Achilles. While evidence of Chaucer's knowledge of the latter is limited to a brief allusion in

HF (1462–3), the former was a significant influence in his work. A quotation from the *Thebaid* (12.519–21), describing the return of *Theseus to *Athens, appears in *Anel* (following 21) as an epigraph before the 'story' – the first stanza of which (22–8) is based on these lines. A slightly shorter version of the same quotation serves as an epigraph for *KnT* (preceding I.859). Two notable allusions occur in *Tr*. While the Theban romance read to *Criseyde (2.78ff.) suggests *Le *Roman de Thèbes*, the Trojan epic of which *Pandarus claims knowledge (2.106–8) suggests the *Thebaid* (on which the *Roman* was based). Subsequently (5.1485ff.), a summary of the story told in the *Thebaid* is provided by *Cassandra. Statius appears among the poets acknowledged in the third book of *HF* (1456–63) and among those named in the dedication at the end of *Tr* (5.1786–92). The allusion to him in the former as a 'Tholosan' (i.e. native of Toulouse) reflects a confusion, common in the Middle Ages, between Statius himself and Publius Sursulus Statius of Toulouse.

Stilboun

Philosopher mentioned in *PardT*. The *Pardoner cites the views of Stilboun in an *exemplum on the evils of gambling (VI.603ff.). The story in question comes from *John of Salisbury's *Policraticus* (1.5.1), where the philosopher is called Chilon. For further information, see Benson (1987: 908).

Stothard, Thomas

(1755–1834)
Painter of a picture of Chaucer's Canterbury pilgrims. Stothard produced his painting in 1808 – in response to a commission, and apparently unaware that he was appropriating an idea on which William *Blake had been work-ing. His picture was accompanied by a pamphlet, written by the art dealer William Carey, which related it to Chaucer's text in some detail. An engrav-ing, by Louis Schiavonetti, was produced at the same time. After the appear-ance of Blake's painting in the following year, the two pictures were often compared (usually, but not always, to the advantage of Blake). A reproduc-tion of Stothard's painting is provided by Spurgeon (1925: 2.facing p. 36).

Stow, John

(c. 1525–1605)
Early editor of Chaucer. Stow was a London tailor and antiquarian, best known for his *Survey of London* (1598). His edition of Chaucer survives

in two issues (*STC* 5075, 5076). The main difference between these is that the former contains woodcuts of the Canterbury pilgrims – mostly derived from *Pynson's edition (1526) – which are omitted from the latter. Stow's edition comprises, in effect, a reprint of William *Thynne's edition, with an appendix. This contains some 23 poems, of which only three (*Gent, Lady,* and *Adam*) have been accepted as definitely by Chaucer, while two others (*Prov* and *Wom Unc*) are often included among poems of doubtful attribution. It is probable that this would have been the edition used by major Elizabethan writers including *Spenser and *Shakespeare. Stow's biographical research contributed substantially to the life of Chaucer contained in the edition of Thomas *Speght (1598).

Further reading: Anne Hudson in Ruggiers (1984).

Stratford atte Bowe

Benedictine priory of St Leonard's, Bromley. The allusion in *GP* (I.125) serves to associate the *Prioress with this institution. For further information, see Andrew (1993: 137–8).

Straw, Jack

(fl. mid–late 14th century)
Prominent figure in the *Peasants' Revolt. Jack Straw, the name (or nickname) of one of the peasants' leaders, is mentioned in *NPT* (VII.3394/ B^2.4584), in a passage which compares the noise of those pursuing the fox as it carries off *Chauntecleer with that made by Straw and his followers as they kill Flemings. While the jesting tone of this allusion has troubled some commentators, it is worth noting that the event alluded to would have been some years in the past by the time *NPT* was written.

Strode, Ralph

(d. 1387)
Eminent philosopher and lawyer. The most significant connection between Strode and Chaucer is the dedication of *Tr* (5.1856–9) to 'philosophical Strode' (together with 'moral *Gower'). While this suggests Strode's career as a philosopher at Oxford (where he was a fellow of Merton College), it is probable that he can be identified with the London lawyer of the same name, with whom Chaucer stood surety for John Hend (future Lord Mayor of London) in 1381 (see Crow and Olson, 1966: 281–2). Given the date of

Strode's death, the tradition that he acted as tutor to Chaucer's son Lewis
*Chaucer, who was born around 1381, is probably false (despite its early
origins, on which see Pearsall, 1992: 217).

Strother

Town in the north of England, mentioned in *RvT*. *Alan and *John are
said to come from Strother (I.4014–15). The uncertainty expressed in the
text as to its exact location has been matched by the inability of modern
scholars to provide a definite identification. It has, however, been established that the family name of Strother is associated with Northumberland.

Studies in the Age of Chaucer

Yearbook of the *New Chaucer Society. *Studies in the Age of Chaucer* has been
published annually since 1977. It provides essays on Chaucer's work and period,
reviews of relevant scholarly books, and an annotated annual bibliography. For
bibliographies of earlier publications, see Hammond (1908), Griffith (1955),
Crawford (1967), Baird (1977), and Baird-Lange and Schnuttgen (1988).

Stury, Sir Richard *see* Lollard Knights

Suetonius

(*c.* 70–*c.* 130)
Gaius Suetonius Tranquillus, Roman historian. Suetonius ('Swetonius',
'Swetoun') was the author of *De vita caesarum* ('On the lives of the caesars').
Though Chaucer cites him in *MkT* (VII.2465, 2720/B^2.3655, 3910), with
reference to *Nero and to *Julius Caesar, Suetonius was probably an indirect
source.

Suharde, Mary *see* Prioress

Sultan of Syria

Husband of *Custance in *MLT*. The Sultan ('Sowdan') converts to
Christianity so that he can be married to Custance (II.204ff.). His mother,
the Sultaness ('Sowdanesse') disapproves of this, and has him killed at a
feast, together with his wife's followers (323ff.).

Sultaness of Syria *see* **Sultan of Syria**

Summoner

Pilgrim and teller in *CT*. The portrait of the Summoner is the last but one of the series in *GP* (I.623ff.). It offers no hint of the quarrel between the Summoner and the *Friar, which develops in Fragment III and provides the motivation for their prologues and tales. The Friar's vitriolic account of the misdeeds of summoners, touched on in *FrP* and developed in *FrT*, describes a pattern of conduct with conspicuous similarities to that depicted in the portrait of the Summoner. Commentators have pointed out that, since the actual work of summoners (also known as apparitors) involved summoning those accused of various offences (including adultery, fornication, and the failure to pay tithes) to appear before the archdeacon's court, the opportunities for bribery, corruption, and blackmail were substantial. In satirical literature, summoners are regularly portrayed as corrupt petty officials. These considerations and influences are clearly reflected in the portrait, which – though mostly genial in tone – represents the Summoner as dishonest, lecherous, cynical, ignorant, and manipulative. He is, however, also given some distinctive characteristics – above all, a propensity for grotesque conduct (lines 634–46, 666–8) and a spectacularly unpleasant skin condition (624–33). The fact that the portrait opens with a detailed account of the Summoner's diseased appearance gives the latter notable prominence. It has generally been taken to indicate the effects of some form of venereal disease, and to symbolize spiritual sickness. An additional aspect of the Summoner emerges in the following portrait of the *Pardoner (669ff.), where these two pilgrims are represented as companions. The description of their song (672–4) has sometimes been taken to imply a homosexual relationship. This implication is not developed later in *CT*; nor is the more general suggestion of companionship between the Summoner and the Pardoner.
  Further reading: Andrew (1993); Mann (1973).

summoner *see* ***Friar's Prologue and Tale, The***

Summoner's Prologue and Tale, The

Prologue and comic tale from Fragment III of *CT*. The opening of *SumP* is unequivocally linked to the end of *FrT*. The *Summoner, enraged by the *Friar's attack on him, begins a riposte which will comprise the whole of his own prologue and tale. Thus he continues – and completes – a quarrel with the Friar which began at the end of *WBP* (III.829ff.), resurfaced after the telling of *WBT*, and provided the motivation for *FrP* and *FrT*. The completion of *SumT* brings Fragment III to a close.

SumT plainly and explicitly attacks the Friar, just as *FrT* had attacked the Summoner. The awareness of this on the part of the two tellers is indicated when they each interrupt the other's tale. In *SumT* (III.1761–3), as in *FrT* (III.1332–7), the interruption takes place early on, and is swiftly dismissed by the *Host. While the two tales thus arise from, and give expression to, the same quarrel, they differ markedly in generic terms. The Summoner's reponse to the satirical *exemplum told by the Friar is a witty and acerbic tale which displays most of the typical features of *fabliau, with the exception of sexual intrigue. Though no source for the main story of *SumT* has been discovered, commentators have related it to analogues which recount the giving of a humiliating gift. Such tales do not include any parallel to the final episode concerning the division of the fart. This has been taken to parody two examples of religious iconogaphy – involving, on the one hand, a representation of monastic vices and virtues by a wheel with twelve spokes, and, on the other, the appearance of the Holy Spirit to the twelve disciples. The account in *SumP* of the final abode of friars, beneath the tail of Satan in hell, has, similarly, been interpreted as a parodic version of a story (apparently first told by the thirteenth-century writer Caesarius of Heisterbach) in which the final abode of Cistercian monks is revealed to be under the cloak of the Virgin in heaven. While the instruction offered by the friar *John on the topic of anger (2017ff.) draws on the *De ira* of *Seneca, the main influence, reflected throughout *SumT*, is that of satire against the friars – which also provides the basis of the portrait of the Friar in *GP* (I.208ff.). *SumT* comprises, essentially, an exposure of the hypocrisy and cynicism of the friar John (and, by implication, of friars as a whole), together with an acount of his humiliation. Like *FrT*, it contains a relatively high proportion of direct speech – dominated, in this case, by John's ingratiating voice. The other figures in the main story, *Thomas and his wife (unnamed, like several other *wives – and *husbands – in *CT*), have relatively minor roles. The same is true (to a still greater degree) of the lord and lady of the manor, and their squire, *Jankin, in the final episode. The emphatic presence of puns in *SumT* – such as those between 'farthing' and 'farting' (1967) and the two senses of 'grope' (search blindly or seek out sin: see 1817, 2141, 2148) – may be related to its relentless exposure of pretension and hypocrisy.

In addition to its emphatic links with the portrait, prologue, and tale of the Friar, *SumT* has been taken to continue the theme of 'glosyng' or the interpretation (and misinterpretation) of biblical texts, initiated by the *Wife of Bath. Indeed, *SumT* and *WBP* have both been seen as parodies of scholastic debate.

It has generally been supposed that *SumT* was written at much the same time as *FrT* and the rest of Fragment III – probably in the early to mid-1390s. The text contains few variants of major significance.

Further reading: Cooper (1996); Walter Morris Hart in Bryan and Dempster (1941); Plummer (1995).

Surrye *see* Syria

Swynford, Katherine

(*c*. 1350–1403)
Third wife of *John of Gaunt. Katherine was the youngest daughter of Sir Paon de *Roet, and thus almost certainly the sister of Philippa *Chaucer, the poet's wife. She served as a member of the household of *Blanche, Gaunt's first wife, before her marriage to Sir Hugh Swynford in 1368. After the death of Blanche (also in 1368), Katherine became governess to her daughters Philippa and Elizabeth. Hugh Swynford, by whom she had two children of her own, Blanchette and Thomas, was killed in 1372. Katherine became Gaunt's mistress around this time, and bore him four children between *c*. 1373 and *c*. 1379 – John, Henry, Thomas, and Joan, who were given the surname of Beaufort. Gaunt publically acknowledged his relationship with Katherine despite his marriage to his second wife, *Constance. After her death, Gaunt and Katherine finally married in 1396, partly in order to secure the legitimacy of their children. Anya Seaton's historical novel *Katherine* (1954) provides a fictional account of her life.

Syria

Country corresponding roughly to present-day Syria, location for part of *MLT*.

Syward, Mary *see* Prioress

T

Tabard

Inn where the pilgrims meet at the beginning of *CT*. The Tabard, mentioned in *GP* (I.20, 719), was a large inn, situated on the eastern side of Borough High Street, *Southwark. The word 'tabard' could signify either the emblazoned tunic of a herald or the sleeveless smock of a labourer (as in *GP* I.541). The sign of the Tabard would presumably have depicted the former. For further information, see Andrew (1993: 29–32).

tail-rhyme *see* **Thopas, The Prologue and Tale of Sir**; Tapicer *see* **Guildsmen**; Tarbe *see* **Antigone**

Tarquinius

Tarquinius Sextus, guilty of raping *Lucrece. In *Lucrece* (*LGW* 1680ff.) Chaucer emphasizes the position of Tarquinius as the son of a king (Tarquinius Superbus, last king of Rome, 539–510 BC), and states that he is banished as a punishment for his crime. He is represented as an arrogant young man whose uncontrolled lust leads to violent and unscrupulous conduct.

Tartary

Land ruled by *Cambyuskan in *SqT*. A passing reference to Tartary as a distant country occurs in *BD* (1025).

Tereus

King of *Thrace and husband of *Procne, guilty of raping and mutilating *Philomela. In *Philomela* (*LGW* 2228ff.), Tereus is presented as an example of exceptional wickedness. His evil conduct – raping his sister-in-law, secretly imprisoning her and cutting out her tongue to avoid detection, and cynically deceiving his wife – are described briefly and with restraint. A passing allusion to his violation of Philomela occurs in *Tr* (2.64ff.).

Tertullian

(*c.* 160–*c.* 220)
Quintus Septimus Florens Tertullian, north African father of the church. Tertullian ('Tertulan') is named among the writers, works by whom are included in *Jankin's *'book of wicked wives' (*WBP* III.676). Several of Tertullian's works contain anti-feminist elements.

'terza rima' *see* Dante; Tesbee *see* Thisbe; Tessaly(e), Tessalie *see* Thessaly; Tharbe *see* Antigone; *Thebaid* *see* Statius

Thebes

City in ancient Greece. The story of the *Seven Against Thebes, as told in the *Thebaid* of *Statius, has significance in several of Chaucer's works, notably *KnT, Tr,* and *Anel.* It is summarized at some length in *Tr* (5.1485ff.) and more briefly in *Anel* (57–63). Allusions to the *Thebaid* itself occur in *HF* (1460–2) and *Tr* (2.106–08) – which also alludes to a romance on this subject (2.99–105), possibly implying Le *Roman de Thèbes. KnT* begins in the aftermath of the conflict at Thebes, as *Theseus takes revenge on *Creon at the request of the Theban widows. *Palamon and *Arcite are clearly identified as Theban princes (e.g. *KnT* I.1009–19, 1202–3, 1791–7; cf. *LGWP* F.420–1/G.408–9). They both comment bitterly on how Thebes has suffered from the enmity of *Juno (*KnT* I.1328–31, 1542ff.) – a point also made in *Anel* (50–6). Passing allusions to Thebes, mainly in connection with the conflict there, occur in several other works, including *WBP* (III.740–6), *MerT* (IV.1715–21), *MLT* (II.200, 289), and *MancT* (IX.116–18). Another story from the *Thebaid* is mentioned in *Mars* (245–9).

Theophrastus

(*c.* 370–*c.* 285 BC)
Greek philosopher. Theophrastus ('Theofraste') was the author of the anti-matrimonial tract, *Aureolus liber Theofrasti de nuptiis* ('The golden book of Theophrastus on marriage'), which survived only in the *Epistola adversus Jovinianum* of St *Jerome. This work is quoted at some length in *MerT* (IV.1293–1310), and included in *Jankin's *'book of wicked wives' (*WBP* III.671).

Theseus

Ruler of *Athens in *KnT*, also mentioned in several other works. Theseus is a dominant figure in *KnT*. As a military leader, he conquers the Amazons (subsequently marrying their queen, *Hippolyta) and overthrows the tyrant *Creon at the request of the Theban widows. The latter conflict results in the capture and imprisonment of the young protagonists of *KnT*, *Palamon and *Arcite, to whom Theseus is thus opposed for much of the tale. Despite this fact, his portrayal can hardly be deemed overtly negative – though the extent to which it should be regarded as positive remains a matter for interpretation. He is clearly represented as a firm and decisive ruler, who nonethless proves capable of mercy, notably when, during the scene in the grove (I.1696ff.), he sentences Palamon and Arcite to death but promptly pardons them when Hippolyta and *Emily beg him to do so. Critics have often seen Theseus as a figure of order – which takes on a philosophical significance in the 'First Mover' speech (2987ff.), where he articulates a Boethian view of the world controlled by a benign providence.

Elsewhere, he appears in a less positive light. In *Ariadne* (*LGW* 1886ff.), which tells the story of Theseus and the *Minotaur, he is portrayed as a resourceful but cynical young man, who completes a dangerous task, but forsakes the devoted and faithful *Ariadne. A summary of the story of her betrayal by Theseus occurs in *HF* (405ff). This unworthy conduct is also mentioned in connection with his son, *Demophoön, who treats Phyllis in a similar manner (*LGW* 2394ff.)

Thesiphone *see* Furies

Thessaly

Region of northern Greece. Thessaly is the home of *Jason, and therefore serves as the setting for parts of *Hypsipyle and Medea* (*LGW* 1368ff.). It is also mentioned in *MkT* (VII.2679/B[2].3869) as the location of the victory of *Julius Caesar over *Pompey in 48 BC. *Alceste was known as queen of Thessaly – though this appears to have been confused with *Thrace in *LGWP* (F.432/G.422).

Thisbe

Noble Babylonian maiden, in love with *Pyramus. The story of the ill-fated love between Thisbe (also 'Tisbe', 'Tesbe', etc.) and Pyramus is told in *Thisbe* (*LGW* 706ff.) – in which, unusually among these 'legends', the male protagonist behaves honourably. There are passing allusions to Thisbe and her story in *MLIntro* (II.63), *MerT* (IV.2128–31), *PF* (289), and *LGWP* (F.261/G.215).

Thoas

Two kings: (1) of Lemnos; (2) of Aetolia. The former is mentioned in *Hypsipyle* (*LGW* 1468), as the heroine's father. The latter ('Toas') is identified in *Tr* (4.138) as the person exchanged, along with *Criseyde, for *Antenor.

Tholeme *see* Ptolemy

Thomas

Bedridden man in *SumT*. The friar *John warns Thomas at length about the dangers of *Ire, and presses him for a donation in support of the friars. Thomas responds with the humiliating gift of a fart.

Thomas à Becket, St

(1118–70)
Archbishop of *Canterbury, killed in 1170 and canonized in 1173. The shrine of St Thomas in Canterbury cathedral was the most popular pilgrimage site in England during the later Middle Ages, and therefore seems a natural destination for the pilgrimage in *CT*. The name of St Thomas is mentioned in Chaucer only in oaths and exclamations (*MilT* I.3291, 3425, 3461; *WBP* III.666; *HF* 1131). There may, however, be a comically disrespectful allusion at the end of *PardT* (VI.946–55) to the hair breeches worn by St Thomas.

Thomas of India, St

(fl. 1st century)
The apostle 'doubting Thomas'. An allusion to the legendary life of St Thomas (which describes how he brought Christianity to India and suffered martyrdom there) occurs in *SumT* (III.1980). His name is also used in an oath (*MerP* IV.1230).

Thomas, Timothy and William *see* Urry, John

Thopas, Sir

Absurd protagonist of *Th*. The conventions of popular romance are satirized in the representation of Sir Thopas, who (for instance) is described in terms more appropriate to a lady than to a knight (VII.725–9/B².1915–19), decides to give his love to an 'elf-queene' (784ff./1974ff.), and flees from a giant because he has failed to put on his armour (807ff./1997ff.). No source has been found for his name, which appears to identify him with a precious stone, and may be intended to suggest (ironically) his great value. It is notable that Chaucer uses 'sir' as a knightly title only in this case, though the *Host mockingly addresses the *Nun's Priest as 'sir John' (VII.2810/B².4000; cf. 2820/4010).

Thopas, The Prologue and Tale of Sir

Burlesque *romance from Fragment VII (Group B²) of *CT*. *Th* is linked with the preceding *PrT* by *ThP* (VII.691ff./B².1881ff.), which describes how, following the 'sobre' response of the pilgrims to the 'miracle' related by the *Prioress, the *Host asks Chaucer himself to tell a 'tale of myrthe'. In the process, he describes Chaucer as a self-effacing man with a rotund figure and an 'elvyssh' countenance. Since the poet does not provide a portrait of himself in *GP*, this constitutes the first description of him in *CT* (and proves to be the only one). It thus invites comparison with the Host's subsequent description of the *Nun's Priest in *NPE* (VII.3447–60/B².4637–50). While Chaucer normally uses *decasyllabic couplets for the links in *CT*, he continues with the *rhyme royal stanzas of *PrT* thoughout *ThP*. The only parallel to this is the (apparently cancelled) stanza at the end of *ClT* (IV.1212a–g).

　Th proves to be a 'tale of myrthe', though hardly in a predictable manner. In it, Chaucer takes the extraordinary step of representing himself as the teller of a totally inept tale, which the Host eventually interrupts out of sheer exasperation. *Th* is, by general consent, a brilliant and hilarious parody of contemporary popular romance, in which Chaucer treats the typifying conventions, motifs, diction, and metre of the genre with acute but good-humoured satire. Numerous analogues have been found among English romances written in tail-rhyme stanzas, including *Guy of Warwick* and *Bevis of Hampton* (both of which are preserved in the *Auchinleck MS), and two works by Chaucer's contemporary, Thomas Chester, *Lybeaus Desconus* and *Sir Launfal*. Some of the relevant heroes are named and related to Sir *Thopas in a stanza towards the end of *Th* (897–902/2087–92). By this juncture, the sustained parody has made Chaucer's intentions entirely clear. He has used, and reduced to utter absurdity, romance motifs such as the journey of adventure (748ff./1938ff.), the love of a fairy mistress (784ff./1974ff.), the confrontation with a gigantic opponent (807ff./1997ff.), and the arming of the knight (845ff./2035ff.). Absurd generalities are supported by ludicrous details, such as the identification of the hare as a beast of the forest (754–6/1944–6) and the sparrowhawk as a songbird (766–8/1956–8), and the allusion to a horse ridden so hard that it needs wringing out (775–7/1965–7). Several versions of the tail-rhyme stanza, with its short lines and insistent rhyming, are used. These stanza forms draw attention to the laboured diction, inexact rhymes, and feeble line-fillers which occur throughout. *Th* is divided into three sections or 'fits', each introduced by an appeal for the attention of the audience, and each shorter than its predecessor.

The interruption of *Th* by the Host has been related to that of *MkT* by the *Knight (VII.2767ff./B².3957ff.). Both involve the exercise of critical judgement. In the present case, the Host expresses contempt for Chaucer's 'rymyng' (919ff.) before agreeing that he should tell a prose tale, which turns out to be *Mel* – a serious work, in marked contrast to *Th*. This has been interpreted as contributing to the discussion of literary forms and processes in Fragment VII. Commentators have also noted that *Th* is the last romance in *CT*, and have related it to the other works in this notably diverse group, which also includes *KnT, WBT, SqT*, and *FranT*.

It has generally been assumed that *Th* was written specifically as a tale to be told by Chaucer in *CT*. There is no evidence to indicate the date of its composition.

Further reading: Cooper (1996); Laura H. Loomis in Bryan and Dempster (1941).

Thrace

Region in the north of ancient Greece. Both *Tereus and *Lycurgus are identified as kings of Thrace – which thus serves as the setting for *Philomela* and *Phyllis* (*LGW* 2228ff.; 2394ff.). In various other allusions, Thrace is associated with the worship of *Mars (*KnT* I.1970ff.; *Anel* 1–4), with hunting (*KnT* I.1638–46), and with cold weather (*KnT* I.1973; *Anel* 2). It is identified as the home of *Aeolus (*HF* 1572ff.) and of Orpheus (*Bo* 3.m.12.4). The designation of *Alceste as queen of Thrace (*LGWP* F.432/G.422) probably reflects a confusion with *Thessaly (see Magoun, 1961: 158).

Thynne, Francis

(1545–1608)
Scholar and antiquarian. Francis Thynne was the son of William *Thynne.
He is known mainly for his 'Animadversions' on the first edition of *Speght
(1598), contained in a long letter to Speght, written in 1599. In this document he insists on due recognition of his father's work and proposes various
emendations and corrections to Speght's edition. Some of these – not all of
which actually improve or correct the original – are adopted in Speght's
second edition (1602).

Thynne, William

(d. 1546)
Early editor of Chaucer. William Thynne, who was an officer in the household of Henry VIII, published his first edition in 1532. It was followed by a
second edition in 1542 and by an undated third edition, each with minor
alterations. Thynne set out to improve the quality of the text contained in
current printed editions and to restore some of the works they omitted.
Though his success in achieving the former objective was mixed, his text,
based on the editions of *Caxton, de *Worde, and *Pynson, was apparently
emended from several manuscipts, some of which have not survived. His is
the first printed edition to include texts of *Rom, BD, LGW, Pity, Sted*, and *Astr*.
He was, however, also the first to include several non-Chaucerian works,
notably *Henryson's *Testament of Cresseid* and *Usk's *Testament of Love*. The
quality of his work was subsequently defended by his son, Francis *Thynne.
  Further reading: James E. Blodgett in Ruggiers (1984).

Tiberius Constantinus *see* Emperor of Rome

Tiburce *see* Cecilia, St; *Second Nun's Prologue and Tale, The*

Tisiphone *see* Furies

Tlemcen

City in present-day Algeria. Tlemcen ('Tramyssene') is mentioned in
GP (I.62) as a place where the *Knight has fought.

To Rosemounde see **Rosemounde, To**; Toas *see* **Thoas**;
Toledo *see* **Arzachel**; Trace *see* **Thrace**; tragedy *see* ***Monk's Prologue and Tale, The***; Tramyssene *see* **Tlemcen**

Treatise on the Astrolabe, A

Astronomical treatise, apparently written for Lewis *Chaucer. *Astr* survives (complete or in part), in 31 manuscripts, seven of which include an attribution to Chaucer – which has not been doubted. In the Prologue, Chaucer states that he is writing *Astr* for the instruction of his ten-year-old son (Prologue 1, 24), to whom he has given an astrolabe, calibrated for the latitude of *Oxford. The work constitutes an elementary treatise on the astrolabe, an astronomical instrument used to calculate the positions of the sun and the stars. Chaucer provides an outline of the five parts of *Astr* (Prologue 65ff.), but appears to have written only the first two of these: a description of the astrolabe in part 1, and instructions on its use in part 2. The three missing parts have been related to *Equat*, which some scholars attribute to Chaucer. It has generally been supposed that the 'supplementary propositions' following part 2 are additions, largely or entirely by another writer.

At a time when scientific treatises were normally in *Latin, it is notable that *Astr* is written in English. Chaucer draws attention to this fact, stating that he will compose *Astr* in simple English to make it easier for Lewis to understand (Prologue 50–9). In the same passage (61–4), he refers to his work as a translation, though a good deal of it does, in fact, appear to be original. Two main sources have been discovered. In part 1, Chaucer uses some material from the thirteenth-century work, the *Tractatus de sphaera* ('Treatise on the spheres') by John of Sacrobosco. Part 2 is based more closely on the *De compositione et operacione astrolabii* ('On the construction and operation of the astrolabe'), a Latin translation of an Arabic work attributed to Massahalla (*c.* 730–815).

Echoes of *Astr* occur in astronomical allusions in several of Chaucer's works, notably *KnT, MLT,* and *FranT*. The most interesting of these is, perhaps, the repetition in *FranT* (V.1123–34) of the idea of judicial astrology as a dubious pagan practice (*Astr* 2.4).

Astr contains two references to the date 12 March 1391 (2.1, 3), and it has generally been supposed that these serve to indicate the year of its composition. This is unaffected by the references to 1397 in the 'supplementary propositions' (2.44, 45), since these are assumed to be later additions (see above).

Further reading: Eisner (2002).

Trevet, Nicholas

(*c.* 1265–after 1334)
English historian and commentator. Nicholas Trevet (or Trivet) was the author of the Anglo-Norman *Cronicles*, a history of the world from the Creation to the fourteenth century, which is the main source of *MLT*. His commentary on the *De consolatione philosophiae* of *Boethius was used by Chaucer in the composition of *Bo*.

Troilus

Son of *Priam and *Hecuba; male protagonist of *Tr* and betrayed lover of *Criseyde. Troilus is represented as a prince of *Troy and younger brother of *Hector, a brave warrior, and (above all) a youthful and passionate lover. Though based on Troiolo in *Boccaccio's *Il Filostrato*, he appears as a notably more thoughtful and sensitive character – an impression increased by Chaucer's handling of his dependence on the help of *Pandarus. This involves not only practical advice and support, but also arranging opportunities for him to meet Criseyde and, at times, even managing the meetings themselves. Since Troilus' love is one of absolute faith and commitment, his sense of loss at Criseyde's departure from Troy and subsequent betrayal of him is devastating. Chaucer portrays this with great sensitivity in the final book of *Tr*, at the end of which, after his death, Troilus looks down from the eighth sphere and laughs at the folly of human conduct.

Troilus and Criseyde

Historical *romance, set in *Troy, on the love affair between *Troilus and *Criseyde. *Tr* appears to have been written during the early to mid-1380s – a period in which Chaucer probably also wrote the first version of *KnT* and translated the *De consolatione philosophiae* of *Boethius (as *Bo*). Like *KnT*, *Tr* reflects a significant indebtedness to *Boccaccio. In *LGWP* (F.332–4/G.264–6; G.344–5; F.440–1/G.430–1), Chaucer refers to *Tr* as a poem about Criseyde. He terms it 'Troylus' in *Adam* (2) and 'the book of Troilus' in *Ret* (*CT* X.1086). There is no evidence to confirm the claim of *Lydgate, made in the Prologue to his *Fall of Princes* (1.286–7), to the effect that Chaucer named the poem 'Troilus and Cresseide', though this is the title by which it has usually been known.

   Towards the end of *Tr*, Chaucer relates his work to that of the great classical poets, *Virgil, *Ovid, *Homer, *Lucan, and *Statius, which suggests his ambition to achieve such recognition himself. He goes on to express concern that its text should be copied accurately (5.1786–98). This might seem to indicate that he had taken a good deal of care over the composition of *Tr* – an impression confirmed by an examination of the text. While Chaucer left several of his major works unfinished, he provided *Tr* with an elaborate conclusion, comprising a succinct account of his protagonist's death and apotheosis, a passage of reflection from a Christian viewpoint (sometimes termed the 'palinode'), a dedication to 'moral *Gower' and 'philosophical *Strode', and a brief final prayer (5.1800ff.). The preceding narrative is designed to emphasize a pattern of rise and fall: of progress towards the achievement of happiness and fulfilment in love, followed by a destructive sequence of separation and betrayal. Chaucer announces this essential pattern at the outset (1.1–7), and clearly articulates it throughout a story told in five skilfully constructed books. All but the last of these is introduced by a proem, which provides brief comments on the appropriate stage of the narrative; in the final book, a broadly equivalent purpose is served by the concluding sequence. The *rhyme royal stanza, which Chaucer had earlier used in *PF*, provides an elegant and flexible medium for the presentation of narrative, dialogue, and comment – and for the moments of intensity expressed through the medium of lyrics embedded in the text (e.g. 1.400ff.; 2.827ff.; 3.1422ff.; 5.638–44). While the manner of *Tr* as a whole is elevated and serious, Chaucer achieves a notable variety of tone, ranging from formality to colloquialism, from the earnest to the ludicrous, and from the tragic to the comic. The poem's generic identity is, similarly, mixed. While *Tr* can legitimately be termed a romance, it lacks both the mysterious element and the happy ending which are typical of this genre. Its engagement with the history (or quasi-history) of Troy, its concern with philosophical issues, and the relentless emphasis on its unhappy ending – encapsulated in the description of it as a 'tragedye' (5.1786) – are all distinctive. They derive emphasis from the presence of a narrator, represented by Chaucer as a learned man, himself a failure in love, attempting to tell a story in praise of love, and anxious to treat Criseyde fairly. Because the outline of its story was already established, one of the characteristic qualities of *Tr* is the presence of retrospective irony, generated as the protagonists speculate about a future unknown to them (except through the partial and uncertain medium of prophesy), but well known both to the narrator and to the audience: essentially, that Troy will fall and that Criseyde will eventually prove unfaithful to Troilus.

The careful shaping of the story combines with the skilful use of the narrator to facilitate the exploration of a wide range of related themes. These include the nature of love and the conventions through which it is expressed; the relationship of love to war and of private experience to public life; the freedom of the individual, specifically in relation to ideas concerning free will and predestination; tensions between ideals of conduct and the practical or contingent; essential values, such as truth, honour, and fidelity; and the corrosive effects of time and change. When Troilus falls in love with Criseyde, he experiences the overwhelming and irresistible passion familiar from romance tradition (1.266ff.). It is notable that he first catches sight of Criseyde in a temple, and that traditional quasi-religious terminology is used to describe both the lady as love-object and the experience itself (e.g. 1.421ff.). The consequent prostration of Troilus, though arguably appropriate in a lover, potentially compromises his effectiveness as a warrior; likewise, it generates a tension between his public and private lives which can be resolved only with the assistance of *Pandarus as go-between. While Troilus blames Fortune for what has happened to him, Pandarus takes the pragmatic view that Fortune's wheel may turn (1.834ff.). These themes and issues are developed in book 2, which describes the wooing of Criseyde, and in book 3, in which the love affair is consummated. The conduct of Troilus continues to be characterized by an intense and somewhat impractical idealism. His tendency to be prostratred by emotion also continues – and is exemplified by his swooning at a singularly inappropriate moment, just as he is provided with the opportunity of consummating his relationship with Criseyde (3.1086–92). This opportunity results from the activities of Pandarus, who demonstrates an aptitude for practical action and manipulative conduct to match the pragmatism of his views. Since the main objective of his efforts is to facilitate the consummation of Troilus' passion for Criseyde, the main victim of his manipulation is Criseyde herself. From the outset, she has been portrayed as a victim of circumstances: a young widow, the daughter of a traitor, *Calchas, who has prophesied the fall of Troy and therefore defected to the Greeks. The lengthy sequence in book 2 (598ff.), in which, having been informed by Pandarus of Troilus' passion for her, Criseyde reflects on the potential advantages and disadvantages of accepting his love, portrays her with remarkable subtlety and understanding, as a woman subjected to pressures far more complex than those experienced by the conventional lady of romance. It is such pressures – specifically, those arising from the war, from the wishes of her father, and from her own disadvantaged position in Troy – which lead to the crucial decision, described in book 4 (64ff.), to send Criseyde to the Greek camp in exchange for the captured Trojan leader, *Antenor. Chaucer stresses the irony of the Trojans' eagerness for the release of Antenor, who later betrays them (197–206); the ironic patterning of a situation in which a man who will betray his people is exchanged for a woman who will betray her lover may also be implied. Criseyde's unfaithfulness to Troilus is, of course, the sad subject of book 5. This describes, with notable delicacy and considerable sympathy, how she succumbs to the pressure of circumstances and to the determined and somewhat cynical wooing of *Diomede, who repeatedly asserts, on the authority of Calchas, that Troy and the Trojans are doomed. As these events unfold in the Greek camp, Troilus, ever the idealist, experiences a gradual and devastating disillusionment, while Pandarus, still the pragmatist, comes to acknowledge that these are circumstances which even he cannot manipulate. The events of book 5 confirm the worst fears of Troilus, expressed in anticipation of Criseyde's departure, which lead him to complain bitterly about the envy of Fortune and assert that divine providence precludes individual free will (4.260ff., 958ff.). Such statements may be contrasted, especially, with the song he sings in the previous book (3.1744ff.), which identifies the fulfilment of human love with the divine order of the universe. In such statements, Chaucer appears to be imagining the mental processes of a worthy pagan – as, more generally, he offers an imaginative recreation of life in a pre-Christian society. Thus he provides evidence not only of a genuine historical imagination, but also of a freedom from censoriousness about the beliefs and understanding of pagans. While the assertions of the protagonists, particularly about Fortune and free will, are plainly flawed from a Christian viewpoint, that viewpoint is, conspicuously, not made explicit until the 'palinode' (1828ff.).

The main source used by Chaucer in the composition of *Tr* was *Boccaccio's *Il Filostrato*. This poem, written around 1335 (when Boccaccio was in his twenties), supplied Chaucer with the outline of the story and with the three main characters. While substantial passages of *Tr* are closely based on Boccaccio, it is notable that many of the most crucial moments and issues in the poem are added or changed by Chaucer. Thus, for instance, the long account of Criseyde's thoughts as she considers becoming Troilus' lover (2.598ff.) is almost entirely independent of *Il Filostrato*. Likewise, though Chaucer bases Troilus, Criseyde, and Pandarus on Boccaccio's Troiolo, Criseida, and Pandaro, he makes some highly significant changes. Troilus is more idealistic, philosophical, and reticent than Troiolo, Criseyde more complex and less frankly sensual than Criseida. Still more significant, Chaucer replaces Pandaro, Criseida's cousin, a young nobleman who lacks any distinctive characteristics, with Pandarus, Criseyde's uncle – and thus (at least by implication) an older man – who plays a far more substantial role, and whose manner, humour, and worldly wisdom are highly idiosyncratic.

Chaucer does not acknowledge his indebtedness to Boccaccio in the text of *Tr*. He does, however, make several references to sources: some to an unnamed author whose account he is (supposedly) following (e.g. 2.18, 49; 3.575, 1325), two to *Lollius (1.394, 5.1653), and one to *Homer, *Dares, and *Dictys as authorities on the Trojan war (1.146–7). Close examination of the text reveals that Chaucer's relationship with his source material can be complex and elusive. Thus, for instance, he claims that his source does not tell him whether Criseyde had children (1.132–3) even though Boccaccio states plainly that she was childless (*Il Filostrato*, part 1, stanza 15). The allusions to Lollius are apparently to a non-existent source, and may constitute deliberate misrepresentation on Chaucer's part. His relationship with the traditional story of Troy – which lies behind Boccaccio's poem as well as his own – is more straightforward. The outline of the story is derived from Homer's *Iliad*, and reached the late Middle Ages though the accounts of Dares and Dictys, the French poem on the subject by *Benoît de Sainte-Maure, and the Latin prose translation of this work by *Guido delle Colonne. Chaucer had no direct knowledge of Homer or Dictys, and probably knew Dares only in the translation by *Joseph of Exeter. The love story of Troilus appears first in Benoît, who names Troilus' love Briseida (a name based on that of Briseis in Homer). Chaucer knew and used both Benoît's poem and Guido's translation. His allusions to the story of *Thebes (2.78ff.; 5.1485ff.) reflect the influence of the *Thebaid* of Statius. Several brief passages are derived from *Dante – notably some words by Troilus in praise of love (3.1261–7; cf. *Paradiso* 33.14–18) and the closing prayer (5.1863–5; cf. *Paradiso* 14.28–30). The song sung by *Antigone (2.827ff.) contains echoes of several lyrics by *Machaut. The influence of *Boethius is more significant. Chaucer probably wrote *Tr* soon after completing his translation of the *De consolatione philosophiae*, and his use of five books may be derived from this work. In addition to Troilus' speech on predestination (4.958ff.), which is based on the *De consolatione philosophiae* (5.pr.2 and 3), *Tr* contains numerous minor echoes and reminiscences of Boethius.

Tr survives in some 16 manuscripts, two of which are fragmentary. None was written during Chaucer's lifetime. In most, *Tr* appears alone – suggesting that it was normally seen as a single work. The *Corpus Christi MS contains a celebrated frontispiece, which appears to depict Chaucer reading to an audience. The manuscripts contain a range of significant variants, in accordance with which they have been assigned to three distinct groups. While these variants have sometimes been taken to indicate that Chaucer revised *Tr*, they could also have arisen from scribal interference.

Familiarity with *Tr* is reflected in *The Testament of Love*, a prose work by one of Chaucer's contemporaries, Thomas *Usk, and in several works by John *Lydgate, especially the *Troy Book*. Robert *Henryson wrote *The Testament of Cresseid* (c. 1475) as a kind of sequel to *Tr*. Though this fine poem not only takes a punitive approach to Cresseid but also alters Chaucer's ending (by having her survive Troilus), it was regularly printed as a sixth book of *Tr* from the sixteenth century to the eighteenth. *Shakespeare is indebted to *Tr* in *Troilus and Cressida*, and appears to echo the story in *Romeo and Juliet*. Two partial translations of *Tr* appeared during the 1630s – one, by Jonathan Sidnam, of the first three books into English, the other, by Sir Francis Kynaston, of the first two books into Latin. *Wordsworth translated part of the fifth book (519–686). The first scholarly edition was that of *Skeat in his complete Chaucer (1894).

Further reading: Windeatt (1992).

Trotula

(fl. 11th century)
Trotula di Ruggerio, female physician of Salerno. Trotula was known as the author of works on gynaecology. Her inclusion among the authors in *Jankin's *'book of wicked wives' (*WBP* III.677) might seem inappropriate, since her works are not anti-feminist.

Troy

Land of the Trojans. Troy is, of course, the setting for *Tr*, where Chaucer envisages it as a fine (but doomed) city, with numerous palaces and temples. He does not describe the surrounding countryside, which serves essentially as a location for battlefields and the camp of the Greeks. Allusions to Ilium ('Ilyo[u]n' etc.), the citadel of Troy, occur in *BD* (1244–9), *HF* (157–61), *LGW* (934–7), *MLT* (II.288–9), and *NPT* (VII.3355–61/B².4545–51), but not in *Tr*. The fall of Troy is mentioned frequently in Chaucer's work: see, e.g., *LGW* (930ff.), *BD* (326–31, 1064–6), *Bo* (4.m.7.1–5), *KnT* (I.2831–3), and *SqT* (V.209–11). The authors who have written on this subject are acknowledged in *HF* (1464–80).

Chaucer does not allude to the idea, current in the 1380s, that *London might be renamed 'Troynovant' (i.e. New Troy). This notion was based on the myth that Britain had been founded by *Brut, a Trojan warrior who escaped the fall of Troy.

Trumpington

Village two miles south of Cambridge, setting for *RvT*. The mill featured in this tale would correspond to the actual water mill, situated during the later Middle Ages beside what is now known as Byron's Pool. (For a map and further information, see Bennett, 1974: 86ff.)

Truth

Moral lyric of 28 lines. While *Truth* survives in 23 manuscripts, an unusually large number, only one of these contains the *envoy. The title was supplied by *Furnivall. A subtitle, 'Balade de bone consayl' appears (with variations) in several manuscripts. *Truth* is a *ballade in three *rhyme royal stanzas; the envoy comprises a further rhyme royal stanza. In this serious and restrained poem, Chaucer advises his reader to turn away from worldly values of the court and embrace those of a simpler and more virtuous life in the country. Though it has no specific source, *Truth* has been related to the tradition of poems on this subject going back to *Horace. It is regularly included (along with *Form Age, For, Gent,* and *Sted*) in a group of 'Boethian' lyrics, which address issues also explored in the *De consolatione philosophiae* of *Boethius, and are generally dated in the mid-1380s. The assertion by *Shirley (in Trinity College Cambridge MS R.3.20) that *Truth* was written by Chaucer on his deathbed, has been disregarded. It is, clearly, contradicted by the envoy (preserved in British Library MS Additional 10340), which was first printed by Furnivall in 1867. This applies the moral of the poem to Sir Philip (de) la *Vache, somewhat lightening its tone in the process. Most recent commentators accept the envoy as genuine, supposing that it was written during the period 1386–89, when Vache was out of favour at court, and added to an existing poem.

Further reading: Pace and David (1982); V.J. Scattergood in Minnis (1995).

Tullius *see* Cicero

Tydeus

One of the *Seven Against Thebes. Allusions to the death of Tydeus occur in *Anel* (57) and *Tr* (5.1501). The latter also mentions his heroism (5.1493) and stresses that *Diomede was his son (5.88, 803, 1513–14, etc.).

Tyrwhitt, Thomas

(1730–86)

Editor of Chaucer. Tyrwhitt was appointed to the post of Clerk of the House of Commons in 1762, but retired due to ill health in 1768, and dedicated the rest of his life to scholarly interests. His edition of *CT* was published in five volumes: four (containing text, introductions, and notes) in 1775, and a fifth (containing the glossary) in 1778. A second edition, in two volumes, appeared in 1798. This has generally been regarded as the first truly scholarly edition of Chaucer. By comparison with his predecessors, Tyrwhitt shows a greatly increased respect for the authority of the surviving manuscripts, together with a determination that editorial interventions should be clearly indicated. He was able, on the basis of manuscript evidence, to present the tales and links in a more coherent and logical order than that in any previous edition. His introductory and explanatory materials demonstrate an understanding of Chaucer's language and metre far superior to that of previous editors. Tyrwhitt also provides some genuinely learned notes, in which he offers explanations and interpretations, many of which have stood the test of time, together with a detailed account of the relevant sources.

Further reading: B.A. Windeatt in Ruggiers (1984).

U

Ugolino

(d. 1289)
Italian nobleman, Ugolino da Pisa (Ugolino della Gherardesca). The story of the death by starvation of Ugolino ('the Erl Hugelyn of Pyze') and his young children, based on *Dante's *Inferno* (33), is related as one of the Monk's 'tragedies' (*MkT* VII.2407ff./B².3597ff.). Chaucer represents Ugolino as the victim of arbitrary misfortune – in the form of false accusations, made by Roger, Bishop of Pisa (Archbishop Ruggieri in Dante).

Ulster, Countess of *see* Elizabeth de Burgh; Ulster, Earl of *see* Lionel of Antwerp

Ulysses

Greek hero of the Trojan war; husband of *Penelope. The encounters of Ulysses with the enchantress *Circe and with the cyclops Polyphemus are related briefly in *Bo* (4.m.3.1ff.; 4.m.7.18–27).

Urban, St

(d. 230)
Pope Urban I, early Christian martyr. St Urban appears as a holy old man in *SNT*, where he is termed both 'Pope' and 'Seint' (e.g. VIII.217, 305; 179, 547). He supports St *Cecilia, the heroine of the tale, and consecrates her house as a church after her death. It appears that the association between St Urban and St Cecilia is based on an erroneous tradition (see Benson, 1987: 942–6).

Urry, John

(1666–1715)
Editor of Chaucer. Urry's edition of 1721 has a poor reputation. Its deficiencies result, in part, from the problems which attended its production: after Urry's death in 1715, his work was completed by various individuals, who neither fully endorsed his methods nor worked as a coherent team. Though Urry had access to several manuscripts, the text of his edition,

largely based on that of *Speght (1602), adds little of significance. Its integrity is, moreover, severely compromised by Urry's attempts to regularize Chaucer's metre. Nonetheless, this edition does contain features which contribute to the development of Chaucerian scholarship – notably a life of Chaucer by John Dart, a chronology of his work by William Thomas, and a glossary by William's brother, Timothy. Of these, the most significant is Timothy Thomas's glossary, which supersedes that in Speght's second edition (1602), and provides a much fuller and more reliable guide to meaning.

Further reading: William L. Alderson in Ruggiers (1984).

Usk, Thomas

(d. 1388)
Author of *The Testament of Love*. This long allegorical treatise in prose (text in Skeat, 1897: 1–145) expresses admiration for Chaucer and reflects knowledge of several of his works, including *Tr* and *Bo*. The fact that Usk was executed in March 1388 (as a consequence of his involvement in the mayoral politics of London) indicates that *Tr* and *Bo* must have been in circulation by 1387.

V

Vache, Sir Philip (de) la

(c. 1346–1408)
Addressee of the *envoy to *Truth*. Chaucer's career brought him into contact with Vache, a knight of the chamber and the son-in-law (and heir) of Sir Lewis *Clifford. It is generally supposed that the envoy to *Truth* reflects the circumstances of 1386–89, when Vache (like Chaucer) was out of favour. Vache's career revived during the 1390s, and he became a Knight of the Garter in 1399.

Valentine, St

(fl. 3rd century)
Early Christian martyr and patron saint of lovers. The association between St Valentine and love (the origin of which remains obscure) is strongly emphasized in *PF* – which may constitute the first celebration of St Valentine's Day (14 February) in poetry. The identification of this as the day on which the birds choose their mates is reiterated in *PF* (309, 322, 386, 683), and mentioned in *Mars* (13), *LGWP* (F.145–7/G.131–3), and the dubiously ascribed *Compl d'Am* (85). The connection between *PF* and St Valentine's day is also emphasized in *Ret* (X.1086).

Valerian *see* Cecilia, St; *Second Nun's Prologue and Tale, The*

Valerius Flaccus

(fl. 1st century)
Gaius Valerius Flaccus, Roman poet. Valerius Flaccus was the author of the *Argonautica* ('The voyage of the Argo'), an epic about *Jason and the Argonauts. Though this work was virtually unknown during the Middle Ages, some scholars have taken the allusion to it in *Hypsipyle* (*LGW* 1456–8) to suggest that Chaucer had first-hand knowledge of it.

Valerius Maximus

(fl. 1st century)

Roman author. Valerius Maximus compiled the *Facta et dicta memorabilia* ('Notable deeds and sayings'), a collection of stories and maxims, arranged thematically. Chaucer cites him in *MkT* (VII.2720/B².3910) with reference to the 'tragedy' of *Julius Caesar and in *WBT* (III.1165) regarding the story of Tullius Hostillius, a legendary king of Rome. The passing allusion to 'Valerye' in *LGWP* (G.280) may signify either Valerius Maximus or the *Epistola Valerii* of Walter *Map.

Variorum Chaucer

Multi-volume edition, currently in progress. The Variorum Chaucer, the first volume of which appeared in 1982, provides conservatively edited texts and lists a substantial body of variants, from both manuscripts and early printed editions. For *CT*, it uses the *Hengwrt MS as the base text. The volumes in this series are significant especially for their commentary, which provides a full account of the development of interpretation, on a line-by-line basis.

Venus

Roman goddess of erotic love. Numerous appeals, prayers, and words of praise, addressed to Venus as goddess of love, occur in Chaucer's work, especially *KnT* and *Tr*. In *KnT*, the ethereal beauty of *Emily initially leads *Palamon to mistake her for Venus (I.1101–11), to whom he later prays for support in his attempt to win her hand (I.2221ff.). In *Tr*, allusions to Venus increase markedly during the third book, which describes the consummation of the love between *Troilus and *Criseyde (e.g. 3.185–7, 705–21, 951–2, 1254–60). The name of Venus is regularly used as a metaphor for love (e.g. in *KnT* I.1534–9; *PhyT* VI.58–60; and *PF* 652–3). She is emphatically realized as an erotic figure in three descriptions of temples dedicated to her (*KnT* I.1918ff.; *PF* 260ff.; *HF* 130–9). The notion of service to Venus covers a range of activities, from enthusiastic participation in sex (e.g. *NPT* VII.3342–6/B².4532–6; *MkP* VII.1959–62/B².3149–52) to the writing of love poetry – in the cases of Chaucer (*HF* 613ff.; cf. *LGWP* F.320ff./G.246ff.) and of Ovid (*HF* 1486–9). The pains of love are associated with Venus both in the description of the temples in *KnT* and *PF* and in particular cases such as those of *Aurelius in *FranT* (V.935ff.) and *Damian in *MerT* (IV.1875–7). The *Wife of Bath identifies her tendency to lust with the astrological influence

of Venus (*WBP* III.603ff., 697–710) – which elsewhere appears, more generally, as propitious to love (e.g. *LGW* 2580ff.; *MerT* IV.1967–76; *Tr* 2.680–3). In
the astrological scheme underlying *Mars*, Venus enjoys a happy love affair
with *Mars, only to be parted from him through the intervention of
*Phoebus. *Venus*, which may be connected with *Mars*, constitutes a woman's
love complaint, but is entirely unspecific. Otherwise, Venus (representing
love) and Mars (representing war) tend to be opposed (especially in *KnT*
I.2438ff.). The support of Venus for her son, *Aeneas, during the period from
the fall of Troy to his affair with *Dido, receives emphasis in *LGW* (930ff.)
and *HF* (162ff.). In *LGWP* (F.338/G.313), she is identified as the mother of
Cupid, god of *Love – a relationship also mentioned elsewhere (e.g. *KnT*
I.1963–6; *Tr* 3.1807–8; *Rom* 1616–19). Later in *Rom* (3693ff.) – in Fragment B,
which was almost certainly not written by Chaucer – she intercedes on
behalf of the Lover. Chaucer uses two other names for Venus, Cypride (also
'Cipris') and Cytherea, reflecting her association with Cyprus and with the
island of Cythera respectively.

verse forms *see* **alliterative verse; ballade; complaint;
decasyllabic couplet; octosyllabic couplet; roundel**

Villanova, Arnold of *see* **Arnaldus de Villanova**

Vincent of Beauvais

(*c.* 1190–1264)
French encyclopedist. Chaucer mentions the *Speculum historiale* ('The mirror
of history'), one part of the vast tripartite encyclopedia compiled by Vincent
of Beauvais, in *LGWP* (G.307). It appears that he was slightly indebted to this
work in *Cleopatra* (*LGW* 580ff.) and in some of the 'tragedies' in *MkT*
(notably those of *Adam and *Samson).

Vinsauf, Geoffrey de *see* **Geoffrey de Vinsauf**

Virgil

(70–19 BC)
Publius Vergilius Maro, Roman poet. While the influence of Virgil on
Chaucer's work is substantial, it is less significant or ubiquitous than that of
*Ovid. Virgil was regarded in the Middle Ages not only as a poet but also as

a figure of wisdom and knowledge – a view reflected in his role as *Dante's guide to the underworld in the *Divine Comedy*. It therefore seems entirely fitting that Virgil should be named first among the group of poets to whom Chaucer dedicates *Tr* (5.1792).

The influence of Virgil on Chaucer's work is at its strongest and most significant in *HF*. Chaucer bases his description of the temple of Venus (*HF* 119ff.) on the temple of Juno in Virgil's *Aeneid* (1.446ff.). He proceeds to quote, in an English version, the celebrated opening lines of the *Aeneid*, and then to offer a summary of the story told by Virgil in this great poem, placing particular emphasis on the episode concerning *Dido. The figure of *Fame herself (*HF* 1360ff.) is based on Fama in the *Aeneid* (4.173ff.). The representation of Virgil later in *HF* (1481–5), standing on a pillar among representations of the other great poets, celebrates him specifically as the author of the *Aeneid*. It is also in these terms that he is praised at the beginning of *Dido* (*LGW* 924–7), though here Chaucer goes on to acknowledge Ovid's *Heroides* – significantly, since his version of this story negotiates the markedly different emphases of his two classical sources. In all, Chaucer alludes to Virgil eight times. Four of these allusions link him with Ovid, as a classical author and authority or (more specifically) the teller of the story of Dido. Two – in *HF* (449–50) and *FrT* (III.1519–20) – associate him with Dante as an expert on hell. All refer to him as the author of the *Aeneid*. It seems that there are no specific borrowings in Chaucer from Virgil's other major works, the *Eclogues* and the *Georgics* – unless the motto, *Amor vincit omnia*, on the Prioress's brooch (*GP* I.162), is taken to echo Virgil's *Eclogues* (10.69).

Virgin Mary *see* Mary, St

Virginia

Daughter of *Virginius in *PhyT*. Virginia unwittingly excites the lust of the unscrupulous judge *Apius. His plan to gain control over her is foiled by the extreme action of Virginius, who kills her. She is named only once in the tale (VI.213), and appears as a representative of innocence and purity victimized as a consequence of lust and corruption.

Virginius

Father of *Virginia in *PhyT*. Virginius chooses to kill his young daughter rather than permit her to fall into the clutches of the lustful and corrupt judge *Apius. He later exercises clemency towards Claudius, who had assisted in the machinations of Apius.

Visconti, Bernabò

(d. 1385)
Lord of Milan. A brief account of the violent death of Bernabò at the hands of his nephew and son-in-law Gian Galeazzo is included among the Monk's 'tragedies' (*MkT* VII.2399–405/B².3589–96). Chaucer had visited the opulent and corrupt Milanese court in 1378, on a diplomatic mission which brought back to England the idea of a marriage between *Richard II and Bernabò's daughter, Caterina. While this did not materialize, it has been suggested that Chaucer's first substantial contact with works by *Boccaccio and *Petrarch, which were to prove so significant to his development as a poet, occurred in the libraries of the Visconti.

Visconti, Galeazzo; Visconti, Violante *see* Lionel of Antwerp

Vitello

(fl. 13th century)
Polish author of a work on perspective. A passing allusion to Vitello ('Vitulon'; Polish name Witelo) occurs in *SqT* (V.232).

W

Walter

Marquis of *Saluzzo and husband of *Grisilde in *CIT*. Walter is based on Valterius, the equivalent figure in *Petrarch's version of the story. Initially, Walter appears as a worthy ruler, whose only fault is his lack of concern for the future. Once, however, he has been persuaded to marry in order to secure the succession, the focus of the tale shifts to his unconventional choice of a wife from a lowly background and, especially, to his relentless and disproportionate testing of her obedience.

Ware

Town in Hertfordshire, about twenty miles north of London. *CT* contains two allusions to Ware. While the first (*GP* I.692), an assertion regarding the skills of the *Pardoner, links it with *Berwick, the second (*CkP* I.4336) identifies it as the home town of the *Cook.

Warton, Thomas

(1728–90)
Scholar and literary historian. Warton was a Fellow of Trinity College, Oxford, and arguably the first writer to provide a scholarly account of Chaucer's poetry. This is contained in the opening volume of his vast work, *The History of English Poetry* (1774).

Watering of St Thomas

First stopping-place on the *Canterbury Way. An allusion to the 'Wateryng of Seint Thomas' occurs in *GP* (I.826). This is generally supposed to have been a place for watering horses at a stream near the second milestone on the road from London to Canterbury.

Webber *see* Guildsmen

Westminster

Seat of government, to the west of the city of *London. Chaucer would have been familiar with Westminster from his work as a servant of the crown. Late in 1399, less than a year before his death, he took a lease on a tenement within the grounds of Westminster Abbey. Records indicate that, a few years after his death, this property was leased to Thomas *Chaucer, his elder son. Chaucer was buried in Westminster Abbey, at the entrance to St Benedict's Chapel. In 1556 his remains were moved to a tomb in the south transept – the area which has since become known as 'Poets' Corner'.

Wicked Tongue

Personification in *Rom*. Wicked Tongue, based on Male Bouche in *RR, is one of the guardians of the Rose, together with *Danger and *Shame (*Rom* 3018ff.).

'wicked wives, book of' *see* 'book of wicked wives'

widows

Several characters, mostly unnamed, in *CT*. Notably: the Theban widows in *KnT*; the woman who runs the poor farm which is the setting for *NPT*; the mother of the boy murdered in *PrT*; and Mabely in *FrT*.

Wife of Bath

Pilgrim and teller in *CT*. The portrait of the Wife of Bath (I.445ff.) is one of the liveliest and most engaging in *GP*. Chaucer represents her as a conspicuous and distinctive figure: a woman who has been married five times, has travelled remarkably widely, runs her own weaving business, dresses in a striking manner, and gives free expression both to her social aspirations and to her liberal views on sex. Many of the features mentioned in *GP* are developed in *WBP* – most notably in her long and detailed account of her five marriages (I.460–2; III.193ff.), but also in the repetition and elaboration of such particulars as her gap-teeth (I.468; III.603–4). It has been widely acknowledged that Chaucer draws on the stereotypes of anti-feminist satire both in the portrait and in *WBP*, and that La Vieille, the old bawd in **RR*, constitutes a model for some aspects of the Wife. The portrait is, on the other hand, full of particularizing detail, which gives an impression of individuality. Such details include the identification of her home – not in, but 'biside Bathe'. Commentators have confirmed that this area was known as a centre of the weaving industry, and have suggested that the allusion could even be to a specific suburb (St Michael's Without, or juxta Bathon). Interpretations of the Wife have been conspicuously diverse. Some critics have taken her to signify the Whore of Babylon or to constitute a parody of the Virtuous Woman of Proverbs (31:10ff.). Others offer negative readings in more general terms, stressing her vices (such as pride and lechery) and her lack of decorum (both social and sexual). Those who take a less censorious view tend to see her as a woman providing a refreshing challenge to male hegemony, and emphasize such qualities as her boldness, frankness, independence, and enterprise.

Further reading: Andrew (1993); Mann (1973).

Wife of Bath's Prologue and Tale, The

Confessional prologue and Arthurian *romance from Fragment III of *CT*. The third fragment begins with the opening of *WBP*, which raises the subject of marriage from a female viewpoint, and has been taken to initiate a discussion of sovereignty in marriage. This has regularly been termed the *'marriage debate', and regarded as involving the *Wife of Bath, *Clerk, *Merchant, and *Franklin. Whatever the strengths and weaknesses of this theory, it is clear both that the Wife raises the issue of sovereignty in marriage, and that her assertions regarding the negative attitudes of clerks to women (especially III.688–91) provides a challenge to which the Clerk responds in his tale.

Such engagement with other pilgrims seems to be a defining characteristic of *WBP* (and, to a lesser extent, *WBT*). Quite early in her prologue (163ff.), the Wife is interrupted by the *Pardoner, who states that her views are leading him to reconsider his intention to marry. At the end of *WBP* (829ff.), the *Friar's observations on the length of the 'preamble' to her tale leads to a vitriolic exchange with the *Summoner. Though order is restored by the *Host, this altercation motivates the mutually antagonistic tales of the Friar and the Summoner, which are told immediately after *WBT*. The satirical comment on the friars near the beginning of *WBT* has been construed as a (fairly mild) rebuff by the Wife to the Friar. She is, notably, the only pilgrim whose views (as expressed in *WBP*) are cited in other tales (see *ClT* IV.1170–5;

MerT IV.1685–8). Chaucer also makes an allusion to the Wife – with reference to a man's feelings about marriage – in *Buk* (29–30).

WBP is distinctive in several ways. It has particularly strong connections with the portrait of the Wife in *GP* (I.445ff.) – including not only central features such as the five husbands, but also relatively minor particulars such as her deafness (mentioned in *GP* 446, and accounted for in *WBP* 634–6). It reverses the expectation that a prologue will be shorter than the tale it introduces: *WBP* is just over twice the length of *WBT*. While (like *PardP* and, to some extent, *RvP* and *CYP*) *WPB* may be termed a confessional prologue, this term does not serve either to identify it with a coherent set of generic expectations or to relate it closely to similar works (since no such works exist). Nor does *WBP* express the repentant and conformist views one would associate with actual confession: indeed, some commentators have envisaged it as a mock sermon or a parody of scholastic debate. Most striking of all, it constitutes (at least overtly) a pro-feminist statement based on anti-feminist materials. *WBP* divides naturally into three parts: an introductory section in which the Wife challenges the teaching of the church on sexuality and marriage; a lengthy description (193ff.) of how she used her sexual skills to manage her first three husbands, struggled to control her fourth husband, and wooed her fifth, *Jankin; and (627ff.) an account of how she engaged with the arguments associated with Jankin's *'book of wicked wives', and finally gained mastery over him. The main sources of *WBP* are anti-feminist tracts, as contained in Jankin's book and specified by the Wife (669ff.) – particularly St *Jerome's *Epistola adversus Jovinianum*, the 'Golden book on marriage' by *Theophrastus, and the *Epistola Valerii* of Walter *Map. Two passages from *RR* are also significant: the complaint of a husband against marriage (8455ff.), and the account of women's wiles by the old bawd, La Vieille (12,740ff.). While the presentation of the Wife reflects all these materials – and La Vieille may be regarded as a partial model – most critics would consider her a notably original creation. Their assessments of her arguments do, however, vary widely – ranging from emphatically positive to emphatically negative views.

The connections between teller and tale are less conspicuous than those beween teller and prologue. There is, however, evidence to suggest that Chaucer originally intended the Wife to tell what became *ShT*; thus it would seem unlikely that he assigned *WBT* to her without due consideration. The tale does, in fact, address several of the concerns expressed in *WBP*. Above all, by relating how a knight rapes a maiden, but is then sentenced to death by a court of women unless he can find the answer to a vital question – what do women most desire? – it sets an instance of crude male domination against a more measured example of female sovereignty. The fact that the source of this essential and life-saving knowledge is the *hag – old, ugly, and poor – enhances the moral potential of the tale, which concerns both the education of the knight and the transformation of the hag. Their lack of names has been taken to indicate that they serve mainly as representatives (of their respective sexes and social positions) rather than as individuals. Though *WBT* ostensibly ends by endorsing the principle of female sovereignty, its final lines describe the relationship of the couple (one morally, the other physically transformed) in terms which first imply mutuality and then male dominance. The setting in the England of king *Arthur seems to have relatively little significance; the tale owes almost as much to the traditions of the folktale as to those of the romance. Three analogues of the main story (unusually, all in English) have been discovered: a fifteenth-century romance, *The Weddynge of Sir Gawen and Dame Ragnell*; a ballad, *The Wedding of Sir Gawaine* (surviving in a seventeenth-century version); and Gower's tale of Florent (*Confessio Amantis* 1.1407ff.). Chaucer's version differs from all three in several significant features, including the rape and the hag's interest in *'gentilesse'. Her lengthy speech on this topic (1109 ff.) reflects the influence of several sources, among them *Boethius (especially *De consolatione philosophiae* 3), *Dante (*Convivio* 4), and *RR* (18,561ff.). Chaucer had previously written on this subject – that is, the distinction between nobility of birth and of conduct – in *Gent*, and returns to it elsewhere in *CT* (notably in *ClT* and *FranT*).

Various pieces of evidence contribute to the dating of *WBP* and *WBT*. The probable relationship with *ShT* (see above) suggests that it was written before these were finalized. The allusions to the Wife in *ClT, MerT*, and *Buk* (see above) indicate that they were almost certainly written after *WBP* and *WBT*. While the dating of *ClT* and *MerT* is not exact, *Buk* may well have been composed in 1396. An allusion to St Jerome's *Epistola adversus Jovinianum* (on which Chaucer draws extensively in *WBP*: see above), not included in the 'F' version of *LGWP*, appears in the 'G' version, generally considered to be the later of the two, and dated *c.* 1394. This would all tend to suggst that *WBP* and *WBT* were composed during the early to mid-1390s. There are signs that *WBP* may have been revised: four passages (lines 575–84, 609–12, 619–26, and 717–20) are missing in some manuscripts. Another passage (comprising the six lines following line 44, often designated 44a–f in modern editions) appears in only three manuscripts, and may not be authentic. Several manuscripts include glosses and scribal comments (some of the latter expressing responses to the views of the Wife). A considerable number of textual variants appear in *WBP*, but relatively few in *WBT*. This would be consistent with the former having been revised, but not the latter. Translations of *WBP* and *WBT* were written by *Pope and *Dryden respectively.

Further reading: Blamires (1992); Cooper (1996); Bartlett J. Whiting in Bryan and Dempster (1941).

William of St Amour *see* Guillaume de St Amour; Wireker, Nigel *see* Nigel of Longchamps

wives

Several unnamed characters in *CT*, notably: the wife of the merchant in *ShT*; the wife of *Simkin in *RvT*; the wife of *Phoebus in *MancT*.

Womanly Noblesse

*Ballade of 32 lines. *Wom Nobl* survives in a single manuscript (British Library MS Additional 34360), where it is headed 'Balade that Chauncier [sic] made'. It was first printed by *Skeat, who supplied the title (from line 24). Several commentators have doubted the authenticity of the poem, pointing out that some of its vocabulary does not appear elsewhere in Chaucer. *Wom Nobl* consists of three nine-line stanzas and a six-line *envoy. A line is apparently missing from the second stanza (probably after line 12); both Skeat and *Furnivall offer conjectural replacements (see Benson, 1987: 1188). This poem does not adhere to the strict form of the ballade, since it lacks a refrain and uses a stanza of nine (instead of eight) lines (which also appears in *Anel*). The rhyme scheme is notably demanding – restricted in the body of the poem to just two rhymes, one of which recurs in the envoy. In this poem, the speaker praises his lady's qualities, promises her his service, and expresses the hope that his love may be reciprocated. No specific source or evidence for dating has been identified, though some commentators take the metrical skill demonstrated in *Wom Nobl* to suggest that this is not an early work.

Further reading: Pace and David (1982); V.J. Scattergood in Minnis (1995).

Woodstock *see* Chaucer, Geoffrey

Worde, Wynkyn de

(d. *c.* 1535)
Early printer of Chaucer's work. De Worde, who came from Alsace, initially served as an assistant to *Caxton, and took over the business on his death in

1491. During the next forty years, de Worde printed several volumes containing works by Chaucer, all based on books previously published by Caxton.

Wordsworth, William

(1770–1850)
Poet; translator of several works by Chaucer. Wordsworth translated *PrT*, *MancT*, and a passage from *Tr* (5.519–686) in 1801–02. He revised the first and the third of these for publication in 1820 and 1841 respectively. His version of *MancT* remained unpublished until fairly recently. Wordsworth's translations are notably conservative, and can reasonably be described as the first genuinely close English translations of Chaucer's work.

Wrath *see* Ire; *Wreched Engendrynge of Mankynde, On the see* Innocent III

Wright, Thomas

(1810–77)
Editor of Chaucer. Wright was a professional scholar and author, whose edition of *CT* was published in three volumes: the first two in 1847, the third in 1851. The most significant feature of this edition is Wright's use of the best-text method of editing – a method which was just making its appearance in the work of classical scholars. While *Tyrwhitt made eclectic use of various manuscripts, Wright based his text on a single manuscript. In doing so, he established the method followed by subequent editors of Chaucer. His choice of base text – MS Harley 7334 – could, however, have been better, and he did not undertake systematic collation of other manuscripts. Though Wright's edition was not well received, it remained the standard text of *CT* until the appearance of *Skeat's edition in 1894.
Further reading: Thomas Ross in Ruggiers (1984).

Wyclif, John

(*c*. 1330–94)
Ecclesiastical reformer. Wyclif spent most of his working life as a scholar and teacher at the University of Oxford. Some of his writings and lectures contained vigorous attacks on the worldliness and corruption of the church and the papacy. He expressed various controversial views, most notably in his rejection of the doctrine of transubstantiation. For some time he enjoyed

the protection of *John of Gaunt. Several of his opinions were, however, condemned in 1380, and he consequently retired from Oxford to the rectorship of Lutterworth (Leicestershire), where he lived (and continued writing) until his death.

There is no firm evidence that Chaucer and Wyclif knew each other, though they both had connections with John of Gaunt and plainly had interests in common. It has regularly been supposed that Chaucer and some of his friends and acquaintances, notably the so-called *Lollard Knights, sympathized with the views of Wyclif. Evidence of such sympathy has often been detected in Chaucer's work – especially in the idealized portrait of the *Parson in *GP* and in various instances of implied or overt anticlericalism (such as the portraits of the *Monk and the *Friar in *GP*, the portrait and the prologue of the *Pardoner, and the tales of the Friar and the *Summoner).

X

Xantippa

Wife of *Socrates. In *WBP* (III.727–34), *Jankin's *'book of wicked wives' is said to include an allusion to Xantippa's disrespectful treatment of her husband. This story would have been derived from St *Jerome's *Epistola adversus Jovinianum* (1.48).

Y

Yeoman

Pilgrim in *CT*. The portrait of the Yeoman in *GP* (I.101ff.) follows those of the *Knight and the *Squire; the three are regularly taken to form a group. The word 'yeoman' clearly indicates a personal servant (as in the case of the *Canon's Yeoman) though there has been some doubt as to whose attendant the Yeoman would have been. Whereas the pronoun 'he' in the first line of the portrait refers most naturally to the Squire, commentators have generally felt that it would be more appropriate for the Yeoman to be the Knight's servant. A partial solution to this problem is provided by the hypothesis that the portrait of the Squire was added after those of the Knight and the Yeoman. Opinion has differed as to whether the Yeoman appears more as a forester or a soldier – his garb tending to support the former view and his weapons the latter. He has thus been related both to the management of estates and to the contribution of archers to English successes during the *Hundred Years' War. It has regularly been noted that the portrait concentrates on the physical particulars of appearance and equipment. While the Yeoman does not tell a tale, some commentators have speculated that Chaucer intended to write one for him, based on the story of Gamelyn: see *Cook's Prologue and Tale, The*.

Further reading: Andrew (1993); Mann (1973).

Yeoman *see* Canon's Yeoman; *Friar's Prologue and Tale, The*

Yevele, Henry

(d. 1400)
Master-mason and architect. Yevele, who supervised various royal building projects during a long and successful career, was employed to design splendid tombs for the Duchess *Blanche, *Anne of Bohemia, and *Edward, Prince of Wales.

Youth

Personification in *Rom*. Youth is represented as a playful and inattentive girl (*Rom* 1281ff.). Personifications of youth are also mentioned in *BD* (797–8) and *PF* (226).

Ypocras *see* **Hippocrates; Ypomedon** *see* **Seven Against Thebes**

Ypotys

Learned child in the pious legend *Ypotys*. A stanza in *Th* (VII.897–902/ B².2087–92), asserting the superiority of Sir *Thopas over several heroes of romance, somewhat incongruously includes Ypotys, who was celebrated not for feats of arms but for instructing the emperor Hadrian in the Christian faith.

Ysidre *see* **Isidore, St**

Z

Zenobia

(fl. 3rd century)
Queen of Palmyra. The story of Zenobia ('Cenobia', 'Cenobie'), based mainly
on *Boccaccio's *De claris mulieribus* (98), is included in the 'tragedies' related
by the Monk (*MkT* VII.2247ff/B². 3437ff.). This account stresses the physical
and martial prowess of Zenobia and her refusal to have sexual intercourse
with her husband, Odenathus ('Odenake'), except for the purpose of achieving conception. It describes their wealth and their conquests, and tells how
Zenobia continues to reign successfully after her husband's death, until she
is defeated by the emperor *Aurelian and brought to *Rome as a captive.

Zephyrus

The west wind in Greek myth. Zephyrus is mentioned several times in
Chaucer's work (e.g. *GP* I.5; *BD* 402; *Tr* 5.10), usually in association with
spring, flowers, and warmth.

Bibliography

Andrew, Malcolm. *The General Prologue: Explanatory Notes*. Variorum Chaucer, vol. 2, part 1B. Norman, OK: University of Oklahoma Press, 1993.

Baird, Lorrayne Y. *A Bibliography of Chaucer, 1964–1973*. Boston: G.K. Hall, 1977.

Baird-Lange, Lorrayne Y., and Hildegard Schnuttgen. *A Bibliography of Chaucer, 1974–1985*. Hamden, CT: Archon, 1988.

Baker, Donald C., ed. *The Manciple's Tale*. Variorum Chaucer, vol. 2, part 10. Norman, OK: University of Oklahoma Press, 1984.

——, ed. *The Squire's Tale*. Variorum Chaucer, vol. 2, part 12. Norman, OK: University of Oklahoma Press, 1990.

Bennett, J.A.W. *Chaucer at Oxford and at Cambridge*. Oxford: Clarendon Press, 1974.

Benson, Larry D., gen. ed. *The Riverside Chaucer*. Boston: Houghton Mifflin, 1987.

——, and Theodore M. Andersson, eds. *The Literary Context of Chaucer's Fabliaux*. Indianapolis: Bobbs-Merrill, 1971.

Besserman, Lawrence. *Chaucer and the Bible: A Critical Review of Research, Indexes, and Bibliography*. New York: Garland Publishing, 1988.

Blamires, Alcuin, with Karen Pratt and C.W. Marx, ed. *Woman Defamed and Woman Defended: An Anthology of Medieval Texts*. Oxford: Clarendon Press, 1992.

Bowers, John M., ed. *The Canterbury Tales: Fifteenth-Century Continuations and Addditions*. Kalamazoo, MI: Medieval Institute Publications, 1992.

Boyd, Beverly, ed. *The Prioress's Tale*. Variorum Chaucer, vol. 2, part 20. Norman, OK: University of Oklahoma Press, 1987.

Brown, Peter, ed. *A Companion to Chaucer*. Oxford: Blackwell, 2000.

Bryan, W.F., and Germaine Dempster, eds. *Sources and Analogues of Chaucer's Canterbury Tales*. Chicago: University of Chicago Press, 1941.

Cooper, Helen. *Oxford Guides to Chaucer: The Canterbury Tales*. Oxford: Oxford University Press, 1989. Second edn, 1996.

Correale, Robert M., and Mary Hamel, eds. *Sources and Analogues of the Canterbury Tales*, vol. 1. Cambridge: D.S. Brewer, 2002.

Corsa, Helen Storm, ed. *The Physician's Tale*. Variorum Chaucer, vol. 2, part 17. Norman, OK: University of Oklahoma Press, 1987.

Crawford, William R. *Bibliography of Chaucer 1954–63*. Seattle: University of Washington Press, 1967.

Crow, Martin M., and Olson, Clair C., eds. *Chaucer Life-Records*. Oxford: Clarendon Press, 1966.

Dahlberg, Charles, trans. *The Romance of the Rose by Guillaume de Lorris and Jean de Meun*. Princeton: Princeton University Press, 1971.

——, ed. *The Romaunt of the Rose*. Variorum Chaucer, vol. 7. Norman, OK: University of Oklahoma Press, 1999.

Dean, James M., ed. *Six Ecclesiastical Satires*. Kalamazoo, MI: Medieval Institute Publications, 1991.

Dillon, Bert. *A Chaucer Dictionary: Proper Names and Allusions Excluding Place Names*. Boston: G.K. Hall, 1974.

Eisner, Sigmund, ed. *A Treatise on the Astrolabe*. Variorum Chaucer, vol. 6. Norman, OK: University of Oklahoma Press, 2002.

Ellis, Steve. *Chaucer at Large: The Poet in the Modern Imagination*. Minneapolis: University of Minnesota Press, 2000.

Ellis, Steve, ed. *Chaucer: An Oxford Guide*. Oxford: Oxford University Press, 2005.

Fisher, John H. *John Gower: Moral Philosopher and Friend of Chaucer*. New York: New York University Press, 1964.

——, ed. *The Complete Poetry and Prose of Geoffrey Chaucer*. New York: Holt, Rinehart and Winston, 1977.

Gray, Douglas, ed. *The Oxford Companion to Chaucer*. Oxford: Oxford University Press, 2003.

Griffith, Dudley David. *Bibliography of Chaucer 1908–1953*. Seattle: University of Washington Press, 1955.

Hammond, Eleanor Prescott. *Chaucer: A Bibliographical Manual*. New York: Macmillan, 1908.

Hanna, Ralph III, and Traugott Lawler, eds. *Jankyn's Book of Wikked Wyves, vol. 1: The Primary Texts*. Athens, GA: University of Georgia Press, 1997.

Havely, N.R., ed. and trans. *Chaucer's Boccaccio: Sources of Troilus and the Knight's and Franklin's Tales*. Cambridge: D.S. Brewer, 1980.

Langlois, Ernest, ed. *Le Roman de la Rose par Guillaume de Lorris et Jean de Meun*. 5 vols. Paris: Firmin-Didot, 1914–24.

Magoun, Francis P., Jr. *A Chaucer Gazetteer*. Chicago: University of Chicago Press, 1961.

Manly, John Matthews. *Some New Light on Chaucer*. New York: Holt, 1926.

——, ed. *Canterbury Tales by Geoffrey Chaucer*. New York: Holt, 1928.

Mann, Jill. *Chaucer and Medieval Estates Satire: The Literature of Social Classes and the General Prologue to the Canterbury Tales*. Cambridge: Cambridge University Press, 1973.

Minnis, A.J., with V.J. Scattergood and J.J. Smith. *Oxford Guides to Chaucer: The Shorter Poems*. Oxford: Oxford University Press, 1995.

Morris, Lynn King. *Chaucer Source and Analogue Criticism: A Cross-Referenced Guide*. New York: Garland Publishing, 1985.

Pace, George B., and Alfred David, eds. *The Minor Poems*, part 1. Variorum Chaucer, vol. 5. Norman, OK: University of Oklahoma Press, 1982.

Pearsall, Derek, ed. *The Nun's Priest's Tale*. Variorum Chaucer, vol. 2, part 9. Norman, OK: University of Oklahoma Press, 1983.

——. *The Life of Geoffrey Chaucer: A Critical Biography*. Oxford: Blackwell, 1992.

Plummer, John F. III, ed. *The Summoner's Tale*. Variorum Chaucer, vol. 2, part 7. Norman, OK: University of Oklahoma Press, 1995.

Price, Derek J., ed. *The Equatorie of the Planetis, edited from Peterhouse MS.75.I*. Cambridge: Cambridge University Press, 1955.

Ross, Thomas W., ed. *The Miller's Tale*. Variorum Chaucer, vol. 2, part 3. Norman, OK: University of Oklahoma Press, 1983.

Rudd, Gillian. *The Complete Critical Guide to Chaucer*. London: Routledge, 2001.

Ruggiers, Paul, ed. *Editing Chaucer: The Great Tradition*. Norman, OK: Pilgrim Books, 1984.

Skeat, Walter W., ed. *The Complete Works of Geoffrey Chaucer*. 6 vols. Oxford: Clarendon Press, 1894.

——, ed. *Chaucerian and Other Pieces: Being a Supplement to the Complete Works of Geoffrey Chaucer*. Oxford: Clarendon Press, 1897.

Spurgeon, Caroline F.E. *Five Hundred Years of Chaucer Criticism and Allusion, 1357–1900*. 3 vols. Cambridge: Cambridge University Press, 1925.

Stemmler, Theo, ed. *The Ellesmere Miniatures of the Canterbury Pilgrims*. Mannheim: Mannheim University Press, 1976. Third edn, 1979.

Whiting, Bartlett Jere, with Helen Prescott Whiting. *Proverbs, Sentences, and Proverbial Phrases from English Writings Mainly Before 1500*. Cambridge, MA: Harvard University Press, 1968.

Wimsatt, James I. *Chaucer and the Poems of 'Ch' in University of Pennsylvania MS French 15*. Cambridge: D.S. Brewer, 1982.

Windeatt, B.A., ed. and trans. *Chaucer's Dream Poetry: Sources and Analogues*. Cambridge: D.S. Brewer, 1982.

——. *Oxford Guides to Chaucer: Troilus and Criseyde*. Oxford: Oxford University Press, 1992.